Why HOW We Do Anything
Means Everything

Why HOW We Do Anything Means Everything

EXPANDED EDITION

DOV SEIDMAN

WILEY

John Wiley & Sons, Inc.

Published by John Wiley & Sons, Inc., Hoboken, New Jersey.
Published simultaneously in Canada.

For general information on our other products and services or for technical support, please contact our Customer Care Department within the United States at (800) 762-2974, outside the United States at (317) 572-3993 or fax (317) 572-4002.

Wiley also publishes its books in a variety of electronic formats. Some content that appears in print may not be available in electronic books. For more information about Wiley products, visit our web site at www.wiley.com.

Library of Congress Cataloging-in-Publication Data:

Seidman, Dov.
How : why how we do anything means everything / Dov Seidman.
    p.   cm.
"Published simultaneously in Canada."
Includes bibliographical references.
ISBN 978-1-118-10637-2 (cloth); ISBN 978-1-118-16768-7 (ebk); ISBN 978-1-118-16769-4 (ebk); ISBN 978-1-118-16770-0 (ebk)
    1. Success in business.   2. Business ethics.   3. Values.   4. Organizational effectiveness.   5. Technological innovations.   I. Title.
HF5386.S4159   2007
650.1—dc22

                                                                            2006103097

Printed in the United States of America.

10   9   8   7   6   5   4   3   2   1

*To my mother, Sydelle, for my first
and lasting sense that HOW matters*

*To my wife, Maria, for the HOW
that matters most to me*

Contents

Foreword

When I was in government, everybody debated two questions: "What are we going to do?" and "How much are we going to spend on it?" After my Presidency, I wanted to bring people together to focus on a more important question: regardless of what we want to do or what amount we have to spend on it, *how* can we maximize our efforts and expand our impact so that our good intentions turn into real change?

My friend Dov Seidman has dedicated his life's work to studying *how* people conduct their business and their lives. As we settle into the twenty-first century with all of its unique challenges, it's clear that we can no longer regard success as a zero-sum game: one group rising only at the expense of another. In this new century people worldwide will rise or fall together. Our mission must be to create a global community of shared responsibilities, shared benefits, and shared values. This new focus will require all of us to think about the *how*, and to find new ways to take action to solve the global issues that none of us can tackle alone.

In 2005, I started the Clinton Global Initiative (CGI) to convene leaders from the public and private sectors to devise and implement innovative solutions to some of the world's most pressing challenges—to answer that *how* question. At events throughout the year, CGI creates opportunities for global leaders to collaborate, share ideas, and forge partnerships that enhance their work. We encourage members to develop specific projects—what we call "Commitments to Action." Commitments are often cross-sector partnerships among organizations dedicated to making lasting change. Physicians join forces with shipping agencies and medical nongovernmental organizations (NGOs) to deliver unused medical supplies—that would otherwise be disposed of—where they are needed most. Unemployed New York City youth are given summer jobs painting rooftops white to lower cooling costs, improve building efficiency, and in the process, raise employment levels. Our work demonstrates that by applying the *how* in the real world, by collaborating around shared values, we maximize the positive impact of our efforts.

I am delighted that Dov has written this essential book articulating his complete philosophy of the *how*, including both the necessary shared values for the twenty-first century and actionable ideas to firmly establish these values in our public, business, and personal relationships. The individuals, organizations, and businesses that understand that *how* we choose to do things matters more than ever before will flourish. When people from different backgrounds, regions, and sectors come together in the spirit of true collaboration, challenging each other to do more and to do better, we find answers to those *how* questions, answers that make the world around us better and our children's futures brighter.

This pivotal book will help all of us who are committed to building that world and creating that future for many generations.

PRESIDENT BILL CLINTON
Founder of the William J. Clinton Foundation and
42nd President of the United States

Preface

This is a HOW book, not a *how-to* book. What's the difference between *how-to* and HOW? Everything.

In the twenty-first century, it is no longer what you do or what you know that matters most.

This is not just true of businesses but of any organization, be it a for-profit, a nonprofit, a government, or even a nation. The same holds true for the way individuals get ahead and accomplish their goals.

In this networked global economy, it is getting harder for organizations and individuals to succeed just on the basis of what they produce or the services they provide. In fact, if you line up all the winners today, you will notice that few win anymore solely by what they make or do. If you make something new (or better, faster, and/or cheaper), the competition quickly comes up with a way to make it still better and deliver it at the same or an even lower price. Customers instantly compare price, features, quality, and service, effectively rendering almost every "what" a commodity.

At the same time, in our hyperconnected, hypertransparent world, there is no longer such a thing as private behavior. For better or worse, everything that happens can now be forwarded, tweeted, and blogged about. We all now have unprecedented power to see over the fences and through the walls past public relations (PR) departments and right into the innermost workings of organizations, even into boardrooms and into the characters of the individuals who comprise and lead organizations. We can evaluate not just what they do, but *how* they do it.

Yet, the drive for differentiation—personal, professional, organizational, even national—lies at the heart of all our endeavors. We all still want to stand out, to be bold, to distinguish ourselves from others, to do things others can't copy. We want to be uniquely valuable, to accomplish things of significance, and to earn a legacy. We always will. But in our commoditized, see-through world, we are running out of areas in which to do so.

There is one area where tremendous variation and variability still exist. There is one place that we have not yet analyzed, quantified, systematized, or commoditized, one that, in many important respects, cannot be commoditized or copied: the realm of human behavior—*how* we do what we do. When it comes to how you do what you do, there is tremendous variation, and where a broad spectrum of variation exists, opportunity exists. The tapestry of human behavior is so diverse, so rich, and so global that it presents a rare opportunity, the opportunity to *outbehave the competition* and create enduring value.

Of course, how we do what we do has always mattered. But today, how we behave, consume, build trust in our relationships, and relate to others matters more than ever and in ways it never has before. The world today, powered by vast networks of information, connects and reveals us in ways that we are only beginning to comprehend. A global data cloud has put us in intimate contact with colleagues, customers, and people from very different cultures. Often, advances in technology have connected us faster than we have developed human frameworks to understand each other. As a result, many of the tried-and-true ways of working together and getting ahead no longer apply.

As we see every day, and as you'll read later on, the most valuable innovations of the twenty-first century are coming not just in new products, services, skills, business models, or public policy programs, but from new ways to create value and differentiation through our behavior both individually and organizationally—innovations in HOW. Individuals and organizations that fail to meet this challenge are already being left behind. Those already getting ahead understand that the best, most certain, and most enduring path to success and significance in these dramatically new conditions now lies in behavior—getting our HOWS right over time. This book illuminates the power and possibility of this very simple idea.

THE ERA OF BEHAVIOR

When *HOW* first appeared in 2007, I argued that we were entering what I called the Era of Behavior.

I was so wrong.

Over the past four years it has become clear that we haven't just entered the Era of Behavior. We're way deep in it. Our behavior matters even more than I thought when I wrote this book, and in ways I never imagined. When I wrote about a New York City doughnut vendor who boosted sales by trusting his customers to make their own change, for instance, I had no idea that giving trust away would become a global business strategy used to forge deep connections in a connected world, or that even countries like Indonesia would adopt it as a tactic to fight corruption. (Indonesia has opened over 10,000 "honesty cafés" throughout the archipelago, and many "honesty canteens" in local schools. Honesty canteens have no cashiers. Instead, students take what they like from the shelves. They deposit payment in an open box and take change from another box. The theory is that honesty canteens will teach young Indonesians habits of probity that will discourage them from sliding into corrupt practices later in life.)[1]

When I analyzed the largest Ponzi scheme to date as essentially being about the abuse of trust, I did not anticipate the possibility of an epic abuse of trust that would reverberate globally far beyond the circle of investors that Bernard Madoff directly betrayed. When I wrote about a pro golfer who disqualified himself from a championship tournament not because he thought he must but because he thought he *should* as a professional *and* as a person, I did not anticipate that one of the greatest golfers of all time would fall from grace because he conducted his professional and personal lives in starkly different ways in a world where public behavior and private behavior have become virtually indistinguishable. And when I evoked a world powered by vast networks of information that revealed us in unexpected ways, I didn't realize that it would take a global financial crisis to expose the real nature and profound implications of our connectedness.

When I described our world becoming interconnected because communication technology had shrunk the distance between people, between countries, and between cultures, I did not fully see the extent to which we also have grown interdependent, even morally interdependent. Moral interdependence is inescapable in a world where mortgage transactions in California can wipe out pension plans in rural Norway, and where global consumer demand for cell phones and videogame consoles fuels genocide in central Africa.

I've come to recognize that we've grown too comfortable describing the world using amoral terms such as flat, connected, transparent, complex, uncertain, and (full of) risk. The world is certainly all these things—and more. Roughly two centuries ago, the Scottish philosopher David Hume observed that the moral imagination diminishes with distance. It follows that the moral imagination should increase as the world becomes smaller with the globalization of information and capital. And so it has. We are no longer distant, and therefore we need to reawaken our moral imaginations.

To frame all of these trends, let me offer a formula for an interconnected and interdependent world:

$$\text{Technology} + \frac{\text{Human}}{\text{Passion}} \times \left(\frac{\text{False}}{\text{Ideas}} + \frac{\text{Bad}}{\text{Values}}\right) = \frac{\text{Extremism and}}{\text{Global Dysfunction}}$$

$$\text{Technology} + \frac{\text{Human}}{\text{Passion}} \times \left(\frac{\text{True}}{\text{Ideas}} + \frac{\text{Good}}{\text{Values}}\right) = \frac{\text{Global Stability and}}{\text{Sustainable Prosperity}}$$

This formula has two constants and two variables. The first constant is that the world is technologically connected. We will never be less connected or less exposed. Privacy, as we've known it, is over. As technology marches on, we will only become more connected and exposed. The second constant is the universal human passion for progress and a better life, and when the forces of technology and human passion combine, as they increasingly do in our interconnected world, their impacts multiply exponentially.

Now consider two variables: our ideas about the world and our values. If you multiply technology and human passion against false ideas and bad values, you get total dysfunction and extremism. You will lurch from crisis to crisis with ever-increasing frequency. But if you multiply those same constants against the right variables—true ideas and good values—you get global stability and sustainable prosperity. In short, you get the things we all want.

The stakes for getting this formula right in our lives and endeavors are higher than ever. In a hyperconnected world, local problems can quickly metastasize into global ones. Whether it's a financial meltdown, a nuclear meltdown, melting ice caps, pandemics, or Internet-fueled terrorism, the rapid pace and global scale of our problems can make us feel that we're facing existential doom every other day. We're like those secret agents in the movie *Men in Black*, clocking in each morning to face yet another threat of annihilation by alien space invaders. However, even though our problems may feel like *end-of-life* crises, they are really *way-of-life* crises caused by the nature of the relationships that connect us to our fellow human beings and to our planet.

In my journey of connecting with people and trying to explain why things happen as they do, I often find it helpful to distinguish between way-of-life and end-of-life crises. The classic end-of-life crisis would be a gigantic comet bearing down on Earth. In that situation, it's perfectly rational to crawl under your bed and pray that the comet somehow misses Earth and hits Venus instead. In other words, an end-of-life crisis is a cataclysm, something you can't do anything about. That's not true of our major social, political, and environmental problems, all of which are caused by human behavior and can only be solved by changing human behavior.

During the financial crisis, for example, many smart people genuinely believed that the world economy was poised on the brink of total destruction. ("Gazing into the abyss" was a popular phrase in those days.) As a result, they hunkered down, avoided exposure, and waited for the storm to pass. Along the way we heard endless calls for a "reboot," "reset," and/or "reform" of the financial system. But we really needed, and still need, a *rethink* of the human relationships underpinning that system. As Albert Einstein said, we can't expect to solve problems using the same thinking that created those problems in the first place. You can solve a way-of-life crisis only by changing the way you live.

Everywhere I go, I've noticed a nearly universal hunger to more deeply understand our changing world and a large appetite to *rethink* how we should forge ahead in a world of frequent way-of-life crises. In this regard, I've often been asked to apply the ideas in *HOW* about the source of human behavior to a global economic disaster caused by stunningly complex financial transactions. For me this all comes down to the distinction between "situational values" and "sustainable values." All behavior is guided by values. There are only two types of values: situational values and sustainable values. Too often we've been connected situationally, as opposed to sustainably. In the housing market, for example, banks got into the habit of providing mortgage loans that allowed consumers to buy houses they couldn't afford. That sounds pretty unsustainable today, right? But at the time it seemed to make sense. The consumers didn't care because they assumed that the value of their home would always go up, allowing them to refinance the loan or sell the house at a handsome profit. The banks didn't care because they quickly packaged their loans into securities that were sold on to investors. The investors didn't care either, because they assumed that only a few of the mortgages they bought would actually default. Nearly everybody assumed, wrongly, that the housing market could only go up, not down. But we also made a more fundamental mistake, which was to assume that we didn't need authentic, sustainable relationships among players in financial markets because financial innovation had insulated us all from risk. We now know that this so-called innovation actually multiplied risk because it encouraged everyone to focus on short-term, situational gain as opposed to long-term, sustainable value.

There's a crucial distinction here. Relationships propelled by situational values involve calculations about what's available in the here and now. They are about exploiting short-term opportunities rather than consistently living by principles that create long-term success. They stress what we *can* and *cannot* do in any given situation. Sustainable values, by contrast, are all about what we *should* and *should not* do in all situations. They literally sustain relationships over the long term. Sustainable values are those that connect us deeply as humans. They include integrity, honesty, truth, humility, and hope. Sustainable values are therefore all about *how*, not *how much*.

What makes an institution sustainable is not the scale and size it reaches, as the collapse of major financial institutions demonstrated. Rather, it's *how* it does its business—*how* it relates to its employees, shareholders, customers, suppliers, the environment, society, and future generations.

HOW GOES GLOBAL

Over the past few years I've been fortunate to present the HOW framework to business leaders and audiences all over the world. I also found myself discussing HOW in unexpected places and applying its ideas to unanticipated realms of life. I was invited on *Good Morning America*, in front of millions of groggy fellow citizens, where I was surprised to find myself talking to host Robin Roberts about the HOWS of parenting. Raising a child is a journey, just like building a career or an organization. In the past, we could control our kids when we needed to by sending them to their rooms and turning off the TV. Today it's nearly impossible to disconnect children from all of the devices that give them access to a socially networked world. Once we hoped kids would naturally model their behavior on that of their elders. Nowadays behavior is in the cloud. Soon after *HOW* was published I became a father. My son is now three years old. As he grows up, virtually everything that he says and does can live online forever. Wherever he goes, his reputation will arrive before he gets there. It is all the more important that I inspire in him the sustainable values that will help him keep his feet on the ground and guide him on a sustainable path in this strange and exciting new world.

Not long after, I sat in a darkened New York studio with Charlie Rose, who asked me how the ideas in this book differed from the Golden Rule. That's a fair question, and the answer is that treating others as we want to be treated always mattered. But how we do so today matters in ways that it never did before. So many more people can see how you behave or be impacted by it. I suggested that we must scale our values to match a world where millions can "friend," "unfriend," and "outfriend" each other with the click of a mouse and gain "followers" in 140 characters or less. It's no coincidence that our rising generations are eschewing social status through conspicuous consumption in favor of gaining currency through conspicuous expression and behavior.[2]

The more I traveled, the more I came to realize that the ideas in this book are universal. I learned a great deal from each audience's unique and creative interpretation of HOW. At a Saturday morning speech in Beijing I made the mistake of telling an audience of Chinese university students that I would stick around after my talk until all their questions had been answered. Four hours later, we were still debating how the theory of sustainable behavior related to classical Chinese philosophy. (The answer: Very closely. A central tenet of Confucian thought, for example, is that laws control the lesser man, but right conduct controls the greater man. If you substitute *company* for *man*, Confucius becomes a contemporary-sounding theorist of organizational management.)

At an international business conference in Europe, I asked a roomful of global CEOs to raise their hands if they could confidently name their top-performing employees. They all raised their hands. Then I asked them to keep their hands up if, with the same certainty, they could name their most principled employees—the ones who most personified the company's core values and best exemplified achieving the right results in the right way. All their hands dropped. Continuing the CEO calisthenics, I then asked if they would be running a better, more sustainable company if they could answer the second question as well as the first. Their hands shot skyward. I finally asked them to keep their hands up if they agreed that the global dynamics now called for them to urgently develop this answer and then embed it in their operations. Their hands remained aloft.

In 2008 I proposed "outbehave" as a new idea at the Ideas Festival, a gathering in Aspen to exchange ideas considered to matter most to our world. I noted that the term *outbehave* is not found in dictionaries, unlike *outperform, outfox, outsmart, outmaneuver, outproduce,* and so on. Language is important because it shapes our thinking. These terms are in the dictionary because they express common habits of mind and behavior. The idea that we can excel in our behavior and that principled behavior can be a source of advantage does not yet have a word for it. We're like bodybuilders who rip their arms and torsos but ignore their legs. We have become top-heavy. We know how to outspend and outsmart our rivals, but we know relatively little about how to outbehave them. Figuratively speaking, it's time to hit the gym and work on the behavioral legs that will both ground and propel us to more meaningful and sustainable lives.

Along the way, I've noticed that a growing community of people, including thinkers and leaders I admire, have adopted and amplified the concept of HOW as an ethic of human endeavor and a platform for creating enduring value. In this vein, they've adopted my use of HOW as a noun (e.g., "getting your HOWs right"; "it's the HOW that makes the difference") instead of an adverb (e.g., "how much market share we can take"). President Bill Clinton has announced that he plans to spend the rest of his life in "the 'how' business" and that he will "leave 'what' to others."

New York Times columnist Tom Friedman added HOW as a "rule" of the flat world in the updated version of his seminal book, *The World Is Flat*. In his next important book, *Hot, Flat, and Crowded*, he embraced the HOW framework of sustainable values as the keystone of a sustainable world. He has also emphasized HOW-based leadership—inspirational leadership—as the key to innovating and thriving in a world marked by increasingly frequent political, economic, and environmental change and upheaval.

HOW VALUES SCALE

I earn my living by running a for-profit company that operates in the open global market. Over the past couple of years I've occasionally found myself debating the merits of capitalism with critics who blamed the recession on greedy bankers, clueless regulators, or incompetent automakers. I would invariably start my answer by noting that economic behavior has always had a moral dimension. In fact, Adam Smith, author of *The Wealth of Nations*, was a moral philosopher and was not trained as an economist. Then I'd argue that in a capitalist society, we naturally tend to assume that economic growth is good for everybody. More growth equals more jobs, more money, and more security for businesses and citizens alike.

Throughout the twentieth century, we saw a pattern of industries consolidating into fewer and fewer huge companies. The assumption here was that growth was good because big companies were ipso facto stronger than small companies. All businesses aspired to become "too big to fail," to use a term that acquired a very different meaning during the mortgage meltdown. An entire ecosystem of business schools, investors, capital markets, business media, and companies grew up and still measures success around this principle. Venture capitalists still ask young entrepreneurs how they plan to scale their start-ups and create hockey-stick growth. Markets still reward companies that grow rapidly, and punish enterprises that do not. But in business, size alone can't guarantee long-term survival. To the contrary, the aggressive pursuit of scale—whether it's more revenues, profits, customers, or stores, or a bigger market capitalization—tempts companies to lose sight of the values that create true sustainability. Show me a venture capitalist that asks entrepreneurs "How do you plan to scale your values?" and I'll be interested in investing in their fund. Show me a company that's "too sustainable to fail" and I'll be interested in buying shares.

If you retain nothing else from this book, remember this: In the twenty-first century, principled behavior is the surest path to success and significance in business and in life. If that seems counterintuitive, it's because we're used to thinking that business and life are somehow different spheres that are governed by different rules. According to this logic, social and environmental responsibility is at best peripheral to the core purpose of business, which is to maximize economic profit. Popular culture reinforces this message in spades. I spent my early career in Los Angeles, love movies, and tend to draw social lessons from them. Think of the Mafiosi characters in *The Godfather*, who justify appalling acts of treachery and violence by defining business impersonally: "This was strictly business. Tell Michael I always liked him."

Or consider the slogan "Greed is good," made famous by the corporate raider character that Michael Douglas plays in Oliver Stone's movie *Wall Street*. Stone did not mean for us to conclude that greed really is good; *Wall Street* was inspired in part by his father, an old-school stockbroker who believed in serving customers honorably. Isn't it ironic that several generations of young capitalists have interpreted Stone's cautionary tale as a rallying cry to get out there and be, well, greedy? The thing is, slogans like "Greed is good" and "This was strictly business" make perfect sense in a disconnected world where people can create a separate sphere—first in their own minds and then in their behavior—in which they relate to one another situationally. The business world, for one, became that sphere. All those subprime mortgages—they were "strictly business." The idea was that there was an amoral space, where as long as you were not breaking the law, your only responsibility was to shareholder value and pursuit of profit. Sadly and painfully, too many of us failed to realize that technology not only interconnected us; it also made us morally interdependent. "Greed is good" and "too big to fail" are rational strategies for a world in which business and personal lives are separate. But they are the absolute worst strategies in a connected world where everything is personal because everyone's behavior affects everyone else.

I think that's why the HOW view of the world is resonating in forums that were traditionally dominated by economic perspectives. The annual World Economic Forum gathering in Davos, for example, was historically about bringing business and political leaders together to gauge the state of the global economy and generate ideas to drive economic growth in order to improve the state of the world. But the title of the 2011 Davos conference was "Shared Norms for a New Reality"—norms as in normative behavior, that which we *should* do. The conference brochure stated explicitly that the meeting would focus on "the question of how." And *Fortune*, the magazine that helped create the too big to fail business ethos through its annual ranking of the 500 biggest American companies, took a break from its more typical *how much* focus to profile the HOW philosophy in an article titled "Why Doing Good Is Good for Business."

Too big to fail logic has always been prevalent in international affairs, where countries race to pile up arsenals and currency reserves in the belief that size equals power and security. But does it? Here again, this book proved predictive in ways that I certainly didn't imagine when I wrote it. The Prologue starts off by describing the spontaneous Wave that stadium crowds perform at big sporting events in order to encourage their favorite team. For me, the Wave is a great metaphor of the kind of human energy and behavior that will thrive in the twenty-first century. And not just at football games, either. The Middle East experienced a series of dramatic, globally televised waves during the early months of 2011, when popular revolutions confronted despotic governments in several Arab countries. Not unlike Wall Street, the politics of the region had long been governed by a too big to fail ethos. We assumed that the autocratic regimes of the Arab world would last forever because they had power and money on their side. Many also benefited from U.S. support, extended not because these regimes shared our values but because we thought that only strong dictators could fight terrorists and keep the oil flowing.

And then something amazing happened. Like millions of other people around the world, I was glued to my TV screen during the

Arab Spring of 2011. In Tunisia and in Egypt, peaceful demonstrators armed with cell phone cameras rose up against the state, using social media channels like Facebook and Twitter to organize their protests and transmit their stories to the world. The protesters wanted the things we all want: justice, dignity, and freedom. And although they didn't have tanks or torture chambers on their side, they quickly succeeded in forcing the old regimes from power. In other words, they created situational freedom, or *freedom from* tyranny. The road ahead is uncertain, and nobody knows whether this situational freedom will lead to sustainable freedom, the *freedom to* live according to their values. But at the very least, we now know that popular movements inspired by sustainable values can triumph against the forces of violence and repression. No dictator is too big to fail.

As I watched thousands of ordinary Egyptians demanding their rights in Tahrir Square, I felt that we received final confirmation that being too big to fail is a myth. Whether on Wall Street or in Cairo, it has certainly proved misguided as a strategy. Instead we need leaders, companies, and governments that are too sustainable to fail, too principled to fail, and too good to fail.

Why? Because in a hyperconnected world, more individuals and small groups can be a stronger force for more good or more evil. One individual can steal millions of personal identities, and one individual can spark revolutions for freedom across the Arab world. Essentially, we've democratized the production of good and evil. The closer we're all connected, the more frequently we should expect the unexpected to happen. In a world of constant, radical change, we all need a bulwark that will act simultaneously as propellant and guide. We need to root ourselves in what we know should never change—our values. That's why now more than ever we need people and organizations rooted in sustainable values. Such values do double duty by keeping you from lurching from crisis to crisis, from greed to fear. They guide you on a sustainable path of progress.

THE RISE OF INSPIRATIONAL LEADERSHIP

If too big to fail is the wrong strategy for a hyperconnected world, then how should we structure our lives and our organizations to make them too sustainable to fail? The short answer is that we need to re-think the nature of leadership itself. Here's why. In today's knowledge economy, the sources of power—information and ideas—are infinite. Google gives them away for free. Because we can't hoard information or have more of it relative to others, the command-and-control leader-ship habits of the Industrial Age are increasingly less effective. When we look at the world through the lens of HOW, we see leaders shift, and others even transform, their habits of leadership from "command and control" to "connect and collaborate." It's a move from exerting power *over* people to generating waves *through* them.

These inspirational leaders have come to understand that as the source of power shifts, how they elicit and guide behavior must shift accordingly. This, too, is quite simple. There are only three ways to generate human connection and conduct: You can coerce, motivate, or inspire.

Coercion says: "Get me the memo by five o'clock. My way or the highway. Just get it done—I don't care how." Motivation says: "If you get it done, you'll get a bigger bonus." Coercive and motivational leaders use systems of external rewards (carrots) and punishments (sticks) to ex-tract performance out of people, generate connection with them, and otherwise get them to play by a set of rules. But in our interconnected world, we are quickly discovering the limitations of carrots and sticks, and that we can't write enough rules to get the behaviors we want for every situation we can imagine, much less for all the ones we can't. We are also seeing the limitations of carrots and sticks as the source of strong connections in a world that readily exposes our connections for what they really are. If the only reason I work at a company is for a pay-check, I'll leave when I'm offered a bigger one. If the only reason I buy something from one company is its price, then I'll switch my loyalty if someone else sells it for less. Motivation also turns out to be an expen-sive way to propel behavior and generate connection, particularly in hard times when there are fewer carrots to go around.

As leaders, we need to rely more on inspiration and less on coer-cion and motivation, especially because we now are asking more of our employees and their conduct than we ever did in the past. We want them to relate to colleagues around the world who come from different cultures and speak different languages. We want them to push beyond merely serving customers to create unique, delightful, and genuine experiences. We ask employees to honorably represent their company and nurture its brand, not only when they're on the job, but whenever they publicly express themselves in tweets, blog posts, e-mails, or any other interaction. We ask employees to be resourceful with fewer resources and resilient in the face of unimaginable uncertainty. We increasingly ask employees to go beyond continuous improvement by conceiving and implementing disruptive innovations that deliver the step changes our companies need to thrive amid global competition. These are not only big asks; they are numerous asks. If you think further about these asks, you will notice that we're asking for distinctly human qualities and behaviors. Carrots and sticks are largely inapplicable to the responses we need.

So what kind of leadership supplies the big answer to these big asks? Connect-and-collaborate leadership that inspires the best in people! Ironically, no industry illustrates this more than professional sports, a realm where too big to fail thinking once reigned supreme. In sports you try to be bigger, stronger, and faster than the other team so that you can outscore them. It's all about peak performance, winning year after year until you've built a dynasty. As you might expect, successful coaches have often been martinets who got results by being highly demanding and screaming at their players. Think Vince Lombardi, Bobby Knight, Tom Coughlin, and a host of other harsh disciplinarians associated with winning in the past. And then consider the Spanish national soccer team, which bounced back from a classic way-of-life crisis sparked by the team's shocking first-round loss in the 2010 World Cup. The Spanish coach, Vicente del Bosque, is the opposite of a screaming drill sergeant. After the loss, he did not impose extra practice drills or other punishments "for the sake of it or to make a show of strength that I am the one in command." Instead he held a series of short team meetings where he reminded his players that selflessness and teamwork had gotten them this far. Del Bosque's quiet leadership apparently united and galvanized his players, who went on to win the World Cup.[3]

If you're a National Football League (NFL) fan, you know that del Bosque is hardly an isolated case. Football is perhaps the ultimate "power over" realm, yet many of the most successful American football coaches today are embracing collaborative leadership styles. One of them, Coughlin, led the New York Giants to an improbable victory in the 2007 Super Bowl thanks in large part to his leadership transformation. Despite Coughlin's long tenure as a pro football coach, critics often attacked his inability to connect with players. They referred to him as an "autocratic tyrant" and a "distant, dictatorial figure." He was nearly fired. So he changed his leadership habits. Rather than screaming more loudly at players, Coughlin sought to forge meaningful connections with them. He began to regularly huddle with the players to gauge their concerns and to learn about their families and lives away from football. His goal of winning the Super Bowl remained the same, but his methods changed dramatically. Coughlin enlisted his players in shared beliefs about being champions and in values that would guide *how* they worked together. An old dog, so to speak, not only learned a new trick, but he also had the courage to transform himself, and he transformed his team in the process.[4]

Am I saying that Coughlin and del Bosque are saints? Not at all. Like many of today's most forward-thinking CEOs, they are smart leaders who have found new ways to elicit peak performance in a world where traditional forms of power are rapidly losing sway. It's all about rethinking the strategic significance of behavior, moving it from defense to offense.

I've presented the HOW philosophy to many corporate leaders. In the past, quite a few of them would listen attentively and then refer me to their "goalies" (i.e., their general counsel, chief ethics officer, chief risk officer, or external affairs officer). CEOs have always wanted to employ the best goalkeepers on the planet, the ones who give up the fewest goals from the perspective of avoiding impeachable conduct and preventing compliance failures. But historically, most business leaders have been less interested in playing goalie than in scoring goals. They have tended to view behavior as a defensive tactic, used to prevent bad things from happening or to demonstrate contrition after their company misbehaves.

This mind-set is understandable. Our initial introduction to the term *behavior* may remind us of the scoldings we received as children. We were admonished to "Behave!" in response to our objectionable actions. From that age onward, most of us developed a perception of behaving as something we need to do only after acting badly. If you're convicted of a crime, for example, you might get sent to prison. And how do prisoners earn reduced sentences? Good behavior.

In recent years, however, I've been heartened to see that many CEOs have stopped referring me to their goalies. Beyond setting the right "tone from top," they have become more directly and deeply involved in shaping their company's culture and their colleagues' behavior. Why? Because these HOW leaders now recognize that sustainable behavior is an offensive strategy that you need to deploy over the entire field. They are also listening carefully to their chief legal or risk officers, who increasingly tell them that there are simply too many shots on goal for them to block, and that therefore the best defense is to keep the ball or puck on offense. Behavior has become a powerful source of excellence and competitive advantage. In the past, bosses could get away with telling subordinates, "Just get it done—I don't care how." The more progressive ones would implore their people to think outside the box, which in their minds was a compliment. In my mind, it's an insult. If you trusted your people, you wouldn't put them in a box in the first place. In our radically interconnected world, leaders need to flip the switch and replace task-based jobs (which are about *what* people must do) with values-based missions. In short, it's about *how* we should get things done.

Think of it as a shift from valuing size to valuing significance. Conversations about "how much" constantly echo throughout business, politics, and our personal lives: How much revenue can we squeeze into this quarter? How much debt can we tolerate? How much growth can we generate? How big should government be? But "How much?" and "How big?" aren't the right questions. Instead we should be asking how we can create organizations and societies that mirror our deepest values. Consider the Himalayan Kingdom of Bhutan, which has long measured its economic and social progress by the yardstick of "gross national happiness," as opposed to gross national product. Today, policy makers in Britain, France, and even Somerville, Massachusetts (where census takers now ask citizens, "How happy do you feel right now?" to help guide future public policy decisions)[5] are debating how similar indexes might measure public happiness and welfare. The fact that governments are increasingly trying to measure happiness as well as material prosperity tells us something about the way the world is going. We are moving from *how much* to *how*.

This leads me back to the third and, I believe, most powerful form of human influence: inspiration. The first syllable of *inspiration* is *in*, signifying that the conduct is internal and intrinsic. Whereas coercion and motivation happen *to* you, inspiration happens *in* you. Inspired people have a deep purpose greater than themselves. They are guided by values they deem to be fundamental—values that sustain their relationships with others in pursuit of shared visions worthy of their dedication and commitment. In other words, inspired behavior starts and ends with people. After all, HOW is an anagram of WHO.

We are not only in the Era of Behavior; we are in the era of behaviors that can only be inspired. We are therefore also in the Era of Inspiration. Inspiration is the ultimate renewable energy resource. And today, inspirational leadership is the most powerful, abundant, efficient, affordable, and shareable source of human connection and guide of human behavior. This kind of leadership can inspire—and reinspire—over and over, without any cost and with dividends that never cease. Clearly, we need more leaders capable of inspiring the game-changing behaviors that map to the world we now inhabit.

We still have a long way to go. Engagement scores among U.S. and many global workers have tumbled in recent years. I think that's because we've been spending too much time engaging workers with carrots and sticks, and not nearly enough time inspiring them with values and missions worthy of their commitment. Leaders and companies need to rethink engagement as a by-product of inspiration. And some are. For example, I recently watched *how* an inspired Southwest Airlines flight attendant connected with an entire planeload of passengers en route to Las Vegas. As we were getting ready to disembark, the attendant came on the speaker and cheerfully announced: "It's a well-known fact that if you fold your seatbelts over your seat when you leave the plane, your luck will improve at the casino tables." Everyone laughed, and then we all did as she suggested. But here's the beautiful part: Federal Aviation Administration (FAA) regulations require seatbelts to be folded on the seats before new passengers can board. She could have taken the time and effort to fold every seatbelt herself. She certainly was not required by her company policy manual nor was she incented by her company compensation program to get us to help her do her job. Instead she was inspired to innovate in her behavior. (When this inspired attendant arrives in Los Angeles, she will likely innovate again in telling her same joke by swapping the number of celebrity sightings for dollars won at the tables.) Through *how* the attendant connected with and enlisted us, she helped her company comply with a regulation, gain an operational advantage in turning the plane around faster (because it would have taken her six minutes to fold the seatbelts by herself), and keep its brand promise of getting us to where we were going with "no frills, fun, safely, and on time."

This kind of creative behavior can't be commanded by a manager or codified in a rule book. It needs to be inspired. You can probably think of several inspirational leaders in your own life and work, but that flight attendant really sums it up for me. She got her point across by connecting with us, not by telling us what to do. She used behavior strategically, not defensively. She wasn't the CEO, an executive, or even a midlevel manager, and yet she exhibited inspirational leadership. To thrive, our companies need to burst with daily demonstrations of inspirational leadership by every employee, regardless of his or her position.

Examples like this one help us rethink leadership. Human qualities like creativity, helpfulness, and hope can't be commanded; they can only be inspired *in people*. You can't order somebody to have a great idea. You can't mandate rich, creative collaborations. You can't command a doctor or nurse to be more humane and show compassion at a patient's bedside. You can't really motivate or coerce a teacher to be more hopeful and create a sense of possibility in the classroom. You can't sufficiently motivate a sales representative to engender trust in every interaction. The lucky ones figure it out early on their own, but others need to be inspired to bring out these qualities.

THE HUMAN OPERATING SYSTEM

Because leadership is now more about inspiration than about coercion or motivation, we need to rethink traditional corporate governance and organization. In recent years, many successful, innovative companies have begun to deconstruct traditional hierarchies and eliminate workplace rules and approvals. These leaders understand that in an open-source world it's no longer practical to run companies as though they were fortresses or jails. But deconstructing hierarchy and flattening the organization chart mark only the first steps—and are the easy part. Once those outdated structures are removed, organizations need to construct and foster corporate cultures that facilitate inspired behavior.

It's about moving from *freedom from* micromanagement and unnecessary approvals to *freedom to* contribute one's character and creativity to *how* the organization pursues its mission.

While I don't think human beings are much like computers, I see a strong analogy between a computer operating system (OS) and the kind of human operating systems we need in order to thrive amid business conditions of the twenty-first century. In both realms you need killer applications to spur adoption of a new system. Just as word processing and e-mail were the killer apps within PC operating systems in the late twentieth century, behavior (as offense) represents the killer app of the human operating system. To implement a human operating system (I think of it as a HOW OS of sorts), organizations first need to build cultures that value humans and behavior at their core. Second, they need to reduce their reliance on traditional command-and-control corporate governance. Finally, they need to harmonize the two models to more effectively put humanity back at the center of business, not just inside every company but across the ecosystems that connect companies with their customers, suppliers, partners, and society.

Today we don't need just technology innovators. We need behavior pioneers who innovate in HOW. One day, not too far in the future, everyone on the planet will be connected by technology. The more that happens, the more the only differentiator will be the quality and depth of your humanity—*how* you connect with and inspire other humans. When everyone has a smart phone, all that matters is the human content of the conversation—not that you have a phone and I don't. That's why more and more organizations are declaring their humanity. Chevron has become the "Human Energy" company; Dow has the "Human Element"; Cisco is the "Human Network." Ally Bank's slogan is "We speak human." To be sure, some companies still honor their humanity in the breach, some confine it to their marketing departments, and others are just beginning the hard work of translating their values into corporate practices and leadership and individual behaviors that gain advantage and forge valuable relationships in the marketplace. It is not enough to proclaim your humanity; you have to live it! The winning organizations are those that deeply understand this. They are placing their humanity at the center of how they operate, lead, and govern, and not only at the center of a marketing campaign. In short, companies must be good in order to be great.

MY JOURNEY

Who am I to be telling you all this? I'm the founder and CEO of LRN, a company that helps global enterprises of all sizes win through *how* they do what they do. My entrepreneurial journey started modestly enough, as many such business journeys do. I graduated from high school with less then a handful of As: One was in phys ed and another was in auto shop. I got a 970 on the SAT. I took it again and my score increased dramatically to 980. Growing up, I struggled with dyslexia. Somehow I talked my way into the University of California at Los Angeles (UCLA). I was accepted very late, and because all the other classes were full I found myself taking remedial English and philosophy.

I fell in love with philosophy, which is fundamentally a discipline that teaches you how to rethink the world using observation and logic. I was particularly drawn to moral philosophy, which addresses some of life's deepest questions, such as the nature of happiness, the difference between good and evil, and the organization of a just society. With my professors' encouragement, philosophy helped me overcome dyslexia. Other academic disciplines rewarded the ability to plow through lengthy reading lists. I couldn't do that, but philosophy rewarded me for the careful consideration of one idea. As a result, my disability became a strength.

Philosophy is also at the heart of my company, LRN. Since many years B.E.—before Enron—and certainly before corporate malfeasance stories became daily headlines, we've been applying philosophy to the rough-and-tumble world of business. We've taught hundreds of business leaders how to inspire principled performance throughout their organizations. We've taught millions of employees how to do the right thing. So my business is an extension of philosophy. I like to think of myself as a philosopher in a suit. (And LRN's conference rooms are named after the great moral philosophers.)

Here's how LRN happened. After studying philosophy as an undergraduate and graduate student, I went to law school. After graduation, I took a job at a private law firm. As I was toiling away in the law library one day, it dawned on me that someone somewhere must have researched the very issue I was working on, and almost certainly knew more about it than I did (which was zero). I saw an opportunity to make legal knowledge accessible to a large number of people in business at a low price, so I built a network of the finest legal minds that could deliver expert knowledge in a far more efficient, democratic way. The business flourished, and we found ourselves helping some of the largest companies in the world confront their legal challenges and manage their risk.

I soon realized, however, that the core of our efforts lay in helping our partners put out fires by responding to legal challenges that had already arisen. I began to believe that we could be of better service by helping them design and build fireproof enterprises, so to speak, to help them develop a new approach to getting their HOWs right and prevent these legal problems from arising in the first place. So we evolved into a company that helped organizations build sustainable cultures at every level, from the executive suite to the shop floor.

For a while, it often felt like we were selling vitamins to companies whose leaders did not realize they could get sick. Then a series of business scandals hit, and suddenly we found ourselves in the middle of a global discussion about values. My alma mater, UCLA, invited me to give the commencement speech, convinced that the power in HOW was the most practical message the graduating class could hear. The U.S. Federal Sentencing Commission asked me to testify about new ways of achieving higher standards of conduct and responsibility in business as they considered revisions to the Federal Sentencing Guidelines. The phone started ringing and the e-mail began to pour in from companies that realized there was an epidemic and they could catch it at any time: I was on TV, traveling the country, and speaking to corporate boards and employee groups of some of the biggest, most venerated companies in the world. LRN quadrupled in size.

Suddenly, it was practical—even fashionable—to be principled. But I saw this as a double-edged sword. Sure, more people acting in a principled way, even if for the wrong reasons (to avoid prosecution, to minimize liability, or to build good PR), still meant more people acting principled, and that was a net good. However, I sensed that people lacked a deep understanding of why they should be principled, and why they should dedicate new energy and emphasis to how they pursue their goals and interests. From that basic notion, LRN has continued to change and expand its vision to help companies of all stripes and sizes the world over to win through principled performance and by outbehaving the competition.

One important way that can you can outbehave the competition is to "outgreen" it. This realization inspired LRN's acquisition of GreenOrder during the depths of the Great Recession, when most companies were hunkering down rather than seeking to grow. GreenOrder was a small but highly successful consulting firm that helped big companies like General Electric develop innovative, environmentally sustainable business practices and products. Like LRN, the team at GreenOrder understood that sustainability is about more than changing light bulbs or fuel sources; rather, it is about changing mindsets and cultures. It is fundamentally about a mode of leadership and behavior that aims to create lasting value as opposed to piling up short-term transactional wins. It's less about wind turbines or solar panels or green buildings than about the reason we want those things: so that our companies and our world will be better off tomorrow than they are today.

Today LRN operates globally, with offices in New York, Los Angeles, London, and Mumbai and colleagues in many other states and countries. We reach, work with, and help shape winning organizational cultures inspired by sustainable values in hundreds of companies with over 20 million people who work in more than 100 countries around the world.

Many of the concepts and strategies identified in this book have been consciously tested in the trenches at LRN, which is why we also tend to view ourselves as a laboratory. We aspire to be the change that we seek in the world. We call it "Living HOW." In this spirit, we tore up our old vertical org chart and designed a flat, self-governing model. We now rely on our Leadership Framework to guide our decisions and interactions, teams to collaboratively drive shared initiatives, and elected councils to provide necessary governance. We endeavor to live our philosophy that you generate trust by extending it to others. One way that we've extended trust has to do with how colleagues spend company money. For example, we want our people to file honest expense reports. Who doesn't? But instead of tightening oversight, we did away with it: no approvals required. We still do random report checks and track aggregate numbers. It helps us arrive at smarter policies on booking airfares, for example. Similarly, our vacation policy is "take whatever vacation you think you need as long as you are considerate of your colleagues." And no one reports to a so-called boss who evaluates their performance. Instead, our principled performance reviews are conducted by a network of colleagues each individual selects to help guide his or her own development. The only boss at LRN is our mission.

As a moral philosopher, I'm pretty well versed in the art of logical argument. But as LRN grew, I kept meeting executives at client companies who were really comfortable only managing what they could measure. Beyond making the philosophical case for HOW, and arguing from our own and our clients' experiences in implementing HOW, I felt compelled to test my arguments and seek statistical confirmation and quantification of my theory and observations—HOW metrics, if you will. So we launched a series of major surveys on governance, culture, and leadership in companies worldwide. These studies on *how* companies and their people operate and conduct themselves stress-tested the HOW Framework, which you'll read about in later chapters of this book. The results indicate firmly that values-based organizational cultures (those with a human operating system and inspirational leaders) much more readily adopt new ideas, are more innovative, deliver better financial performance and customer experiences, enhance their recruiting success, are less plagued by employee attrition, and find lower levels of employee misconduct and retaliation—all well-established building blocks of long-term sustainability and success.

THE PURSUIT OF SIGNIFICANCE

As I said, this is a HOW book, not a *how-to* book. *How-to* books tend to offer *Five Rules of This, Ten Practices for That,* or *Seven Ways to Get More of Whatever It Is You Want.* Follow all the rules exactly, these books promise, and the end goal—be it career success, losing weight, or becoming a millionaire—will be yours. I believe that a truly useful book must deliver something more—more lasting, more essential, and more applicable to the full range of life. Instead of rules, steps, or an instruction manual, this book offers an approach—a framework and a way of seeing—to help you navigate the globally interconnected and interdependent world in which we now live and work. It offers a more positive, hopeful vision that will guide you beyond short-term rewards toward lasting success.

A new vision of HOW requires a new way of embracing why we get up every morning and go to work. I believe that the inspiration to do so lives in the thought that there is a difference between doing something *so as to* succeed and doing something *and* achieving success. Inspirational leaders understand this important distinction. They are mindful of the paradox of hedonism, which I discuss in this book, the philosophical idea that if you pursue happiness directly it eludes you. But if you passionately pursue a higher, more meaningful purpose, you can achieve happiness. I have learned from my work that there is a corollary to the paradox of hedonism. I call it the paradox of success—that you can't achieve success by pursuing it directly. Inspirational leaders understand that real, sustainable value can be achieved only when you pursue something greater than yourself that makes a difference in the lives of others. The word I use for this is *significance.*

How we manage this relationship between success and significance will determine our ability to not only survive, but thrive in the new conditions of the world today. This book seeks to help you discover this idea in everything you do. Throughout the pages that follow, we explore a new lens through which to view the world, business, and human endeavor. I have learned this way of seeing from my conversations with everyone from thought leaders, scholars, CEOs, and corporate managers to professional cheerleaders, sports stars, and New York City street vendors. I have filtered these conversations through the challenges I face leading a growing company that must contend every day with competitors that also want to get ahead. I deal with the pressure to get better, make the numbers, take care of every customer, and, above all, make a difference, while challenging myself to do the right thing even when it's inconvenient, unpopular, or seemingly less profitable.

Through anecdotes, case studies, cutting-edge research in a wide range of fields, personal experience, and interviews with a diverse group of leaders, experts, and everyday folk—some familiar, others completely unexpected—we explore in this book HOW we think, HOW we lead, HOW we behave, and HOW we govern ourselves to uncover the new HOWs that unlock and create value in the twenty-first century and beyond. People and organizations that get their HOWs right will rise to the top today and stay on top tomorrow. They will be rewarded, promoted, and celebrated. The world has changed to make this idea more relevant than ever, and I believe it now represents the most powerful way to chart a course of enduring personal and organizational achievement.

No doubt you've heard the old business cliché that hope is not a strategy. It's an expression used to belittle managers who don't do their analytic homework before embarking on a course of action. But inspirational leaders understand that hope is very much a strategy. Franklin Delano Roosevelt understood that in the depths of the Great Depression, when he galvanized a despondent nation by telling Americans that they had nothing to fear but fear itself. Roosevelt was urging not to lose hope. Hope is a sustainable value that inspires us to see the world as a source of meaning and to connect with people in valuable ways. Hope is a catalyst. When we lose hope, we retreat into ourselves; we detach and despair. When we have hope, we lean into the world, and a sense of possibility takes root that allows us to connect with others and collaborate with them to bring these futures about. Like trust, hope is fundamental to how we connect in a connected world. Without hope there can be no progress, no innovation, and no lasting prosperity. Hope impels people to get up out of their chairs, and inspires them to take on challenges that they never dreamed of taking on before—and to stick with them however hard things get. Of course hope alone is not a strategy, but it is the essential starting point for any sustainable strategy. In this way, hope inspires the pursuit of significance. And that's the ultimate HOW.

DOV SEIDMAN
Founder and Chief Executive Officer, LRN
July 2011

Why HOW We Do Anything
Means Everything

Making Waves

On October 15, 1981, in the stands of the sold-out Oakland Coliseum, Krazy George Henderson had a vision. It was the third game of the American League play-off series between the Oakland Athletics and the New York Yankees, and the A's had lost the first two. Krazy George was a professional cheerleader, in the A's employ for three years or so. No pom-pom shaking college rah-rah, George roved solo up and down the aisles of the stadium clad in cutoff shorts and a sweatshirt, a manic Robin Williams character with Albert Einstein hair, banging with abandon a small drum, inveigling the crowd, and leading cheers with an infectious intensity that had endeared him to fans throughout the Bay Area. Most shouts were familiar, like *"Here we go, Oakland, here we go!"* But this day was different. On this day, Krazy George imagined a gesture that would start in his section and sweep successively through the crowd in a giant, continuous wave of connected enthusiasm, a transformative event that later proved historical. October 15, 1981, is the day Krazy George Henderson invented the Wave.[1]

Everything has to start somewhere.

I had long been fascinated by the Wave, so I wanted to find Krazy George and ask him about the story of that first Wave. "The day I

1

started it, I already knew what I wanted," he told me. "I knew what was gonna happen, but nobody else in the stadium did.

"First thing, I hit my drum. That focuses everybody within three to four sections of me. It's the secret to why I am successful. See, the drum shows energy and emotions; it shows I am personally involved with the fans. I move everywhere in the stadium (I am constantly moving), and I pound the drum. They see me sweating, they see the energy, they see that I love the game, and that I love the team. I act like a fan wants to act, and it releases something in them.

"So that day, I had to tell them what I envisioned. It's so important to set the cheer up. If everybody doesn't do it, it won't go. You have to have almost total participation for it to go, and that's the point. I pounded the drum and I started screaming, '*Here is what we're gonna do. We're gonna stand up and throw our hands in the air. I want to start with this section, and we're gonna go to this section,*' and I yelled down to the next section. '*I'm gonna start it and it's gonna keep going.*'

"I knew it would die. I didn't know how far it would go before it died, but I knew it would. No one had *ever* seen this before. So, I prepared them. I told them that when this thing died, I wanted all three sections to boo as loudly as they could. I couldn't reach out to the whole stadium myself, but I thought as a group we might. Then I said, '*We're gonna start on three, this section first; then you are gonna go, and get ready down there.*' I yelled as loud as I could, and I knew what was gonna happen, and I started it, and the first section stood and threw their hands in the air . . . then the second section . . . the third . . . the fourth; it went about five sections and it just tailed off to nothing. People were looking at the game and they didn't know what was happening. So it died.

"Right on cue, three sections just went '*Booo!*' and I pounded my drum. I was screaming and waving my arms. They can't hear *me* across the field, but they can hear my drum. They saw me flailing my arms and shaking my drumstick at them, and they got the idea. So, I started it a second time and it went about 11 sections—about a third of the way around—and it died behind home plate. Suddenly, the hugest '*Booooo!*' you ever heard, maybe six, eight sections, came out. But it focused everybody, and they figured out what I wanted to do. So I said, 'We're gonna try it again.' I didn't say 'try'; I said, 'We're *doing* it again,' and I started it the third time.

"By the time I looked around, all three decks in the stadium were doing it, all in unison, throwing up their hands, a giant wave of human energy going around the stadium. It swept behind home plate. It kept going, and it got stronger and stronger. The people were screaming and yelling. It came around, went behind home plate and then all the way through the outfield, through the bleachers, and back to our section, and it just kept going. It swept right back, and it got even more powerful. Everybody was going crazy. Nobody had ever seen this before.

"The great left fielder for the A's, Rickey Henderson, known as 'The Man of Steal' for his prowess running the bases, was coming up to bat at the time. He looked up and saw this thing going around and around the stadium, and he stepped out of the batter's box and adjusted his gloves for about two minutes, watching this thing. He just stood there, looking at this thing, adjusting his batting gloves. I don't know how many times it went around—four, five, six times—it was that powerful.

"After the Wave, the crowd was noticeably different, hyped up and involved in the game. They knew they'd helped out. They felt the energy. When I did the next cheer, the defense cheer or the clapping, it was *much* louder. That's the thing I saw that day, and still see today after almost 25 years of leading the Wave, the added energy that it brings to the stadium or the arena or whatever venue I'm at. The fans start feeling that they are part of the game and they're adding to it."

The Wave is an extraordinary act. All those people, spread out over a vast stadium, with limited ability to connect or communicate, somehow come together in a giant cooperative act inspired by a common goal: to help the home team win. It defies language and culture, occurring with regularity throughout the world at Tower of Babel events as diverse as the Olympics and international soccer games (in fact, it's often called the Mexican Wave or La Olá because of its first appearance on the international stage at the Mexico City World Cup Finals in 1986).[2] It transverses gender, income, and societal status. It is a pure expression of collective passion released.

When I started LRN Corporation in 1994, I thought it would be extraordinary if I could capture in the workplace something of the spirit of the Wave—that rich, cacophonous tapestry of human beings coming together to create that home court advantage. Was there some way to foment that kind of creative energy focused on our business goals? *What does it take to start a Wave?*

If you consider the Wave as a process of human endeavor, you realize immediately that anyone can start one—an enthusiastic soccer mom, four drunken guys with jellyroll bellies and their bare chests painted Oakland green, or eight adolescents who idolize the team's star player. You don't have to be the owner of the stadium, the richest or most powerful person there, or even a paid professional like Krazy George. No one takes out their business card and says, "My title is the biggest; let the Wave start with me." Anyone can start a Wave; it is a truly democratic act.

So, how do you do it? Let's have some fun for a minute and break it down. Say, for instance, that you are sitting in the stands at a football game and the home team is down by a touchdown. You see your team huffing and puffing, and you are disappointed that your fellow fans seem lethargic and complacent. Suddenly, you have a vision, a vision to help your team win, to make them feel like they have a home field advantage. You imagine a certain esprit de corps, a massive wave of energy. But you are honest with yourself. You realize that you don't own the stadium. The people there don't owe you anything—they are free agents; they have other agendas. They are munching popcorn, eating hot dogs, slurping drinks, or cheering for the opposing team. They might be highly inconvenienced by your vision. The guy next to you may not feel like getting up; he might be thinking, "I'm mad as hell that our prima donna wide receiver wants to be traded." So, what will it take?

First, you need people's attention. Starting a Wave requires an act of leadership, so you must be willing to stand up and lead. You have to stand up, communicate your idea, and inspire others to help you achieve it. But how? Krazy George uses his drum, but the security guard at the metal detectors made you leave yours in the car. You could, perhaps, turn to the guy next to you and say, "Hey, here's 20 bucks—let's stand up." He might go along, but really, unless you are Bill Gates you will probably run out of money before you get all 60,000 fans to buy into your plan, and you certainly don't have enough money to motivate them to get up more than once. You will soon exhaust whatever loyalty you might have bought and they will sit down or start negotiating for more. Money as a motivator has its limits.

You could turn to the people around you and say, "Listen, I'm a lot bigger than you, and if you don't get up when I say so I'm gonna punch you out." Your impressive display of brute force might get some people to follow you. Coercing by fear, however, is limited in its reach. You might get local buy-in, but the people three sections over or across the stadium probably feel securely remote from your threats, and will likely continue to do as they please, which may include simply leaving. The pumped-up bicep and snarling tone inspire little beyond a desire to flee. More important to your vision: If they do comply, with what gusto will they stand up? To create a great and powerful Wave, one that can make a difference to your team, you need enthusiastic participation. Threatened, will they leap up or, in a state of reluctant acquiescence to your superior brawn, get up slowly? Will it be a glorious Wave or a so-so Wave?

Having ruled out money as a motivator and force as a coercer, your best option to reach out to the strangers around you is probably verbal communication (although you are basically strangers, you are united in a common activity of watching the game, so you do start from a place of common interest). So what do you say and, more important, *how* do you say it? Again, you have some options. You could think, "Information is power. The more information I control, the greater my advantage over these other fans." You have a vision and you don't want anyone to steal it, so you turn to the next guy and say, "I'm going to ask you to do something, but I can't tell you why; it's on a need-to-know basis. Trust me." By playing your cards close to your chest, of course, you ask a bunch of people to risk making fools of themselves—or worse, engage in a waving and screaming activity that makes no sense to them—on the word of someone they hardly know. Krazy George may have built up enough personal capital from three years of banging that drum at Oakland As games to pull it off, but few others in the stadium have, and even George runs the risk of encountering a bunch of newbies from out of town who think he's just another Northern California nut job with a drum. If *you* try it, people will probably think, "How do I know this is going to work? Why should I trust him?" Your CIA operative approach will do little to allay suspicions of your motivations.

So you think, perhaps, it might be more effective to *share* your vision with the other fans. Maybe a PowerPoint presentation on the Jumbotron explaining the complex and fascinating physics of human interaction that form a Wave would win you converts:

Hungarian Research[3] Shows That the Wave:

❑ Usually rolls clockwise.
❑ Is 6 to 12 meters wide (average—15 seats).
❑ Moves about 12 meters (20 seats) per second.
❑ Is generated by no more than a few dozen people.
❑ Acquires a stable, near-linear shape as it expands through the crowd.

Credit: Vladimir Rys/Staff, Alemannia Aachen v Borussia Monchengladbach, 2006.

slide 13

Probability of Wave

Well-established approaches to the theoretical interpretation of excitable media can be generalized to include human social behavior. By analogy with models of excitable media, people are regarded as excitable units.

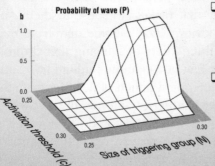

❑ Units are activated by an external stimulus—a distance- and direction-weighted concentration of nearby active people exceeding a threshold value (c).
❑ Once activated, each unit follows the same set of internal rules to pass through the active (standing and waving) and refractory (passive) phases before returning to its original resting (excitable) state.

slide 14

Clearly, while the PowerPoint presentation may stand as a testament to your superior research and computer presentation skills, it lacks something in its ability to inspire 60,000 people. Even if this were a baseball game, which, let's face it, can be as slow as molasses, a well-made PowerPoint slide is less interesting than the peanut guy every time.

Clearly, *how* you communicate your vision—how you connect with those around you—directly affects the outcome, so all these approaches miss the point. The essence of a Wave, what makes it such a forceful expression of human desire, is that it is powered by a common passion to help the home team win. That value lives larger than any individual's actions and unites all the fans in the stadium. No one followed Krazy George's idea because they thought it was about *George*; a Wave is leadership, but the most important thing about a Wave is that you forget where it started—Section 32? 64? 132? The fans followed because he got everybody enlisted, and when you get everybody enlisted, it doesn't matter where your Wave starts. It just goes. And no one followed Krazy George's idea because people booed (that was just a good-natured way of getting attention in a big stadium). They followed because they liked what he stood for and the way he banged his drum for it.

To start one, then, you need to *reach out* to those around you, to *share* your vision with them, to *enlist* them in a common purpose. You must lead this Wave not by wielding formal authority, punitive power, or the threat of a small thermonuclear device under the stands, but with a touch of charisma. To get them to join you, you must be earnest and transparent, hold nothing back, and earn their trust. "Hey!" you might yell, charged with passion and commitment, filled with the unbridled emotion that you want to uncork in others. "I've got this idea! If we all stand up, wave our arms, and yell, I think it might help us win!"

Who doesn't want to win?

I like the Wave as metaphor because it is about what a diverse group of people can accomplish when united by a common vision. It illustrates the power that moves through a group of people when they perform at their best, their most unbridled and passionate. People often don't realize that there's a powerful way of accomplishing something—a HOW—that incorporates being transparent, being revelatory, declaring your intentions, and being very open about everything it means to you; and that HOW affects the Wave you create. The best HOWs make a Wave continue long after it has moved beyond your reach. I've found that anyone willing to do so can understand, focus, and unleash that power in business (if not in all aspects of life) regardless of position, status, or authority. This is the first point of this book.

Individuals start Waves by acting powerfully and effectively on those around them. For the Wave to take off and go, however, the conditions in the stadium must be such that the energy generated by the few can flow easily to the many. Studies show that Waves begin more easily and travel further in circular or oval stadiums than they do in lineal ones. Crowds at a high school football game, where crosstown rivals sit on opposite sides of the field according to fan loyalty, are less likely to cooperate, even though they all live in the same town. Not so in oval soccer stadiums, despite equally intense partisan feelings. Organizations can build stadiums that allow Waves to happen. Teams can create environments that allow Waves to happen. This is the book's second point.

Recently, I ordered a bracelet for my wife from a New York jeweler for our upcoming wedding anniversary. The jeweler shipped it to me in Los Angeles via UPS overnight so that I would be sure to have it on the day (missing your anniversary, as we all know, may be an even greater screwup than not delivering for your customer's just-in-time supply chain). I met our UPS delivery guy, Angel Zamora, in my office lobby the next morning, eager for the package, but it wasn't there. Angel registered my disappointment immediately, and told me to sit tight. Though his shift ended when he emptied his cart at my building, an hour later he was still on the phone with the central warehouse in downtown Los Angeles. Finally, he traced the package down to a warehouse problem and arranged for a special run to get it delivered that night. He then gave me his personal cell phone number and the cell number of his supervisor, and told me he would stay with it until it was done. By five o'clock that afternoon, the package was in my hands.

When I saw Angel again, some days later on his regular run, I told him how impressed and grateful I was with the way he owned the situation and did what was necessary to keep the commitment

UPS had made. He didn't hesitate with his matter-of-fact reply: "It's what I do." It reminded me of the old story about two guys doing masonry work on a building. The first one, when asked what he was doing, says, "Laying bricks." The second replies, "Building a cathedral." Some people see themselves as bricklayers. Angel builds cathedrals. He doesn't define himself narrowly, as simply a package delivery person. He sees himself as the instrument by which UPS keeps its promises. He makes Waves that make UPS a leader in its field. By thinking of himself in the broadest, most purpose-driven terms, he distinguished not only his company, but also himself, not by WHAT he did—get me the package—but HOW he did it, with forthrightness, concern, passion, initiative, and a sense of being part of something larger than himself. Those HOWS, the quality of his endeavor and the way he was able to reach out to others, allow Angel to make Waves, to enlist those downtown who found my package and got it on a special delivery van to my office.

UPS, in turn, creates the culture that allows those Waves to happen. Angel did not have to go through a chain of sign-offs and approvals to get his overtime okayed or his extra work validated. UPS understands and institutionalizes the HOWS that allow its frontline personnel to get the job done right and to fulfill commitments to its customers with a minimum of drag on the system. UPS and Angel were aligned on common values and behaviors that inspired Angel to do what he did.

In today's business world, those companies building lasting success, those that seem to be getting it right in highly competitive markets, have something going on in them, a certain energy, very much like a Wave. Waves result from HOW we do what we do. If, sitting in a company's stadium, gripped by a vision of the way something should be, someone in the crowd feels comfortable enough, inspired enough, and able enough to reach out and connect powerfully to those around them, then great things can happen. To build and sustain long-term success in the new socioeconomic conditions that define our world, you must embrace a new power, the power in human conduct, the power in HOW.

Build success based on how people interact? You may think, *Come on! Business is a rough-and-tumble world. Competition is fierce, the pressure to make the numbers intense, and the environment slippery and full of potential downfalls. Sure, it's great to think about an ideal world where everyone is transparent, is driven by values, is inspired by common goals, treats each other well and fairly, and unites behind the common good; but that's just not the way it is.*

I would be insulting you if I did not acknowledge that we all carry a set of personal experiences that make it seem like some of the ideas I present throughout this book are an idealist's pipe dream of a world that will never be. But in the pages that follow, I hope to show you that the world that formed and informed most of these prior experiences—the business-is-war, information-is-power, to-the-victor-go-the-spoils world of run-and-gun capitalism—no longer exists. Advances in technology, communication, integration, and connectivity have converged with predictable cycles of history to create a sea change in the way we do business, and in the way we live our lives. Things have changed faster than we have developed new frameworks to understand them, and I hope to show you in great detail exactly how radical—and permanent—these changes are. To thrive in the hypertransparent, hyperconnected world of the twenty-first century, we need to change, too.

Throughout this book, I show you how qualities most people think of as soft—trust, respect, transparency, purpose, reputation—have become the hard currency of achievement in a connected world—the drivers of efficiency, productivity, and profitability. You will come to understand that the HOWS of human conduct will be the determining factor in your long-term success. At first blush, these ideas may seem to contradict much of what you believe or seem counterintuitive. By book's end, you might feel differently.

Waves are fun; that is their greatest benefit. Standing up, waving your arms, screaming your head off for the home team, and, most important, *being connected to everyone else in the stadium when you do so*, that's fun. But Krazy George told me that the most significant thing about his first Wave, and every Wave he has made since, is how it changes everything that comes after. For the rest of the game, the crowd cheers more vigorously. They are more excited and engaged in the outcome. They feel more a part of the experience. The Wave is not only powerful in itself; it unleashes long-term, enduring power in its wake. That is an essential property of power; once the circuit is complete, the current continues to flow.

There is a Wave pounding through the people who work in companies like UPS and many others that everyone there enthusiastically perpetuates. It represents a sea change, an approach to how we do what we do that generates lasting, quantifiable value. I believe it is a power that every individual and group of people can understand, master, and learn to apply, and this book will try to help you do that. This book is about the tidal power in HOW.

Part I

HOW WE HAVE BEEN, HOW WE HAVE CHANGED

INTRODUCTION: THE SPACES BETWEEN US

Consider, for a moment, our brains. Individual working units in the brain are called neurons. Some neurons are highly specialized to perform certain cognitive functions. Others are arranged in groups of varying size to accomplish more complicated tasks. Some are charged with storing things, and others with just passing information along. Neurons have *excitable membranes*, a unique cellular characteristic that allows them to generate and propagate electrical signals. When a neuron wants to act, it sends out a small signal, like an e-mail, to the parts of the brain with which it wants to connect. That signal, in order to get where it wants to go, must jump a series of small gaps, each called a synapse, that separate one neuron from another. A child's brain contains as many as 1,000 trillion synapses, but by adulthood age and decay pare that number back significantly to between 100 trillion and 500 trillion. What occurs in our synapses—in other words, *in the space in-between*—is a key determiner of successful brain function. So-called *strong synapses* pass messages—called *action potentials*—easily to the neurons around them. Where synapses are strong, they allow for the free-flowing transmission of energy from neuron to neuron that enables the vast range of human capability. Where synapses are weak, however, messages don't get through. A weak synapse drops the ball, so to speak.[1]

Now, imagine a football stadium, full of people. It functions in a remarkably similar fashion. Each fan is like a neuron. Each has an excitable membrane capable, should the individual desire, of reaching out and connecting with others. The space between them, where one person's skin leaves off and another's begins, is like a synapse. It's the space *in-between* where we connect. There are places in the stadium where people have strong connections—they know each other, hold season tickets, or share a similar enthusiasm for the home team—and places where the connections are weak. When the space between people is capable of connecting them strongly, cheers start with little encouragement, food purchased from strolling vendors gets passed along quickly, and rapport develops easily between strangers sitting nearby; in short, they thrive. When those junctions are weak, however, action potentials die. Fans cheer alone and must push down the row to get their own peanuts.

A single synapse in the brain, just like the space between people in a stadium, connects to many different neurons, like an intersection where many roads converge. This allows it to receive action potentials from many sources simultaneously. Subjected to these multiple simultaneous stimuli, even a weak synapse can be coaxed to pass along messages. In a stadium, we experience something similar. The combined stimulation of a lot of people doing the Wave often sweeps up and involves those less interested or connected to the cheer. In fact, what we colloquially call a "brain wave" is an electroencephalographic impression of a bunch of neurons all firing together, sending their action potentials across synapses weak and strong to get things going—essentially, the brain doing the Wave.

By analogy, in the realm of human behavior, everything that affects the spaces between us affects our ability to get things done. Put 60,000 people in a stadium blindfolded with earplugs, and making a Wave becomes extremely difficult. Ask them to whisper something from person to person while the organist plays at full volume and the message becomes unrecognizable before it leaves the section. Introduce a complicated emotion between two people and everything they say to one another can get misconstrued. To make Waves, then, to begin to generate the sorts of interpersonal interaction that can carry our initiatives throughout an organizational entity (like a brain, a stadium full of people, a team, or a business), we must not only understand the power it takes to start them, but we must also understand the things that affect the spaces between us, that make our interpersonal synapses strong or weak.

On October 13, 1994, Netscape Communications released the first version of its World Wide Web browser, heralding the dawn of the popular Internet and effectively spawning the information age.[2] At that moment, the free flow of information began to radically alter how we fill the spaces between us, bringing changes so significant as to have almost completely reshaped how the world works. Our understanding of these changes, however, has not kept pace with their rapidity. To adapt and succeed in these new conditions, then, we need a new framework, a new understanding of how we have been and how things have changed.

In this first part, we explore the recent (and not-so-recent) past to connect the dots between a series of disparate events that have shaped and informed our present world. We begin with the birth of the information age and the shift it brought from a command-and-control business model to one of collaboration and sharing. Then we look at how technology trespasses into the synapses of our relationships, both helping and hindering us. Finally, we talk about the shifts in our world that have intensified the importance of how we do what we do.

The next three chapters chart the geography of a very different world, a world of HOW, which requires new powers and new skills to traverse. By the end of this part, it is my hope that you have a greater understanding of the radical ways our landscape has changed, our critical need for a new lens with which to see our way through it, and the way HOW can guide us on our journey.

CHAPTER 1

From Land to Information

*Where is the wisdom we have
lost in knowledge? Where is the
knowledge we have lost in information?*
—T. S. Eliot

ometimes, to look ahead we must look back, in this case, way back,
to feudal Europe circa 1335 A.D. In the 1330s, England needed wine.
It needed wine because in the century before, Norman fashions had
become all the rage and your average noble Joe had given up his daily
pint of beer for a glass of *vin rouge*. It needed wine because wine provided vitamins, yeast, and calories to get the English through the long
winters. And it needed wine because, well, wine is fun. Given that England was too cold to grow a decent grape, the English required a system
of foreign exchange to get their spirits from France. They traded English
fleece to Flanders for Flemish cloth (the good stuff at the time), then
brought that to southern France to trade for the fruit of the vine. Luckily,
the English controlled both Flanders and Gascony (on the west coast of
France) at the time. Thus they were able to trade freely, transport safely,
and drink to their hearts' content. For these reasons, and a million other
feudal details, the French hated the Brits. In 1337, they attacked Flanders
to regain control of the mainland, beginning the Hundred Years' War,
which really lasted 116 years until 1453, when the Brits were finally

17

expelled from continental Europe and went back to drinking beer, a habit they largely retain to this day.[1]

What does all that have to do with us, doing business in a high-technology information age? Well, beer is not the only habit that has hung around since the Middle Ages. Back then we were a land-based world, and the people who controlled more high-value land than anyone else ruled. Land is a zero-sum game: The more I have, the less you have; and the more I have, the more powerful I am relative to you. Land meant crops, and land meant rent from serfs—tradesmen, farmers, and craftspeople—who created the goods and consumables that drove the economy. There was a one-to-one correlation between the most powerful people and the ones who had the most land. To this day, Queen Elizabeth remains one of the richest people in the United Kingdom based on her family's landholdings.[2] In a time of finite resources, feudal nobility learned that to succeed and gain more power, they needed to protect and hoard what they had. They built castles with moats around them to protect their fiefdoms, conquered everything they could, and built their wealth one furlong at a time, habits that served them well for centuries.

Fast-forward a few hundred years to the birth of the industrial revolution. The invention of machines, powered mainly by the steam engine, brought a host of innovative ways to make things. The rate and scale of manufacturing increased exponentially. A savvy entrepreneur could suddenly mass-produce goods efficiently and bring them to market at lower prices than his craft-guild cousin. Machines created a systematic way to get rich relatively quickly. One no longer needed a lifetime to amass wealth or had to risk a dangerous voyage in search of treasure. Anyone with money to invest could identify cutting-edge inventions, build an efficient factory to make them (or make with them), and take market share from his old-world rivals. Initiative and innovation became wealth, and old gave way to new, all powered by a new investor class able to make money with money. In 1776, Adam Smith wrote *The Wealth of Nations*, and capitalism was born.[3] The word *capital*, by the way, comes from the Latin word *capitalis*, meaning head. Under capitalism, you could use your head to get ahead.

As we shifted from land to capital as the engine of wealth, however, the zero-sum mentality of feudal times remained. Capital, too, is finite, and the more capital I had the less you had. With more, I could innovate, expand, and do things that you could not. Capitalists developed habits of power, certain rules of thumb about how to succeed in the new economy. When we had stuff, we hoarded it; we did not share. We did not give it away; we meted it out and only for high returns. We extracted interest. For hundreds of years, assets meant power, and to succeed we controlled them zealously. Generally, we built a fortress around our holdings and defended them against all invaders. We dominated markets, protected trade secrets, and made sure everything we did received a patent or copyright. We could also control information flow to the market, and so developed a host of one-way communication habits to control how it viewed us. We invented the press release, perfected the arts of *messaging* and *spin*, and learned to divide and conquer, telling one thing to Customer A in one market and something different to Customer B in another. Company structures mirrored these impulses with command-and-control structures and top-down hierarchies. The habits of fortress capitalism soon permeated every facet of enterprise.

LINES OF COMMUNICATION

Let's pause in our brief rush through history to note a couple of specific industrial age events whose significance to our discussion will become quickly apparent. With the coming of the telegraph to the United States in the mid-1850s, some savvy entrepreneurs tried to strike it rich by stringing up thousands of miles of copper cable connecting both the established mercantile centers of the East and the rapidly developing Midwest. In their helter-skelter pursuit of wealth, the enterprise produced a glut of transmission capacity without the market to sustain the infrastructural costs of its installation. Prices collapsed, as did the fortunes of those who invested. Call it the dot-dash explosion. Suddenly, the cost of transmitting a word of text dropped to a then-unheard-of penny per word. This leap in connectivity and economy had some unintended consequences, as journalist Daniel Gross reported in *Wired* magazine: "Reporters could file long stories from the Civil War battlefields, fueling the great newspaper empires of William Randolph Hearst and Joseph Pulitzer. Likewise, the spread of the ability to send cheap telegraphs spurred a national market in stocks and commodities and made it much easier to manage international business."[4] These were world-altering developments. Half a century later, American Telephone and Telegraph extended that network dramatically when it introduced the telephone, although they were savvy enough to protect themselves by soliciting monopoly protection from the U.S. government in 1913, thus assuring profitability. The telephone was the telegraph on steroids, and its impact on business was similarly huge.

Fast-forward to 1994, and reflect on the birth of the information age. Technology again allowed multifold leaps in the way we did things. Opportunity was everywhere, and though few had a clear vision of where it would lead, inventions, products, and processes made things possible that were previously only a dream. Once again, entrepreneurs jumped in all over the place. A host of entrepreneurs (seemingly ignoring the lessons of the dot-dash era) invested heavily, laying fiber-optic cable around the world. Fiber-optic cable provided a quantum leap in transmission capacity from the copper cable originally installed by Ma Bell and her telegraph brethren. A single pair of optical fibers can carry more than 30,000 telephone conversations for distances of hundreds of kilometers, whereas a pair of copper wires twice as thick carries 24 conversations about 5 kilometers. When you apply new technologies like wavelength division multiplexing (WDM), fiber capacity increases by up to 64 times. With the new technologies on the horizon, scientists believe fiber-optic cable's theoretical transmission capacity to be infinite. Laying fiber-optic cable was like replacing every bathroom faucet with something the size of a missile silo. Suddenly, total global electronic communications consumed just 5 percent of transmission capacity. Transmission prices again collapsed (along with a lot of the companies hatched with the idea of getting rich quick on the back of this new technology), and we found ourselves in a world in which information flowed around the world instantly and cheaply like light through a darkened room.

GETTING FLATTENED

This changed everything. Information, unlike land and capital, is not zero-sum; it's infinite. The more I have, the more you can have, too. And, unlike money, it is elastic; a dollar is worth a dollar no matter how much you desire it. Knowledge, in contrast, becomes more valuable directly in proportion to your need or desire for it. If you were told that you had a disease, for instance, you would pay much more for the information to cure it than you would if you were healthy.

In the days of fortress capitalism, a professional class of lawyers, doctors, accountants, and other gatekeepers of knowledge took advantage of information's elasticity and profited from it in two significant ways: They hoarded knowledge (like any other commodity) and meted it out in small doses for high fees (typically, to people who really needed it because they were in trouble, ill, or their metaphoric houses were otherwise on fire). Simultaneously, they built indecipherably specialized language and complex codes—like legalese, the tax code, and other "fine print"—as barriers to keep people from gaining easy access to what they knew. This increased their value. The more someone needed certain information, the more they were willing to pay a specialist to explain it.

The wired world, by conducting information so quickly and cheaply, in contrast removed the layers between individuals and knowledge, making the professional specialist somewhat less valuable and the information itself more so. The unit cost of information dropped dramatically, from the $300 you might pay a private investigator to locate a deadbeat dad, for instance, to the $50 or so you might spend to do a nationwide online records search yourself. Power and wealth shifted from those who hoard information to those who could make it available and accessible to the most people.

This simple fact makes the habits of fortress capitalism obsolete. With the ascent of information as the engine of commerce, power has shifted to those who open up, who share information freely. The young titans of the information economy—Yahoo, Google, Amazon, eBay—understand that it is no longer about hoarding, no longer about creating secrets, no longer about keeping things private; it is about reaching people. Google, now a company with one of the largest market capitalizations in the world, trumpets its corporate mission as nothing less than "to organize the world's information and make it universally accessible and useful."[5] Think about it: a multibillion-dollar enterprise organized around giving stuff away. Amazon.com also gives it away: not its products—it sells books and other stuff, just like thousands of others—but its knowledge. Its success lies in the novel and inventive ways it has developed to share information. Wish Lists, Search Inside!, and Listmania Lists use information to powerfully connect Amazon customers in common-interest communities. EBay takes this idea a step further, organizing its entire market into a self-governing community based on the free flow of information about its users. The new information-based economy affects everyone, not just those in the information business. Every business, in almost every industry, has undergone a major transformation in how it accomplishes its goals. Manufacturers no longer employ assembly-line workers; they employ trained knowledge workers who can keep the automated manufacturing systems running.

Pulitzer Prize–winning *New York Times* journalist Thomas L. Friedman, in his seminal book *The World Is Flat*, comprehensively details the global effects of this newly unfettered flow of information. He describes some of the unprecedented possibilities suddenly available to us, many of which are being exploited by the business world: new paradigms of collaboration, specialization, supply and distribution, and expansion of core competencies.[6] We can partner, "plug and play," and work together in totally new ways because we can share information as never before. Collaboration itself—our heightened ability to *connect*—serves as an engine of growth and innovation. Sharing not only drives the relationships companies maintain with customers, it also drives the companies themselves. Friedman details many forward-thinking companies pursuing new business paradigms to exploit this new reality: UPS uses the efficiency of its shipping system to run the repair center for Toshiba less expensively than Toshiba can itself; call centers in Bangalore seamlessly provide Dell Inc. computer customers vital product support; housewives from the comfort of their own homes in Salt Lake City interface directly with JetBlue Airways' central booking computers to take and process reservations. Clearly, the maglev bullet train of zeros and ones has left the station and no one knows where it will stop.

Friedman's macroeconomic and social analysis of our newly "flat," interconnected world presents a vision of the forces reshaping global business in the twenty-first century. The free flow of information significantly changes the way internal business units perform and are governed, and how individuals work together every day. Fading away are the days of the vertical silo model, when departments and programs within a corporation ran independent fiefdoms organized in top-down, command-and-control hierarchies in the spirit of feudal systems. Increasingly, our typical workday involves relating to people of relatively equal status in an ever-evolving array of teams and partnerships between units throughout the globe. Since knowledge allows people to act, companies that can instantly deliver more high-value information to their workers can enable more of them to act on it.

Companies are flattening, like our world, so that many activities that were once the province of one department are now everyone's job. In 2005, for example, Computer Associates International, Inc., a company struggling to rehabilitate itself after being tainted by scandal, product deficiencies, and management problems, eliminated all 300 of its customer advocate positions worldwide.[7] CEO John Swainson explained that the goal was to make the company's sales workers "more accountable," but the underlying message was clear: Advocating for the customer is no longer the special responsibility of customer advocates; it is now a part of everyone's job description.[8] In company after company, managers are eliminating so-called "Centers of Excellence" and "Centers of Innovation," making these jobs the province of all workers. Everyone now must increase company excellence and everyone must innovate. How can you make a Wave of innovation if only the 20 or so people in your Skunk Works stand up?

As traditional job silos break down and become horizontal, command-and-control hierarchies begin to lose their relevance. A new model emerges: connect and collaborate. To succeed in this new model, workers and companies alike need to develop new skills and harness new powers within themselves. Companies—and the people who comprise them—need to recontextualize how they do business. Individuals must develop new approaches to the sphere of human relations. Both companies and employees must learn to share in whole new ways.

The world has become even more like the game of chess. Every piece on a chessboard is highly specialized, with virtues and vices, strengths and weaknesses, assets and liabilities. Some move diagonally and some move straight; some roam free and unfettered while others are tightly regimented. But, with a few exceptions, you can't typically achieve checkmate with fewer than three pieces. Most accomplishments in chess are team-based; only when you position pieces properly—and in communication with one another—do they start to win. Two rooks, if communicating, are very powerful, even if they are very far apart; without close communication, rooks are far less powerful. Business is now much more like that. Success depends on how people of diverse backgrounds and skills communicate with and complement one another. In a connected world, power shifts to those best able to connect.

Six hundred years ago, people succeeded with barter arrangements on street corners. Today, most business takes place in formalized organizations; a corporation, for the most part, is nothing more than a society of individuals who share a common interest to get something done. (The corporation itself is for the most part a legal fiction. Many of them are incorporated in Delaware, but few of us commute to Delaware every morning, do we?) While not everyone works in a company—some people are independents: accountants, contractors, agents, consultants, entrepreneurs, and the like—everyone working in the world of exchange and commerce needs to connect with others, be they customers, clients, vendors, suppliers, team members within our companies, or subcontractors. No man or woman, as poet John Donne famously said, "is an island, entire of itself"; we are all part of a larger landscape of people, because most of what we do cannot be done alone.

I cannot accomplish anything by myself. I find myself a member of an organization. I find myself in a marketplace, competing, trying to do something that depends on other people. That is quite a place to find yourself. It stands to reason that, in such a world, your success will depend on your ability to relate to others in powerful ways. The information economy places new emphasis on how we bridge the spaces between us. How do we reach out? How do we create strong synapses capable of making our action potentials real? With the fundamental shift from land to capital to knowledge and information as the currency of business, we've seen a concurrent shift from the power of command-and-control hierarchies to the power of collaborative, horizontal effort. The necessity to work together like pieces on a chessboard places a new premium on our ability to conduct ourselves successfully in the sphere of human affairs.

More profoundly than just getting things done, strong connections with others represent a value unto themselves. Relationships lie at the heart of who we are as humans; they give our lives meaning and significance. When we die our headstones seldom read Sylvia Jones, 1960–2042, VP of Strategic Planning and Implementation. Made the numbers 16 quarters in a row. Instead, we write Stan Smith, Beloved Husband, Father, Brother, Uncle. He made the world warmer with his smile. Though our jobs may make us wealthy, our relationships give us lasting value and enduring worth. Building stronger relationships, then, can lead to more than success: It can lead to a kind of significance.

2

Technology's Trespass

*Computers are useless. They can
only give you answers.*
—Pablo Picasso

R elationships. Communication. Connection. Collaboration. This is
how we fill the spaces between us. *Communicate* comes from
the Latin word *communicare*, meaning "to share." So it follows
that as the nature of the way we communicate changes, so too does
the nature of our relationships. Over the past decade, the intercession
of technology into our interpersonal synapses has radically altered
what goes on in the spaces between us, has changed the way we do
business, and has given us easy access to information, creating a double-
edged sword that cuts both for and against us.

THE TIES THAT BIND US

Back in the days of feudal capitalism, running a company like IBM was
a far simpler proposition than it is today. Remember the blue suits? IBM
used to be famous for its strong corporate culture, so impressed on

everyone who worked there that the blue suit became the de facto uniform of the workforce. Everyone knew when Big Blue walked into the room. Their suits stood out as strongly as a coat of arms draped on the backs of a medieval lord's archer brigade. If you worked at IBM, you knew what armor to put on every morning. Enforcing a company-wide point of view was easier when the old fortress mentality still held sway. You could communicate policies, values, rules, goals, and perspectives to your workforce through vertical channels. You could post notices, hold meetings, and have retreats for managers, and your messages—explicit and implicit—would travel their way throughout the workforce. Strategies would shift in lockstep, and blue suits would be worn. Both corporation and employee benefited from this way of operating; orders were given and everyone knew where to march.

Few businesses have fortress walls that shield and contain their workforce anymore, especially the larger ones. Communication technology has replaced the concept of workforce with an array of laborers affiliated in myriad, open relationships. Full-time employees work hand in hand with members of joint ventures, colleagues in independently managed subsidiaries, on-site independent contractors, remote representatives of outsourcing companies, consultants working from their homes, and as many more creative interrelationships as you can imagine. Add to that a global supply and distribution chain and you get an organic tangle of human relationships difficult to easily control.

In place of the nice, tidy company-as-city-state, the population of corporations more closely resembles a Central American rainforest. Tall, old-growth trees define the greater geography while vines twist this way and that, connecting one tree to another, to a bush, to the ground. Lichen and moss grow in patches everywhere, often on top of one another. Bushes, fungi, saplings, and parasites abound. Flowers sprout, often in unpredictable places, as countless species of birds, bugs, and animals find a home in its dark, fertile recesses. The forest has subsumed the stone fortress of businesses, leaving in its place an organic ecosystem filled with possibility. Not only don't your co-workers wear the blue suits, but some, who work from the privacy of their homes, work in pajamas. Traditional ways of categorizing people have gone away, along with the traditional ways of reaching out and communicating organizational goals and values to them. Few give or receive inflexible marching orders; many more of us must navigate day to day on our own. The workforce has become an *ecosystem* comprised of mutually reinforcing independent agents. An ecosystem, by definition, *interacts* or it does not survive. To thrive in a business ecosystem, you must be able connect with those in it—one way or another—as never before.

Returning to our organization-as-stadium metaphor, a Wave must work with everybody in the stadium. Full-time employees are like season ticket holders, with a significant investment in the success of the team, and that stake might be sufficient motivation for them to participate in your Wave. Others—consultants or on-site contractors, say—might completely depend on what you pay them, and they, too, might stand up when you ask. But there are many people, five rows down, who do not and will not. They depend on other things. Some came just for this one game. They might have a lesser stake, or even competing interests. Some might be cheering for the visiting team. They can all stop your Wave. If all non–season ticket holders refused to get up with your Wave, you might be left standing and raising your arms alone.

Organizations have always been constituted of complicated interrelationships of mutual interest. Today, however, we have both thinner and thicker bonds with our various shareholders, stakeholders, and partners. They are thinner because the diverse types of relationship and connection we form with suppliers, freelancers, part-timers, outsourcers, free agents, and cooperative partners are no longer strong enough on their own to impel total cooperation. They are thicker in the degree to which we now may depend on these bonds to achieve critical goals. Despite newly complicated and quickly evolving relationships, we still need to reach out and connect with our related communities in a way that can unite us in a common goal, to make a Wave powerful enough to sweep up and unite the many competing interests in play.

DISTANCE UNITES US

Business in the information age is complicated not only by the myriad new forms of relationship upon which it is built, but also by the increasing remoteness of those with whom we build it. The philosopher

David Hume once said that the moral imagination diminishes with distance.[1] By this he meant you don't feel the same sense of connection or obligation to someone halfway across the world that you do to someone halfway across the room, halfway across town, or even halfway across the country. In fact, our personal survival systems *depend* on not feeling implicated with things that are far away. Doctors, for instance, do not drive around randomly from county to county treating people. They say, "My responsibilities extend to this hospital, and over there is another doctor's responsibilities." A person in Senegal lives so far away from most of us that we can think of him in the abstract and believe we do not need to feel responsible to an abstraction. This is the logic, if you can call it that, behind Joseph Stalin's horrible formulation, "A single death is a tragedy; a million deaths is a statistic."

For centuries, local proximity determined the majority of our social functions, containing us in relatively homogenous environments. We dealt on a day-to-day basis with people with whom we generally shared a common culture and therefore understood easily the behaviors and signals that occurred in the spaces between us. Global connectivity sets that whole idea on its ear. We now find ourselves in a world where we are thrust together in all aspects of our lives without borders and without the homogenizing pressures of locality. The fiber-optic strands that enmesh us pierce the protective membranes of local culture like needles popping soap bubbles. They create a whole new set of interrelationship challenges. From purchasing items from a seller on eBay to online dating to video chats with team members halfway around the world, at any time you might find yourself interacting with people with whom you have never before broken bread, who don't necessarily speak the same language you do, who don't necessarily recognize your patterns of behavior, and vice versa. That guy in Senegal? Your company just bought the Internet start-up for which he works and folded him into your business unit. You will now manage him and his team in Dakar remotely.

Before all information became zeros and ones, our lives moved at a slower pace. We had more time to get to know each other and the luxury to value personal contact in nearly all our dealings. Now, multinational companies commonly form teams of employees chosen from various divisions, various countries, and various cultures. Global supply chains and international customer bases multiply and mutate faster than a flu virus. Mergers and acquisitions fuel growth and value creation with little regard to how the individuals involved will interrelate each day. We often build our business relationships in a collage-like construct of flyby hotel meetings, video chats, cell calls, e-mails, and faxes. While I was editing this chapter, one of my researchers working across town instant messaged me about a file she was looking for, and I was able to drag-and-drop it to her faster than if she had been working across the hall. We take such things for granted.

Opportunity conjoins us faster than we have developed frameworks for understanding each other and getting along. Distance no longer separates us; new communications capabilities render distance irrelevant by connecting us instantly. In this proximal world, the opportunities for misunderstandings abound. How do you write an e-mail to someone if you can't tell from their e-mail address if they are a man or a woman, what country they are from, what upbringing they had, or if they believe cows to be sacred or just lunch? In the United States, if two managers of different seniority find themselves in conflict they are most likely to approach each other directly and communicate frankly to try to resolve the issue. In Indonesia, the direct approach will only make it worse. In Jakarta, the concept of *asal bapak senang*, keeping the boss happy, comes into play.[2] Indonesian subordinates typically feel personally responsible for solving problems without notifying their superiors, even if it means lying about a situation rather than addressing it directly.

Dr. Fons Trompenaars and Charles Hampden-Turner, authors of *Building Cross-Cultural Competence*, conducted a worldwide study of cultural attitudes that revealed startling differences among the countries now commonly linked in global enterprise. They posed the following problem to workers in dozens of countries in order to better understand cultural dispositions toward loyalty and regulation:

> You are riding in a car driven by a close friend. He hits a pedestrian. You know he was going at least thirty-five miles per hour in an area of the city where the maximum allowed speed is twenty miles per hour. There are no witnesses other than you. His lawyer says that if you testify under oath that he was driving only twenty miles per hour, you will save him from serious consequences.

What right has your friend to expect you to protect him? What do you think you would do in view of the obligations of a sworn witness and the obligations to your friend?[3]

Before you read the results, take a moment to think how you would respond.

In countries with a strong Protestant tradition and stable democracies, like the United States, Switzerland, Sweden, and Australia, nearly 80 percent thought the friend had "no" or only "some" right to expect help, and would choose to tell the truth in court. In South Korea and Yugoslavia, fewer than 20 percent felt this way; 80 percent felt that helping their friend was the right thing to do. "When we posed this question in Japan," Hampden-Turner told me when we spoke, "the Japanese said this was a difficult problem, and they wanted to leave the room. I thought this was an unusual way for people to answer the question, but let them leave the room to discuss it. They came back in 25 minutes and said the correct answer is to say to your friend, 'I will stick with you; I will give any version of events that you ask me to, but I ask you to find in our friendship the courage that allows us to tell the truth.' I thought this was a wonderful solution. They wanted to be universalistic—to tell the absolute truth, a characteristic of the Western world—but their culture is particularistic and values the love and loyalty to a particular friend. They made the move from one to the other, but approached it from the opposite direction than a white Anglo-Saxon Protestant would."[4]

Complicating these differences in perception is the concurrent tendency of each culture to view negatively the values of the other. A Swiss person might tend to distrust a South Korean because, in the Swiss person's view, Koreans don't respect authority, and that Korean might in turn disrespect the Swiss believing that they do not sufficiently value friendship and loyalty. How does that bode for your ability to communicate to the wide variety of people throughout your global supply chain or on an e-mail distribution list? How about a company trying to disseminate and acculturate a uniform code of conduct throughout its global organization? How do you get people to do the Wave if, at a foundational level, they either mistrust or don't understand your values?

When software development company Lotus sought to expand its well-known business collaboration products—Notes and Domino—to support a global user base, it ran headfirst into these questions. To extend its "global virtual watercooler" to successfully interface with business in Japan, for example, it designed a space within the software for users to share the extensive social pleasantries that Japanese culture demands prior to doing business.[5] Bridging these gaps can be a mind-boggling task. Imagine how many different options it would take to accommodate the bridging requirements between every possible pair of cultures, and then remember that a single group meeting on a project might involve representatives of four or five different cultures.

CAN YOU HEAR ME NOW?

Business is an ecosystem, distance no longer keeps us apart, the ties that bind us are looser than ever, and there is a new *us* whose members change almost daily; and it is all made possible because electronic communication fills the synapses between us. Electronic communication is both a boon and a bane. It makes these new, powerful networks of collaboration possible, but does so in a strange and fractured language.

What separates humans from other creatures is our uniquely complex ability to create symbols. Symbols allow us to understand the world, and are the primary means by which we create social and psychological relationships. Human interaction is a symphony of symbolic gestures of which language is just a small part. Physicality, intonation, facial expression, volume, and body language play an important role in our ability to interrelate and understand the intention behind the words we use. In the days before electric communication (telegraph and telephone), the majority of our communication took place face-to-face. We were generally able to look someone in the eye and interpret what he or she was telling us. Over the past 75 years or so, technology systematically removed many of these interpersonal behavioral cues from our dominant modes of interaction. First the telegraph and then the telephone allowed us to hook up more easily—but only partly, as many symbolic social cues were missing. The slower pace of change characteristic of the industrial age, however, gave us time to adapt to these new modes of communication and to develop the new symbol decoding ability they demanded of us. Still, we never came to fully trust them. The unwritten rule was that much could be accomplished on the telephone, but when it came down to really important communications, nothing beat looking someone in the eye and shaking that person's hand.

Step back for a moment and think about the myriad and fantastic ways business communicates in the twenty-first century: e-mail, instant messaging, cell phones, personal digital assistants (PDAs), text messages. Each mediates our message in subtly different ways, distorting some parts, magnifying and diminishing others. Each technology works like a filter allowing some symbols to pass through and others to be left behind. Now think about how fast these changes have come upon us. E-mail, as strange as it is to think now, has been with most of us for around a decade. In the mid-1990's, some of us wore numeric pagers, and if we even had a cell phone, it was often larger than this book.

When we communicate electronically, we communicate less dynamically, with less give-and-take. Electronic communication tends to be unidirectional and sequential. When it does overlap, like in an instant message chat, it often ceases to make sense:

MarkTheCEO [11:16 AM]: Hi Cindy.
CindyCEOAssist [11:16 AM]: Hello Mark.

MarkTheCEO [11:16 AM]: RU prepared for the mtg w/ counsel?
CindyCEOAssist [11:16 AM]: Think so.

MarkTheCEO [11:17 AM]: Think so? I hope so. Can you brief me on our client's situation?
CindyCEOAssist [11:19 AM]: You don't believe I've been working on it?

MarkTheCEO [11:20 AM]: I'm seeing them in five minutes.
CindyCEOAssist [11:20 AM]: They broke the contract on many levels, but they are claiming that we made it impossible for them to fulfill the contract.

MarkTheCEO [11:20 AM]: Of course I believe you.
CindyCEOAssist [11:20 AM]: Well, not we, but us. I mean not me, but you and your board.

CindyCEOAssist [11:20 AM]: It's your rescision.

MarkTheCEO [11:20 AM]: I apologize.

MarkTheCEO [11:21 AM]: So, we are going to sue them for breach of contract.

CindyCEOAssist [11:21 AM]: No problem. I'll go set up the conference room.

MarkTheCEO [11:21 AM]: Rescision?

Auto response from CindyCEOAssist [11:21 AM]: CINDY is online but may be away from the service right now.

MarkTheCEO [11:21 AM]: I'm not sure I understand. What rescision?

MarkTheCEO [11:22 AM]: Hello? Are you still there? The video conference is in three minutes!

Though we now work more cooperatively, like pieces on a chess-board, the electronic communication that passes between us is a game of incomplete information, more like poker than chess. In chess, both players can see complete information about the game. In poker, you can only see the cards that are face up. But unlike poker, the goal of most of our communication is not to confuse our opponent but rather to be clear with our partner; we want, to varying degrees, to put our cards on the table. It's the paradox of the information age: Technology connects us more than ever before but those connections are more fractured and incomplete than we are accustomed to. Missing are many of the clues we need to fully decode the intentions of others.

Another pressure of instant communication could be called the Expectation of Response Factor. In the industrial age, we wrote letters deliberately, knowing that even if we dashed off a quick note from point A it would take its own sweet postal time to arrive at point B. The recipient, in turn, could take a commensurate amount of time crafting a response. The pace of information flow allowed enough time for even time-sensitive writing to receive a modicum of consideration before being sent. Not so with the various gizmos and gadgets we now find strapped to our belts or planted on our desks. Messages appear instantly, implicitly insisting on a quick response. The Expectation of Response Factor exerts an influence on the quality of our communication, often forcing us to respond in less considered ways. In media whose nature transmits only parts of our intended symbols at best, the virtual ticking of the electronic clock cheats us of the time we need for careful or meaningful expression.

THE AGE OF TRANSPARENCY

In the olden days (before about 1995), when people wanted to buy, say, a toaster, they would pick a local store known for its good selection or good pricing of small appliances and buy the one that seemed best for their needs. If they were particularly industrious, thrifty, or enamored of the process, they might call or visit two or three stores before making their purchase, dig out back issues of consumers testing magazines, or consult a catalog or two to compare price and features. As more businesses went online, people suddenly had the ability to shop not only within their local area, but almost anywhere. Large and trusted online retailers were added to the shopping mix, giving consumers a few more options if they wished to pursue them. Between June 2004 and March 2005, however, as e-commerce began exploding worldwide, people who bought online suddenly became more prone to visiting 10 or more web sites before returning to a favored location hours or days later to make a purchase.[6]

It has been said that information is like a toddler: It goes everywhere, gets into everything, and you can't always control it.[7] Someone should have told that to David Edmondson, former CEO of RadioShack. For consumers, easy access to information about vendors has become an advantage; for those like Edmondson, who had something to hide, it has meant devastation. When he joined RadioShack in 1994, Edmondson invented a couple of lines for his resume in the form of college degrees in theology and psychology from Pacific Coast Baptist College in California that he never earned. In February 2006, after just eight months at the top of his profession, he was forced to resign. Though the school had relocated to Oklahoma and renamed itself, a reporter from the *Fort Worth Star-Telegram* tracked it down and uncovered the discrepancies. Edmondson's career, built on the foundation of these lies, lay in pieces at his feet.[8]

He's not alone, of course. The news is full of examples of the mighty who have taken the fall. Kenneth Lonchar, former CFO and

EVP of Silicon Valley software storage firm Veritas (the Latin word for *truth*), got caught in 2002 claiming a false Stanford MBA.[9] University of Notre Dame head football coach George O'Leary resigned when it was revealed that he had not only lied on his resume about playing football at his alma mater, but he had also falsely claimed a master's degree.[10] Even Jeff Taylor, founder of online job-search company Monster.com, posted on his own web site an executive biography touting a phony Harvard MBA.[11]

We live in the age of transparency. In 1994, it might have been easy to get away with such shenanigans, but with the massive shift of personal records and personal profiles to databases easily accessed over the Internet, virtually everything about you can be discovered quite easily. The fact that *The New Oxford American Dictionary* lists "Google" as a verb makes this perfectly clear, as does the sample sentence it uses to illuminate its meaning: "You meet someone, swap numbers, fix a date, and then Google them through 1,346,966,000 Web pages."[12] The *Pittsburgh Post-Gazette* recently reported a Harris Interactive poll showing that 23 percent of people routinely search the names of business associates or colleagues on the Internet before meeting them.[13] The DontDateHimGirl.com web site allows a woman to post the name and photograph of a man she says has wronged her. As the web site's founder, Tasha C. Joseph, told the *New York Times*, "It's like a dating credit report" for women.[14] Anyone with a video camera can share with the world your worst moments by posting them on YouTube.com, a revolution that within just a couple of years of its launch has had a dramatic effect on politics, entertainment, law enforcement, music, and countless people's private lives. Political pollsters can compare your age, income, party registration, type of car you own, charities you donate to, and a glut of other readily available personal information to predict with a very high degree of accuracy how you will vote.[15]

These facts exert a profound influence on business. Before transparency allowed them to peer through the tall trees, outside observers could discern the outline of a forest, but thought little about what was growing beneath. Companies, for instance, could form a joint venture to protect themselves from the ramifications of a dubious enterprise, believing that if the unit got into trouble it would not hurt the reputation of the parent company. In a transparent world, however, when your joint venture transgresses, everybody knows who owns it. In the past, training its managers in proper conduct was sufficient to protect a company's reputation because line employees had little contact with the outside world and rarely got a company into trouble. Now, any employee can say something about a company in a chat room or in a blog and the next day it might appear on DrudgeReport or The Smoking Gun. There's even a new word for it—whistleblogging—when employees create personal online journals to report company wrongdoing. The new transparency doesn't allow you to hide in the dark underbrush, to have a joint venture here, or hire an agent there. Observers can easily tell the trees from the forest.

An information society also breeds a surveillance society. People are more curious and they *look* a lot more. They look because it is suddenly easy to do so; looking costs little, requires even less effort, and pays off with everything from the best prices for goods and services to revelations of the unsavory. Around the world, viewers are glued to their television sets by "reality TV," programming that purports to give true glimpses of private lives (the United States now has a whole network dedicated to it, and the British version of *Celebrity Big Brother* touched off an international incident[16]). We've always been interested in what was happening next door, but now we can actually see it. It's like examining a drop of water under a microscope. When you first place the drop on the slide, it looks clear and pristine. But the microscope's lens reveals a hidden world. With each adjustment of the magnification you see organisms and objects that before you could only have imagined; what first appeared clear and unpolluted suddenly appears messy and complex. Microscope technology changes the way you look at water, and with your curiosity thus piqued, you can't help but wonder what worlds might exist within other familiar objects.

People look more often because the looking is easier and there has been more to find. Imagine the gratification of Heather Landy, the *Fort Worth Star-Telegram* staff writer who uncovered David Edmondson's embellished RadioShack resume. She began her investigation "into Edmondson's credentials after learning that the executive, who started two churches before making the transition to a full-time business career, [was] scheduled to go to court . . . to fight his third drunken-driving charge."[17] Corporate scandals, celebrity breakups, political corruption: Each day's news—delivered instantly via television, radio, web site, cell phone, RSS feed, and BlackBerry—exposes the transgressions of the icons of the age. Whether the media are addicted to it because they have so much bandwidth/airtime/column space to fill or we're hooked by our newfound access, in the information age, once we've gotten a taste of scandal we can't seem to get enough.

THE PERSISTENCE OF MEMORY

When Paul Chung hit the send button on an e-mail message to his friends, he sent a promising career in investment banking into a tailspin. The Carlyle Group had recently hired the 24-year-old Princeton graduate and relocated him to their Seoul, Korea office. Three days later, he used the company's network to boast to his buddies in New York about his lavish new lifestyle. "I know I was a stud in NYC," he wrote, "but I pretty much get about, on average, 5–8 phone numbers a night and at least 3 hot chicks that say they want to go home with me every night I go out." Later, he bragged about using one bedroom in the apartment his employer provided as his "harem" and another for sexual activities. Astounded recipients forwarded the message to thousands of people on Wall Street, until it finally ended up in his boss's in-box. Chung lost his job—and his reputation along with it.[18] That was in 2001. Five years later, people are still talking about it. I googled "Paul Chung Carlyle," as his future employers and colleagues undoubtedly will, and found the story cited five times on the first page returned. It will follow him the rest of his life.

The brain forms and stores memories by building networks of neurons. Each network imprints and stores the millions of detailed impressions that make up a memory. The World Wide Web works exactly the same way. Its vast, interconnected database has a persistence of memory that will long outlive us. Even web sites that are pulled down or deleted live on forever on a site called Wayback Machine, which archives 55 billion web pages dating back to 1996.[19] The persistence of memory in electronic form makes second chances harder to come by. Before the information revolution, a quack doctor could move to another town and hang out his shingle without fear of repercussion. Now, states keep instantly accessible databases detailing every charge and investigation lodged against him. The same holds true for companies, stores, and eBay sellers. In the information age, life has no chapters or closets; you can leave nothing behind and you have nowhere to hide your skeletons. Your past is your present, and it catches up with you like a truck backing over what it left behind.

It's not just smoking-gun e-mails like Chung's that get people into trouble in the information age. With the democratization of information, anyone can publish whatever they think at whatever time he or she thinks it, true or false. The standard of information verification has been lowered. In the mass media age of the 1980s and 1990s, large media companies still acted as the gatekeepers and watchdogs of public information. A professional class of journalists and editors vetted most claims and accusations for veracity before broadcasting them, applying a standard of independent proof and corroboration, or they paid the price for neglecting to do so. Information technology takes this responsibility out of the hands of trained professionals and places it in the hands of anyone with a keyboard. Any disgruntled employee can strike back. A dishonorable accuser with a false accusation can gain instant currency. As was prophetically said in a time before electronic communications (attributed to Mark Twain by some), "A lie can travel halfway round the world while the truth is putting on its shoes."[20] Now, it can circle the earth numerous times in the time truth takes to simply think, "shoe." Reputations formerly carved in stone now seem easily besmirched by anyone with access to a keyboard. Accusations still uninvestigated gain as much currency as proven truth and, even if they are untrue, consume significant resources to defend against. Technology provides just about everyone the ability to quickly and cheaply compare and contrast reputations before making decisions. As reputation becomes more perishable, its value increases. As it becomes more accessible, it becomes a greater asset—and liability.

THE INFORMATION JINNI IS OUT OF THE LAMP

The free flow of information has irrevocably changed the ways we interrelate, both for the positive and the negative. According to a recent Pew study, for example, 40 percent of the 11 million people who use instant messaging at work feel it increases teamwork, but 32 percent say it encourages gossip, 29 percent say it has been distracting, and 11 percent say it has added stress to their lives.[21] Unquestionably, communications technology has upended centuries of traditional practice, weakening the effectiveness of many habits that used to make us strong. It has changed the structure of how businesses operate and how people in businesses interoperate.

And we can't go back.

We will never become *less* connected. We will never become *less* transparent. The information jinni is out of the lamp and he's paying attention to no one's wishes. Tired of living in the dark recesses of a tarnished copper fixture, he's built himself a new house, one with transparent and permeable walls, framed by the new realities we've discussed in these two chapters: the destruction of the fortress, the flattening of the world, the rise of the business ecosystem, the fractured nature of virtual discourse, uncontrollable transparency, the destructive power of accusation, and the importance of reputation. With all these changes to the way we live, connect, and conduct our professional and personal lives, the questions become: How do we now thrive? How can we turn these challenges into strengths? We'll answer these questions in the chapters ahead, but first there are a few more important issues to consider: changes in what society values, trusts, and relies on for stability in times of uncertainty.

3

The Journey to How

It isn't what you do, but how you do it.
—John Wooden, Hall of Fame
basketball coach

nformation is king, hyperconnectedness puts that information in
the hands of the many, and transparency reveals all: this is our new
reality. Thus far, we've looked at some of the external forces working upon us as we struggle to adapt to changing times. There are
other forces at work, though, powerful internal shifts that affect how
we feel about ourselves as individuals, companies, and any group of
which we are a part. The new needs and perceptions bred by these
changes also exert a powerful influence on our future business success. To fully consider the rapid changes to the geography of business,
then, we must also open our minds to how these strong forces have
created a new playing field for success.

JUST DO IT

At the end of the twentieth century, new conditions left little doubt
that we were but a mouse click away from having everything about

us—good, bad, and indifferent—revealed. From our hobbies to our bank account information, personal identification numbers to details about what we spend or owe, lots of facts we might not feel comfortable discussing with friends routinely find their way to the public eye without us being able to stop them. Increased exposure brought increased unease, vulnerability that has affected us in ways many of us have not yet had time to fully consider. With all the *looking* that became possible, we began to look more, and at different things. We began to question whether the world in which we lived matched the values we held most dear. That's when things began to change.

In 1996, writer/director Cameron Crowe made a film that insightfully captured the values of the go-go 1990s, *Jerry Maguire*. In the film, Tom Cruise plays an amoral sports agent who wakes up in the middle of the night with an epiphany about the corrupt core of his business practices. He stays up all night typing his manifesto-cum-mission statement, "The Things We Think but Do Not Say." In it, he argues that the future of business success lies in having fewer clients and treating them in more meaningful, humane ways, in reconnecting with the timeless values of human relationship. He distributes copies in the middle of the night to the entire office. The next morning, when he arrives for work, the entire company stands and applauds him, moved by the passion of his convictions. During the uproar of the ovation, one fellow agent turns to another and out of the corner of his mouth asks, "How long do you give him?" The second agent replies, "Mmmm. A week." Sure enough, a week later, he is gone, his clients stolen, and his career in ruins.[1]

Jerry Maguire tells the story of a man fighting back against the dehumanizing forces of the era. Upon its release, it became one of the top-grossing films of all time because it struck a chord in people tired of cutting corners.[2] We were in the Just Do It decade. The world was accelerating rapidly, and "Just Do It," the advertising slogan of sport shoe maker Nike, captured the self-centered zeitgeist of the decade. The market was booming, and a huge new investor class experienced the particular easy-money thrill typical of speculative bubbles. Many leapt in as fast as they could, afraid the train would pass them by. Millions of people gambled in the market, and millions more saw their 401(k) accounts and retirement savings boom. People took chances, buoyed by the security that increasing prosperity brings. Everyone seemed to be in it for number one.

With the seemingly limitless possibilities of the dot-com era, the spirit of the age infected business. Managers, to answer the short-term demands of an increasingly insistent capital market, looked for short-cuts and easy solutions, managing for the here and now in ways that often neglected long-term goals. The habits and tendencies of the industrial age—efficiency, speed, and a focus on the bottom line—became all-consuming priorities. The message to subordinates was clear: Just get it done. Managers didn't care how. As long as it fell within the limits of legality, Just Do It. Often, they ignored the methods employed. In the same way that the era of industrial capitalism rewarded and encouraged certain habits of mind, like hoarding, the 1990s seemed to call forth other qualities. In the 1990s, you got ahead by developing habits of ingenuity and cleverness, ways to dance around obstacles in fast-changing times. The winners danced elegantly; everyone else just danced as fast as they could. Business, in general, focused on managing initiatives and tasks and became obsessed with Gantt and Program Evaluation and Review Technique (PERT) charts. Its approach to people was the same. The watchword of the day was *performance*, and human resources departments everywhere got focused on *performance management*. It became important to always answer the phone on the third ring, to always have a smile on your face, and to always perform any number of prescribed behaviors that managers felt would get them closer to their goals.

Along the way, however, we lost the value of leadership. You manage things; you lead people. And we felt it. Just Do It was no longer enough. As *Jerry Maguire* seemed to show us, by the end of the decade people started to care about *how* you did it—how you treated people and how you achieved your goals. The winds of public opinion shifted, and, importantly for business, the shift started to affect the bottom line. As early as 1997, a global public awareness campaign buffeted Just Do It Nike by exposing the substandard factory conditions at its manufacturing facilities around the world.[3] Information about the HOWs of business became increasingly easy to obtain and share. Change was in the air, but its scent was often overpowered by the heady rush of the times. It was not until the turn of the century that the natural cycles of boom and bust began to expose the new realities, and things got shaken up.

THE CERTAINTY GAP

We all carry in us a vision of ideal stability and security, an idea in our minds and hearts of what it would feel like to live a perfectly secure life. We never achieve this ideal state because at any given time the conditions of our lives or the world around us create varying degrees of uncertainty and disequilibrium. This opens a gap between our ideal state and the realities of life. I call it the Certainty Gap, and I believe it exerts a profound influence on our ability to succeed. The Certainty Gap never disappears entirely; it gets larger or smaller as conditions change. When it is small, we hardly pay it any attention; we feel in our guts that we can take any hit that befalls us. As it grows, however, we close ranks and protect ourselves from the threats around us. The larger it becomes, the more help we need as we attempt to fulfill our life's desires (because even when times get rocky and we feel at risk personally and professionally we still need to carry on with our lives, grow our businesses, and pursue our goals).

I have always thought that three pillars give life integrity: physical security, material prosperity, and emotional well-being. Like the three legs of a stool, when they sit soundly on the ground life is authentic and meaningful; the stool has integrity. When something damages any leg, however, the stool becomes wobbly; life becomes unsafe and insecure. At the beginning of this century, concurrent with the growth of the information age and the sudden connectedness and transparency technology brought to people the world over, the Western world experienced a series of shocks that collectively rocked our stools.

First, the dot-bomb fell, exploding the bubble economy and setting off a severe economic recession that exerted persistent dislocating effects on employment and financial security. Although we knew that expansion and contraction cycles are normal for the economy, we newly sensed that factories closing would never reopen. The economic realities of a new global economy pushed jobs in larger economies overseas where others could perform them at lower cost. These developing countries in turn experienced rapid growth and increased wealth, often challenging the traditional values that had long provided them with stability and continuity. The underlying economic assumptions of much of the world shifted, and somehow we sensed that, unlike previous business cycles, the pendulum would not swing back to nearly the same place as before.

Then, in rapid succession, a series of corporate scandals came to light and rocked global business, abuses so egregious that the mere mention of the names brings back the whole history: Enron, World-Com, Parmalat, Hollinger International. Corporations became among the least-trusted organs of society, according to a study conducted by Harris Interactive and the New York Institute for Reputation.[4] We started paying closer attention to everything business was doing, and the emerging transparency allowed us to see more deeply into its workings. In another study, conducted by LRN/Wirthlin Worldwide in 2003, 71 percent of Americans polled said that "none," "very few," or "only some" corporations operated in a fair and honest manner, despite the fact that relatively few had transgressed.[5]

The disappointments we felt came not only from the lapses in the business world and failures in the economy; we began to feel the revealing power of technology throughout the culture. Every facet of society seemed suddenly laid bare, flaws exposed for all to see. Scandals in the Catholic Church, fabrications by college football coaches, professional athletes on steroids, reporters for the *New York Times* inventing stories; icons at every level of society seemed suddenly vulnerable. These were the people and institutions we looked up to and held as paragons of meaningful life. People who could normally be trusted had let us down. As the foundations of their success became exposed, we saw that many successes were built on the same Just Do It habits of expediency and short-term values. The instruments of society that gave us our emotional center began to crumble around us, filling us with doubt about the structures of our beliefs. It is against our nature to accept that long-term success can be built on a corrupt foundation, but in such a world, on whom could you rely?

And then the World Trade Center towers fell, ushering in a series of global attacks against civilians—Madrid, London, Bali, and others—that, coupled with destabilizing regional wars, left much of the world uneasy. The needs and procedures of physical security suddenly intruded into the day-to-day lives of many who had long felt safe.

This was by no means the first time a confluence of events had rocked the three legs of the stool. World War II, the Vietnam era, Watergate, and the Mideast conflict and oil crisis of the 1970s, to name a few from just the previous half-century, all brought similar disruption and instability. Boom times, tough times, corruption, and fraud were by no means new to us, but the deeply dislocating difference this time around lay in our startling new ability to see it all in real time. Much of what happens around the world is now present in our daily lives. This flood of undigested and unprocessed information bombards us minute by minute, giving us little time to regain our footing. When our stools wobble, the Certainty Gap grows, and when that happens, we reach out for reassurance, for things that can stabilize us and give us confidence to go on. We look for something to fill the gap.

THE LIMITATIONS OF RULES

To pursue our endeavors and achieve our desired success, we need certainty, consistency, and predictability, a hard floor from which to take a leap. Basketball players can jump higher than beach volleyball players can because they play on a hard wooden floor. It is much more difficult to leap high with the sand shifting beneath your feet. The Certainty Gap describes not only our internal relationship to sureness, but also our relationship to the societies in which we live. In democratic societies, we look to rules—in the form of laws—to provide the certainty, consistency, and predictability we require. In the days of fortress capitalism, we got very good at writing rules, but as the century came to a close, we began to sense that rules were letting us down.

There are good reasons for this. For one, the way we write rules often makes them inefficient when governing human conduct. Rules, of course, don't come out of thin air. Legislatures and organizations adopt them usually to proscribe unwanted behaviors but typically in reaction to events. They lower speed limits after automobile accidents become too frequent, regulate pit bulls after a series of dog bites, or institute new expense-tracking procedures after someone is caught trying to get reimbursed for their new iPod. Rules have been established for a reason, but most people are out of touch with the rationale and spirit of why. They don't read legislative histories and so have a thin, superficial relationship to the rules. This, given the proper set of circumstances, leads people to explore ways around them, to find loopholes. Steve Adams, for instance, is an Alaskan postal clerk who wanted to express his individuality by showing up for work wearing ties decorated with the Three Stooges and Looney Tunes characters. That didn't sit well with his bosses, who fought with him for months before finally ordering him to follow the rules specifying permissible neckwear. So he did. Then, he examined the rules thoroughly and discovered that they contained no special prohibitions about suspenders. Now he proudly wears suspenders with "Taz," the Tasmanian Devil, on them.[6] Rules fail because you cannot write a rule to contain every possible behavior in the vast spectrum of human conduct. There will always be gray areas, and therefore, given the right circumstances, opportunities, or outside pressures, some people might be motivated to circumvent them. When they do, our typical response is to just make more. Rules, then, become part of the problem.

Rules react and correlate to vulnerabilities and infirmities. Companies don't have rules to tell employees that they must remember at all times to breathe; the company suffers no vulnerability to breathing; people just naturally do it. Companies *do* have rules that tell people when to come to work, because absent those rules, people would come to work whenever they felt like it and it would be harder to get things done. Rules achieve good floors, minimum standards of behavior, and they prevent bad things from happening—if people follow them. But people transgress, so we write rules to prevent further transgression, yet because rules are inherently limited, people find a way to transgress again. People who feel overregulated in turn feel distrusted. They lose fealty to the rules (and those who make them) and search for ways to avoid their yoke, like Steve Adams did. This creates a downward spiral of rule making which causes lasting detriment to the trust we need to sustain society. With each successive failure of rules, our faith in the very ability of rules to govern human conduct decreases. Rules, the principal arm of the way we govern ourselves, lose their power, destroying our trust in both those who make them and the institutions that they govern.

There is something in the nature of rules and laws that reduces their effectiveness in certain realms of human behavior. How do you legislate fairness? What enforceable language can we use to enshrine into law a powerful value like that? You can (and we do) write long lists proscribing a number of behaviors you think are unfair, but it is impossible to write them all without creating hopeless contradictions, inequities, and loopholes. In business, for example, how do you write a contract that obligates you to *delight* a customer? To exceed expectations, or even surprise customers? You can't. You can set minimum deliverables, optimum schedules, and basic compensation, but you can't construct language that will mandate that extra measure of performance that builds long-term, successful relationships. By setting floors of behavior, rules unintentionally also set ceilings.

When we lived in a Just Do It world, we did not care how you got things done if you generally played by the rules. As long as you did not drop beneath the floor set by rules, we let it slide. Society was content to judge people by their ability to make the numbers—in other words, by WHAT they did, not HOW they did it. As the world became more transparent, however, we began to distinguish compliance from behavior; or, to put it another way, because everyone could see your methods, HOW you did something became as important as WHAT you did. It was suddenly insufficient just to *follow* the rules, because we could now see and understand people's *relationships* to rules. In a hyperconnected and hypertransparent world, you can no longer Just Do It; you must Just Do It Right.

OUTBEHAVING THE COMPETITION

No matter how the world changes or the Certainty Gap grows or shrinks, there are certain traits in us that do not change: We all like to be unique, we like to be valued, we like to be complimented, and we like to achieve things, for ourselves, our families, our communities, and our society. We still must find a way to achieve our goals and desires, to leap as high as we can. Business, as an expression of human aspiration and achievement, mirrors these same goals. It is about being great, about achieving something, and sometimes even about changing the world. Gallup polls in fact show that people's happiness at work is integrally tied not to their wages, but to recognition, praise, and the opportunity to do what they do best every day.[7] And if you look at the companies that make up *Fortune*'s 100 Best Places to Work, almost every one of them distinguishes itself in its employees' eyes by the value of its endeavor.

As the world becomes ever more connected, however, the challenges to success grow. A bachelor's degree from a good college was all you used to need to secure a career. Now, Starbucks employs baristas with master's degrees and PhDs. Engineers used to be in great demand, but with universities in India and China turning them out in droves, an engineering degree is no longer a guaranteed ticket to success.[8] As a company, proximity to your customers used to provide a competitive advantage, allowing you to deliver goods or services more cheaply than competitors that were more remote. Now, you find yourself competing against suppliers from around the world, and the equation is often reversed. To succeed in a crowded, global market of companies and people, we must find a way to differentiate ourselves from the competition in an enduring fashion. As the market becomes more crowded, however, the possible areas of differentiation become fewer, creating new questions about the personal qualities the new world requires of us in order to thrive.

Leaders in twentieth-century capitalist enterprises historically differentiated themselves by WHAT they did. We used to be very *inventive*; those who could invent something and patent it won, and those who could not do so gleaned the fields for survival. I call it Innovating in WHAT. The market provided great incentives and protections to Innovate in WHAT. That is where the spoils went, that is where the publicity went, that is where government protection was focused, and those inventors made the front cover of *Forbes* and *Fortune* magazines. We used to celebrate them, the people who made the best WHATS—like Chester F. Carlson, who in the late 1930s was puttering around in an improvised lab he had set up in the back of an Astoria, New York, beauty salon owned by his mother-in-law when he got some fungus spores to transfer from an electrostatically charged sheet of metal to a piece of wax paper. After patenting the process, he tried to sell it to 20 of the largest corporations in the country. They all turned him down. In 1947, a little photographic products manufacturing company in Rochester, New York, called Haloid bet a quarter of its yearly profit (profit of $101,000 on $6.7 million in revenue) on developing the idea. In 1959, Haloid introduced the first practical application of Carlson's invention, which Haloid called the Xerox 914. Two years later, revenue topped $60 million. Four years after that, Xerox was a half-billion-dollar corporation.[9]

Or people like Noah and Joseph McVicker, who in 1956 invented a pliable plastic composition they hoped would clean wallpaper. When their sister, who taught preschoolers, seized on the stuff to replace the modeling clay her students found too difficult to play with, they formed the Rainbow Crafts Company to manufacture the stuff as a toy. To date, Hasbro, the corporation that eventually bought out Rainbow Crafts, has sold more than two billion cans of Play-Doh. Its odor has been named one of the top five most identifiable smells in the world, and it is one of the most successful toy products of all time.[10]

Innovating in WHAT powered twentieth-century capitalism, but those days are gone. If the McVickers came up with Play-Doh today, someone could take it to China, reverse engineer it in a week, and deliver it around the world at a fraction of the price. A Xerox machine might suffer a similar fate in just a few months. It is difficult to invent a better product in a world of commodities, and that is where we find ourselves. Starbucks unleashes a newfound appreciation for coffee drinks, and now every diner and greasy spoon serves caffe lattes. Dell makes an inexpensive personal computer, and Hewlett-Packard is soon doing likewise. Johnson & Johnson finds a way to protect the integrity of Tylenol, and nearly instantly every analgesic bottle has the same antitampering device.[11]

It is harder now to Innovate in WHAT. It takes a lot of luck and money to be a pioneer, and even if you pull it off, the ability for someone to reverse engineer you in six months and not in six years eliminates a lot of the incentive for doing so. In 1999, two companies, ReplayTV and TiVo, simultaneously rolled out the first consumer versions of the digital video recorder (DVR), an invention that so completely revolutionized the television-watching experience that it held the power to fundamentally undermine the business model of the entire broadcasting industry. Seven years later, ReplayTV is gone and TiVo still struggles to be profitable with a medium-sized share of a small market. The DVR has become a generic commodity, made by any number of companies worldwide, and TiVo struggles to redefine itself as less about its hardware (its WHAT) and more about the experience its software delivers (how you use it).[12]

Many companies have no desire to Innovate in WHAT; it is simply too expensive. They say, "I'll wait until *he* invents it and I'll copy him." Jack Welch, former CEO of General Electric (GE), was fond of pointing out that the game is not structured to reward the innovator.[13] It is very hard to build path protection for your WHATS. Many throughout the world regularly infringe on copyrights, and numerous countries pay no attention to property rights or the concept of intellectual property. In many cultures, there is no word that translates as "intellectual property"; they cannot address the concept that someone can own an idea. Welch was so convinced of his idea that it is pointless to try to protect WHATS that he would continually disclose many details of GE's business model and strategies in the company's annual report—essentially making public GE's WHATS. "We went to Jack and asked him why he was giving away the secret sauce by revealing our business models," my friend Steve Kerr, GE's former chief learning officer (CLO) and vice president of leadership development, told me over lunch on Wall Street near Goldman Sachs' headquarters. Steve is also the former CLO of Goldman Sachs and a co-author of *The GE Work-Out* (McGraw-Hill, 2002), a leadership approach he developed as head of GE's famed leadership development center at Crotonville, New York. He has long been recognized as a thought leader in the world of corporate management. Steve recalled about Jack Welch, "He told us, 'There's no secret to the *what*; the secret is in *how*. They can know our model, but they cannot do it. They can't copy our *hows*.'"[14]

Welch was right. Beginning in the 1980s, American businesses began to Innovate in *how*. They focused intensely on process management, which I call the *hows* of *what*. We now live in a time where winning is about HOW generally. Total Quality Management (TQM), six sigma, just-in-time (JIT) inventory, *kaizen*, Enterprise Resource Planning (ERP), customer relationship management (CRM), human resources information system (HRIS), process reengineering, zero defects, supply chain management, customer service, safety management, BPO— process culture now dominates business practice, aiming to improve profitability by reducing inefficiencies at every stage of the product development process. Business recognizes what Welch saw so clearly: There is going to be one genius in a crowd of 100 who is so smart that she invents a cure for cancer; the other 99 people are going to win on *how*. The journey is as important to profitability as the goal, and process is the Way.

But a funny thing happened on the way to the Way. Everyone got pretty good at it. As companies reached the limits of process improvement, they leveled the playing field. Almost everyone now can reduce quality defects to infinitesimal levels, almost no one gets killed on the job when it can be prevented, everyone answers the phone on the second ring, we all have the same antitampering devices, and we are all drinking caffe lattes. We have commoditized process and performance in the same way we have so much else, possibly to the point of diminishing returns. (Wharton professor Mary J. Benner argues persuasively that the results of her 20-year study show that process management, which has risen to the level of fad, might even be strangling innovation. Benner argues that it encourages short-term, exploitive thinking that stifles bold invention.[15])

There is one area where tremendous variability still exists, however, one place that we have not yet analyzed and commoditized, and which, in fact, *cannot* be commoditized: the realm of human behavior—HOW we do WHAT we do. Think about it. Behavior you can control. If you reach out and inspire more people throughout your global network, you win. If you collaborate more intensely with your co-workers, you win. If you keep promises 99 percent of the time and your competitor keeps promises only 8 out of 10 times, you deliver a better customer experience, and you win. When it comes to human conduct there is tremendous variation, and where a broad spectrum of variation exists, opportunity exists. The tapestry of human behavior is so varied, so rich, and so global that it presents a rare opportunity, *the opportunity to outbehave the competition.*

Look at the kinds of business behaviors we have seen in the past few years. Who could conceive that the founder of the job-search web site Monster would embellish his own resume? That the former executives at Tyco would turn a publicly traded corporation into their personal piggybank to pay for, among other things, an ice-sculpture cherub spouting vodka from his private parts?[16] On the other side of the coin, look at Angel Zamora, the UPS driver I met who went the extra yard to deliver not only an important package, but also a great experience. Or the pilots of Southwest Airlines. I recently flew to Phoenix to visit a client and I noticed that when it was time to board the plane, the pilot appeared at the gate to help the ground personnel take tickets. Later, as I was exiting the aircraft after we landed, the co-pilot appeared on the ramp carrying a stroller for a mother and her child deplaning ahead of me. How extraordinary, I thought. It certainly isn't in the job description of the pilot to help board the plane. And I can't imagine the Southwest Pilots Association union rep negotiating a clause requiring the co-pilot to carry strollers. There is no rule that says, "To stay employed here you must help board the plane and hand out baby strollers." It seemed as though there was something bigger than a job description or a rule guiding those Southwest employees.

Of course, you still need great products and great business models. You still cannot succeed, thrive, or become number one without having good WHATS. But those WHATS used to be enough to excel; now you need them just to stay in the game. To thrive, you need something more. "Anything times zero is zero," said Steve Kerr. "If you do something useless in a really elegant way, it is no more profitable than if you do something important in an inefficient way. The reason to emphasize the HOWS *now* is that they are the underattended part of the equation. They can take you to a different place." It is not that HOW is necessarily more important than WHAT, Steve was telling me; it is that we live in an A-times-B world, and HOW is the X-factor. The greater your command of HOW, the greater are the results of your efforts.[17]

The world today, powered by vast networks of information, connects us and reveals us in ways we have only just begun to comprehend. Through it all, one thing has become crystal clear: It is no longer WHAT you do that makes a difference; it is HOW you do it. Not every team gets to win. Not every employee becomes an executive. Many do not even get to survive. Some last, some end, some outperform others.

The emerging trend among leading-edge businesses today involves delivering not so much a better product, but a better experience to their customers. The opportunity to differentiate by outbehaving the competition is the central raison d'etre for both this book and my life's work. This concept, applied broadly to company/customer/supplier relationships and worker/boss/team relationships, is what I mean what I talk about innovating and winning through HOW.

HOW WE GO FORWARD

Human behavior always mattered in the way we conducted our affairs and pursued personal fulfillment but, unquestionably, it now matters in a new way. In 2005, Merriam-Webster reported that the number-one most looked-up word on its world-renowned dictionary web site was *integrity.*[18] Our new networks of connection allow enormous innovation, but only for those who understand how to send current through these networks and how to make Waves with other people. Frameworks change; paradigms shift. Business, like life, often seems to exist in a bowl full of splinters; movement in one place has a profound effect on dozens of others. Sometimes, tectonic forces bring about new alignments in the world. Sometimes, it is just our ability to see familiar things in a different way that reveals a new world order lurking not far beneath the surface of the one we thought we knew so well. If the world has changed, how we conduct ourselves within it must change, too.

In this part of the book, we have explored the conspiracy of forces that define the parameters of a new framework, a new reality for twenty-first-century business. We've looked at the shift from land to capital to information and the old habits like hoarding, dividing and conquering, and command-and-control that have clung to us despite profound change; the trend in business toward horizontal connections that puts us into increasing contact with those of relatively equal stature working in teams around the globe, the ways in which we have been jammed together across time and cultures faster than we have developed frameworks to understand and operate productively with one another, and how information and communications technology trespasses upon and alters how we fill the spaces between us.

We've talked about the many ramifications of transparency, how it inflates the value of reputation and how it combines with the free flow of information to make reputation more vulnerable to inaccurate or unfair charges. We've charted the end of the Just Do It era, with its focus on bottom line results and transactional behaviors, and the limitations of rules to govern human conduct. And we've considered the profound way that these changes have shifted our focus from WHAT to HOW.

The picture of the world these forces and dynamics paint reveals a sea change, not a pendulum swing, in how we do what we do, and places unprecedented focus on human conduct as a process full of value. There is no going back. It bears repeating that we will never be *less* transparent, will never have *less* information, and will never be *less* connected than we are today. No matter what our vertical specialty—sales, marketing, manufacturing, finance, administration, management, service, and on and on—achievement in the twenty-first century dramatically depends on our ability to thrive in a system of connections more vast, more varied, and more exposed than any before in the history of man. We do not live in glass houses (houses have walls); we live on glass microscope slides, flat as flat can be, visible and exposed to all.

Success now requires new skills and habits, a new lens for seeing, and a new consciousness for relating. In our see-through world, there's an overabundance of information and it flows too easily for anyone to control it and outfox everyone. You can no longer game the system and expect that no one will find out. You need to stop dancing around people and start leading a dance that everyone can follow. Long-term, sustained success is directly proportional to your ability—as a company or an individual—to make Waves throughout evanescing networks of association, to reach out to others and enlist them in endeavors larger than yourself, and to do so while everyone watches you. In the chapters that follow, we'll explore HOW.

Part II

HOW WE THINK

He who has a hundred miles to walk
should reckon ninety as half the journey.
—Japanese proverb

INTRODUCTION: THE PARADOX OF JOURNEY

As a law student, I was a teaching fellow in a class taught by Alan Dershowitz, Stephen J. Gould, and Robert Nozick called "Thinking about Thinking" to undergrads at Harvard College. It was a highly conceptual, cross-disciplinary class that combined science, philosophy, and law to confront the big issues of the time: drugs, abortion, euthanasia, gun rights, and others. At the end of the semester, I began to notice an interesting trend in my grading patterns, something surprising about who earned Bs and B+s, who earned the As, and, most interestingly, who earned the Cs. I discussed it with my fellow teaching associates, and in the process confronted an interesting paradox about how we learn and the journey to deep knowledge.

The B/B+ students in my class demonstrated good command of

the material. They started their intellectual journeys at the beginning of the semester and climbed a hill of understanding. They did all the reading, they were industrious, and they were able to lay it out very clearly on the final exam. They climbed diligently, as one does on all journeys, ever upward toward knowledge. At the end of the semester they displayed a basic understanding and basic knowledge, made no major mistakes, showed little confusion, and repeated it all back clearly. Basic knowledge deserved a grade of B.

Those who received A grades had mastered, synthesized, and integrated the material into their being. They thought deeply, developed counterarguments that weren't part of the readings, internalized the material, and put it to work. They took charge of what they had learned, took it further, challenged it, and created new, innovative thoughts: thinking outside the classroom, if you will. In short, they had developed a power—a power informed by what they had read and heard, and amplified by the way they saw it at work in the world. They were not just *taking* the class; they were in some respects *teaching* it, and I found them inspirational. They deserved a grade of A.

Those who got Cs, however, really caught my attention. As you would naturally assume, some were lazy and did the bare minimum to get by. But I was surprised to realize that a good number of them were every bit as industrious as those who got As. They, too, did all the reading and understood the material well. And like those who got As, they exuded flashes of brilliance, often trying to take their understanding to the next level. But when it came to coalescing it into an understanding and expressing their thoughts, they were stuck in a deep valley of confusion, struggling to get out. They had taken the extra step and had gone for the deep knowledge, but missed it by a degree or two or kept slipping back, and couldn't express their thoughts in clear or cogent ways.

When I plotted it out on a graph it looked like Figure II.1.

The paradox was that the C students were actually further along than the B students. They had traveled more ground and gone past the first peak of basic understanding achieved by the Bs. They were unable to command the power of the As, sure, but they were closer to the As than the Bs, further on the intellectual journey than the Bs. The good news/bad news story for those C students was, at semester's end, I had to give them a C for *confusion*. But they revealed a com-

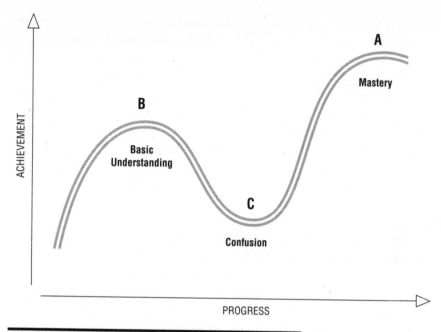

FIGURE II.1   The Paradox of the Hills of Knowledge

pelling analogy for the path of knowledge. It is easy to stop on the Hill of B; you feel like you made a climb, can see the lay of the land below you, and think that perhaps you deserve a little rest. It feels safe there, too; on that first hill, things seem clear. You have demonstrated a reasonable amount of effort and achievement, and exposed yourself to relatively little risk.

B, however, is not a winning grade. If you stay at B while others accept the challenge of continuing on to A, you get left behind. B is stasis, and, as we all know, success lies in consistent progress. To gain true understanding requires struggle in the deep Valley of C. If you don't struggle there, you'll never get to that second, much higher, peak. You can skip around in this book, for example (as many people do with business books) and come to a superficial understanding that Innovating in How is good business, that HOW we do what we do holds the key to long-term, sustained success, and that the winners in the twenty-first century will outbehave the competition, but all you will achieve is a *basic* knowledge. Those are thin concepts. Despite the old cliché, knowledge doesn't have wings; we can't fly from peak to peak. To gain a true understanding of the world of HOW, you must be prepared to struggle and wrestle with complexity and uncertainty and new ways of seeing.

It takes courage to keep going, and more courage still to descend into the Valley of Confusion and wrestle with what lies there. Most of us have experienced this before, unintentionally, when we set out to truly master something. We found ourselves in the Valley of C but didn't understand why we were confused. Some of us struggled on, and some got demoralized and gave up. You might experience this again as you read this book. To get from the Hill of B to the Hill of A, you need more than directions and you need more than rules; you need bravery, tenacity, and emotional intelligence. You need to struggle and be confused so when clarity comes, the knowledge is deep. The only thing wrong with the Valley of Confusion would be to get stuck there. Zen Buddhist scholar Daisetz T. Suzuki said, "If one really wishes to be master of an art, technical knowledge of it is not enough. One has to transcend technique so that the art becomes an 'artless art' growing out of the Unconscious."[1]

Power in a world of HOW is not power *over* something, but power *through* something, like a network, or a synapse, or a circuit; a power that connects, not a power that commands. I want to lead you to the Hill of A, and, as the Chinese philosopher Lao-Tzu said, "A journey of a thousand miles must begin with a single step."[2] Change, progress, and personal growth require a journey, and I use that word consciously throughout the book. To be on a journey means to focus on process not product, on HOW not WHAT, and on the road not the destination. Journeys are by their nature curvilinear; they have highs and lows and require more effort for the climb than the descent. From this point on, then, I will use this two-hill model to illustrate the journey from old to new, from getting it to mastering it, and from knowledge to understanding. Since that wavy line picture I first drew seems a little less than inspirational, I've created Figure II.2 to illustrate these ideas. The point, of course, is exactly the same.

So let's briefly summarize the first three chapters of this book, putting the knowledge and behaviors that are easily attained or widely known on the Hill of B, and our newer concepts we have discussed on the Hill of A.

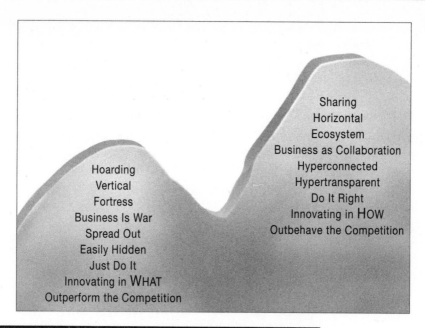

Hoarding
Vertical
Fortress
Business Is War
Spread Out
Easily Hidden
Just Do It
Innovating in WHAT
Outperform the Competition

Sharing
Horizontal
Ecosystem
Business as Collaboration
Hyperconnected
Hypertransparent
Do It Right
Innovating in HOW
Outbehave the Competition

FIGURE II.2   How We Have Been, How We Have Changed

The shifts in society and business over the past decade—from hoarding to sharing, from fortress to ecosystem, from spread-out and easily hidden to hyperconnected and hypertransparent—combine to put new emphasis on the HOWs of human behavior, the way we fill the synapses between us and others. In this second part, we begin our journey to understand and command these HOWs and to put them to work in everything we do. The first step leads us inward, to the thought processes and understandings that shape our decisions and actions toward others. A little biology, a little sociology, a little linguistics, and a little golf: This section is called "How We Think," and in it, we're going to begin to build a new framework for understanding a world of HOW.

4

Playing to Your Strengths

*We can't solve problems by
using the same kind of thinking we
used when we created them.*
—Albert Einstein

In the movie *Cast Away*, actor Tom Hanks plays Chuck Noland, a fictional FedEx employee marooned on a deserted island for four years after the delivery plane on which he has hitched a ride plummets into the ocean.[1] He survives armed with nothing but his wits, what he can scrounge on the island, and the contents of several FedEx packages that float ashore after the crash. If you ask most people what the film is about, they will typically mention mankind's heroic struggle to survive or—propelled as Noland is by the desire to reunite with his fiancée—the power of love to overcome all obstacles. There were two events in the film, however, that sent me a different message. These events so intrigued me that I e-mailed the film's screenwriter, William Broyles Jr., to ask him what they meant.

The first thing that struck me was the friendship Noland forms with a half-inflated soccer ball rescued from the crash, which he names "Wilson," after the ball's manufacturer. Broyles told me that to research the film, he spent time alone on a beach by the Sea of Cortez. During his solitude, he found a volleyball washed up on the shore. "So much are we a social animal," Broyles wrote me, "so much do we need the spiritual connection to another human being, that I was endowing a volleyball with human characteristics, just because it was so hard to be alone."[2] You have no need for morals or values when you are stranded on an island (unless you believe you have duties or obligations to palm trees and bananas, a legitimate concern, but off the point). You have no one but yourself to answer to, so how you survive is entirely up to you. By creating this imaginary friend, Broyles acknowledged that there is something in man that calls him to be greater than just himself, to have a purpose to others beyond himself.

The second event that jumped out at me came at the very end of the film, when, four years after he was stranded, Noland completes the delivery of one package that survived the crash, and includes a note that says, *This package saved my life.* "It was a crucial part of who he'd been," Broyles said. "Noland had been someone who 'connected' the world, who made it work, who kept the simple promise of delivering a package from one human being to another. This man of connections, who'd been so long disconnected, reestablished himself as part of the world by fulfilling this commitment." To survive his ordeal, Noland needed purpose. He realized he was not just a person who moved packages; he was a person who kept promises. *Cast Away*, in my view, is a film about keeping promises to others, about our inherent need as humans to be connected with and to do for one another, and to fulfill what seems to me to be a biological imperative to be more than ourselves alone. I began to wonder, is this something that we have learned as a species, or is there some sort of biological underpinning that makes us this way? Are we, in fact, hardwired to connect to others?

When we talk about the interpersonal synapses between people in a stadium or our horizontal collaborations across global supply chains, we are in a sense talking about biological networks. The brain—that spongy mass between our ears—processes a tremendous amount of information throughout the average day, both consciously and unconsciously. It is responsible for everything from our intake of breath to the kiss we place on a loved one's cheek at night. The unconscious aspects of the brain's ability to absorb subtle clues from our environment and to process them through what both nature and nurture provide gives us our ways of acting in and reacting to the world. It is the most complex biological network we know. Academics and scientists, it turns out, have begun to marry advances in their ability to see the brain at work with behavioral research in economics, politics, and other sociological activities, to reveal an inherent, biological human predilection for certain behaviors that increase our ability to be effective and prosperous.[3] The networked brain and the networked world of business have more in common than we ever thought possible.

First, we'll examine some of this groundbreaking research, and then try to draw some conclusions. Though it may seem at first counterintuitive to launch into a deeper discussion of HOW in an internetworked world by discussing neuroscience and evolutionary anthropology, the workings of the brain can provide us with some keystone understandings about how we think and act. Since most people concede that you get better results from energy invested in improving on what you already do well as opposed to energy spent improving on your weaknesses, understanding the brain's biological proclivities can give us new perspective on where best to concentrate our efforts. Good science points to the fact that getting your HOWs right may, in fact, mean playing to your strengths.

HELP

You are shopping in a supermarket, pushing your cart, minding your own business, thinking about what brand of soup to buy, when you pass a fairly short person taking a can down from the top shelf opposite you. In so doing, he accidentally knocks a few cans of minestrone off the shelf. He grabs for the falling cans, instinctively trying to steady the other cans on the shelf while catching the falling ones. Without thinking, you reach over and help him steady the cans on the shelf, and when they are secure, reach down and pick up the fallen ones, while he stammers his thanks. Without any conscious thought, you help.

Humans routinely help one another, even if there is no payoff for the helper. We help strangers as well as those we know. This behavior—called *altruistic helping*—is one of the things that separate us from most other animals. Altruistic helping requires a rather complex set of cognitions: You must see another person's action, understand his intent, understand what is needed to achieve that intention, evaluate his ability to achieve it, evaluate his willingness to accept assistance, and make the decision to intervene despite the fact you receive no immediate or physical reward for so doing. For a long time psychiatrists believed that altruistic helping was a socially induced phenomenon, something learned over time from parental modeling and the observation of human society. This belief sprang from the fact that, at first blush, all this would seem to require higher brain function—reasoning, syntax, empathy, and decision-making skills—abilities that take years of childhood development to achieve.

Recently, however, Felix Warneken and Michael Tomasello at the Max Planck Institute for Evolutionary Anthropology did a revolutionary study that demonstrated that children as young as 18 months of age—prelinguistic or just linguistic and not generally possessed of these complex cognitive abilities—readily helped an unknown adult achieve a series of goals in a variety of situations and, amazingly, were able to make complex judgments about whether help was needed.[4] Children helped a stranger reach out-of-reach objects, though not if he had purposefully discarded them. They aided him in stacking books if it appeared he had not yet met his goal. When he struggled to open a cabinet with his hands full, the children opened the door for him, though not if he made an effort to unload his burden on the cabinet top and was therefore able to open it himself. Finally, they retrieved objects from a box for him, though not if they felt he threw them there on purpose. Children with barely developed verbal skills were able to tell the difference between an individual needing help and one who had made a decision that made help unnecessary. From their study, Warneken and Tomasello concluded that "even very young children have a *natural* tendency to help other persons solve their problems, even when the other is a stranger and they receive no benefit at all." This contradicts the widely held misconception that humans, absent the mitigation of social necessities, tend to act in their own self-interest. It turns out that greed, in the sense of doing *only* for yourself, others be damned, is not only not good, it is not natural.

YOU CAN JUDGE A BOOK BY ITS COVER

On September 26, 1960, 70 million people watched the presidential debate between Richard M. Nixon and John F. Kennedy. This was the first of four so-called Great Debates, and the first ever televised.[5] For the first time, the nation as whole was able to watch both candidates interact. Millions more listened on the radio. Nixon—who had been hospitalized most of August with knee surgery—showed up at the studios thin and pale in an ill-fitting shirt, and refused to wear makeup to enhance his complexion and disguise his not-inconsiderable five o'clock shadow. In contrast, the senator from Massachusetts had spent the previous weeks campaigning in California. He was tan, fit, and impeccably tailored. Polled after the debate, radio listeners proclaimed Nixon to be the clear winner. Television viewers, however, came to a different conclusion. Kennedy's charisma and poised delivery presented television viewers with the marked impression that his vigor and charm discomforted the then vice president, and it swung their allegiance to Kennedy. Viewers were more persuaded by what they saw than by what they heard, according to polling organizations' results analyzed at the time by Earl Mazzo, head of the Washington bureau of the *New York Herald-Tribune*.[6] According to Mazzo's analysis, in the West, which Nixon carried, 9 percent of adults heard the debate on radio; in the East, which Nixon lost, the radio audience was about 2 percent.

In order to help strangers—or vote for them—you have to overcome the biological fear response that they will harm you when you approach. In other words, you have to decide to trust them. We know that babies bond intensely with their mothers shortly after birth, but how can they know to trust a stranger enough to help them? Isn't that another series of complex cognitions? Researchers set out to find out. Peter Kirsch, Christine Esslinger, and others at the Cognitive Neuroscience Group, Center for Psychiatry and Psychotherapy, Justus-Liebig University showed adult subjects a series of photos of various Caucasian men, each displaying basic, neutral facial expressions, while simultaneously scanning their brains with functional magnetic resonance imaging (fMRI). Scientists asked the test subjects to label the faces as "trustworthy" or "untrustworthy." The scans showed that a certain portion of the brain, the amygdala, lit up in subjects when they viewed faces they felt to be untrustworthy.[7] The amygdala, an almond-shaped set of neurons located deep in the brain's medial temporal lobe, is part of the limbic system, the section of the brain that forms neurological structures involved in emotion, motivation, and emotional association with memory. The amygdala enables you to experience fear. (When your father-in-law arrives unannounced for dinner, the amygdala signals fear to the brain stem, the center of arousal and motivation, which conveniently remembers that you left some work at the office that you must immediately leave to retrieve.) Later, the researchers asked the same subjects to rate various characteristics of the faces they had seen. The faces deemed untrustworthy in the first portion of the experiment received more negative ratings for these other characteristics than those deemed trustworthy.

One of the first objects that capture the attention of newborns is the human face, and now, it seems, there are evolutionary, survival reasons for it. First impressions, it seems, do count. Humans are biologically hardwired to make snap decisions to trust or distrust others. Like the 70 million people who watched the Nixon-Kennedy debate, we do tend to judge a book by its cover.

LOOKING OUT FOR NUMBER TWO

If trust isn't something that results from high, rational functioning, what is it?

Trust, it turns out, is a drug called oxytocin. The so-called bonding hormone is a peptide chain of nine amino acids (nanopeptide) secreted by the pituitary gland and most famously released during the orgasms of both sexes and by mothers during birth and nursing. When released, oxytocin fills the synapses between neurons and floods the brain with a feeling of well-being. This brief bliss (the effects of a cerebral oxytocin buzz last just three to five minutes) reduces the connectivity of the amygdala to the upper brain stem; in other words, it overcomes fear. Kirsch and Esslinger demonstrated this effect. They showed two groups of people identical pictures of fearsome faces and fearsome situations and, like similar studies, mapped their brains' reactions with fMRI scans. One group received oxytocin via nasal spray (you can synthesize it in a lab); the other group did not. The unmedicated group was predictably afraid of the scary faces; the oxytocin group was not.

Oxytocin, when produced, does not flood the whole brain. It works on specific regions associated with memory, as well as those that control involuntary functions like breathing, digestion, and heart rate. Amazingly, these brain regions connect powerfully to a different portion of the brain associated with attention and identifying errors in the environment, which in turn sends messages to the decision-making region. In other words, oxytocin influences decision making in a way that is largely outside the realm of our conscious perception.

What can we draw from all this? So much of our thinking about the highly competitive world of global business is predicated on the assumption that maximum profit and success flow from the pursuit of self-interest. Business is war, goes the old saying; the strong survive and the weak fail. We commonly assume that, left alone on a deserted island like Tom Hanks in *Cast Away*, man would revert to this basic instinct to look out for number one, that we are biologically hardwired to do so, and that we only cooperate with others *because the conditions of society demand it*. But this assumption may be incorrect. It would seem that humans, at a very early stage of mental development, are hardwired with the ability and desire to connect with and help others, despite the fact that doing so engenders great risk and returns no obvious reward. Moreover, in order to do so, we have an amazing biological gift that allows us to overcome our animal, prerational fear of the unknown.

In light of some of this new thinking about the biological basis of trust and altruistic helping, Paul Zak, chair, department of economics at Claremont Graduate University and adjunct professor of neurology at Loma Linda University, School of Medicine, set out to learn, once and for all, whether maximum profit in fact flows from the pursuit of self-interest, as we have long assumed. Zak is the founding director of the Center for Neuroeconomic Studies and a leading light in the emerging field of neuroeconomics, the place where economics and the mind meet. Neuroeconomics draws on neuroscience, endocrinology, psychology, economic theory, and experimental economics to try to better understand economic decision making. Zak staged an experiment based on a game theory form called *the trust game* first used by Joyce Berg, John Dikhaut, and Kevin McCabe in 1995,[8] and made some fascinating discoveries that stand conventional thinking about self-interest on its proverbial head.

The basic trust game goes like this: Random subjects are paired up and placed at computers in different rooms, unable to see each other. Each is paid $10 to participate. The first decision makers (DM1s) are told they can send any portion of their $10 to their partner (DM2) and the amount they send will be tripled in DM2's account; if DM1 sends $4, then DM2 receives $12. The DM2s are told they can then send any, all, or none of the money they receive back to their partner. The money DM1 sends is, in effect, an expression of trust; the amount DM2 returns is an expression of trustworthiness.

The economic thinking prevailing at the time about how each person should play the trust game to achieve optimum profit comes from the work of John Nash, the noted mathematician portrayed by Russell Crowe in the Academy Award–winning movie *A Beautiful Mind* (based on the biography by Sylvia Nasar).[9] His famous formula— called the Nash equilibrium—represents mathematically the correct action to achieve maximum profit in a world of perfect self-interest.[10] For Zak's game, Nash's reasoning concludes that, if each person acts in perfect self-interest, neither should send the other any money at all; DM1 should send no money because he has no reason to believe that his anonymous partner will return any and to do so would require sacrifice without guaranteed return, and DM2 should not return any because he gains nothing by doing so.

Zak ran this experiment a vast number of times, both in the United States and in developing countries, using various amounts representing, in some cases, a large percentage of the subject's monthly income (to make sure that the significance of the amount involved did not influence the outcome). Amazingly, typically 75 percent of DM1s sent some money to their unknown partners, and an even *higher* ratio of DM2s sent some back.[11] I spoke to Zak and asked him about this counterintuitive result. "The trust game is embedded in social interaction," he told me, "and the Nash equilibrium does not take that into account." Nash, Zak points out, suffered from schizophrenia, a neuropsychiatric disorder characterized by, among other things, social withdrawal. To some extent, Zak believes, Nash's illness affected his economic theories. "Cost isn't the only reason people buy product A versus product B," Zak said. "There are any number of social, human-based reasons involved, and Nash never calculated those into his equations."[12]

Zak theorizes that we trust others because doing so activates social attachment mechanisms; in other words, it seems the right thing to do. Trust appears to be driven by a *sense* of what to do, rather than a conscious determination of what is most profitable to do. To understand this hypothesis better, Zak performed blood tests on his subjects after they had played the trust game and made a phenomenal discovery: The more money DM2s received from DM1s, the more their oxytocin levels rose, and the more they returned to DM1s. Put another way, when you trust someone, their brain responds by making more oxytocin, which allows them to trust you in return. *Reciprocity—doing unto others as they do unto you—seems therefore to be a biological function; trust begets trust.* (Interestingly, Zak pointed out, roughly 2 percent within the groups did not share any of the wealth, a number roughly corresponding to the percentage of sociopaths in a population.[13])

Furthermore, remember, oxytocin directly affects the areas of the brain associated with memory. When you extend trust, which is at times an unconscious behavior, you not only bathe this area of the brain with soothing chemicals, you create memories of having done so. This concurrence of activity led Zak to conclude that it is possible to restimulate and reinforce trusting behaviors over time. In other words, trust *builds* trust, as well, on a biological basis.

How does that translate into the modern marketplace? If trust is, as Zak explains, "a tangible, intentional act in which you cede power over resources to another person," both sides can recognize extending trust as cooperation for potential gain. We generate feel-good hormones in the people we trust, and they reciprocate by trusting us in return. We, in turn, consciously or unconsciously acknowledge their trust with a similar biological response. Fear dissolves, cooperation ensues, and an upward spiral of mutual reinforcement thrives. We are on some level, it seems, hardwired to seek connections with others, to build biological networks to achieve greater personal gain.

THE EVOLUTION OF WHAT IS VALUABLE

Survival of the fittest is an evolutionary concept we take for granted. Yet, when it comes to humankind, what defines the fittest? Is it the strongest? When early man was walking around in animal skins and living in caves, did the biggest ones rule the littlest ones? Did they get more food or a reproductive advantage because of their size? Though this is, I think, a common assumption, the cutting edge of social anthropological thinking suggests that it may be false. If modern man is so much more than brute force and the ability to use tools, then at some point in our evolution mustn't we have selected for other traits? What if humankind's greatest strength is not the size of our muscles but our seemingly irrational embrace of connection and cooperation— our ability to form societies of like-minded individuals? We have already seen that we have a biological predisposition to do this and, it turns out, we have an evolutionary one as well. Like so many things that make us who we are, our predilection to form human networks and work together is a result of both nature and nurture.

Let's think about what binds groups of people together. One of the primary ways societies and organizations fill the interpersonal synapses between their members is with common beliefs or values. These could be as simple as "If we hunt together, we will get more food," as primal as "We take care of each other no matter what," or as psychologically complex as "Our spiritual beliefs prescribe that we act in a certain way toward one another." Like trust, values are to some extent also hardwired into our brains; they are the outgrowth of the neurological effect of trust on our attention-focusing, memory, and error-recognition faculties. However, they are more flexible and more learnable, a more conscious process than automatically released oxytocin and its neurological by-products. We learn values like a vocabulary, from the people around us, and their behaviors set an example of the behavior norms of the group.

Children absorb their society's values in the same way they learn the language of their society—a child in France learns French, a Saudi child learns Arabic, and so on. Culture exerts a powerful influence on values formation. A behavior obligatory in one culture could be prohibited in another culture, while a third culture might not care one way or the other. The content of values is largely culturally determined and culturally sensitive. Each society reinforces its own hierarchy of values: what is important and what is less so. The traffic accident study we discussed in Chapter 2 demonstrated that both U.S. and Korean cultures prize the values of respect for law and obligations to friendship, but each society assigns them a different priority in its hierarchy of values. Likewise, a child raised in one society may have certain moral boundaries that do not translate into another society.

Below the surface of the societal norms, however, there are certain values that translate across sociopolitical boundaries. Historically, societal values have had evolutionary impacts on how human societies have flourished. Anthropologist Joseph Shepher, for example, studied people raised communally on kibbutzim in Israel, where children spend much of the day in a group. He discovered that people have a strong tendency *not* to be sexually attracted to those with whom they were raised, irrespective of genetic relationship.[14] Something in the group experience over time interrupts the biological urge toward procreation. Shepher's work reinforced the nineteenth-century hypothesis by Edward Westermarck that this tendency is a mechanism for incest avoidance. Back in the earliest human societies, someone you knew from childhood was probably your cousin, and thus not a prime candidate for reproduction. Therefore, the cultural aversion to incest stems from our physical hardwiring.

So it seems that culture and values are not *solely* learned; evolution also ingrained them in our biology. Dr. Richard Joyce from the Australian National University, author of *The Evolution of Morality*, calls this "fitness-survival."[15] Joyce is a remarkable thinker, as anyone who speaks with him would quickly realize. His work combines the study of evolutionary anthropology with the study of moral philosophy to provide another model that has far-reaching implications for how we function in organizations and networks. "*Moral thinking* [the capacity to conceive of social behavior in terms of values] can be found in every culture and throughout history, tracing back even to the *Epic of Gilgamesh* or ancient Egyptian writings," he said.[16] Joyce believes this ubiquity of moral thinking raises an important question: "Is there a biological predisposition toward values-based thinking," he asks, "or are we just smart, rational creatures who are social and sort of naturally invent morality as a way of getting on as social beings?"

In other words, if we want to play to our strengths, to which strengths should we play?

Joyce's conclusion? Moral thinking goes back to our earliest ancestors and through a process of natural selection has become part of the fabric of our biological beings. Joyce explains that there are two schools of thought about the evolutionary benefits of values-based behavior: the *benefit-to-the-group* model and the *benefit-to-the-individual* model. In a group model, our fictional caveman ancestor—call him *Ook*—and his tribe-mates somehow developed a cooperative, altruistic, value-based society that allowed them to function more efficiently than their neighbors; they could farm or hunt or defend themselves better, or shelter themselves in such a way that they were able to grow their tribe. Their neighboring tribe, two hills and three caves over, had no sense of values, and thus would be more disorganized and less capable of cooperation, trust, and sharing. Eventually, starvation, exposure, or other factors eliminated the other tribe because they were unable to produce a smoothly functioning society. This "survival-of-the-fittest-group" scenario has obvious ramifications for developed societies—like corporations—but it leaves something out: How did we get to be a group of moral thinkers if we weren't born that way?

"Benefits can accrue to the individual from acting in a moral way and thinking in moral terms," Joyce explains. In other words, Ook, by acting in an altruistic, self-sacrificing way—sharing, cooperating, and helping others—engendered trust, which, as we know from Professor Zak's work, would prompt his tribe-mates to reciprocate. Ook would reap the rewards from a shared harvest, a shared shelter, and the people who watched his back, and thereby would gain a reproductive advantage over other members of his group. He would make a boodle of baby Ooks, propagating his genes throughout the culture, which would mean more moral thinkers. According to Joyce, this idea of individual selection is a more likely explanation for our ability to think about behavior and cooperation in terms of values.

Biology is not the only transmitter of Ook's values orientation, of course. Being a social leader, Ook talks to his comrades, they observe him, and he exerts influence over them. His friends, Nook and Took, see that Ook is building a pretty good life; he has lots of food, a warm cave to sleep in, and good luck with women. If they are smart enough to observe what he is doing, his fellows will imitate him. Thus, value-based thinking may not be purely a biological adaptation, because these tribes' people are talking to each other and sharing ideas; they can influence each other's behavior. So, Nook and Took develop a moral capacity, as do their offspring. The tribe gets bigger and more able than the tribe two hills over not because they are stronger, but because they work together better. The actual details of *how* early man got from morality to having more babies could have gone a variety of ways, Joyce suggests, but it seems clear that values evolved because they do provide reproductive advantage.

What strikes me as interesting in this theory is how it, too, stands the notion of survival of the fittest on its head. Ook might not have been the strongest or the fastest cave dweller on the rock, but his ability to work well with others and inspire them to do the same could have made him very popular, in a nice-caveman-gets-the-girl sort of way. The more offspring Ook produced, the greater the chance that he passed his propensity for values-based thinking along with his genes, throughout the eons. Nice guys—genetically speaking—finished first.

Now, here is a leap: Our biological propensity for values-based thinking leads directly to Adam Smith's vision of ideal capitalist enterprise: the development of a free and fair market system based on mutual advantage.

A far-fetched statement? Think about it.

Since Smith wrote *The Wealth of Nations*, the book that birthed the idea of capitalism and free markets, many have misapplied or misinterpreted his theories to justify various versions of business-is-war, laissez-faire capitalism. The key thought many overlook, however, is the concept of *mutual* advantage that lies at the very heart of his vision: Forming the basis of all markets is the idea that goods, money, or work can be exchanged for other goods/money/work and that both parties can benefit from this exchange. This cannot occur without the presence of moral values because, in order to trade, both parties must have a sense that one cannot simply take from the other without giving something in return. A mammoth tusk, for example, might belong to Ook or to his tribe as a whole; Natto, the shaman from the tribe two hills over, may want the tusk. He can take it without Ook's knowledge or permission, or he can exchange some of his (or his tribe's) corn for the tusk. Thinking of something as mine/ours is a value-based admission, implying an awareness of rights; that is, if you have earned/created something, then other people are obliged to respect your ownership. Ownership engenders rights, obligations, and prohibitions. To create a market, both trading parties must be capable of this sort of values-based thinking and see the mutual benefit in exchange. The rise and success of market-based economies, therefore, might never have occurred without the biological success of collaborative, values-based thought.

BELIEVE IT

There is one last piece of the brain puzzle to touch on: belief. A belief occupies a very special place in the human intellect: It can exist in the absence of any objective proof, and often in the face of direct contradiction. We all have something of a system of beliefs. Religious doctrine, cultural myth, even narrative history often sustain and propagate stories and beliefs that have no basis in fact. Some people even depend on it. For instance, flat-earthers know from study that the earth is round, but believe it to be flat nonetheless. Many people teach their children to believe in Santa Claus although they have not ridden in his flying sleigh.

A big part of our humanness involves our ability to hold both factual knowledge and belief in our consciousness simultaneously. In the case of Santa Claus, some even ascribe benefit and power to our very ability to believe. The other side of this belief coin, however, is that belief can also negate fact. We can know a fact but refuse to believe in it, and to reconcile this conflict we decide that the contradicting knowledge is wrong. Some people believe in ghosts and spirits, and their dedication to that belief—right or wrong—leads them to discount a substantial body of evidence to the contrary. I'm not here to question or refute anyone's particular beliefs, but it is important for our discussion to understand that *believe* and *know* have two different definitions and employ two different parts of our brains.

Belief can have a powerful, uncontrolled chemical effect on how we think and process information. The starkest illustration of this is called the placebo effect. In studies done at the University of California, Los Angeles, researchers told two groups of subjects that they were to receive an antidepressant drug; one group got the drug, and the other received a placebo instead. The placebo group experienced the same physiological response as the group getting the real drug.[17] Though a drug and a placebo may both affect a specific brain region, the drug does so directly; placebo effects are typically activated by belief alone. The belief causes the brain to act as if it were fact. In another experiment at the University of Michigan, scientists injected the jaws of healthy young men with enough saltwater to cause painful pressure, while positron-emission tomography (PET) scans measured the impact in their brains. During one scan, the researchers told the men that they were also getting a pain reliever, although it was actually a placebo. Typically, pain relievers mimic the effects of endorphins or cause them to be released, thus blocking pain. In this case, because the subjects believed they were getting a pain reliever, the unconscious portion of the brain that controls the release of endorphins simply acted "as if." Immediately, the subject's brains released more endorphins and the men felt better.[18]

These findings bolster previous research indicating that expectations play an important role in placebo effects. *Expectations typically involve affective thoughts about current and future experience.* In other words, our expectations can affect our experiences; beliefs can alter how we perceive information, and sometimes these beliefs manifest themselves *unconsciously*, separate from our conscious thought processes. Children confronted with the image of their parents wrapping presents in the living room on Christmas eve will create extraordinary fictions to explain why this sight does not refute their belief in Old St. Nick and not see themselves as doing anything illogical or out of the ordinary. Likewise, cynics who believe that everyone is motivated by self-interest will create narratives of self-serving interest in almost everything they see—*even altruistic helping*—often unaware of the influence that belief exerts on the mind. The first instance affects little but the fairy dreams of a child; the second affects your ability to succeed. You can absorb new information and let it alter your beliefs, *and* you can alter your beliefs and thereby apprehend new information.

Let's think back to Paul Zak's trust experiment for a moment. It had one more interesting result: *People who extended trust to others made more money than those who did not.* On average, DM1s who sent money made $14, and DM2s who returned some made $17 (those who sent nothing walked away with their original $10). The only way to make more money was to take a risk and give it away. In Zak's game, money functioned as a metaphor for trust. In the end, the message of the game is that if you hold the right model of human nature—that people are basically good and can be trusted—you can extend more trust and make more money. Here is where belief enters the picture. If you *believe* that people are generally good and trustworthy, people sense that about you (because, as Kirsch and Esslinger showed us, humans are very good at that); they make quick judgments about your trustworthiness; and they return the trust more easily. *Belief* in trust created the conditions for trust, and the profit that results.

PLAYING TO YOUR STRENGTHS

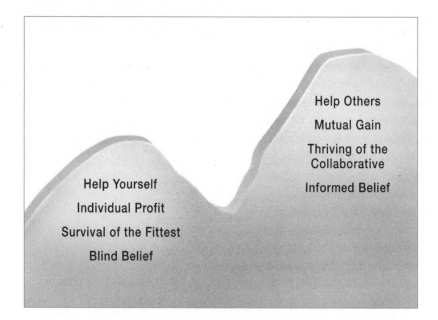

Belief is a powerful force of inspiration and energy, but it can also get in the way of seeing clearly. Belief and perception are integrally connected. To make the journey up the Hill of A to a new understanding, you have to be willing to bring your beliefs into play and acknowledge their tremendous influence—both positive and negative—on HOW you think.

Evolution has provided us with a complex brain and a collection of peptides and hormones that act in symphony to ensure the survival of our species. That survival is not facilitated now, as it was thousands and thousands of years ago, solely by fear-based responses that cause our hearts to race, our stomachs to churn, and our faces to flush, but rather by our feeling good about each other and ourselves. Altruistic helping. Trust. Reciprocity. Values-based thinking. Belief. These behaviors, which have the power to fill the interpersonal synapses between us, seem to be hardwired to some degree into our DNA. To focus your attention in these areas seems to mean playing on your biological strengths, which is actually the path of least resistance. One theorist called it "doing what comes naturally." Like the prelinguistic children helping a stranger, we naturally, instinctively, unconsciously seek to better our fellows. Understanding this natural proclivity leads naturally to exploring the world of HOW.

This, in the end, is why *Cast Away* moved me so deeply. Despite his solitary journey, Tom Hanks's character was a promise keeper, invested in his connections with others. We feel in our guts that keeping promises and connecting with others are what gives our lives meaning, and most of us seek meaning in our lives. These connections give our lives significance. That is why, both biologically and culturally, mastering ways of building better interpersonal synapses with the people around us by getting our HOWS right is so germane to our success today. If we live now in a world more connected than ever before, shouldn't we all find ways to connect better?

CHAPTER **5**

From *Can* to *Should*

> *[There is a] difference between what you have*
> *a right to do, and what is the right thing to do.*
> —Potter Stewart,
> U.S. Supreme Court Justice

Everyone loves tax time, that special time of year when we sit down with our loved ones and measure our financial commitment to society. Around the world, people throw joyous tax parties, where we celebrate our dedication to funding a fair, just, and honorable society. Feasts are made, wine uncorked, and people dance with gleeful abandon in appreciation of society's goodness.

Well . . . maybe not.

I pay taxes in the United States, so that's the system I know the best. According to U.S. Internal Revenue Service (IRS) estimates, taxpayers in the United States spend about 45 hours on average on paperwork per tax return filed each year, very little of it, I'm sure, in celebration.[1] Every hour requires a small dialogue with yourself. As distasteful as it might be, recall it for a moment. You consider each receipt. Can you deduct it? Should you report it? Can you ignore it? What if you alter the number a little to your benefit? As you massage the numbers, do you quietly wrestle with the likelihood of being audited versus the potential gain of a little inaccuracy? Does the stress of potential discovery add an additional, nonmonetary cost to the process? Do you carry that concern with you, even when you are not actively engaged in the process? How about the emotional costs? Do you argue with your spouse or partner, or stress over the amount of money you've spent or not saved to pay the tax man? How much time do you spend actively *not* doing your taxes, procrastinating because they are such a drag? While you are not doing them, aren't they still in the back of your mind? Do you carry them around with you even when you're avoiding them?

Now consider the so-called flat tax. Imagine how little thought, energy, and time you would spend each year meeting your civic obligation to fund the government if you had but a single payment to make that equaled, say, 20 percent of gross earnings no matter what your income, with no deductions or loopholes. My guess? About half an hour. The savings to the nation in productivity gained? Billions of dollars. This argument, put forth strongly by proponents of a flat tax, not only would save the objective time it takes to file tax returns, but seemingly would also quiet the internal conflicts that sap focus and concentration from other things. It seems like a no-brainer. Of course, it is not that simple. Rules like the tax code function as proxies for the desires of a society. They approximate a value or standard that a culture deems important, and attempt to achieve it in a clear and unambiguous way. A progressive tax code—where those who earn more pay a higher percentage of their income in taxes—is an attempt to codify a vision of the equitable redistribution of wealth and the responsibilities of the wealthier in society to the poorest members. In other words, the tax code exists to legislate a vision of fairness. If utility, economy, and ease of compliance were the sole aims of the tax code, anything but a flat tax would seem wasteful and inane. When you consider the proxy duties of the tax code, however, the issue becomes far more complicated.

It's difficult to instill values like fairness and respect throughout a population as large and diverse as the populations of most nations. Yet fairness is a powerful idea, and one most people would agree brings benefit to all. So legislatures create a tangled and inefficient set of rules they believe approximates the prevailing sense of what is fair.

This creates a paradox. Almost everyone can argue that, from his or her perspective, one part of the tax code or another is *unfair*. Whether you feel corporate loopholes benefit the powerful over the individual, the mortgage interest deduction favors the middle class over the working class, or the earned income credit favors the poor over small businesses, every line drawn by tax rules to be fair to one group immediately creates a negative space of unfairness to another. A rule, for instance, that gives a tax break to a small business for buying a needed small truck or sport utility vehicle (SUV) inadvertently benefits extremely wealthy people who buy gas-guzzling Hummers for their personal pleasure.[2]

Rules are rules, but unlike our desire to connect with others and our tendency toward value-based thinking, our brains are not hardwired for rules. They are a social phenomenon.

We grow up as children in a world of external rules—"Don't touch the stove" or "Don't run into the street"—determined and administered by their parents and accepted, for the most part, on faith. As we get a little older, we begin to incorporate rule formation into our imaginative play. At first, those rules are in our complete self-interest. "Okay, the rule is you can't tag me!" We form rules much as we experience them, as expressions of limits imposed by others—in other words, what mommy and daddy want. Pretty soon, though, we begin to realize that our friends don't like rules imposed on them any more than we do, and so, in the interest of getting along, the rules become more neutral. We learn to "play fair." Still later in life, most of us begin to find some joy and challenge in playing within the rules. Checkers becomes fun because pieces can only do certain things at certain times, card games add more complexity, games like chess and Go add nearly infinitely more, and sports add specific parameters to physical activity. The relationship to rules that we individually hold by the time we become adults is deeply informed by these early experiences with rule formation and group play.

Civilization itself developed along similarly organic lines, as adults developed ever more complex rules in response to the pressures of living together. We began in small tribes and, as our tribes grew in size and interrelationships became more complex, they began to invent rules to guide, manage, and sometimes control each other. Rules became codified in the form of laws, like the tax code, designed by a cadre of leaders and held up as the structure of civil society. To this day rules, in one way or another, govern the spaces between us, and as we discussed earlier, serve us well in many areas. However, as we begin to consider in depth the new thinking needed to succeed in a world of HOW, we need to examine more deeply our relationship to rules, how our thinking about them helps us and, sometimes, holds us back.

RULES AS PROXIES

Why do we employ rules as proxies? Because rules seem efficient, and modern society (and industrial age capitalism) was built on the foundations of efficiency. Most democratic societies, for example, confer the right to vote based on age. In the United States it is 18, in Japan it is 20, and in many other countries it is 21.[3] (The right to vote at 21 also originates in long-forgotten feudal habits—it was the English age for knighthood.) Age, however, does not necessarily correlate to a person's intelligence, maturity, or sense of civic duty, qualities that arguably comprise a much better standard by which to judge a person's qualification to vote. If you want to hold an election that will produce the best possible outcome for society, as judged by its ability to do the greatest good for the greatest number of people, you would allow only mature, civically responsible citizens to vote. Instead, we choose a proxy—age—as an objective, easily quantifiable substitute for intelligence and civic-mindedness, and hope that this somewhat arbitrary marker includes enough quality voters to get a good representative government. There are, however, many 25-year-old voters who have little idea of what comprises good government and lots of 15-year-olds with a highly developed sense of civic responsibility. By relying on a proxy rather than a value, we include many who, by the standard of holding the best possible election, should not be enfranchised, and we exclude many others who should. Rules like a voting age, when they act in this way, are both over- and underinclusive.

Though an election including only qualified voters would be a much better election, it would be extremely difficult to administer. It is relatively simple to administer an election if the rule says that you need to be 18 to vote. You verify everyone's age and citizenship when they register; then they show up with their registration and vote, and the entire election throughout the country takes but one day. Determining a qualification like maturity and civic-mindedness, on the other hand, would be far more complex and time-consuming, not to mention subjective. In a rules-based society, we often choose efficiency over value, but, while rules-based governance systems may often serve well the values of fairness and representation, their seeming efficiency hides a deep and important flaw: *We often rely on rules when they are not, in fact, the most efficient or effective solution to getting the result that we desire.* Understanding that flaw is vital to thriving in a world of HOW.

Another problem with rules lies in the fact that they are not created in a very efficient, or systematic, way. Elected bodies, vulnerable to the demands of the political process, write them; those who wield or seek to wield power over others, either militarily or professionally, write them; owners or boards of companies, or a manager chosen by professional meritocracy write them. William F. Buckley once joked that he would rather be governed by the first 2000 people in the Boston telephone directory than the Harvard faculty, and those Harvard folk are pretty smart people.[4] Despite the best of intentions, people create rules variously and often in *reaction* to behaviors deemed unacceptable to the larger goals of the group. That is why we often find ourselves revising the rules when new conditions reveal their loopholes. Again, let me share a couple of examples.

In 1991, the U.S. Congress issued federal sentencing guidelines to incent good corporate behavior.[5] At that time, the Congress laid out a number of steps and programs corporations could adopt to mitigate their potential liability should they be found guilty of criminal violations. It was a rules-based solution proposed by a rules-based organization: the U.S. government. In response, companies spent enormously on compliance programs (proxies for good behavior, really) and grew large and costly bureaucracies of compliance in an attempt to inoculate themselves against future penalties. This carrot-and-stick approach, however, did not lick the problem. Companies added more enforcement, more penalties for getting it wrong, and more incentivizing rewards for getting it right, and yet they did not see substantially more compliance. Despite this huge investment in more compliance programs, since 1991 there have actually been more companies that have run afoul of the law. In 2003, the ad hoc advisory committee to the Federal Sentencing Commission concluded, after studying these compliance programs, that they failed to achieve "effective compliance."

In the wake of a seeming abundance of corporate scandals at the turn of the twenty-first century, the U.S. Congress hastily wrote a new set of rules to govern corporate conduct, the Sarbanes-Oxley bill (commonly called *SOX*), and revised the sentencing guidelines to react to those transgressions. Corporations again immediately allocated billions to figure out how to comply with the new regulations, just as they did a dozen years before.[6]

Consider this smaller example of the same phenomenon: A manager puts up a sign in your company lunchroom that says, "Please Clean the Microwave after You Use It"; then another, "Do Not Put Your Feet on the Tables"; then a third, "Don't Eat Other People's Food." All these rules, and the myriad more little lunchroom dos and don'ts that your manager madly prints out and posts, attempt to codify a single value, *respect.* Rather than declare a common value, such as "Respect Our Common Spaces," most rules makers spend their time chasing human ingenuity, which races along generally complying with the rules while blithely creating new behaviors that exist outside of them.

What does the persnickety lunchroom manager and his signs have in common with the U.S. government and Sarbanes-Oxley? Both reveal a startling truth about rules: Rules respond to behavior; they don't lead it. *Rules don't govern human progress; they govern the human past.* This essential truth shapes our thinking about rules: To succeed, it seems to imply, we must learn to dance with the rules.

DANCING WITH RULES

I believe in the rule of law, and I believe we need rules and laws. Certain laws work. Laws have done a good job of regulating easily quantifiable human actions. Environmental laws, safety laws, child labor laws—these are areas where society unquestionably benefits from hard floors that regulate action. We do not select a bottled water based on how few people it has poisoned, nor do we buy the car least likely to spontaneously combust. If extensive and reliable science exists about how to build a house to best withstand earthquakes and hurricanes, society benefits by codifying that science into law. We should not give builders four options for building something when we know that only one will work. Remember that this book is not about crime, sociopathic behavior, or the desire to undermine or destroy civil society; it is about the habits of mind and behavior that can lead to long-term, sustained success in a hyperconnected, hypertransparent information age. When I talk about rules, I'm talking about the rules that regulate behavior within the mainstream of socially acceptable action.

Likewise, I believe that we should all master the ability to live well within the rules. Mastering the rules is a Hill of B accomplishment. It's safe, well-defined, and basic. Like all basic knowledge, it is a necessary stage on the path to real understanding. But too many of us get stuck on the Hill of B.

We live in a rule-of-law society, and due to our history of ever evolving toward fairer rule making, we have grown very comfortable with rules. In fact, our reliance on them has become part of the problem; we turn to law to solve too much. If the law says we *can*, then we do. We're very good at *can* versus *can't* thinking. Our habits of mind are so strong in this area, in fact, that we've become musclebound, as overdeveloped as a bodybuilder trying to touch his toes—strong, but inflexible. We overrespect rules, which leads us into a quagmire where all our actions get mucked up in the spectrum of legal permissibility. We're so strong in this way that we begin to feel like we can do anything as long as we obey the law. We become like Microsoft was in the 1990s, believing that we can crush the competition as long as we don't break the letter of the law.

As Supreme Court Justice Potter Stewart suggested, we've conflated legal permissibility with permission. Dancing with rules often leads to losing your sense of what is right for the long term. Since rules often blow around with the winds of political expediency, they don't provide a stable reference with which to steer a true course, especially when the seas are rough and changeable. Microsoft never got into trouble for being a monopoly. There is, in fact, no law in the United States against *being* a monopoly. No one minded Microsoft being a bull—we like bulls in business—but no one could stand the company conducting itself like a bully. When Microsoft used its position as a virtual monopoly to act unfairly and with belligerence in the marketplace, the U.S. Justice Department and the European Commission prosecuted the company.[7] Microsoft never got into trouble for its WHATS; it got into trouble for its HOWS.

It might be easy to assume from all this talk about the limitations of rules that I'm an advocate of breaking them. "Rules are meant to be broken" is a familiar strophe in popular culture and conventional entrepreneurial wisdom. "I believe in rules," said legendary baseball coach Leo Durocher. "I also believe I have a right to test the rules by seeing how far they can be bent."[8] When we "get around" the rules, we feel we are free of constraint, but this is a dangerous illusion.

My central conflict with rules lies in the essential nature of our relationship to them; *rules live outside of us.* Because of this, we spend a lot of time and effort wrestling with them, trying to find ingenious ways around them or creative ways of living within them. No one internalizes the tax code, not even the accountants who make their living interpreting it. Human beings are natural problem solvers and enjoy the challenge of puzzles. We will always invent new loopholes, and no rule can govern all the cracks.

Time spent dancing with the rules builds muscles of mental agility, cleverness, and ingenuity—Just Do It muscles, and the time of Just Do It has passed. Dancing with the rules turns you into a legal technician, constantly looking for loopholes. Some even think that breaking all the rules qualifies as creative thinking, but it is quite the opposite. *Working in opposition to rules is simply the negative space of working within them;* thinking just in terms of what a rule excludes is as limiting as being bound by what it includes. Too much time spent in the realm of law limits truly creative thought.

An excess of rules breeds an environment where we are less conscious about what is right. We become dependent on the rule book to govern our behavior. Where no rule exists—in those gray areas that we come up against every day—we sometimes feel we can do what we like. "If it mattered," we think, "they would have made a rule." Overreliance on rules also tempts people to play close to the edge. "How close can I go?" we wonder. We focus on exactly where the rule is and try to toe the line without exceeding its limits. When the wind blows, however, and conditions change, we can easily find ourselves on the wrong side of things, paying a stiff price. When the chairman of the board of Hewlett-Packard (HP), Patricia Dunn, resigned in the wake of the scandal created by her decision to authorize electronic surveillance of other board members, the *Los Angeles Times* reported that "she was not concerned that anything illegal was taking place because HP lawyers were overseeing the investigation."[9] Meanwhile, Kevin Hunsaker, an HP senior counsel and ethics officer, was trading the following e-mails with HP security manager Anthony Gentilucci, who was overseeing a team of private investigators performing the investigation:

> From: Kevin Hunsaker
> To: Anthony Gentilucci
> Hi Tony. How does Ron get cell and home phone records? Is it all aboveboard?
>
> From: Anthony Gentilucci
> To: Kevin Hunsaker
> The methodology used is social engineering. Investigators call operators under some ruse to obtain the call record over the phone. The operator shouldn't give it out, and that person is liable in a sense. I think it's on the edge, but aboveboard.
>
> From: Kevin Hunsaker
> To: Anthony Gentilucci
> I shouldn't have asked.[10]

Leaders must be rigorous about the truth, but Dunn and her HP colleagues got so wrapped up in what they *could* or *could not* do that they lost track of what they *should* or *should not* do; they lost track of "The HP Way," the values that had built the company and made it strong and unique.

Human conduct is more complicated than what the language of law can describe. Human conduct, in its infinite variety and creativity, defies reduction. It has a lot to do with aspirations and intentions, with back-and-forth interactions. Our interpersonal synapses are two-way streets, and the interactions that travel through them are dynamic. Rules, because they are made reactively, have difficulty keeping up with the infinite permutations and various shades of meaning that pass between people in the course of life.

THE PROBLEMS WITH RULES

RULES ARE EXTERNAL
They are made by others.
They present us with a puzzle to be solved and loopholes to be found.

WE ARE AMBIVALENT ABOUT RULES
We know we need some and we want others to play by them,
but we say, "Rules are meant to be broken."

RULES ARE REACTIVE
They respond to past events.

RULES ARE BOTH OVER- AND UNDERINCLUSIVE
Because they are proxies, they cannot be precise.

PROLIFERATION OF RULES IS A TAX ON THE SYSTEM
Few people can remember them all.
We lose productivity when we stop to look them up.

RULES ARE TYPICALLY PROHIBITIONS
They speak to *can* and *can't*.
We view them as confining and constricting.

RULES REQUIRE ENFORCEMENT
With laxity, they lose credibility and effectiveness.
They necessitate expensive bureaucracies of compliance.

**RULES SPEAK TO BOUNDARIES AND FLOORS
BUT CREATE INADVERTENT CEILINGS**
We can't legislate "The sky's the limit."

THE ONLY WAY TO HONOR RULES IS TO OBEY THEM EXACTLY
They speak to coercion and motivation.
The inspiration to excel must come from somewhere else.

TOO MANY RULES BREEDS OVERRELIANCE
We think, "If it mattered, they would have made a rule."

This presents us with a question: In a fast-changing world, is there a way to govern human behavior that proactively embraces change?

Despite Winston Churchill's quip that democracy is the worst system of government except all the others, it does work. But it works as a social contract because democratic countries are not founded on a set of rules, but rather on a set of shared values, on constitutions. Constitutions are powerful documents because they are filled with the values and principles of the people they govern, such as free expression, liberty, enfranchisement, fairness, justice, the pursuit of happiness, or the rule of law. These core, foundational values can be interpreted and reapplied to new situations as they arise. The more profound the document, the more durably it can adapt to changing times. *The key to long-term, sustained success does not lie in breaking all the rules; it lies in transcending the rules and harnessing the power of values.*

ON THE TIP OF YOUR TONGUE

To fully understand how limited we can be by our overreliance on rules, let's examine for a minute how they affect the way we think. To do that, we must consider the process of language. When you invest yourself in a relationship to rules, you invest yourself in their language as well, and language exerts a powerful influence on the way we think. Most people believe, for instance, that words follow thought: Something occurs to you and then you find the words to express it. In fact, studies have shown that the exact opposite is true; we think in language. The greater our vocabulary and command of the syntax of language becomes, the more refined and nuanced becomes our cognition. If, for instance, you knew only two words to describe a surface, *hard* and *soft*, you would be likely to classify it only in one of two ways. The whole world would be hard or soft, and all the degrees of hardness—firm, rigid, stiff, supportive—and all the different kinds of softness—spongy, fleecy, downy, satiny—would tend not to occur to you. You conceive of those qualities mostly because you know the words for them, or, to be more precise, according to linguists, *you are more likely to make certain kinds of assessments because of the nature of the language you speak.* Although Indian philosopher Bhartrihari first argued this idea in the fifth century C.E., modern linguists call it the Sapir-Whorf hypothesis, derived from the work of linguist and anthropologist Edward Sapir and his colleague and student Benjamin Whorf.[11] They posited a systematic relationship between the grammatical categories of the language a person speaks and how that person both understands the world and behaves within it. As Sapir put it, "We see and hear and otherwise experience very largely as we do because the language habits of our community predispose certain choices of interpretation."[12]

To see how language influences the way we solve problems, consider these two examples and the way a predisposition to certain language shaped their outcomes:

In the 1970s and 1980s, during the Cold War, East German athletes won a slew of Olympic medals, far out of proportion to the size of their population. After the fall of communism, what the world widely suspected quickly became well known: They built their success on a regimen of enforced use of performance-enhancing drugs, more commonly known as anabolic steroids.

These drugs later wreaked havoc on the health of the athletes forced to take them, and in 2005, a small group of these former East German Olympians banded together to seek restitution and compensation for their progressive medical problems and expenses.[13] Since the East German government no longer exists, they sued JVE Jenapharm, the company that manufactured the drugs, seeking $4.1 million to pay for medical costs.[14] Jenapharm is an old-line, family company dating back to the nineteenth century, that is now owned by pharmaceutical giant Bayer Schering Pharma AG. The firm is known today for its expertise in reproductive medicine, and manufactures a line of oral contraceptives and postmenopausal hormone replacement therapies.

Jenapharm's response to the lawsuit was clear, immediate, and unambiguous. The company argued that, under the command economy of East German communism, the state forced it to manufacture the drugs and then distribute them to athletes without warnings or options. Facing the shadow of potentially bankrupting legal action from the nearly 10,000 other athletes who were similarly harmed, Jenapharm said, essentially, "It's not our fault and we'll see you in court." Given international and German legal precedent, this position contains potentially strong legal merit, and fighting the suit was clearly an option, something, they seemed to say to themselves, they *could* do.

On the other side of the globe, the University of Michigan Hospitals and Health System (UMHS) in Ann Arbor consists of three hospitals, a medical school, and numerous other health facilities. In 2001, UMHS, like many similar institutions, suffered under a budget-busting load of medical malpractice litigation that had seen exponential growth nationwide over the preceeding decade. Given the increasingly transparent nature of medical care, better-educated patients, and opportunistic personal injury lawyers, it realized that it was going to incur liabilities in some percentage of cases despite doing everything it could to eliminate systemic errors. That year UMHS fought many malpractice claims and lawsuits in court, but also settled more than 260 others at a cost of $18 million.[15]

As the administrators at UMHS considered ways to reduce their potential liability, they realized they could do little about lawsuits stemming from catastrophic errors that result in loss of life or limb. They focused instead on suits involving less serious consequences, like a patient with epilepsy admitted for surgery whose doctor forgot to note his postoperative need for antispasmodic medication. When that patient had a seizure in the bathroom and bumped his head, requiring a few stitches, typically a lawsuit quickly followed. In cases like these, they asked themselves, what *should* we be doing for our patients?

Continuing to fight malpractice claims in court remained an option, but they chose a different course of action. They encouraged their doctors to say, "I'm sorry." Using their established doctor/patient interaction education program, they developed scenarios to help doctors understand how to step up and promptly admit when a mistake was made. Now, when they discover an error like the prescription oversight for the epileptic patient, the doctor apologizes on the spot. Unlike Jenapharm, when UMHS announced this new approach, the strategy was widely ridiculed as legal suicide.

It is critically important to realize that in a hyperconnected world, where information about your actions travels instantly to any interested party, people watching you will judge not just *what* you do, but *how* you do it. They're not going to sit back and wait to see if you win or lose; they're going to watch the manner in which you pursue the case. If these two companies were people—your colleagues or potential business partners—the opinion you form about them would certainly affect the way you choose to interact with them. So let me ask: Given just what you now know about these two similar legal situations, what judgment have you formed about the character of these two companies? Do you think that Jenapharm took a reasonable, prudent, and legally defensible position that represents a legitimate strategy to save the company from bankruptcy and that UMHS must be out of their legal minds for admitting liability immediately when mistakes are made? Or do you think that Jenapharm made the situation all about impersonal legal rights, potentially alienating its customers by acting strictly within legal limits, while UMHS upheld its values and put the best interests of its patients first and the risk of higher legal costs second?

Here is where things stand in the marketplace. In late 2006, Jenapharm agreed to pay 184 of the thousands of affected athletes 9,250 euros ($12,200 each) and donate 170,000 euros ($224,000) to organizations providing support to victims of East German doping.[16] Admitting no wrongdoing, Jenapharm CEO Isabel Rothe said in a statement that "the agreement will avoid a drawn-out legal argument." The long-term effect on Jenapharm's reputation and relationship with the market is unknown. (Interestingly, a week before Jenapharm's announcement, the German Olympic Sports Union and the federal government announced they would pay a similar amount to 167 victims. Striking an altogether different tone, union president Thomas Bach said, "We take the moral responsibility and we want to make sure that something like that cannot happen again.") In the three years following UMHS's decision to apologize, in contrast, medical malpractice claims and lawsuits against them dropped by nearly 50 percent and the per-case cost of defending against the remaining suits dropped 50 percent as well, saving UMHS millions of dollars. One company attempted to limit its exposure by shutting down all challenges, while the other opened itself up to challenge and, in so doing, actually reduced its exposure.

How did UMHS arrive at a counterintuitive solution like apologizing, a choice widely seen at the time as legal suicide? UMHS employs a values-based approach to pursuing corporate goals. Respect, compassion, trust, integrity, and leadership—the stated values—inform everything from the way they treat their patients to the way they treat their staff, and they articulate these values in their Seven Strategic Principles.[17] As an organization whose very core was grounded in the language of values, they tackled their mounting litigation problem by asking themselves not "What *can* we do?" but rather, "Based on our values, what *should* we do?" This train of thought led them to see that medical care is fundamentally an interaction between two people—the doctor and patient—just like any other business relationship, and to examine what was "sick" in the cases that resulted in litigation. They quickly learned that the overwhelming majority of plaintiffs were generally able to forgive the error itself—doctors are only human, after all—but that the doctors who had betrayed their trust by denying culpability filled them with rage. The real illness in these cases lay in the interpersonal synapse between doctor and patient. Armed with the knowledge that the destruction of trust was contributing to retributive consequences for unavoidable mistakes, UMHS looked for ways to heal this core dysfunction; healing, after all, is what they do best. The new approach realized unexpected additional benefits as well. With the working atmosphere now free of retribution, doctors no longer have to duck and dodge to avoid the appearance of guilt when errors occur. They enjoy greater opportunity to explore what went wrong and devise innovative solutions to prevent future occurrences. The culture of transparency bred by UMHS's new openness has brought error rates down throughout the hospital and measurably improved the quality of patient care.[18]

All organizations of people need a way to govern (companies, societies, and even families are alike in this way), and most governance systems benefit from the inclusion of at least some rules. In our workgroup-as-stadium metaphor, we might agree, for instance, that everyone needs a ticket to get in, people will sit in their own seats, and the game will start at 9 A.M. Without some rules, anarchy rules; fans rush the gates and sit where they please, and people come to work when they feel like it with little regard for the work schedules of others. The game is never played. Most groups articulate their system of governance as a code of conduct. Some of these codes read like the tax code, a set of rules designed to anticipate, prescribe, and proscribe certain behaviors. "Clean your cubicle at the end of every day." "Always wear blue pants." They, like all aggregations of rules, seem at first blush to be an efficient way to codify and communicate the floors of human conduct throughout the hierarchy of the company. Other codes of conduct read more like constitutions, filled with the values and principles that propel the company's efforts. Clothing maker Levi Strauss's code of conduct states, "We are honest and trustworthy. We do what we say we are going to do. Integrity includes a willingness to do the right thing for our employees, brands, the company, and society as a whole, even when personal, professional, and social risks or economic pressures confront us."[19] These general statements of principle can, at first blush, seem vague and not immediately or easily applicable to the various day-to-day decisions a worker must face. The nature of the language a group chooses, however, exerts a remarkable and powerful influence on the conduct that follows from it.

The language of laws and rules is the language of *can* and *can't*, *right* versus *wrong*. It's a binary language with little room for nuance or shades of meaning. That is why it is inadequate to describe the full richness of human behavior. We are, as people, so much more than right or wrong. When you get stuck in the language of permissibility and prohibition (*can* versus *can't*) you get stuck thinking in relation to rules rather than in the realm of true human potential. You can discuss a lawsuit in terms of utility—"*Can* we fight this effectively in court?"—but it is quite another thing to discuss it in terms of your values—"Given what we believe, *should* we fight this in court?" The first approach prompts thinking in relation to rules and codes; the second opens up thinking in relation to what is most important to an organization's or individual's core values and long-term success. In that difference—the difference between *can* and *should*—lies an extraordinarily important step toward thriving in a world of HOW: *True freedom lies not in the absence of constraint; true freedom lies in the transcendence of rules-based thinking.*

Thinking in the language of *can* versus *can't* predisposes you to perceive challenges in a certain way and respond within narrow avenues. Thinking in and speaking the language of values—the language of *should* and *shouldn't* instead of the language of *can* and *can't*—opens up a wide spectrum of possible thought, a spectrum that encompasses the full colors of human behavior as opposed to the black-and-white responses of rules. This spectrum can lead to truly creative and innovative solutions to challenges.

UNLOCKING *SHOULD*

I offer the legal challenges faced by Jenapharm and UMHS here because they paint a fairly black-and-white picture of the difference between thinking in *can* and thinking in *should*. Being presented with a lawsuit is usually far more serious than our daily confrontations with rules and regulations; however, our responses are in many ways identical in nature. We go through each day avoiding or complying with as much nimble grace as we can. The boss compliments you for a task you know was done by a junior associate on your team. Do you stop her and give the credit where the credit is due? You certainly *can* say nothing and let the moment pass unmentioned. There is no *rule* that requires you to credit a junior colleague; in fact, the unwritten rules of business permit you to take credit for the accomplishments of those who report to you. So you let the moment pass. This is rule-based thinking in its most insidious form.

I would guess that most people think that taking unearned credit is not right, even if you didn't solicit it. It's not something one *should* do, nor a value we agree with. And yet I would also hazard to guess that, if you think hard enough, you can think of a similar moment in which, either because of the absence of a specific rule or the presence of an ambiguous one, you let your actions be guided by your relation to a rule and not by what, in reflection, you *should* have done to be consistent with your values. Transcending the rules-trapped language of *can* and embracing the values-inspired language of *should* illuminates the pathways to truly innovative solutions like those of UMHS, as well as simpler choices like sharing the credit. UMHS achieved dramatically lower litigation costs; you, by sharing credit, earn the loyalty and increased dedication of a junior associate who, the next time your team needs an extra measure of effort to accomplish its goal, happily steps up and puts in the weekend hours necessary to get you there. To thrive in a world of HOW, you must balance your muscles of casual avoidance—as strong and developed as they are—with the ability to think in the language of values, in terms of *should*.

There is little in rules that inspires; by definition, you comply with them. All it takes to honor a rule is to do what it says, and nothing more. Rules breed a culture of acquiescence in which everyone comes to terms with them and finds a way to live within them or a way to circumvent them—in other words, to live in their positive or negative space. While giving someone the advice to "break all the rules" is terrible counsel, giving them the opposite age-old counsel to "just play by the rules" is now not that much better advice. It consigns them to a life of external servitude and a compliant mind-set. Thinking in the language of values frees you from the tyranny of rules and from the illusion of freedom you have when in their negative space.

To be capable of making Waves, you need an organizing principle more inspirational and compelling than rules. You can't start a Wave by making a rule that Waves will happen every Tuesday after lunch. And if you could, what kind of a Wave would it be? Thinking and communicating in the language of *should*—values-based language—by its very nature inspires. The landscape of values is vast and unbounded, and creates a genuinely free space of creativity in which you can see new ways of accomplishing your goals. Values matter to us, and they matter to others, so they fill the synapses between us and others with greater meaning. Values provide floors plus propulsion because we think they are important, and because we tend to spend our energy on what matters most to us. *Justice. Truth. Honesty. Integrity.* Values have texture. *Fairness. Humility. Service to others.* The language of values inspires us because values are aspirational in nature. They propel us to higher ground. We don't believe in rules but we all hold a belief in our values. They speak to the core of what makes us human. Values do double duty; they inspire us to do *more than* while simultaneously preventing us from doing *less than.* To betray them is to betray ourselves. They create natural floors without creating inadvertent ceilings.

We all have a core set of values, formed over time either by the influence of others—parents, teachers, mentors, friends—or learned through life experience. Unlike rules, which act as proxies for the things we care about—like a voting age approximates maturity and civic-mindedness—values are not a mechanism or device that approximates what is important or mediates between us and what is important; they connect us to it directly. Values play to our strengths as humans. Similarly, thinking of what we do in values terms imbues it with greater meaning. If two masons are paid equally for their day's labor, which one walks away the richer, the one who was hired and managed as a bricklayer or the one enlisted and enfranchised as a cathedral builder?

There are myraid reasons why it is important now, more than ever before, to rethink our relationship to rules. First, twenty-first-century business craves creativity and innovation over almost all else, and freeing yourself from the constraints of rules-based thought unleashes new pathways of exploration and possibility. More important, in a transparent world we are judged as much by the process of HOW we solve problems as by the results we achieve. In a world where we have any number of competitors or potential competitors, HOW we do what we do is the thing that increasingly differentiates us from the other guy. There is hardly a business that doesn't suffer from "the grocery store syndrome." We can choose from any number of grocery stores, each one offering competitive prices. After price, the choice of where to shop usually boils down to customer experience, the quality of the human interaction that occurs there. We want to shop where it is pleasant, where the goods are easily seen and obtained, and where the employees respond positively to us. To provide this sort of experience in everything you do, to discover ways to outbehave the competition, you need to think in ways that inspire your best achievement, to think in the language of *should*.

RISK AND REWARD

Thinking in the language of values unlocks powerful possibilities for growth and action, but at first blush it can seem dangerous to some. For the senior management of companies, shifting the way you lead and govern people from rules-based to values-based thinking sometimes brings the fear of losing control. Governing by rules shifts less power down the hierarchy, allowing those at the top to believe they can easily control the actions of those below them. This is a habit of mind left over from the days of fortress capitalism and feudalism. Leading from values, on the other hand, decentralizes power and shifts the responsibility for decision making into the hands of individuals at all levels. Values are not black-and-white or quantitative. Values are like trust; they empower others to honor or betray you. They open up avenues of possibility and leave room for interpretation.

Surprisingly, though, values-based leadership has a tremendous upside. As business units spread around the world and more and more interactions take place among equals in the organization, top-down governance strategies become less effective. The trend of twenty-first-century business to become more horizontal, in fact, creates fertile conditions for leadership strategies that thrive in decentralized environments. While this shift of power may at first seem to make values-based thinking dangerous for businesses of all sizes, it ultimately makes them more powerful. The new conditions of the world of HOW call out for exactly this sort of approach. Values-based thinking truly frees the individual to act in the interests of the organization.

When Harry C. Stonecipher, the president and CEO of Boeing, was asked by Boeing's board to resign after having an extramarital affair with another employee, for example, the company could have responded by amending its code of conduct to prohibit or restrict certain kinds of relationships between employees. Instead, Boeing did something far more interesting: It enshrined and enforced a value. Lead director and former non-executive chairman of Boeing, Lewis Platt, said, "The board concluded that the facts reflected poorly on Harry's judgment and would impair his ability to lead the company . . . the CEO must set the standard for unimpeachable professional and personal behavior, and the board determined that this was the right and necessary decision under the circumstances. We have fought hard to restore our reputation. Everyone should know that if we see any improper activities, we will take decisive action."[20] Boeing sent the message that employee behavior does not answer to a set of rules, but to a much more powerful standard: *repute*. In a stroke, Boeing employees understood that part of their job involved bringing the company positive repute, and that integrity was so central to what Boeing is that it could cost even the highest executives their jobs. By celebrating a value rather than instituting a rule, Boeing gains much tighter alignment with its workforce. Every employee must internalize this value, wrestle with it on an ongoing and individual basis—deep in the Valley of C—and thereby develop a much more active relationship to the company's desires and a tighter alignment with its goals. The value, while seemingly less direct than a rule, achieves a greater result.

Even within a lower-skilled, service-oriented workforce like fast-food giant McDonald's, values provide a means of tighter integration with company goals. "The whole experience at McDonald's boils down to the moment of truth at the front counter or drive-through, that 30 seconds of interaction," CEO Jim Skinner told me when we met at the company's Oak Brook, Illinois, headquarters. Skinner built his career on knowing that moment. He began his career with McDonald's in 1971 as a restaurant manager trainee in Carpentersville, Illinois. "The development of that relationship between our people and the customer is probably the hardest thing that we do. With hundreds of thousands of employees serving more than 50 million customers a day across 119 countries, common values are essential. They are efficient. They form the link among all our moving parts, allowing everyone who serves the McDonald's brand to understand what it means to be successful at that moment of truth with a customer."[21]

FROM *CAN* TO *SHOULD*

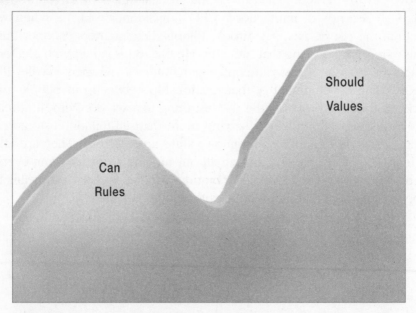

Can versus *can't* thinking substitutes for genuine time spent considering the HOWS of a given situation (HOW can I best delight my client? HOW can I bring the company greater repute? HOW can I make this meeting more successful?) and fosters a passive relationship to interaction with others (WHAT does the manual say to do? WHAT is my job description? WHAT is on the agenda?). In this mode of thought, you believe you can do what you want as long as you comply with the contract or the code. When you think in the language of values, however, you must actively engage each situation. Values propel action toward others. This creates an energy focused on HOW you do WHAT you do, and that energy becomes a propeller, driving a Wave of action toward others. In an information economy, where more power lies in the network than in the individual, outwardly focused energy makes sense as a propeller of success.

From *can* to *should*. From rules to values. These fundamental shifts in language exert a profound effect on the way you think, orient your energies, make decisions, and, therefore, achieve. New language may seem awkward at first, like learning to communicate in something other than your native tongue. But people who learn a second language often develop better grammar than native speakers, because they do so as a conscious act of will. Understanding the interplay of rules and values, and freeing yourself from the tyranny of *can* versus *can't* are essential steps toward mastering the grammar of the new world of HOW.

CHAPTER **6**

Keeping Your Head in the Game

*The shortest and surest way to live with honor in the world
is to be in reality what we would appear to be.*
—Socrates

The Open Championship, held each summer in Britain, is the oldest and perhaps most prestigious title in professional golf. In 2005, the tournament was held at the birthplace of golf, the Royal and Ancient Golf Club of St. Andrews in Scotland. Former Professional Golfers' Association (PGA) champion David Toms, with one win and six top-10 finishes so far that season, was among a handful of players with a great chance to win. Then something unusual happened.

On the morning of the second round, Toms walked into the officials' tent and explained to the bewildered officials (and later to the press) that the day before he might or might not have done something for which he should have taken penalty strokes. On the famous 17th hole, the Road Hole, he missed a medium-length putt, then strode to the hole and tapped it in. He was unsure, however, whether the ball might have been wobbling in the wind slightly when he did so. It is against the rules of golf to hit a ball while it is still in motion, and because he was not sure, David Toms disqualified himself from the Open.[1]

To disqualify yourself from a major tournament is an extraordinary act of sportsmanship; to do so for something that may or may not have happened, and that nobody else saw, is downright remarkable. Toms has always been known as one of the good guys on the PGA Tour. His charitable foundation works with abused, abandoned, and underprivileged children throughout the country, and was heavily involved with on-the-ground support for the victims of Hurricane Katrina in 2005. He's easygoing and direct, and you'd be hard-pressed to find anyone with a bad word to say about him. When I heard about his sportsmanlike act, I sensed there was something important going on in Toms's head, something key to achieving the highest levels of performance and success. So I called him on his cell phone while he was driving through the backcountry, returning to his Louisiana home. I asked him, essentially, "What were you thinking?" Here's what he told me:

DAVID TOMS: When I got back to my hotel room that night after the first round and cleared my head a little bit, I started thinking about the 17th hole. I thought: If I hit a moving ball when I tapped in, it's a penalty. There was a lot of gray area there, whether or not it wobbled, and I didn't have anybody to call and ask. I'd already signed my scorecard, so I knew that if it was determined that it had happened, I would be disqualified.

I woke up early the next morning and went into the rules officials' tent and told the head official the story. He went and looked at it on the tape and said he really couldn't see anything. He finally said it was up to me; I could call it a foul or just move on to the second round. He was fine with me going ahead and playing.

But then he asked me, unofficially, "If you did finish first, how would you feel?" He just wanted to know my gut reaction. And I said I felt like I would be getting away with something, and I would feel like that for a long time, regardless of how I do. If I won the golf tournament, if I made the cut, or whatever, it still wouldn't be fair to the rest of the field and it certainly wouldn't be fair to me because I would have to live with it forever.

You just couldn't continue the tournament?

DAVID: No.

Why not?

DAVID: Because I plan on playing golf for a long time. It's not like it would just go away. What would the decision be the next time that there was a controversy like that? I wouldn't have felt right, especially if I was the one to lift the claret jug [the winner's trophy], and then all of a sudden, you know, it hit me.

That's not the way golf is; that's not the way I am. The organizers of the event, you know, they hated to see it happen, but I was really the only one that could make the call; so . . .

You made the call on yourself?

DAVID: I did. You know, there are things that only the golfer sees. Whether it was a breach of a rule or not, there was a doubt there that I just didn't want to live with. I decided to disqualify myself and flew home. I felt like I did the right thing.

Is there something about your feelings here that you think would affect your ability to play golf?

DAVID: Sure. My actions there were going to affect me and affect the rest of the players playing in that golf tournament, just like in anybody's line of work, whether it's sports or business or whatever.

I understand, but those are your competitors. Your job is to beat them.

DAVID: (Laughing) In golf, we just call these [infractions] on ourselves; we don't try to hold or try to foul until the refs call it on us, like in basketball. That's not what our game is about. I'm not saying that there's not sportsmanship in other sports, but it's on a different level in golf. That's just the way I was brought up. That's the way golf teaches you to be.

When I got home, there was a lot of media attention, but after it was over, I felt fine. It's kind of like confessing your sins, you know. You just feel better after it's all said and done.

Is there something about the clarity you feel that you think impacts your game? Or perhaps the better way to ask the question is the opposite: Is there something about that conflicted feeling that you think would impact your game?

DAVID: It's very hard to perform without a clear head or a clear conscience. You have to be mentally and physically ready and prepared to play.

Why?

DAVID: I think it's the power of the mind. You just can't narrow-focus when you have a lot of other stuff cluttering your mind. I know that carries over to a lot of other things, but it's certainly very important in our sport. It's all about being able to focus, having a clear mind no matter what the situation is. I think the bounce-back statistic—being able to make a birdie after you make a bogey and being able to bounce back—is one of the most important ones. It shows really the heart and mind of the player.

Somebody once told me that golf is the most difficult sport mentally, because in every other sport you react to the ball—you swing at the pitch, catch the pass, and so on—but that golf ball will sit on the grass until Hell freezes over or until you hit it.

DAVID: (Laughing) Yep.

And it seems to me that the brilliance of golf, and why it's so revealing of character, is that how you bring yourself to the ball is almost more important than what you do when you get there.

DAVID: Yeah, sure, it is. It's what goes through your head on that journey. Bob Rotella, the sports psychiatrist, reminds me of this every time I've ever talked to him. He says, "We know you can talk yourself into a bad shot, so why can't you talk yourself into a good shot?"

I don't know what the secret is, but I know that the really successful people, whether it's on or off the golf course, wherever it might be, have something special there, an inner peace. You can learn skills and be trained and everything; but there's something else inside that separates the good, the really good, and the great from the just mediocre. If we could bottle that, we'd make a lot of money (laughing).

How does integrity figure into that equation?

DAVID: It goes back to knowing you are doing the right thing and feeling good inside about your works. I've always gotten a lot of pleasure out of helping other people and trying to give them the same type of chance that I had. It's important for me to feel like I am giving back to society, whether it's through my integrity and the example that I set, or through giving, or whatever. I can't speak for everybody, but for me, knowing that you are leaving a mark adds a little spring to your step.

So to hark back to St. Andrews, did you walk away with a spring in your step?

DAVID: I walked away feeling that I did the right thing, and to be able to say "I did the right thing" means a lot the next time that I tee up the ball. It means my head will be clear of that distraction. It also means a lot to me to set the right example. If there is a young boy playing at his club, and he has always had the problem of keeping his score correctly but didn't think much of it, I want him saying, "Look what Toms did. Maybe I need to stop trying to get away with something."

I think you are a rare individual, David. Golf is an individual sport; it's you against the world. Yet you express yourself as being constantly connected with everybody else on the tour, your community, your fans, and the people who might look up to you. Do you carry that responsibility within you in everything you do?

DAVID: People are watching. How you act, what you say, even how you say it, is not always interpreted in the right way. It's not that you don't want to speak your mind and express your opinion; but at the same time, it's being measured by what it's going to look like and how it's going to affect others. What you want others to think of you plays a big part in what you do on and off the golf course. If you live to try to set a certain example, you have to live by that all the time. You have to live in a way that others can be proud of.

The pressure is always there to perform and to be a certain way, and we fail every day. You always come up short of your expectations. Even in a round of 61, you kind of look back and say, "Well, why didn't I shoot 59?" But it ends up becoming ingrained in you. "Hey, this is the way I live my life. This is what I need to be like 24/7. I need to do right by my family and friends and by the people that support me."

If your real personality is one thing and your on-the-golf-course, on-camera personality is something totally different, then you'd always be looking over your shoulder. For me, it's the same, so it's really not that hard.[2]

People like David Toms, people who operate day in and day out at the top of their games, who win major championships, who are consistently ranked in the top 10 of their chosen occupation, and who sit at the top of the money list every year, know how to keep their mind in the game. In the preceding two chapters, we've looked at what the mind does well as a biological machine and how language exerts a powerful influence on the way we conceptualize events, both freeing and constricting our thinking, creativity, and success. In this chapter, we look at another thing the mind does well: get in the way. At the end, we'll return to this remarkable conversation with David Toms to see how these ideas all come together.

DISTRACTION

Though most of us are not schizophrenics, we all have voices in our heads. Each represents a part of our personality or experience—like integrity, insecurity, resistance or comfort with authority, or compassion—and at different times each voice exerts primacy or influence over our actions. Our boss asks us in a dismissive tone to do something fairly simple, but because it reminds us in some vague way of the way our sixth grade teacher used to speak to us, we grumble and fuss to ourselves far out of proportion to the severity of the slight, despite the fact that we are adults and know better. We have a noisy conversation with the voice inside that still resents that teacher.

Some of these voices speak consistently louder than others, and some are quiet by their nature or because we do not yet trust the guidance they offer. Often, they cooperate with each other, and when they do all is calm in our heads and our thoughts seem like a well-ordered conversation among friends: Our focus is keen, our concentration sharp, and we operate at our best. But at other times, for most of us, one or another voice will try to shout down its competition. Then they sound more like siblings arguing at the dinner table: They distract us, hinder our progress and efficiency, and ruin the casserole our mom spent an hour preparing. This distraction is all part of the normal everyday experience of being human.

Distraction comes from within, but it also comes from without, in equal measures throughout the day. Often, we don't even realize when it is at work. As an experiment to demonstrate this, let me give you a little test. As you read, try not to cheat by looking ahead for the answer.

Can you guess the most searched term on Google in 2005?

It was a newsworthy year. Hurricane Katrina crippled New Orleans and much of the Gulf Coast. A tsunami decimated the lives of millions in Asia. A beloved Pope died and a new one was chosen. Terrorists attacked London's Underground. There was a lot on our minds and much important work to be done, but none of these subjects topped the list.

Here's a hint: Can you remember who played in the 2004 NFL Super Bowl? It was one of the most exciting, closely contested games in Super Bowl history, won in the final seconds by a field goal. Can you remember if you watched the game? Can you remember who won?

Unless you're a dedicated football fan, I'm going to guess you cannot. But I'll bet you remember what happened at halftime.

The number-one term search term on Google in 2005 was "Janet Jackson," the entertainer whose lapse the year before in January 2004 was still on everyone's mind all through 2005.[3] Few remember who won the game, but still, years later, the phrase "wardrobe malfunction" resonates around the world. Hundreds of athletes had toiled a full year to become the best at what they do, producing a dramatic showdown between the two very best teams, the New England Patriots and the Carolina Panthers. Around the world, millions tuned in to watch the confrontation, a spectacle that has become a national ritual in America and routinely the most watched U.S. sporting event of the year. But all most people can remember about that day is a two-second flash of star-shaped jewelry. Jackson's lapse obscured the accomplishments of those on the field (the Pats beat the Panthers 32 to 29 on a 41-yard field goal made with four seconds left to play).[4] Why do we remember a two-second compliance failure during halftime but not the enormous effort and achievement represented by the championship game itself?

Did you cheat?

About our experiment: It has nothing to do with Janet Jackson. Rather, having just read the inspiring story of David Toms at the British Open, how did you feel when I asked you not to cheat and look ahead to the answer? Did it enter your mind as you were reading?

Were you insulted by the intimation that you *might* cheat? Did you read the passage more lightly? Lose focus and have to read part of it again? Or perhaps just read a little slower in order to *make sure* you wouldn't cheat by reading ahead? People are sensitive about cheating, and rightly so. To casually tell someone not to cheat immediately raises questions of trust. "What does that person think of me, that I'm a *cheat*?" In the few moments immediately after a small comment like that, those voices in your head get activated, and without necessarily realizing it, you get distracted.

Janet Jackson's wardrobe malfunction prompted 500,000 or so complaints to the Federal Communications Commission (FCC) and the largest fine ever levied by the FCC on a television broadcaster at the time, and whether you judge the action innocent, misguided but harmless, inappropriate, or offensive, the total amount of productivity lost while people discussed it over the watercooler (or e-mail, or instant message, or the blogosphere) was probably in the hundreds of millions of dollars.[5] The actions of any single individual can drain significant resources from a company and affect the fortunes of many. Major failures of conduct can bring about the downfall of a company or cost it millions in fines, legal fees, and lost business. But far more significant (and ultimately more detrimental) are the million small events—like that comment about cheating—that crowd our attention each day, activate our inner voices, and pull our minds out of the game.

SMALL LAPSES, LARGE COSTS

The game doesn't stop, of course, when your head leaves it; it goes merrily on without you, leaving you to play catch-up. If the passion and integrity of Krazy George can make a positive Wave, one that propels innovation and success, the Janet Jacksons of business can make a negative one, a Wave of distraction and de-focus. Both positive Waves and negative Waves derive their force and power from the ways we choose to interrelate. Our experiment demonstrates the many ways in which small lapses of HOW can harm us in significant ways.

Business consultant Stephen Young made popular a new management buzzword about these small moments; he calls them *micro-*

inequities.[6] Bad body language in a meeting, a question asked in a mocking tone, an off-color joke told at an inopportune moment—all lapses in how you fill the spaces between you and those with whom you work—can subtly leech productivity from any organization. Checking your messages while speaking with colleagues devalues their time and thus them. Glancing at your watch while someone makes a presentation dismisses his or her effort. You can frame performance reviews in a way that sends underperforming colleagues back to their desks inspired to improve or in a way that leaves them demoralized and revising their resumes. These microlapses create distraction by infecting interpersonal relationships with doubt and fear. Doubt and fear increase the Certainty Gap between us and others. Energy that should be focused on the task at hand or a common goal gets diverted to concerns of politics and survival. An individual or team distracted and without focus will almost always lose.

Let me ask another question (no test this time). In the past week or two, how many times have you opened an e-mail and had one of the following reactions?

- This is not what we agreed to.
- This pisses me off.
- Why did you cc: my boss?
- Are you trying to make me look bad?
- I'm offended.
- I don't find this all that funny.
- Why are you filling my in-box with this stuff?

Did you forward this e-mail to someone? Did you call a friend or loved one and say, "How's your day going, honey? Let me tell you about this e-mail I just got." Or did your annoyance pop into your head again the next time you saw that person and prevent you from relating to them? These things happen all too frequently in the course of a business day. They generate bad feelings, and those feelings accumulate and take their toll. In business, distractions caused by lapses in human conduct reduce everyone's ability to focus, and thus to function well. It is hard enough to succeed in the competitive world of global business, but if you can't focus on winning, you don't stand a chance. One distracting e-mail or phone call can break your concentration on the task at hand.

Such distractions happen all the time. An inappropriate comment by one worker to another during lunch gets escalated into a charge of sexual harassment. The entire team and the focus of the managers immediately get diverted into an investigation. Relationships that were easy and cordial become strained and formal, and productivity quickly suffers.

Distraction can be quantified in all sorts of ways, some anecdotal—like the loss of productivity one can easily imagine following the wardrobe malfunction—and some scientific. Studies have shown, for instance, that the distraction of talking on a cell phone while you are driving exerts a more powerful negative influence on driving performance than alcohol consumed at the legal limit. Some drivers in one study actually reported that it was *easier* to drive under the influence than while talking on a cell phone, a powerful testament to the mental resources necessary to balance attention and distraction while pursuing a goal.[7]

In Chapter 5 we looked at Jenapharm and the University of Michigan Health System and their different approaches to a legal challenge. The time, money, and organizational concentration that go into fighting legal battles are nothing but distraction. People go into business to make things, provide services, solve real problems, create more efficiency, and even better mankind. No one goes into business in order to make better lawsuits. A friend told me a story about a businessman who left an extremely high-paying career selling enterprise software to major corporations in order to strike out on his own.[8] With his wife and brother-in-law, he opened a gelato store in a hip Los Angeles neighborhood to sell epicurean Italian ice cream with flavors like lemoncello with basil and chocolate martini. The store was an immediate success, tripling all expectations right out of the gate. But when I asked him how the first month went, he told me they spent almost their entire profit in legal expenses fighting with a litigious neighboring bakery owner about whether the ham-and-cheese croissant they were selling technically qualified as a "sandwich" or a "pastry," and as such whether it violated their lease by impinging on the bakery business. It was all he could think about. Major corporations suffer the same fate on a much grander scale. The demands of discovery for even the most frivolous of lawsuits can cost corporations millions of dollars and, more crucial, thousands of man-hours' worth of distraction.

Humans have good and bad days, distractions at work and distractions at home. Wardrobe malfunctions happen. Recognizing this and learning to reduce the distractions that take your mind out of the game can make you a step quicker than your competitor, make you more focused, and help you to use your energies more productively. Keeping your mind in the game—learning to recognize and tame both the voices in your head and the HOWs that affect others—is a constant challenge, but more important than ever in a time when small lapses can mean large costs.

DISSONANCE

You walk into a bakery to buy a roll. Behind the counter in plain view is a sandwich preparation area, and on it sits a large bread knife. You order your roll, and when the counterperson hands it to you in a bag, you ask her if she will cut it in half and butter it for you. She looks at you sweetly and tells you, "I'm sorry, but we don't cut." You look again and, just as sweetly, point out that there is a bread knife sitting in plain view obviously used for cutting bread. She again refuses, telling you it is against bakery policy to cut rolls. Then she hands you a plastic fork and some butter. How do you feel?

A bakery with a bread knife that sells sandwiches should have no reason not to cut a roll for a customer. They represent one value—bread service—and yet enforce a policy that blatantly contradicts it. Perhaps the store manager believed there was a good reason for this seemingly inane rule—an employee once injured herself cutting that type of roll, a customer with a plastic knife might take someone hostage and rob the store, or the manager, a bread connoisseur, believes rolls should only be torn by hand and never touched by a knife—but no rationale will ever resolve the basic incongruity of the situation. So you react. Maybe you get angry, feel put upon, or feel disrespected. You might yell at the counterperson and make a scene. Or maybe you just grumble about it while you sit and have your roll and tea. This emotional response is called *dissonance* or, more precisely, *cognitive dissonance*.[9] It results when the mind is asked to accommodate new ideas that conflict with already held beliefs.

As silly as the bakery story might sound, it actually happened to a colleague of mine, and it illustrates well the effects of dissonance on how you think. Despite our best intentions, we are sometimes confronted with messages we can't avoid whose contradiction creates tensions that activate an emotional response. The voices in our heads go wild. This is not just a psychological effect; it's a change in how our synapses fire. Studies have shown that when confronted with situations like these the reasoning parts of your brain—normally employed for effective decision making and sound judgment—actually turn off, and the emotional parts of your brain turn on. Dissonance physically impedes your ability to think clearly, act with reason, and make good decisions.[10]

Businesses send conflicting messages all the time, unaware that the dissonance they cause brings negative results. How many managers say they encourage the input of their subordinates but interrupt them by taking three phone calls, including one from a golfing buddy, while meeting with them? How does it feel to sit in that office, seemingly secure in the belief that your well-considered suggestions are desired, and receive undermining signals to the contrary? Do you lose your train of thought, start stumbling over your words, or bail out in the middle of your proposition, no matter how important it seemed when you entered the office? The next time you have an idea, do you just keep it to yourself? How many companies talk about trust and individual empowerment, and yet require their employees to get the boss's signature on every expense reimbursement or multiple signatures on a purchase order? If they claim to trust you, shouldn't they show they trust you? How do you feel when you have to fill out a form, get it signed by your boss, and then get it approved by accounting before you are reimbursed for a $10 business lunch? How much do you grumble, procrastinate, or resent the system for making you go to such extremes? Do you look to find ways to get paid back for your trouble, maybe slip in a personal receipt or two?

How about the retail store that, with a smile and a swipe of a credit card, takes your money in seconds, but requires you to stand in line for 10 minutes, fill out a form, surrender personal information, and obtain a manager's approval to return your purchase? Are they still smiling? Does that affect your purchasing decision next time you need something? The message management is sending to their retail salespeople is just as dissonant: "We trust you enough to take their money, but not enough to give it back." One might try to explain away this dissonance by suggesting that businesses require a higher level of scrutiny in matters of money because of the commensurately higher potential for abuse and fraud. But trust, as we know, begets trust. Employees who feel truly trusted are less likely to betray that trust because they understand innately that it works to their benefit. Employees who feel disrespected or not trusted by their management and companies are more likely to strike back in subtle ways—like cheating on expense reports or dipping into the till—to get payback for the burdens they feel unjustly placed upon them. The layers of additional rules in fact create the conditions that prompt people to game the system.

The opposite of dissonance is *consonance*, a sense that things belong together. Consonant messages inspire in those around you a greater sense of alignment to a common cause. That creates strong synapses and makes more Waves. It is more profitable in the long run to send signals of trust to employees submitting expense claims, verify them in a random and diligent manner, and deal harshly with the few people who betray that trust than to institute layers of procedure that send the message that you don't really trust anyone. When people are subject to dissonant messages that seemingly make no sense—like the bakery that doesn't cut rolls—they lose their sense of connection to whoever is sending them and strike out on their own, either physically or intellectually. They view your Wave with suspicion and a wait-and-see attitude; then they may get up slowly or without passion, or they may leave the stadium entirely.

Even more damaging is the profound, deleterious effect dissonance exerts on people's ability to learn and adapt to new information. French developmental psychologist Jean Piaget gave this phenomenon specific language to describe it. *Accommodation*—the ability to reconcile conflicting ideas—is more difficult than *assimila-tion*—the ability to accept a new idea as wholly true.[11] In other words, if someone is called upon to learn something that contradicts what they already think they know—particularly if they are committed to that prior knowledge—they are likely to resist the new learning. Studies of the brain have shown that not only will they reject the dissonant message, but, amazingly, will feel good about so doing; their brain actually *rewards* them.

Emory University professor of psychology Drew Westen demonstrated how this works.[12] He put self-described partisans from opposing political parties in brain scanners and asked them to evaluate negative information about various candidates. Both groups rapidly identified inconsistency and hypocrisy in the candidates, *but only in the ones they opposed.* When Westen confronted them with negative information about the candidate they supported, the parts of the brain associated with reasoning and learning switched off and the parts associated with strong emotions kicked on. These strong emotional reactions allowed them to easily reject the information they found dissonant. Then something really interesting happened. Their brains released endorphins, the body's natural opiates, flooding them with a sense of warmth and happiness. In other words, subjects *rewarded themselves* for finding a way to resolve dissonance without having to change their beliefs.

Business in the internetworked world moves faster each year, and the conditions of the marketplace reward organizations and teams most able to adapt to changing circumstances. Companies who subject their employees to mixed messages, repetitive policy changes, or incongruent practices may actually be causing the workforce they so desperately want to be nimble and adaptive to instead become hooked on resistance to adaptation and change. When things get *really* out of hand, you end up in the Kafkaesque reality of the bakery that won't cut. Other studies of cognitive dissonance have shown that when learning something has been difficult, uncomfortable, or even humiliating enough, people are *less* likely to concede that what they believe is useless, pointless, or valueless because to do so would be to admit that they had been duped.[13] Thus the counterperson at the bakery can, with a sweet and genuine smile, tell you that it is against policy to cut a roll, no matter how long or vociferously you attempt to convince her otherwise. For her to see your logic and admit to the folly of the policy would be to admit to being a fool, which, obviously, she will naturally resist.

Though companies desperately want employees to keep their heads in the game, it turns out that generally they do a terrible job at creating the conditions necessary for employees to do so. A three-year survey of about 1.2 million employees at Fortune 1000 companies conducted by Sirota Survey Intelligence concluded that, although the vast majority of employees are filled with enthusiasm when they begin a new job, in about 85 percent of companies morale declines dramatically after six months and continues to do so for years afterward.[14] The Sirota research lays the fault squarely at the feet of management and its inability to create policies and procedures that satisfy the three sets of goals that the great majority of workers seek from their work:

1. *Equity:* to be respected and to be treated fairly in areas such as pay, benefits, and job security.

2. *Achievement:* to be proud of one's job, accomplishments, and employer.

3. *Camaraderie:* to have good, productive relationships with fellow employees.

These statistics illuminate the ultimate cost of dissonance: cynicism. When a company breaks trust and fails to live up to the representations it makes and the values it professes, the enthusiasm new hires bring to the company gets eaten away until nothing is left but the dry bones of cynics. Cynics believe that people are motivated by pure self-interest rather than acting for honorable or unselfish reasons. They create a space of suspicion between themselves and the actions of others—a permanent and unfillable Certainty Gap—and habitually question whether something will happen or whether it is worthwhile. While it is not necessarily corrosive to question things—skepticism can be a healthy response in the right circumstances—to do so reflexively, out of unconscious habit of mind instead of honest consideration, places you at a distance from the events around you.

Cynicism hampers more than just the intangibles of the way people interrelate; it directly affects the bottom line. Studies indicate that highly cynical employees are more likely to file grievances against the company, show lower levels of commitment, and be less likely to believe management would reward good work.[15] (This last fact is particularly relevant to cultures that govern primarily through carrot-and-stick motivational models. When the power of the carrot becomes moot, the stick becomes the only means management has to achieve progress.) Cynicism consumes energy like a sport utility vehicle consumes hydrocarbons. You can't make a Wave in a stadium full of cynics. No matter how passionate and transparent your persuasion, or how much integrity you bring to your initiative, the cynics will sit on their hands convinced that your desire to help the team is nothing more than self-aggrandizement. Though you may cajole until you are blue in the face, the corrosive drag of cynics will eventually wear you down to a stub. "Cynicism can poison a company," said John Wanous, professor of management and human resources at Ohio State University in Columbus. His three-year study of more than 1,000 workers concluded that "Cynicism spills over and colors how employees see everything about the company and their jobs."[16]

DOING CONSONANCE

You don't have to be a passive victim of dissonance; you can learn new HOWS of thought that can help you to see it coming and employ conscious strategies to minimize its ability to colonize your brain. The first step, obviously, is to become aware of how dissonance affects the mind and the emotions, which we have already done. The second step is to interrupt that emotional reaction, and then substitute one of several strategies to resolve the conflict.

The most common resolution strategy involves *changing* one of the held ideas.[17] Say, for instance, that you hold the belief that, in general, suppliers cannot be trusted and must be carefully monitored at all times. Suddenly, you realize that a number of your suppliers recently caught ordering mistakes and, rather than exploit them for their own profit, reported them to you for correction. In order to reduce the embarrassment you might feel from having misjudged the situation, you could choose to review your contract monitoring procedure in light of your new perception. In this way, you turn emotion into improved decision making.

Another technique is to *bolster* the new idea, thus giving it more weight in relation to the previously held idea. One study demonstrated this quite clearly. Researchers told a group of subjects a sexist riddle and, after they laughed at it, made them aware of its discriminatory nature. They then gave them a test to measure their attitudes toward feminism and compared the results to those of a group who had not been told the joke or confronted about its derogatory nature. The joke group tended to overemphasize answers that demonstrated sensitivity to equal treatment. By having the new idea bolstered, the joke group was more easily able to balance their previously held, sexist beliefs with their newly sensitized notions of gender equality.

When the desire to achieve is strong enough, you sometimes *trivialize* a conflicting idea that prevents action. A rock climber faced with a fear of heights might find a way to mock or ridicule his fear in order to accomplish his goal. Once the goal is accomplished, the emotions from the two dissonant ideas tend to dissipate. When the challenge to deeply held beliefs activates strong emotional responses to new information, *emotional expression* can also remove the mind-clouding effects of dissonance. Talking about the emotions helps to normalize them, which minimizes their distracting influence. Lastly, if you can identify the source of dissonant ideas, sometimes simply *avoiding* the cause of them can be an effective strategy for keeping your head in the game.

All of these techniques of dissonance reduction can improve decision making and learning and help you actively reduce the internal noise that dissonance brings.

FRICTION

Imagine a dynamic and successful young businessperson with a major university MBA and a bright future. Her boss has been entrenched in his position for some time. One day, she receives a seemingly innocent e-mail from her boss about a job opening at another company. The note says something like, "I heard of this great opportunity. Do you happen to know of anyone who might be interested?" The job, suspiciously, fits her to a tee. One of the things they teach you in big college MBA programs is that a superior threatened by a rising young star will often try to protect his or her own position by indirectly removing the threat. Recommending a job at another firm fits that bill nicely. Could the e-mail from the boss, while masquerading as an innocent gesture, in fact be a stealthy attempt to undermine his competition?

Try as she might, she can't get the e-mail, and its possible implications, out of her thoughts; it pulls her head out of the game and begins to affect her productivity. Uncertain, she can't help but forward the e-mail to others to get their opinions. She discusses it with friends, and worries about her position and what she would need to do to protect it: all the classic signs of distraction. The dissonance it breeds is equally destructive. Instead of the calm confidence and trust in her position she formerly felt, now her workdays are filled with insecurity and tension. She questions her choices and spends more time making them, sacrificing some of the nimble agility that made her such an asset to the company.

Finally, the emotions she feels make it impossible for her to relate to her boss in a free and unfettered way. Their relationship becomes uncomfortable, a fact noted by the rest of her team. What had once been a smooth-running unit begins to falter. Instead of filling the synapses between them with trust and support, this boss has just gunked up the works. Communication breaks down as spaces previously filled with trust became clouded with doubt. Political tensions arise, people start bickering, and morale plummets. The friction worsens as people become irritated or insulted, then get more people involved, who in turn grow counteraggressive, clouding the synapses with more real conflict.

It's difficult to gauge who is hurt worse by this political maneuver (if, in fact, it is a maneuver), the woman whose productivity suffers or her boss, who sacrificed the cohesion of the entire unit on the altar of his own insecurity. Perhaps the e-mail was entirely innocent and the whole situation could have been avoided if the boss had found a more direct and transparent way to reach out, if he had gotten his HOWS right. In either case, what is perfectly clear is how destructive these forces can be. In a transparent world, where your HOWS are as closely scrutinized as your WHATS, keeping the interpersonal synapses between you and your co-workers in an optimal condition for making Waves is crucial to meaningful action. It takes constant care and attention. When distraction, dissonance, and cynicism overflow the boundaries of the mind and manifest themselves in conduct they contaminate these spaces. That's where *friction* comes from.

In the mechanical world, friction is the force that occurs when two surfaces in contact rub against one another in oppositional ways. In organizations, it results when the forces of distraction and dissonance infect the spaces between people trying to work together. We know from the laws of mechanics that friction slows progress. Friction extracts energy from the system and creates a by-product: heat—wasted energy released into the atmosphere. Excess heat makes people uncomfortable. It requires more energy—in the form of air-conditioning—to cool things down. Without stretching this metaphor too far, we all know what happens to worker productivity when people are hot under the collar. We know, too, how much additional managerial energy it requires to keep an overheated working atmosphere cool and comfortable.

Though distraction, dissonance, and friction can each develop independently in an organization, often they compound each other, like in the situation just described, and set off a self-perpetuating spiral of destruction. Small or large distractions set up powerful dissonance that leads to overt friction. If the situation continues to deteriorate, the heat generated by friction will lead to combustion. Suddenly, your energy will be diverted from the task at hand or there will be two teams working at odds where there used to be one in common purpose. Thriving in a world of HOW involves recognizing and avoiding the conditions that cause distraction, dissonance, and friction; learning to break these cycles when they occur before they can spin out of control; and finding ways to rebuild situations where they already have.

PUTTING IT IN THE WHOLE

It is one thing to talk about reducing distraction, resolving dissonance, avoiding friction, and expunging cynicism from your life, and another to actually do it every day. That is why I began this chapter with my extraordinary conversation with golfer David Toms. Toms sits proudly atop the Hill of A in this area, a master over those forces and events that could pull his mind out of the game. He wrestles with the voices in his head and gets hot under the collar when he is disappointed in his performance, but at a deeper level he recognizes the potential pitfalls that would impede his greater goals and either chooses a course of action that prevents these corrosive forces from entering the fragile machine of the mind or tames them when they do.

What guides him? First, he realizes that rules and rule keepers are just a floor of what he does, not the ceiling. The officials at the Royal and Ancient Golf Club of St. Andrews, the same officials who established and have governed the rules of golf for hundreds of years, would have allowed Toms to continue in the tournament if he had so wanted; according to the rules, he had done nothing wrong. But, prompted by a wise official who undoubtedly understood, too, that rules have limits, Toms knew that he should not. He knows the rules, the *can*s and *cant*s, and plays within them when they apply. But he lives in *should*s. His values—honesty, obligation to others, leadership, and integrity—transcend the rules. Rules can't touch the spirit of golf, his love of the game, or the purity of his pursuit of excellence. These values keep him focused on higher goals.

It also strikes me that, as individual a sport as golf is, Toms does not separate his personal success from the larger world in which he exists. He sees himself connected and responsible not just to himself and his self-interest, but to his family, his fans, his fellow competitors, and even to the young person just learning the sport who might be struggling with the easy temptation to cut a few corners and ignore a few putts. He knows that, in a transparent world, everything you do is on the record and stays with you throughout your career. Toms seems to understand innately that his public and private behavior are inseparable, and that to live any other way is to set up the conditions for dissonance to thrive. That internal calm he believes so essential to the constitution of winners is nothing less than consonance, the ability to act in harmony with oneself. Dissonance creates internal tensions that others can sense and, like the free flow of information in a transparent society, those tensions cannot be fully masked or controlled. He stands as a living example that external congruence flows from internal consonance.

Altogether, David Toms seems to crave something more than success, something more than just winning tournaments. He strives each day to fill the synapses between him and all the others in his personal stadium with trust, integrity, and consonance in order to be *significant* in the eyes of those who watch and are influenced by his actions, and it is this pursuit of significance that guides his journey through life.

KEEPING YOUR HEAD IN THE GAME

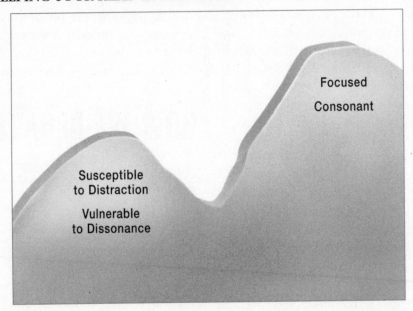

Focused

Consonant

Susceptible
to Distraction

Vulnerable
to Dissonance

We all face choices every day like David Toms does, several times a day. To build long-term sustained success we too must learn to take the paths that reduce distraction and dissonance and keep our interpersonal synapses clear. Rules keepers are not always there and the rules don't always keep us clear. We can seek our advisors and mentors, and they can guide us, but at the end of the day, we are all metaphorically left in that lonely hotel room late at night, with nothing but ourselves to depend on to do the right thing. It is there that we must seek consonance between the various voices in our heads, be guided by those that help us, and turn away from those that pull our heads out of the game. The guidance we need in that moment is not circumstantial (what can I do now?) but rather foundational (what do I believe?), and that foundational knowledge flows from values, connection, and the pursuit of something larger than immediate success.

The ability to keep your head in the game is closely married to the ability to get your HOWs right, to build strong synapses between yourself and others, and to keep them clear and unpolluted in everything you do. If the challenge of living in a connected world requires us to make strong connections with others, we can only do so if we first accept the challenge of making strong connections within ourselves.

Part III

HOW WE BEHAVE

INTRODUCTION: HOW WE DO WHAT WE DO

A friend of mine since law school, David Ellen, is the senior vice president and general counsel for cable, telecommunications, and programming at Cablevision Systems Corporation, a leading telecommunications and entertainment company. In 2005, David and I had a conversation about what LRN was doing and, subsequent to that conversation, I prepared and sent him a personalized packet of information about the solutions I thought might support Cablevision's journey, including the card of one of our sales executives responsible for David's area. In mid-2006, Cablevision hired a new senior vice president of corporate compliance, Adam Rosman, to establish and develop a new compliance initiative. In the course of getting the lay of the land, Adam reached out to David. "David had good things to say about the company in general," Adam said when the three of us got together to recount this story, "and he was candid and up-front about his relationship with Dov."[1] During their conversation, David reflected on the work we were doing at LRN, and he gave Adam the packet I had sent him the year before.

On David's recommendation, Adam called me and left a message with my temporary assistant, which for some reason I never got. "When I got no response, I thought it reflected poorly on the company," Adam said, leaving no doubt that he thought something quite a bit stronger. Nonetheless, he was impressed by the materials I had put together specifically for them, and there was David's recommendation, so he took a second step and left a message for the rep listed on the business card in the packet. "No one in their right mind would do this," Adam said. "Without David's additional recommendation, I probably wouldn't have made the second call." Lots of people want Cablevision's business, and Adam is used to getting his calls returned.

But again, no one called back. In the intervening time between when I had sent David those materials and Adam called the second time, the sales executive had left the company. Through a technical glitch, his voicemailbox had never closed and forwarded (another example of the ways technology both connects us and keeps us apart).

A few months later, David bumped into Adam, and asked in passing what had come of his conversations with us. Much to his surprise, Adam told him that, despite leaving a couple of messages, he had never received a return call and that, frankly, he was surprised. "It was inconceivable to me," David said. "It was totally out of character. I told Adam, 'Something must be wrong. That's not Dov. You should give them another chance.' "[2] The force of David's reaction impressed Adam. A couple of weeks later, he found himself at a conference with Chris Kartchner, one of my colleagues at LRN. Because of David's comment, he approached Chris and told him the story. "He was mortified," Adam said. "A couple of days later, he followed up and explained that they had discovered the unreturned voicemail message sitting in the dead mailbox. He took my ribbing on the subject in good stride."

When I found out, I immediately called David and apologized. Adam Rosman had basically written off LRN when his call was not returned, and I don't blame him. How strange it must have seemed to be ignored and disrespected by a company whose business it was to help others get their HOWS right. Although my initial conversation with David Ellen had started a Wave of interest that Adam's original call perpetuated, our oversights stopped it dead. We didn't get our HOWS right.

Any possible collaboration between us could have ended right there, but there were a few powerful forces at work in this small, but common, interaction. The first was the reputation and trust I had built with David over the years. He knew that I placed the highest premium on getting my HOWS right. That reputation bought us a second chance. "It was not the ordinary benefit of the doubt you extend to companies," David told me. "In the ordinary course of things, you make a call or two and you move on. Too many people want our business to waste time with those who don't seem to." The second force lay in David's HOWS with Adam. He was transparent about our prior relationship when he first recommended us to Adam as a company he should definitely meet with, and equally forceful about that fact in his immediate response after learning of our failings. Adam could sense that David truly believed we were a company for Cablevision to know more about. The third force, of course, was Adam's perseverance and thoroughness in his search for the right company to assist Cablevision.

When Adam met Chris at that conference, he was impressed with the way Chris immediately owned the situation, discovered the miscommunication, and made it clear that it was out of character with what we believed in as a company. Chris was able to restore the reputation that had been damaged. In the ensuing months, Cablevision conducted a selection process during which they gave us full and honest consideration on the merits of what we had to offer. In the end, they selected one of our competitors that they felt better met their current needs. But I believe that we built a strong and trusting relationship, and as their needs evolve, I believe our dialogue will continue.

A small moment. A technical glitch. In a hyperconnected world, where the Expectation of Response factor is almost instant, such small moments can mean the difference between sustained, ongoing success and looking for your next job. Me to David, David to Adam, Adam back to David, Adam to Chris: To thrive in business today, these are the sorts of interpersonal synapses that we must seek to strengthen and extend. This is the sort of Wave that we need to make every day. Ours continues because, despite the "wardrobe malfunction" that almost killed it, our synapses were filled with some powerful forces.

Frameworks of understanding begin in the mind, in the actual chemical processes that fill the synapses between the active neurons in our brains, in the way we choose to see events and interactions, and in the language we choose to craft our thoughts. As we begin to see the connections and connectedness of the world around us in the light of HOW, we begin to look for ways to act on those connections, to affect them in powerful and productive ways. This part looks at the HOWS of behavior, the ways of conducting ourselves in an internetworked world: transparency, trust, and reputation.

Doing Transparency

Sunlight is the best disinfectant.
—Supreme Court Justice
Louis Brandeis

For years, the bicycling community considered the locks made by Kryptonite, now a division of Ingersoll Rand, the gold standard in bicycle security. In 2001, *Bicycling* magazine made its New York 3000 lock an editor's choice, saying, "The company that invented the U-lock just never quits raising the bar on theft prevention. . . . if you want peace of mind when securing your pride and joy this is about as good as it gets."[1] Kryptonite confidently marketed the U-shaped devices as "tough locks for a tough world."[2] Then, in 2004, Chris Brennen came along.

Brennen, a 25-year-old cycling enthusiast, regularly posted to a small online bulletin board for fellow bike nuts, and on September 12 he posted a small notice claiming that Kryptonite's famously impenetrable locks could be opened by anyone with a 10-cent BIC pen and a few seconds to spare.[3] Fourteen hours after Brennen's initial post, another user posted video using Brennen's instructions to demonstrate how quickly and easily he could compromise Kryptonite's star product. The impact was astonishing. Details of the product failure crossed the globe within hours. Within two days of Brennen's first posting, more than 11,000 people had visited the discussion thread and 40,000 had downloaded the video. Early on in the crisis, concerned forum users contacted Kryptonite's public relations manager to alert the company to this critical product failure; Kryptonite had built terrific customer loyalty over the years, and these lock owners wanted to help Kryptonite to protect their bicycles before savvy thieves caught on. What did Kryptonite do? Not much. It was, after all, just a bunch of online nuts. But other online forums linked to the posts, and bloggers trumpeted the failure loudly. After a week, the numbers jumped to 340,000 views and three million downloads.[4] Worse, the *Boston Globe*, *New York Times*, and Associated Press grabbed the story and nearly instantly transformed what years ago might have been a quiet-but-manageable embarrassment into a multimillion-dollar hit to Kryptonite's reputation. By the time Kryptonite developed its definitive response 10 days later, it was in the midst of one of the first large-scale, Internet-spawned public relations (PR) disasters on record. Their entire brand promise, years of work, lay in ruins.

Patricia Swann, assistant professor of public relations at Utica College, studies this phenomenon, known as *issue contagion*, and published a paper on the Kryptonite debacle. "Kryptonite's decision not to respond provided the bike forum's posters even more motivation, as the fear grew that the company would ignore their concerns unless many people complained," Swann said. "The Internet has totally changed the rules of the game. You used to get a couple of days, or at least 24 hours, to prepare a response to something like this. Now, it goes everywhere, fast like wildfire. You have no control of the story."[5]

The mass-media society of the twentieth century was built on a discursive, top-down model of communication. Information flowed through centralized channels and was easily dammed and harnessed. As Swann suggested, you had time to control the story. Powerful organizations, powerful societies, and powerful people were built on this vertical information structure. Now, consider the following, an eloquent summation of the world as we now know it, reported in May 2006 by Kevin Kelly in the *New York Times Magazine*:

> From the days of Sumerian clay tablets till now, humans have "published" at least 32 million books, 750 million articles and essays, 25

million songs, 500 million images, 500,000 movies, 3 million videos, TV shows, and short films, and 100 billion public Web pages. . . . When fully digitized, the whole lot could be compressed (at current technological rates) onto 50, 1-petabyte hard disks. Today you need a building about the size of a small-town library to house 50 petabytes. With tomorrow's technology, it will all fit onto your iPod.[6]

Knowledge is power. That old adage is as true today as when philosopher Francis Bacon first said it in the seventeenth century. When knowledge—enabled by this unprecedented access to information—was controllable, those who controlled it accrued power and became leaders. Now that information is virtually uncontrollable, the power has shifted to those who share it. We must adapt to take advantage of the new realities.

We have discussed how business in the twentieth century is busy remaking itself in order to profit from the strengths and efficiencies of the free-flowing internetworked world. More people in more places can collaborate freely, sparking innovation and invention. There is less functional disparity between the top and the bottom of an organization, so more and more of our business relationships become horizontal collaborations between equals. Skills and habits that helped us thrive in top-down hierarchies are less vital in collaborative networks. The strong-but-silent leader, the sycophantic yes-man, the hard-sell salesperson are all fast becoming relics of the old world. No longer can you make a Wave, that powerful image of initiative flowing unrestrained into the organization, simply by having the biggest title in the stadium. It now requires a different set of skills, the ability to build strong interpersonal synapses capable of reaching out through these horizontal networks and bringing people together around ideas and initiatives.

As the world transitions to a bottom-up and side-to-side model in which each individual can contribute to the free flow of ideas, it opens up and becomes more transparent. An information society is a dialogical society, one based on the interactive sharing of information among mutually interested parties. Equalized access to information allows more people to act in an informed manner, a lesson Kryptonite learned the hard way. And though it was able to eventually repair the damage to its reputation with a product recall and redesign, in an information world, Kryptonite discovered it is harder to hide from the truth. Everything we do, say, or represent can be verified or disproved easily and relatively cheaply. While Kryptonite's underestimation and lethargy was a big, public spectacle, it is also an example of a million small interactions that happen every day in business. A salesman tells one potential customer one thing in Chicago and a different lead another thing in Phoenix, believing that the information will never be compared or exchanged. You tell your boss one thing about your recent business trip, forgetting that her easy access to your expense receipts tells her something different. A job applicant exaggerates a university degree he never received, and is easily discovered by a $10 background check.

Transparency—the new conditions of the world that allow us to see past the medium to get to the heart of the message—fundamentally changes almost every way we conduct our lives in public (and in private), demanding a new set of HOWS if we really want to thrive. To understand these changes, we must consider two types of transparency: technological and interpersonal. *Technological transparency* describes the ever-evolving state of the networked world, the transparency that happens *to* us—transparency as a noun, if you will. These are the conditions that Kryptonite fell prey to. *Interpersonal transparency* centers on the realm of HOW we do what we do—transparency as an action, as a way of being, as a verb *to be transparent*. This is the active transparency we bring to our interactions with others. These two forms of transparency live in a symbiotic relationship, each fueling the other synergistically. The question before us as we consider what we need to thrive in the internetworked world is: How do we conquer our fear of exposure and turn these new realities into new abilities and behaviors? How can we become proactive about transparency?

BEYOND PROXIES AND SURROGATES

I was watching CNN when the jury in the Scott Peterson murder trial, one of the most publicized celebrity trials of the past few years, handed down its death penalty verdict. In the aftermath of the verdict, I happened to catch an interview with one of the jurors. When asked how the jury reached its decision, the juror said that the testimony of Amber Frye, Peterson's mistress, about their tawdry extramarital dalliances, had little to do with convicting him of the crime of killing his wife and unborn child, but everything to do with giving him a death sentence. Her testimony revealed the most about his character and intentions.[7] This statement struck me. In legal terminology, Frye's testimony went to "malice aforethought" and "depravity of the heart," and these amorphous unprovable notions were the key information the jury needed to consider. Jury foreman Steve Cardosi, when asked if Peterson could have helped himself by testifying in the case, said something just as remarkable. "You know, given his past and his level of honesty," he said, "it probably would have done him more harm than good to talk to us, because I don't believe we would have believed him even if he was being honest."[8]

This got me thinking about some other celebrated cases of the past few years. In the securities fraud and obstruction of justice trial of media maven Martha Stewart, Judge Miriam Goldman Cedarbaum considered whether Stewart showed remorse in deciding how to best mete out justice after her conviction for lying to investigators, but her postconviction social gallivanting to awards shows and parties in the Hamptons did little for her cause.[9] Hotelier Leona Helmsley displayed negative attitudes toward the court. Her famous quote "Only little people pay taxes" displayed an egregious disrespect that proved a factor in her punishment as well.[10]

Character is a difficult thing to judge, and yet we judge the character of individuals day in and day out, both casually when deciding in our own interests and in the extreme cases when deciding someone's fate. It is a deeply held, long-standing tradition that informs who we are in profound ways. The importance of the outcome, from the trivial to the most dire, does not change the criteria we use. Whether it be meting out the ultimate punishment or giving a dollar to a homeless person on the street, character, that soft quality of a person's worth, plays a huge role in our dealings with others.

Then in 2006, when public mortgage corporation Fannie Mae was fined $400 million for financial irregularities, what I heard on the news made clear to me how the world had changed.[11] Reuters reported that the enormity of the fine had a lot to do with the fact that "Fannie Mae's 'arrogant and unethical' corporate culture led employees to massage earnings," and that "Fannie Mae's faults were not limited to violating accounting and corporate governance standards, but included excessive risk taking and poor risk management as well."[12] James B. Lockhart III, director of the Office of Federal Housing Enterprise Oversight, made it very clear when he appeared on PBS's *NewsHour.* "This whole company's culture needs to be changed," he said. "We're really demanding sort of a top-to-bottom look at this company."[13] It struck me that if he had been speaking three years before, Lockhart would have said something like "They lacked proper internal controls or compliance mechanisms." Now he was saying that they had looked deep into the soul of Fannie Mae and decided that something was rotten at the core, that the transgressions arose from an "arrogant and unethical corporate culture." We habitually judge people's characters, but when it came to companies, this was not the case until very recently. We did not judge an organization's "character," because we couldn't impute a character to it.

In the days before information transparency made almost everything easily knowable, all we could really know about a company's "character" were the programs and procedures that stood as proxies for it. When companies could be fortresses, they had much greater control over what outsiders could see. The walls were high, and it was highly effective to post proxies on the parapets like flags that could be seen from a distance. A jury assessing a company's complicity when one of its employees broke the law had to assume that if it invested heavily in, say, a compliance hotline, then it must be honest and diligent. The hotline served as proxy for self-policing. Since people couldn't see deeply into the corporation's true, everyday behaviors, they had to pick a surrogate, a proxy, something that would indicate whether it was good. Often these took the form of programs or departments charged with duties such as compliance or safety. When a company like Fannie Mae became embroiled in a scandal or was accused of wrongdoing, we would judge its culpability on the programs it had in place. The thinking went: Like every city has some criminals, every organization has some bad apples; you judge a city by its laws and efforts to root out crime, and you judge a company by the programs and policies it has in place to keep people in line. City laws and company programs served roughly the same function in this respect, as proxies for their leaders' efforts to stop crime. You don't arrest the mayor or penalize the company for the transgressions of its bad actors. In legal terms, they call this the due diligence standard. Judging the actions of an organization centered around answering the question of whether it took reasonable precautions and preventive measures to protect against what ended up occurring; had the organization shown due diligence?

In Chapter 5, we explored the nature of rules as proxies for the desired values of an organization or society. Industrial age capitalism developed many such proxies and surrogates to stand in for all sorts of things. A resume served as a proxy for your work history. A compliance program told Wall Street and regulators that you are vigilant about regulation. The salary you made at your last job communicated by proxy your value in the marketplace. In the pretransparent age, proxies and surrogates were an efficient way of representing information to others, and we selectively put them forth for the world to see as the best indicators of our worth. Both companies and individuals operating successfully in the age of fortress capitalism had good reason to create and manage by proxies and surrogates: They provided efficient and demonstrable leading indicators. By tracking the indicator, you could easily track progress. A company aiming to improve its customer service response could institute a training program to introduce a set of rules and standards. Since monitoring and tracking the actual performance of each of the thousands of employees who graduated from the program was expensive and time-consuming, the graduation rate became an efficient measure of success, and efficiency, as we know, was the opium of the industrial age. Through much of the twentieth century, contemporary culture relied on proxies and surrogates as crutches because of how difficult or expensive it was to get real-time, in-depth information.

Those days seem to be gone. Think how easy it is to see through to the inner workings of a company today versus just a few years ago. Chat rooms, online forums, instant access to financial reports and transactions, news coverage from around the globe—almost nothing goes unreported or unvaulted somewhere online, where it can be quickly retrieved. I know of a lawyer who works with companies to reduce their risk profiles in the human resource and worker safety areas, and in explaining how he tries cases almost immediately said, "Do you know how many hard drives I cart off each month? It's the first thing I do. We just pick them up and pour through everything that's been said or thought about the case. Seeing the inner workings of a company is just a subpoena away." At every level of society now, the easy access to information has changed both how we judge organizations and what we expect of them. Simply having a hotline does not suffice when we can easily poll your employees to determine whether people are scared to call it or do not trust that it is confidential. Increasingly, we can discover and impute character to an organization to evaluate its norms, values, and practices.

Consumers, customers, regulators, judges, and juries have now begun to view companies from a characterological viewpoint. They pay more attention to, and care more about, the inner life and character of the companies with which they do business. They've begun to ask themselves whether the company has integrity. Does it have a character? In such an environment, programs and proxies alone no longer suffice. Those passing judgment in our newly transparent age look past programs and proxies deep into the culture of the company. It already happens every day, in almost every business transaction. Global businesses look deep into the workings of potential partners as trust becomes vital to the transparency they require to open themselves to new forms of collaboration. The best and brightest MBAs profess to be willing to forgo substantial compensation to work for companies with reputations for fair dealing and cultures that value the individual. According to a recent LRN study, an overwhelming majority of employees—94 percent—say it is critical that the company they work for have a strong commitment to values. In fact, 82 percent said they would prefer to be paid less and work for that values-driven company than receive higher pay at a company with questionable commitment.[14] Business in general has become far more precise and concrete about issues—like conduct, character, and reputation—that it formerly considered "soft."

Soon these judgments will become pervasive and ingrained, affecting every evaluation of a company's prospects and its ability to perform in the marketplace. People will habitually ask: Does this company have a culture that is nimble and responsive, or one full of friction and dissonance? Are its team members free to create and achieve at their top level or encumbered by a governing system and culture that discourages their best efforts? Is it a company of talent aligned with shared beliefs, attitudes, and aspirations, or one with competing interests who jockey for internal advantage? Due diligence will take on new and added dimensions, with these formerly soft issues weighing as heavily in the mix as balance sheets and assets.

ICU, UC ME

Technological transparency has lifted the veil of proxies and surrogates, leaving individuals and organizations exposed as never before. This new vulnerability has profound ramifications on how we do what we do. In an attempt to quantify the way transparency affects the HOWS of business, Professor James A. Brickley of the William E. Simon Graduate School of Business Administration at the University of Rochester considered a typical deal between a buyer and a seller. The seller contracts to buy a certain product, say a chemical compound, of a certain high quality. It is more expensive for the seller to produce a high-quality compound than a low-quality one. If the conditions of the world are such that the purity of the compound can be easily and cheaply tested prior to the transaction, the buyer probably will do so, so the seller, in these conditions, has little incentive to cheat on quality. The seller would be easily discovered and lose the deal. If testing is difficult or expensive, however, things get trickier. The seller gains a strong incentive to cheat on quality, especially if the gain by cheating exceeds the expected costs of delivering as promised.[15] In other words, if it costs $10 to make a product of promised quality and $5 to make one of lesser quality, the seller will gain $5 if he is reasonably sure he won't get caught before the deal goes through.

Testing, in this example, is information, and easy access to information changes everything. In a nontransparent world, it was generally far easier for a seller to look at each deal as an individual transaction, with few ramifications for future sales. For buyers, it was far more difficult for the right hand to know what the left was doing (i.e., to get information about the seller or the product). Thus the costs of cheating remained low and easily determinable. The more rapidly, widely, and inexpensively information about a product can be distributed, however, the higher the long-term costs of cheating. Cheating will quickly be discovered and broadcast, resulting in long-term loss of reputation and sales. Further, a high-information culture creates the expectation of high information. When sellers can't provide reasonable and substantiated assurances about a product, buyers will want to pay less to protect against higher uncertainty. *The very presence in a market of cheap and easy information changes the costs involved in every transaction, providing the seller with a strong incentive to do the right thing.*

Although Brickley's analysis uses quality as a variable, quality as a process is not the issue at hand; it is trust and transparency, getting your HOWS right. Whether it be recruiting the best talent, negotiating with a potential customer, or defending a workers' compensation claim, more than ever companies now have to answer for their culture both in the courts and in the court of public opinion. Today, a company is no longer judged merely on the quality of its WHATS, but also on its HOWS. It is not enough to make a good tennis shoe if you exploit workers in Vietnam to do so. It is not enough to pay a good salary if you institute policies that make workers feel devalued. It is not enough to keep promises 80 percent of the time when your competitor keeps them 100 percent of the time.

If the company is a stadium and its workers fill the seats, the gates to the field have been thrown wide open and anyone can now wander in, look up, and watch how you do the Wave. They can see who is leading and how they are leading, who is or isn't following, how section 38 communicates with section 52 and what they say. The way the outside world now views a company has irrevocably changed, and this new framework of understanding has profound implications for the way business is conducted in the twenty-first century. Now, HOW you do WHAT you do matters most.

THE MARKET DEFINES YOU

Nowhere in the internetworked world is our changing relationship to proxies and surrogates better illuminated than in the world of advertising. Advertising and marketing are proxies as well, up-front representations of a company's best effort to reach out to its customers. Back in the early days of radio and television, when advertisers broke free of the printed page and began to employ images and sound, ads were by and large conversational approaches to the consumer, an attempt to replicate the experience of everyday life. People talked about things to one another, and those who could appear more sincere, more folksy and down-to-earth, were often most successful. Ronald Reagan, for example, then a B-movie actor, would come on the radio and tell you in his relaxed tone how Boraxo Waterless Hand Cleanser would clean everything from paint to grease from your hands. "The whole crew swears by it," he said, "and so will you."[16] Messages were simple, informative, and direct.

As television grew in popularity, people began to realize the power of the image and manipulate it accordingly. Decade by decade over the next 40 years, ads became slicker, images more polished and manipulated, and commercials more frequent and overwhelming as marketers attempted to perfect methods to define their product identity in the market. The era of folksy friends evolved into the world of abstract icons. The Marlboro Man, Colonel Sanders, Joe Camel, and even real-life characters like Michael Jordan for Nike became highly evolved and crafted symbols representing the feelings and aspirations of consumers. Powerful "brand image" became the marketer's goal, with "brand awareness" following close behind. By the 1990s, brand messaging had become so abstract and sophisticated that the product itself often became less important than the image or associations that our most talented marketers could wrap it in.

The connected world is changing all that. Easy access to information makes consumers smarter today; they can easily get past the image and get to the truth of a company's product. In the United States, movie marketers were one of the first groups to feel this. Twenty-five years ago, the biggest movies of the year would open on a few screens in New York and Los Angeles, and then, buoyed by positive word of mouth and the praise of critics (themselves surrogates for the audience), would roll out across the country week by week, with foreign markets to follow. According to the *Los Angeles Times*, top box office hits made just 12 percent of their total gross in the first week of release.[17] With the growth of the cineplex and the introduction of the wide release, studios became able to flood the market with their product, opening on thousands of screens on a single day around the world. Since only critics and a scattered few test audiences around the country actually saw a film before it was released, movie marketers could almost completely control the branding of a film, and no industry got better at defining its product for the marketplace. The power in Hollywood shifted from the creators of motion pictures to those who marketed them. Big films now routinely make one-third of their total gross the first weekend, essentially cashing in on their marketing before word of mouth can correct the perception in the marketplace.

But along came such web sites as aintitcool.com (or Ain't It Cool News), accompanied by blogs and boards catering to those who loved to talk about movies. Members of a test audience in New Jersey who saw a sneak preview of a film still in production could go online and share what they had seen. Even films that had just opened could suddenly become widely discussed. Marketers lost control of the message. "Instant communications technology has completely changed the role of word of mouth," Nancy Utley, COO of Fox Searchlight Pictures, told the *Los Angeles Times* recently.[18] "Word of mouth used to be confined to cities. Now, thanks to e-mail and text messaging, it crosses continents. It's revolutionized what word of mouth means." A recent *Los Angeles Times* poll backs up this notion, revealing that nearly 40 percent of teens and young adults (the largest percentage of the moviegoing audience and the most wired generation) share their opinions during viewing, right afterward, or on the same day they see a film. Instant communication can build an almost immediate national consensus about a film, creating an instant hit or dooming it to a quick DVD release almost before opening weekend is over. In other words, you no longer define yourself in the market; the market defines you.

This trend is pervading other areas of society as well. Yelp, a web site that touts "Real People. Real Reviews," is building a community of nonprofessional reviewers who log on and share their immediate impressions of everything from hot dog stands to five-star restaurants to corner hardware stores. When it launched in San Francisco in late 2004, it had an almost instant impact. Unlike the anonymous reviewers of the Zagat and Michelin guides, Yelpers post detailed profiles of themselves and bond around common interests. This transparency builds almost immediate trust, and a "good Yelp" can get cash registers ringing almost overnight. "No longer is each customer transaction a one-off interaction," media analyst Ken Doctor of Outsell Inc. told the *Los Angeles Times*.[19] "Any customer who has a great or horrible experience now has, as soon as they walk out the door, a megaphone to tell the world they had a great or horrible experience, fairly or unfairly." Rather than being passive beneficiaries or victims of this new trend, smart businesses there are taking advantage of the feedback to instantly improve their products. "It's changed the way I run my business because I get feedback right away," said chef-owner Ola Fendert of restaurant Oola. "You used to find out too late, when your business was slowing down. Now it's almost instant: Something happened, you see it on Yelp the next day, and you can fix it." (Interestingly, as an even greater sign that we are reaching a critical mass of these trends, both of these *Los Angeles Times* reports—on movies and Yelp—appeared in the same day's paper, August 25, 2006, in completely different sections edited by different people.)

The easy explanation for the trend toward the increasing effectiveness of word of mouth would be to assume that people are just overwhelmed and cynical about corporate messages and Big Media. After all, why should someone believe Joe from Berkeley over a reviewer from the *San Francisco Chronicle* or their own experience of a movie trailer? But if you dig deeper, the reason is far more profound. Proxies succeed in their function as messengers only when those receiving them endow them with trust and have no other sources of information with which to compare them. In a world where everyone is connected and has ready access to a flood of information, people can look past the proxies to get at the truth. Why accept what Hasbro says about how much your child will enjoy their newest toy when you can go online and read reviews by other parents who have already bought it describing the real-life experiences of their kids? In a time where the Certainty Gap is large, people yearn for a more immediate and authentic impression before they part with their hard-won dollars.

Today's leading-edge companies know this, and are putting their marketing money where other people's mouths are. They spend less and less each year on big television ad campaigns and more and more on direct approaches enabled by new media. In 2005, advertisers spent about $47.4 billion on newspaper advertising, according to the Newspaper Association of America. That is comparable to $46.2 billion for broadcast television and $52.2 billion for direct-mail advertising. These mass media outlets are seeing meager year-over-year growth of about 5 percent. By comparison, year-over-year spending on targeted interactive advertising—dialogic marketing—is projected to be up nearly 30 percent, from $9.7 billion to over $12.5 billion, according to industry estimates.[20] Smart companies are targeting more and more marketing dollars to efforts to connect more intimately with their markets—efforts like word-of-mouth marketing, defined by the Word of Mouth Marketing Association (WOMMA) as "Giving people a reason to talk about your products and services, and making it easier for that conversation to take place." WOMMA joins together cutting-edge efforts to perfect "the art and science of building active, mutually beneficial consumer-to-consumer and consumer-to-marketer communications."[21]

New and innovative strategies for reaching the market seem to pop up each day. *Viral marketing* focuses on creating entertaining or informative messages designed for customers to pass along in an exponential fashion, often electronically or by e-mail. *Evangelist marketing* cultivates advocates or volunteers and encourages them to take a leadership role in actively spreading the word on a company's behalf. *Cause marketing* involves supporting social causes to earn respect and support from people who feel strongly about the causes. *Mobile marketers* use cell phones to achieve a huge range of objectives—from text-to-win competitions to direct-response handling, customer service management, and brand building—to build a two-way conversation with new or existing customers, "extending the brand into the pocket."[22] Interestingly, these more direct, personal approaches are in many ways a throwback to the early days of media, when people got their messages from people they trusted, like Ronald Reagan.

Mass media advertising is losing its effectiveness because people don't believe it (the information age has given them ample access to objective facts that disprove advertising claims), and, more important, they just don't need it as much anymore to make buying decisions. Gallup's 2005 annual governance survey reported that "[Only] half of Americans say they trust the mass media when it comes to reporting the news fully, accurately, and fairly," down substantially from the peak in 1976, when nearly three-quarters felt that way.[23] A recent study by Intelliseek reported that 88 percent of consumers trust advertising via word of mouth, but only 56 percent said newspaper ads were trustworthy, and 47 percent said the same for television and radio (27 percent trust "experts" and 8 percent trust celebrities, for what it's worth).[24] "The shift is happening because consumers and customers are rather cynical," Linda Wolf, former chairman and CEO of advertising giant Leo Burnett Worldwide, told me recently over break-fast in Chicago. During her tenure at Burnett, Wolf oversaw global op-erations that spanned more than 80 countries and more than 200 units. She is widely considered one of the most influential executives in the world of advertising. "They're more sophisticated in their interactions with brands and with products. Based on that sophistication they can see through the phoniness of what is going on. They are connoisseurs of authenticity, so savvy and so sophisticated, and I think people are looking for more authenticity."

The new challenge for marketers is to find ways of facilitating *au-thentic impressions* on their potential consumers. Authentic impres-sions come from human interactions where people get their HOWS right, without attempting to manipulate the message or the market. "The world is so transparent today that the minute you're not honest and authentic with what you stand for, the damage can be done so quickly," Wolf said. "Your customers feel like they've been fooled or tricked; they absolutely do feel like they've been betrayed. When a company has done such a good job in building up the trust in this re-lationship and then does something to crack that, the sense of betrayal is just huge."

Marketing today is all about making Waves through the market-place by connecting in direct, transparent, dialogic ways with con-sumers. It is the new HOW of brand messaging. You might think that putting shills in dance clubs to talk up your product is just another manipulative way to get your highly crafted message out, but amaz-ingly, a recent study showed that evangelist marketers who *identified* themselves as paid shills to those with whom they had contact actually made a stronger impression than those who kept their affiliation a se-cret. In other words, even in the highly crafted message world of ad-vertising, those who reach out personally *and transparently* to the market benefit more than those who seek to manipulate it in covert ways. If the message is the proxy, an actively transparent proxy wins.

Mass information access has fundamentally changed the way we perceive the messages we receive. Technological transparency renders living, governing, and representing yourself through proxies and surro-gates obsolete. "Winning customers is now all about building authentic and relevant relationships," Wolf said. "The extreme fragmentation in the media world today creates an opportunity to clearly reach different customers based on their interests and desires, and build those relationships. It's a very exciting time. You can have a much more one-on-one, richer relationship, a much deeper relationship with those who believe most strongly in your brand, and work with them."

Connecting with the market is no longer about propagating brand image or brand awareness; it is about asserting *brand promise*, a direct relationship between business and the market. Brand promise is deeper than image, it encompasses what you stand for, the expectations you set for yourself, and how you honor that promise with action and behavior. "It's all about trust," Wolf said. "Trust is key, and brands that consistently stand for something build that trust and build that credibility and build that relationship. When they do, it's a rock-solid relationship that is very difficult to be broken."

All of this points to one simple conclusion: what you say about yourself now takes a backseat to how you create a rewarding and reliable experience for your customers. And the key to that? "We all need to be very clear and transparent in what we stand for, and what we stand for with our company," Wolf said in closing. "That clarity will immediately communicate to whoever that customer is. That's the simplicity of it."

SAY YOU ARE SORRY

Fear of exposure is a real concern in a transparent world. Transparency is not just a WHAT, however, something that happens *to* you; it is a HOW that any group or individual can embrace and master.

To see how this can work, let me say, "I'm sorry."

Those are difficult words to say, especially in a business context. And yet there's a lot of it going around. In June 2005, Charlotte, North Carolina–based Wachovia Corporation, the fourth largest bank in the United States, issued an apology to all Americans, and especially black Americans, because a historical search it commissioned revealed that two of its ancestral banks owned slaves before the Civil War.[25] "While we can in no way atone for the past, we can learn from it, and we can continue to promote a better understanding of the African-American story, including the unique struggles, triumphs, and contributions of

African-Americans, and their important role in America's past and present," the company said.[26] Also in early 2005, another large U.S. bank, JPMorgan Chase & Co., did the same, admitting that two of its predecessor banks accepted thousands of slaves as collateral against loans. It apologized for contributing to "a brutal and unjust institution."[27] When the stock option backdating scandals broke in mid-2006, Apple Computer conducted a three-month internal investigation and published its findings on its web site. It included an apology from co-founder and CEO Steve Jobs, who took full responsibility for the issue. "I apologize to Apple's shareholders and employees for these problems, which happened on my watch. They are completely out of character for Apple," said Jobs. "We will now work to resolve the remaining issues as quickly as possible and to put the proper remedial measures in place to ensure that this never happens again."[28]

In a dramatic gesture that underlined his sensitivity to the values of other cultures, Citigroup's chairman and chief executive officer, Charles Prince, traveled to Japan, where ritual apologies are deeply ingrained in the culture, and bowed in public to show regret for the company's regulatory wrongdoings there.[29] Speaking at the Japan Society in New York a few days later, he said, "We've had some examples where people thought very short-term without considering the need to extend the legacy of the organization. . . . It is not the Citigroup way, and it is not reflective of how we do other business. . . . How we do business is at least as important as how much business we do."[30]

To apologize is inherently a dangerous act, but one with latent power. To apologize is to accept responsibility, this we all know, but it is also to cede power to the wronged party. You place in their hands the decision to forgive you or not. Apologizing requires willful vulnerability. It is the ultimate act of transparency, which makes it an extremely interesting example of turning the new realities of the hypertransparent world in your favor. Apologies always follow wrongdoing, and that means loss—loss of respect, loss of credibility, and loss of trust. Apologies, by their nature, are remedial; they seek to mitigate damage that has already been done. When admitting wrongdoing can cost an organization significant revenue or an individual his or her job, life, or liberty, the temptation to avoid this gesture is enormous. Since the damage is done, the reasoning goes, why expose yourself to further liability by admitting your wrongdoing? The old cliché from the CIA rings in the ears: "Admit nothing. Deny everything. Make counteraccusations."[31] (That is another relic of fortress mentality brought to us by an organization whose primary purpose is to control information.) The structure of law in highly litigious societies, however, disincentivizes apologies. The rules are written so that both sides deny responsibility and then go to court, where each forces the other to prove fault. That's the position Jenapharm took in its suit with the former East German Olympic athletes.

In a transparent world, the truth will win out. "All of us must recognize that there are now hundreds of thousands of watchdogs out there who can gain access to what we write and what we say," Robert Steele, of the Poynter Institute, a journalism think tank in Florida, recently told the *San Diego Union-Tribune*. "All of us will be held accountable more quickly and easily because of the scope and reach of the Internet."[32] This puts a higher premium on the ability to stanch the flow of loss that results from a misstep, to be proactive in the face of error. In Chapter 5, we saw how University of Michigan Hospitals and Health System, one of the most respected medical establishments in the United States, decided to train its doctors to apologize, lowering its litigation and malpractice costs. That's an important and powerful metric to consider, but it is only the most important result if you believe the mission of your organization is to increase the bottom line. Far more important for the long-term sustained success of that organization was the reparation of trust it achieved with the community. The decrease in costs serves merely as an easily quantifiable indicator of the far greater gains achieved in its relationship with the community it serves. How much more does the organization accrue by the reputation it gains for its actively transparent stance?

In 2002, TriWest Healthcare Alliance, a health insurance company that serves primarily active military personnel, suffered the theft of two laptop computers from the company's main offices. These weren't just any two laptops; they contained the personal information of 550,000 TriWest customers. Names, addresses, birth dates, Social Security numbers, and in some unfortunate cases credit card numbers—essentially everything needed for a highly successful case of identity theft—

walked out the door. At the time the theft occurred, it was the largest information theft to ever have taken place in the United States.[33] The blow to TriWest was potentially mortal. What is an insurance company without trust?

Dave McIntyre, president and CEO of TriWest, did something remarkable. "The first thing I thought was, 'What is the quickest way to tell 550,000 people that something has gone terribly wrong?'" He decided to immediately inform those affected customers and then launched a $2 million effort to correct the error. TriWest contacted the affected customers and set up an information hotline where people could call with their questions and concerns. Then McIntyre took it a step further, devoting himself to teaching both the public and business owners alike how to correct and prevent future security breaches of this sort. He did this so well, in fact, that he transformed a monumental mistake into an award of excellence from the Public Relations Society of America for the campaign against identity theft.[34]

Public apologies such as this understandably make an easy target for cynics. Cynics believe that people act almost exclusively out of self-interest. There is no doubt that an apology is an attempt to right a wrong, ideally with the result of lessening its harm to the transgressor. In a case like this, the admission and attempt at restitution can easily be seen as an attempt to create the illusion of due diligence. The cynic might say, "Where was the due diligence when the hard drives walked out the door? Why was the personal information of these customers left somewhere susceptible to a security breach and theft?" Apology is an antecedent act, to be sure. It answers the questions: "How can we best go forward from here? How can we rebuild the trust we have lost?" In this, studies show, to apologize is not only the right thing to do; it is the smart thing to do. Roy Lewicki, professor of management and human resources at Ohio State University's Fisher College of Business, led a study published in the *Journal of Management* in 2004 that suggests that "a willingness to take blame and offer amends . . . may be necessary to help repair a loss of trust in a business relationship."[35] Cynicism exists, in all its corrosive forms, but this kind of proactive transparency flies in the face of cynics precisely because its authenticity disarms them. *I'm sorry* put McIntyre out ahead of the curve. By asking himself not "What can we do?" but rather "What *should* we do?" McIntyre was able to act swiftly and transparently to save his company.

Sure, an apology contains a measure of self-interest, but truly offered, it contains an equal measure of concern for others, and its nature of transferring power to the receiver tips the scales in its favor. In Chapter 6, we touched on the Ohio State University study that illuminated the corrosive effects of employee cynicism, and how that cynicism was responsible for the destruction of the tremendous goodwill employees bring to a new company when they are hired. But the study also revealed ways that companies and managers could reverse the destructive trend, concluding that managers need to be honest and open to their employees about both their successes and failures. "When plans fail, management needs to give credible and verifiable reasons for the failure to employees," the study's author, Professor John Wanous, said. "If management made a mistake, then say so."[36] In other words, transparency can be the *antidote* for cynicism. And because an apology extends trust, the natural response is to reciprocate that trust with trust, just as the subjects of Paul Zak's trust game experiments reciprocated altruistically. It won't reach everyone—some people's walls are just too high—but those it does reach can provide the foundation for new, restorative trust that will lead you to the future.

An apology in the context of business demonstrates how much of our current success is tied to our ability to be actively transparent with those to whom we are connected. Transparency builds strong synapses by increasing trust and reducing the corrosive factors that weaken them. Active transparency is not just about ameliorating liability or diffusing potentially explosive regulatory missteps, however. It puts you out ahead in a lot of situations.

INTERPERSONAL TRANSPARENCY

When I was in law school in Boston, I rowed crew with a guy I had met at Oxford, a smart guy named Sig Berven. I remember him as a fun guy, a scholar-athlete. He did well in school, was very well-rounded, but was by no means head of his class. One day, he told me the remarkable story of his admission interview for Harvard Medical School, where he was then studying. "I went into the dean's office and sat down," he told me. "There was so much riding on this interview, and the air in the room was stifling. The dean sat there, behind his desk, with my transcript in his hands, and said nothing for a moment or two. Finally, he looked me right in the eyes, held up my transcript, and said, 'You know, I've seen better grades than this before.' I caught my breath, looked right back at him, and said, 'So have I . . . So have I.' Then we kept talking."

At the time, I didn't understand Sig's candor with the dean. It seemed foolhardy, given his overall level of qualification. Later, I came to recognize how extraordinary was this simple act. Sig got accepted, and he is now a distinguished assistant professor at University of California, San Francisco's department of orthopedic surgery. He aced his interview in large part because he was simply honest when the situation and the expectations in the room screamed at him to be otherwise. He didn't say, "Well, let me tell you, my mom was sick, so I took this semester off and my GPA dropped." He offered no excuses, no puffery, no lies, but simply acknowledged that he, too, had seen better grades.

Most people in Sig's situation—applying for a new position, whether in a school or with a company—portray themselves as something they are not. They succumb either to the pressure of being on the spot and feeling like they need to say the right thing to please their superior or the pressures of the old get-ahead-by-any-means-necessary culture. This is easy to understand. Nowhere in business are you more vulnerable than when you are trying to find a job. Landing a new job means forming a relationship that will have a substantial impact on your life. The majority of your waking hours will be spent there, a hefty percentage of your physical and mental abilities will be applied to its endeavors, the money that supports the rest of your life activities will flow from there, and the time you spend there will be part of your path through life toward the goal of whatever your eventual success will be. It's a little like marrying an elephant: You must trust them enough to climb into their back pocket, but you can only hope that they don't forget you are there and sit down on you. The wrong choice could push you off the success track. An environment that stifles creativity and growth could hold you back from reaching your full potential. A bad relationship could burn valuable bridges or create an indelible blot on your work history (business doesn't believe in no-fault divorce, and elephants have long memories). It's a process fraught with risk and reward, and even the most talented and in-demand candidates feel vulnerable.

In the days before hypertransparency, the hiring process could be described as a carefully orchestrated dance between company and recruit, each trying to control and mete out information about themselves in a way that achieved their desired outcome. Interviewees would construct an image of themselves on paper in the form of a resume, and then dress themselves up and put their best face forward, highlighting their strengths while hoping that their weaknesses were well hidden. Many simply make things up. A recent *New York Times* Job Market research team study indicates that an astounding 89 percent of job seekers fudge their resumes. Typical embellishments include exaggerated job responsibilities, falsified employment dates, and manufactured reasons for leaving a former employer.[37] According to a recent article in *Time* magazine, InfoLink Screening Services, a company that performs background checks on potential hires, estimates that 14 percent of applicants lie about their education. Organizations, in turn, would do their own dance, presenting their greatest successes and painting a picture they hope will seduce the recruit.[38]

These sorts of common obfuscations no longer fly in a world where almost everything you say can be easily verified. Information technology has driven down the cost of uncovering applicant fabrications to almost nothing. Fully 96 percent of businesses now routinely perform background checks on potential employees. The third-party screening industry, just a handful of firms in the mid-1990s, in 2007 numbers around 700 companies doing $2 billion worth of business per year. On the other side of the coin, almost any candidate can search blogs and message boards and chat rooms, look deep within an organization, and gain accurate information about not only its prospects, but what it is like to work there day to day.

Success in any business relationship flows from the alignment of the parties involved. The more closely an organization and recruit share the same vision for the future, the more productive and fulfilling that relationship will be. In the new, more vulnerable world of business, where innovation and growth spring from the leadership of every stakeholder, achieving synchronicity, alignment, and common goals can cement a relationship that creates enormous value for both parties. So let us ask ourselves a question: On what vision can we truly align? Job description? Salary? Benefits? Production goals? Can we truly align in a way that inspires us to achieve at our highest levels on the basis of these measures of success?

Paradoxically, *success* is the worst possible answer. People who seek their next job on the basis of these external measures stay in a company's foxhole only as long as their career goals and aspirations stay in line with what's happening to the company. Their alignment is coincidental, not deep. They continue to work hard for the company's mission only as long as the mission works for their resume. Success, in this way, is a WHAT, and in any business journey, the WHATS will change. If, though, you see your career decisions as fueled by the desire to build a legacy, to construct and provide values to others—in short, to do something *significant*—then you begin to open the doors to the possibility of a deeper form of alignment, alignment on HOW. People and companies align on values, on the HOWS of pursuing a goal, not on personal success or the success of the effort. Values are inspirational, and last long after short-term WHATS expire. Long-term alignment can best be achieved when individual and organization align and mutually embrace the HOWS that drive the enterprise. According to a Watson Wyatt Worldwide WorkUSA study, companies whose employees understand and embrace the corporate mission, goals, and values enjoy a 29 percent greater return than other firms.[39]

That's the paradox of success. You can achieve it only by pursuing something greater: *significance.*

If thriving in the workplace flows from close alignment with the HOWS of the organization you work for, then you must bring yourself to the table in a way that lets them see who you truly are. At his Harvard interview, Sig understood instinctively what most of us need to learn: interpersonal transparency is the best way to present yourself authentically to the world. Sig won that place in their program in part because at the moment of truth, he was able to present himself transparently. His honesty allowed Harvard to see the whole person, a person of confidence and personal integrity, despite the fact that his grades were so-so by their standards. I've personally interviewed dozens of high-level candidates for positions at LRN, and I often ask people to share with me something they consider a weakness. Too many times, I hear something like "I care too much" or "I'm a workaholic," pat interview answers that are designed to be strengths masquerading as weaknesses. Seldom do I hear an honest appraisal of skills that need improving. When I do, it makes an impression. In our transparent age, there has never been a better time to resist the pressure to cut corners and shade the truth, not only because you will probably be caught, but because transparency is now understood as the way to accountability, strength, and mutual understanding. You no longer need to have a Master of the Universe costume on. Trying to be Superman, or all things to all people, no longer defines strength. Hiding weakness, like controlling information, swims against the current of business in a transparent age.

There has never been a better time to turn your weaknesses into strengths, like Sig did, because strength now comes with this type of vulnerability. Instead of puffing yourself up in an interview or trying to be something you are not, what if you say, "I'm actually not so good at these two things, but I am pretty good at these other two things." Are you more likely to get a job at that company? Employers are looking for skill sets, yes, but more importantly they are looking for someone who can align with their goals. Yvon Chouinard, the founder of Patagonia, a leading values-based company, said in a recent interview on NPR's *Marketplace*, "When we hire employees, we look for a passion. That passion tells me that they're alive, and there is potential there."[40] As information-based job skills become increasingly transferable between industries and job descriptions, companies looking for the best talent put far less emphasis on specific expertise—a candidates WHATS—and far more on their HOWS. A potential employer, hearing you being candid, thinks, "Wow, this candidate really seems to know herself and what she can bring to the table. I can work with someone who is self-aware."

SIG, DON'T ZAG

It is no longer possible to make and sustain a Wave by telling the people sitting next to you that you'll pay them to participate, telling the people two rows back that you think it will help the team win, and telling the little guy in front of you that you'll punch him if he doesn't stand up. The free flow of information creates a dangerous playing field for those whose game is to shade the truth. When people are connected—when they can share notes and communicate horizontally among themselves—the ability to spin and manipulate information disappears. Co-workers, customers, suppliers, and strategic partners are all sitting in the same stadium with you, integrally connected. Information becomes powerful when you get everybody on the same page with you, and it is the *most* powerful thing if you spread a consistent message to more and more people. The only way to make that powerful Wave that starts in one place and then flows throughout the stadium in a self-sustaining way is to get everyone you can reach directly aligned in a common goal. In a horizontal, connected world nothing achieves alignment and common purpose faster then active transparency. In fact, without it, they are almost impossible to achieve.

Transparency in its active form has a remarkable effect on people. It calls them out to meet you on the plane of openness, it speeds and encourages trust and collaboration, and—here's the surprising part—it is incredibly disarming. I'm talking about something greater than just telling the truth. Rather, the new conditions of the world can become a competitive edge if you aggressively embrace transparency in its verb form, *to be transparent.* If business is no longer war, then you need to practice skills that take the war out of business. That's what makes active transparency so effective. As we have seen, active vulnerability with others creates the conditions in which they can be vulnerable with you, and trust creates trust, on a biological and an organizational level, with mutually beneficial results. Vulnerability, in this way, is actually strength.

Last year, I had a "Sig moment." I was having a business dinner with Alan Spoon, a managing general partner of Polaris Venture Partners, a venture capital firm that invests in growth companies around the world, and former president of the Washington Post Company. He was interested in investing in LRN, and I was interested in him becoming part of the team. During the meal, Alan asked me frankly what my board thought of a certain aspect of my performance. Without hesitation (thank you, Sig!) I found myself saying, "I think they'd give me a pretty low grade; I don't know—C-minus."

He was clearly very surprised.

I didn't tell him that because he would have found me out; I was up-front with him because I was trying to inspire him to join in with me, to see that I understood the work ahead and could be honest about what's working and what's not. I employed the power of transparency toward creating a more intimate collaboration, toward getting aligned faster. Any truth I shaded was going to be something we'd have to talk about later, something that would undermine the trust in our future dealings, and something that would stifle any inspiration for him to be part of what I'm trying to do—ever. I could have let him take six months to drill down to the truth, but by just putting it out there I extended a powerful invitation. This worked to my advantage in the long term.

Some months later, Alan was at a meeting also attended by some members of my board. He called me soon after. He had indeed quizzed them about the very subject that I had opened up to him about, he told me, and was even more impressed with my transparency as a result. The board was less critical of me that I was. Now, you can imagine someone playing games with this. The Machiavellian schemer in us could say, "Set him up. Tell him something negative because you know he'll get something rosy when he checks." But trust me on this: *You don't want to do the right thing for the wrong reasons.* It will inevitably backfire later. People sense when you are trying to game them or the system, and they react with suspicion. The power in this sort of candor lies precisely in its guilelessness. You can imagine how much more negatively someone will react if they've been lulled into a sense of security and trust by guile and subterfuge. From that place, there is no going back. "Fool me once, shame on you," the old maxim goes. "Fool me twice, shame on me." To tell a potential investor "You know, the board would give me a low grade on that" is a dark point to make. But when you're aware of the power of honesty and transparency, you get inspired to be more honest.

I had an even more powerful reason to take off my Master of the Universe suit and open up to Alan. Vulnerability creates true opportunities for deep collaboration, a much more profitable relationship than just making money. Being transparent with him created a moment that made it clear that I thought Alan was more valuable than the money he could potentially invest. After all, in the same way I want my journey and the journey of LRN to be more significant than just our bottom line, Alan wants to be more than just a money man. The opening I extended allowed him to see an opportunity to pursue his own journey of significance, to share his knowledge and wisdom in a more substantive way. Instead of just showing him a bright shiny wheel, I showed myself as a gear, with powerful teeth but also with spaces into which he could intermesh. My transparency gave him a vision of what we could accomplish together in one machine, to create an intimate collaboration that had the potential to set off an upward spiral of meaningful endeavor. Not long after, Alan and Polaris did invest in LRN, and I asked him to sit on our corporate board, where he is now an integral part of who we are.

What does it mean to be truthful? To be open? To act from principle rather than for a desired effect? For one thing, it's simpler. As Mark Twain once wrote, "If you tell the truth you don't have to remember anything."[41] More importantly, in a world accustomed to falsehood and deception, in which daily we receive hundreds of commercial messages inveigling us to one act or another, transparency and forthrightness can be tremendously refreshing. No one can copy your HOWs, and within the wide spectrum of human behavior, the HOW of active interpersonal transparency can become a powerful differentiator.

DOING TRANSPARENCY

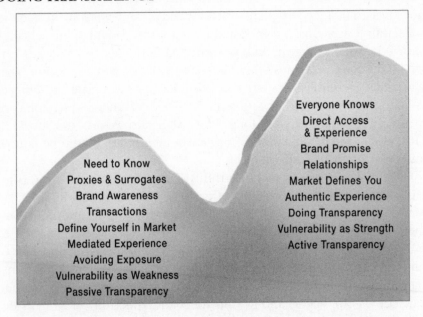

Need to Know
Proxies & Surrogates
Brand Awareness
Transactions
Define Yourself in Market
Mediated Experience
Avoiding Exposure
Vulnerability as Weakness
Passive Transparency

Everyone Knows
Direct Access
& Experience
Brand Promise
Relationships
Market Defines You
Authentic Experience
Doing Transparency
Vulnerability as Strength
Active Transparency

The Certainty Gap does not just describe a condition of the world; it also describes our relationship with those around us in business. There is a Certainty Gap between people, too. Business relationships are formal relationships, and just like companies use programs or advertising as formal layers between themselves and their market, people rely on personal surrogates and proxies in their dealings with others each day. When a buyer in a negotiation tells a potential vendor, "We're talking to your competitors," when it isn't true, the buyer is using the illusion of false action to secure a better price. When a boss says, "Get it to me by four o'clock," without sharing the reasons and benefits of the action, the boss is relying on the proxy of his or her position to get things done. When the world is opaque and you can't see beyond people's personal proxies, there is a Certainty Gap in your interactions with them. But when active transparency is in the room and people show you what's behind the curtain, it raises the floor, the Gap is smaller, and the conditions that breed the trust you need to fill it rush in. The conditions of general uncertainty in the world make transparency—both technological when you can turn it to your favor and interpersonal when you can bring it to the table—into one of the most powerful HOWS there is.

8

Trust

*For it is mutual trust, even more than mutual interest
that holds human associations together. Our friends
seldom profit us but they make us feel safe.*
—H. L. Mencken

few years ago, in the early days of the blogging phenomenon, a
New York–based web designer named Jason Kottke told a fascinating story on his blog, Kottke.org, about his experience with a
coffee-and-doughnuts street vendor he called Ralph.

"I stepped up to the window, ordered a glazed donut (75 cents),"
Kottke writes, "and when he handed it to me, I handed a dollar bill
back through the window. Ralph motioned to the pile of change scattered on the counter and hurried on to the next customer, yelling 'Next!'
over my shoulder. I put the bill down and grabbed a quarter from the
pile." Kottke was intrigued by this behavior, so he decided to investigate. "I walked a few steps away and turned around to watch the interaction between this business and its customers. For five minutes,
everyone either threw down exact change or made their own change
without any notice from Ralph; he was just too busy pouring coffee or
retrieving crullers to pay any attention to the money situation."[1]

As he observed and considered what may be gained or lost by this unusual policy, Kottke noticed that Ralph was serving an extraordinary number of customers. To confirm this suspicion, he went and watched two other similar vendors nearby. On average, both spent twice as much time with each customer and served half as many in a given time period.

Kottke is no economist, but it was immediately apparent to him "that Ralph trusts his customers, and that they both appreciate and return that sense of trust (I know I do)." He also noticed something that often eludes us. "When an environment of trust is created," he writes, "good things start happening. Ralph can serve twice as many customers. People get their coffee in half the time. Due to this time-saving, people become regulars. Regulars provide Ralph's business with stability, a good reputation, and with customers who have an interest in making correct change (to keep the line moving and keep Ralph in business). Lots of customers who make correct change increase Ralph's profit margin. Etc. Etc."

Kottke observed, in a firsthand anecdotal way, a quantification of trust in action. Because Ralph trusts his customers to make honest change, he is able to serve far more of them than his competitors serve. In economic terms, Ralph reduced his transaction costs by substituting trust for the labor of making change. A cost-benefit analysis would probably reveal that what he loses in dishonesty or error he more than makes up for in gross sales volume. Additionally, although increased volume results in less of the person-to-person service time that you would suspect is necessary to build customer loyalty, Ralph's customer loyalty seems anecdotally to have increased. The introduction of trust had an unintended consequence for his business: It made customers more likely to get their daily doughnut fix from him rather than his competitor down the block.

Trust is a funny thing, one of those soft things that we often rush by. What's not so funny is how often it lies at the center of our challenges and opportunities. "Trust is like the air we breathe," Warren Buffett said. "When it's present, nobody really notices. But when it's absent, everybody notices."[2] That is because trust allows us to function in times of uncertainty. When the Certainty Gap—that space between the unpredictable nature of the world and our ideal vision of stability—grows, we look for something to fill it. That something is *trust*. Trust calms the fears that uncertainty breeds. In times of high uncertainty, therefore, we pay more attention to the source of trust: human conduct—HOW we do what we do. Trust becomes, more vitally than ever, the currency of human exchange.

Business has long known about the benefits of trust, but absent any real metrics or data found itself at a loss to be able to do anything about it. Similarly, we as individuals innately seek trusting environments and trusting relationships in order to enrich our lives, although we often don't give much conscious thought to how to create them.

THE SOFT MADE HARD

We have two ways of calculating the value of trust: subjectively (how it makes us feel) and objectively (in dollars and cents). Subjectively, almost all of us would rather live and work in a world where the Certainty Gap is filled with trust, predictability is high, and we feel safe and secure. So we accept prima facie that trust plays an important role in the way we live our lives. Trust makes us feel safe. It allows us to function and thrive in an uncertain world. To fully understand the value of trust in business, however, we must begin to quantify it objectively, to move it from the realm of feelings to the realm of observable benefit. Trust, for instance, allows us to rely on each other, to divide up labor and form teams knowing that each will do his or her part, and to share confidences with others. Without trust, how could you send a confidential strategy e-mail to a partner and know that it will remain confidential? Business, for its part, has long suspected that trust could, in fact, be objectively quantified, but it is only recently that researchers have done so. Their findings reveal a startling truth: Trust, to use an old cliché, makes dollars *and* sense.

In a groundbreaking 2002 study, Professors Jeffrey H. Dyer of the Marriott School at Brigham Young University and Wujin Chu of the College of Business Administration at Seoul National University proved empirically what the blogger Jason Kottke observed on the streets of New York. Dyer and Chu surveyed almost 350 buyer/supplier relationships involving eight automakers in the United States, Japan, and South Korea and found a direct, and dramatic, relationship between trust and transaction costs. The least trusted buyer incurred procurement costs *six times* higher than the most trusted: same parts; same sorts of transactions; *six times more expensive*. These additional costs came from the added resources that went into the selection, negotiation, and compliance costs of executing deals. Dyer and Chu point to Nobel Prize–winning economist Douglass C. North's findings that these sorts of transaction costs account for more than a third of all business activity They also found, perhaps to no surprise, that the least trusted companies were also the least profitable.

But Dyer and Chu didn't stop there. They also studied the relationship between trust and certain value-creating behaviors, specifically the willingness to share critical information among business partners. Though it was unclear, in a chicken-or-the-egg sort of way, which led to which, their data clearly demonstrates that trust extended by one company to another increases value-creating behaviors, like information sharing, which, in turn, leads to higher levels of trust. One executive they interviewed put it like this:

> We are much more likely to bring a new product design to [high-trust Automaker A] than [low-trust Automaker B]. The reason is simple. [Automaker B] has been known to take our proprietary blueprints and send them to our competitors to see if they can make the part at lower cost. They claim they are simply trying to maintain competitive bidding. But because we can't trust them to treat us fairly, we don't take our new designs to them. We take them to [Automaker A] where we have a more secure long-term future.[3]

Like the oxytocin response between one person and another, trust between companies leads to more trust. It sets off an upward spiral of cooperative, value-creating behaviors. "This phenomenon makes trust unique as a governance mechanism," Dyer and Chu conclude, "because the investments that trading partners make to build trust often simultaneously create economic value (beyond minimizing transaction costs) in the relationship."

I was struck by these stories about transactions both small, like Ralph's doughnuts, and medium-sized, like Dyer and Chu's study, but I wondered if the same principles applied at the highest levels of business and the biggest deals. This reminded me of a story told to me by Mike Fricklas, executive vice president, general counsel, and secretary of Viacom Inc., one of the largest media conglomerates in the world, when we met recently at Viacom's headquarters in Times Square. After a successful career in mergers and acquisitions (M&A), Fricklas came to Viacom to negotiate their purchase of Paramount and Blockbuster, two of the biggest media deals of the 1990s. Since then, he has played a central role in Viacom's growth and acquisitions. Mike and I have worked together for many years, and I have found him not just a first-rate lawyer, but a true adviser to those at the highest levels of business. So I asked him how trust factors into the work he does every day. "Transaction costs are not such a big deal in large commercial transactions," he told me. "What's much more strategic is if people want to do business with you in the first place."[4] When we spoke, Mike confessed that Viacom was currently pursuing a strategy of modest-sized acquisitions, but pointed out what he felt was a significant advantage that Viacom, by virtue of its square dealing, enjoyed. "People trust us enough that at the beginning of the relationship, when we first reach out to potential acquisition targets, we're getting a series of exclusivities—in effect, 'trust me's'—where companies are taking themselves off the market because they want to move forward with us."

This is an example of how existing trust can fill the Certainty Gap between two companies, especially when one is the target of an acquisition and may have a lot to lose. Obviously, having an exclusive, first-look opportunity to transact business represents a significant advantage in the marketplace. But it is another soft, anecdotal example of the value of trust, and I wanted to know if Mike could make a direct connection between trust and profit at the highest levels of business. "Absolutely," he immediately replied. "In economic terms, trust is important to the cost of capital. When you need money to finance a large deal, you often can't clue the market in to the exact specifics of your business plan without compromising your competitive advantage. So the market relies on trust and your past consistency. With trust, they lend you money at a lower rate. So a multibillion-dollar transaction will close at a lower price when you are a preferred partner, rather than going to the stock market and paying with the same green as everyone else."

This same relationship of trust to economic advantage scales up to the macroeconomic level, too. Studies show that economic growth and prosperity within a given society require a certain minimum level of generalized trust. Without it, investment ceases and economic activity stalls. Francis Fukuyama first hypothesized this in his seminal 1995 book, *Trust*. The wealth of a nation, "as well as its ability to compete," he wrote, "is conditioned by . . . the level of trust in the society."[5] Neuroeconomist Paul Zak extended Fukuyama's thoughts about the relation of trust to general prosperity. "Our analysis also shows that if trust is sufficiently low," Zak reports in the *Journal of Financial Transformation*, "then the investment rate will be so low that income will stagnate or even decline."[6] Economists call this a "poverty trap," and once a society has slipped into one, a downward spiral of trust deficiency results. "We show that the primary reason for a poverty trap is ineffective legal structures that result in low levels of generalized trust, and therefore little investment," says Zak. "Further, the threshold level of trust necessary for positive economic growth is increasing in per capita income; that is, the poorer a country currently is, the more trust is required to generate sufficient investment to raise living standards. This makes the low-trust poverty trap difficult to escape from." In other words, when the societal Certainty Gap gets too large, it becomes almost impossible to fill.

Laws do many things well, and one is to create the reasonable amounts of generalized trust necessary for economic prosperity. This is one of those "floors" I spoke about. Zak's research shows that general trust is high in Scandinavian and East Asian countries and low in South America, Africa, and the formerly communist countries. In a worldwide survey designed to measure the general ability of any two random people to trust each other in a society, only 3 percent of those surveyed in Brazil and 5 percent in Peru say their compatriots are trustworthy, while 65 percent of Norwegians and 60 percent of Swedes believe this to be so. The United States comes in at 36 percent, down from 50 percent in 1990; the United Kingdom has been holding steady at 44 percent since the mid-1990s.

Zak also found direct, quantifiable relationships between trust and prosperity. Business investment in a given society directly mirrors levels of trust. Where general trust is high, the national rate of investment—gross investment divided by gross domestic product (GDP)—is commensurately high, and vice versa. The same direct relationship also exists between trust and GDP growth. For each 15 percent increase in the proportion of people who find others trustworthy, per capita income rises 1 percent. If trust in the United States grew from 36 percent to 51 percent, for example, the average income for every man, woman, and child would grow about $400 per year from the parallel rise in investment and job creation. That adds up to about $30,000 over the course of a working life.

There is something of a paradox in this marriage of trust and prosperity. Those who have misread Adam Smith's principles of reciprocal capitalism often clamor for truly unregulated, laissez-faire markets. They work under the illusion that, free of regulation, they could achieve anything they put their minds to. This is simply another form of rules-bound thinking: defining your ability to achieve in relation to regulatory constructs. But in fact, the certainty and predictability created by strong legal systems and regulatory apparatuses support achievement. Consider traffic signals as a metaphor. Traffic signals allow us to get around as speedily, efficiently, and safely as we can. They help to create a reasonable level of certainty that other drivers and pedestrians will behave in a predictable fashion. Like those free-market types, we all wish at one time or another while driving that the traffic laws did not apply to us. Occasionally, we even take the law into our own hands, so to speak, and choose to roll through a stop sign or exceed the speed limit in order to get where we're going faster. But interestingly, when law breaks down—for example, if there's a blackout and all the signals stop working—people do not suddenly go charging off at breakneck speed. Traffic, in fact, slows down. The absence of predictability makes everyone more cautious. People tend to prioritize safety over speed. In the absence of law, nobody enjoys driving because the risks suddenly start to weigh heavily against the rewards. The same holds true in the vastly less controllable sphere of human relations, and, by extension, in the marketplace. When we experience states of high uncertainty, everyone slows down, as does economic activity. Our circle of trust shrinks, as does our tendency to take risks, even, interestingly, if they may lead to greater rewards.

Dr. Peter Kollock, associate professor and vice chair of the department of sociology at the University of California at Los Angeles, conducted a study in the mid-1990s that demonstrated this. He set up a trading game where people traded goods in two different environments. In one environment (low uncertainty), participants knew the value of what they were trading, and in the other (high uncertainty), they did not. Kollock's study achieved two fascinating results: (1) people have a greater tendency to form interpersonal commitments in a high uncertainty environment, and (2) they tend to forgo potentially more profitable exchanges with untested partners in favor of trades with partners who have demonstrated their trustworthiness in previous transactions. In short, economic activity in times of high uncertainty slows down and traders become risk-averse.[7]

HOW HIGH IS THE CEILING?

If the Certainty Gap is the space between our ideal state of security, certainty, and predictability and the state that exists in the world, and the confluence of destabilizing factors in the world today has lowered the floor of certainty, what defines the ceiling of the Gap? What defines an ideal state of certainty?

Actually, it is a trick question, because I believe there is no ceiling. When we create sufficient trust to take risks, innovate, and progress within current global or market conditions, why stop there? Why not keep going? Security and certainty are not heights to be dreamed or attained, but rather something that spreads out around you horizontally. Picture an archery target sitting on a table, with you standing in the bull's-eye. Around you are circles and circles stretching out to the horizon. Each represents a trust gap to be filled—red, blue, green, white, and so on. The more rings of trust you can fill around you, the more secure you can be. The horizon is limited only by your imagination. Now take that same mental picture and instead of a target, imagine a football stadium with you standing in the center. All around you are the people you work with, play with, live with, and love. Instead of rings, imagine circles of connection, interpersonal synapses filled with trust, stretching out to the very lip of the stadium. The more powerfully connected you can be to this expansive mass of people, the more secure you can be, and, more importantly for your ability to thrive, the more Waves you can create throughout the stadium.

It is easy to draw and imagine pictures, but much more difficult for many of us to implement what they represent in daily life. Those who have had long and satisfying experiences with trusting environments can envision a very high level of certainty, while others, who have perhaps suffered in environments of betrayal and self-interested action, can imagine only distrust. But everyone has the ability to expand their vision of a trust-filled world. Like all journeys of knowledge, we can't just leap from the Hill of B to the Hill of A; we must build our ability to imagine trust circles incrementally, one relationship at a time, one group at a time. Sometimes we will struggle in the Valley of C, where we have trusted the wrong people and been betrayed. But we can push out from where we are, no matter what our previous experience with trust has been, to reach the furthest limits of possibility. Perhaps you can accomplish one ring of your target, perhaps three. But when you get to the edge of one ring, and only when you get there, will you suddenly see the next ring to fill. Like climbing a mountain, you must crest one peak before you can see the next. Trust isn't a switch you can turn on and off at will, but the power to envision it is strength you can build over time.

GOING ON A TRIP

So, what do we know about trust? We know that it fills the brain with powerful chemicals that strengthen interpersonal bonds by reducing fear. We know it fills the Certainty Gap, thereby defeating the arresting forces of insecurity and timidity that make us go slower when—to really thrive—we need to go faster. We know that trust begets trust between individuals and between corporations and that it builds more trust over time and repetition. We know it stimulates an upward spiral of cooperation and value. We know that trust fuels Waves that bring people and organizations closer together. It gives back as much energy as it takes to create, if not more, and enables risk-taking behavior. In short, we know that trust is active and propulsive; it is nothing short of inspirational.

It takes a journey to envision and learn about trust, but trust also propels its own trip. No book like this would be complete without an inspirational acronym and, not to be pedestrian, I'd like to offer just one that I have found encapsulates a lot of these ideas about trust:

> **TRIP**
> **T**rust
> **R**isk
> **I**nnovation
> **P**rogress

Trust

The "T" in TRIP stands for trust. If we have just met, and I choose to extend you my trust, who is virtuous: Is it me for trusting you or you for being trustworthy? Aristotle said that the one who extends trust is virtuous. When I trust you (even though I've just met you), I'm giving you the power to let me down or do right by me. I'm the one who's vulnerable, who takes the risk. Trusting, in a sense, means giving something away and ceding power to others, an essential step in achieving the outward focus needed in a hyperconnected world. Trust empowers others but, because it is a virtue, it also empowers one's self. Trust at its very essence involves risk and provides the engine that powers this TRIP.

Risk

"R" stands for risk. We know that in business and in life, risk is directly proportional to return. "No risk, no reward," says the cliché. The more rational risk you can take, the more you can accomplish. In environments of high uncertainty, forming trust circles becomes very difficult. Peter Kollack's study demonstrated this clearly. We look closer to home for partners and limit our exposure to those with whom we've done business in the past, those to whom we are related, or those with whom we can reinforce trust ties with through personal and direct means like reputation and recommendations. Without trust, the Certainty Gap looks like the Grand Canyon. We drive slower, act more cautiously, shrink our circle of friends and associates, and generally default to more conservative impulses. When there is trust in the room, however, all of these tendencies are reversed. We are secure and so can act boldly. We feel free to invent a new process, for example, without being scared our boss will be angry with us for messing with the status quo. We experiment more, confident that even if we fail we will have learned something valuable and improved. If the very nature of trust involves risk, then the more trust there is, the more risks we can take. Studies have shown that if teams have a lot of trust, they outperform teams that don't have trust.[8] If you trust people's vision for making a Wave, you'll stand up with them. If you don't trust it, you're going to keep eating your hot dog. To take risks, then, the Certainty Gap must be filled with trust.

Trust enables risk. If I were to stand you on a sandy beach and ask you to jump as high as you could, try as you might you would not get very high. If I put you on a hard surface, like a basketball court, you could jump higher. It's difficult to jump off of sand. That's why we respect beach volleyball players; we know intuitively that their jumps are more difficult. In building construction, the more solid the foundation, the more stories that can be added to a skyscraper. The same holds true for leaps forward in business: The firmer the ground is, the more innovation can spring forth. The dynamic relationships between living things—like colleagues, partners, or companies—are like the shifting sand on a beach. But trust creates solidity. It stabilizes relationships and creates the hard floor from which you can walk or leap. This soft thing called trust is actually the hardest thing of all. When it's there, it allows you to take a risk, to leap higher.

Innovation

In a hypertransparent, hyperconnected world, we are more exposed and discoverable. Opening up and letting information flow inherently involves more risk, less control, and increased vulnerability, so current conditions require us to be more comfortable in high-risk environments. A horizontal world, where teams collaborate across space and specialty, is unbounded and much more diverse. To function well—to take risks and reap rewards—you must have enough trust circles around you to allow you to work laterally in many directions at once. You've got to get good at heterogeneity, at developing the kinds of strong synapses that allow you to cover a much larger geography of interrelationships.

In a trusting environment, everyone feels emboldened to take more risks. They challenge the system more, they solve problems, and they don't stay in small boxes afraid to venture into new territory for fear of criticism (by bosses or colleagues). Innovation flows from this creative spirit. Business is all about constantly pushing the edge. It asks us daily to go to uncharted territory; to take more chances; to leap higher or run faster; to create innovative new strategies, products, and systems; and ultimately to think more deeply than our competitors. To reap these sorts of rewards, we must take risks and create the environment in which others can do so as well. Some bright marketing people, comfortable in their high-risk environment, conceived of viral marketing. What could be more risky or counterintuitive than to expose a brand to the manipulations of consumers? Leaps of consciousness like this happen only in environments of trust.

Resting in the status quo leads to stasis and decline. For all great innovations, someone took a risk. They risked capital; they risked their energy; they risked their opportunity cost; and most important, they risked failure. We can't innovate without the belief that we can succeed, the confidence that others will be there to help us on the journey, and the security that we will not be punished if we fail to reach our goal. A fast-moving world demands innovation for long-term success. Leaders who want employees to take risks must create an environment where risk can flourish, a trust-based environment. Trust enables risk, and risk leads to innovation, the "I" in TRIP.

Progress

What happens if you innovate? You create progress. "P" stands for progress—not just progress in goods, services, and profit, but also personal progress. We toil each day for the satisfaction when we achieve great things, when we help the team, and when we make others' lives better. Progress is, in this way, intimately related to the pursuit of significance. We go on TRIPs because we want to accomplish big things. We go on TRIPs because we want to solve real problems and because we want to create lasting value. We also progress when we take risks and succeed. When we struggle through the Valley of C and climb the Hill of A, we know that we have grown as a person, that we are stronger and more capable, and, most important, that we have the strength to set out on the next journey, to an even higher hill, and beyond. And isn't that what the journey is about?

TRIPPING

Trust enables risk, which leads to innovation, which creates progress. TRIP. This is the basic formula for thriving in the hyperconnected, hypertransparent world of twenty-first-century business.

There's more to this TRIP, as well. The "T" also stands for transparency, which creates trust. Interpersonal transparency is a necessary power to thrive in a connected world, and not coincidentally, it creates trust. I was discussing trust with Roger Fine, former vice president and general counsel of Johnson & Johnson (J&J). I had the privilege of working closely with Roger during his time at J&J, and learned a great deal from him. When we spoke, he zeroed right in on this. "The main way people create trust," he said, "is by being transparent and being honest. Transparency lets people know when you are telling them the truth, the whole truth, and nothing but the truth, and they know that in a minute. That's why we believe in the jury system. Jurors can sniff that out. All it takes is a lot of common sense and some basic human instinct; you know when somebody is putting you on and when somebody is really being transparent with you. We all feel that."[9] When you are employing the power of active transparency, people feel that you've told them everything—the bad with the good, the negative with the positive—and that you are the kind of person who wouldn't lie to them and hide something that was against your own interest. So trust and transparency go hand in hand.

"R" also stands for reputation. Reputation both derives from trust and engenders it. We'll discuss its importance more in Chapter 9.

Trust also frees instinct, another "I." As humans, we have animal instincts, but unfortunately for our decision-making apparatus, most of our true biological animal instincts have either disappeared or become vestigial. What most people consider instincts are simply a complicated interweaving of experience, judgment, and sense perception that takes place in the synapses of the brain when faced with making a decision. When you are in a trust-filled situation, these synapses are strong. The various centers of your brain communicate seamlessly and rapidly, and you can then make split-second decisions that often pay off.

Athletes know this well. In golf, hitting your ball along a more aggressive line might get you to the hole in fewer strokes but also might lead you closer to hazards that can penalize you. When your swing is working well and you trust it, you feel more confident about taking such risks, so you swing away; you go for it. When you have less trust in your stroke, you take a safer line or shoot for the center of the green rather than for a flagstick tucked behind a bunker. The same principle applies to more reactive games like tennis or basketball, where the action happens so quickly that you often do not have time for considered thought before making a play. If you trust your stroke in tennis you are more likely to attempt a dangerous drop shot or a passing shot down the line. When the trust isn't there, you'll make a safer shot to keep the ball in play. All of these instinctual decisions happen in milliseconds because trust builds strong synapses, and these instinctual decisions can often be more powerful and successful than more considered ones. Trust creates the environment where instinct can thrive.

And finally, if you are always on this TRIP and you constantly progress, then "P" stands for perennial prosperity as well. You'll notice I did not say that "P" stands for profits. The pursuit of progress seldom flows from the pursuit of profit, but rather from the pursuit of creating something of value to others.

DOING TRUST

The $64 billion question (it used to be $64 million) of our time is how do we get this TRIP going? Where does it start? What's the Big Bang? We've already shown that it's not through rules, because rules can't inspire that type of certainty and risk taking. If not with rules, then with what?

The answer, of course, lies in the realm of HOW. We tend to trust people who get their HOWS right, people who are transparent, forthcoming, and open, and honest; who share credit and opportunity with us; and who communicate fully, build strong interpersonal synapses, and keep their promises. In short, people with integrity. They collaborate, they embrace, and they engage. If you want trust, you need to find people and companies that create circles of trust around themselves. Like the Olympic rings, the more interlocking circles within a stadium, the more Waves you can make there. We live in a time when trust is the currency of the age. Trust is more valuable than ever before, so you should produce a lot of it. Those who can engender and wield more trust will win.

Mike Fricklas knows that from experience. "In the late 1990s," Mike told me, "I was negotiating the terms of a major joint venture for Viacom. It involved the acquisition of a business from a major entertainment company in exchange for a stake in the venture. I was leading the team, and the deal had a number of moving pieces. The people on the other side were under a lot of pressure to get a transaction done, but between the time we negotiated the general deal and the time we were to close it, the valuations had moved. At the last minute, their negotiator came to me and said, 'We really need something more on this because the numbers have really moved dramatically.' We weren't prepared to renegotiate the price at that point because it wouldn't have worked for our shareholders."

"We had all the leverage, but were also under a lot of pressure to close, so the dynamic was tense. Someone on the other side of the table asked for a major price concession that I did not feel they were entitled to. The dynamic could easily have been somebody pounding away on the table and taking a hard line. I mean, in this sort of situation, you often see little more than efforts to assert every piece of obvious leverage that they have and not a view toward the bigger picture. But this guy had been really straight with us, and when you deal with someone like that, I am more inclined to say, 'You have been reasonable with me, so let's figure out a way to deal with your situation.' I came up with a creative way of adding a lever that would give him a certain degree of additional protection. It allowed him to report to his team the change he had achieved and made his people more comfortable. I didn't have to go back to my boss and tell him that the price was going to change, and, as it turned out, the protection we gave up didn't cost us anything in the end.

"A few years later," Mike continued, "I was negotiating the M&A side of a complicated deal involving a different Viacom asset to an entirely different company. Another Viacom team was negotiating a related but separate part of the deal. Across the table from our folks was that same guy I just told you about with whom I had done the deal years before. This negotiation, for a million complicated reasons, also got bogged down on some intractable point unacceptable to us, which I also felt was unreasonable. Because of my previous relationship with this other negotiator, I considered calling him directly, but instead decided to let our team take one more shot at it.

"Later that day, the team called me back. They had spoken to their counterpart, and in the course of the conversation told him that I thought his position was unreasonable. He immediately changed his mind. 'We'll do this for Mike,' they reported him saying. I ran into him at an industry event a few months later and thanked him."[10]

I told Mike what a terrific example of the currency value of trust this was, and he was extremely modest about it. "Having those good, trusting relationships dramatically facilitates your ability to get things done," he said. "My wife, with our children, always refers to a 'ladder of trust.'

You go up one rung at a time, but when you slip you come all the way back down to the bottom. I think there is a lot of truth in that for making deals as well. Once you catch someone not telling you the truth or not dealing fairly, then the trust element really disappears and it's hard to build back. Things get a lot more difficult from that point on."

Extensions of trust can occur both as conscious and as unconscious actions. Some people you meet just feel trustworthy to you, and at some level you choose to extend them trust without too much conscious thought. This is the trust that happens at what the neurobiologists call the amygdalic level, that complex interface of oxytocin, error detection, and decision making in your brain. You can become one of these sorts of people. On a one-to-one basis, you can conduct yourself in a way that activates what Paul Zak and others call social attachment mechanisms, behaviors that create physiological responses, release oxytocin, and increase trust. Meeting with people in person when the occasion is important, greeting them with a warm handshake, making frequent eye contact, sharing a meal together, and demonstrating concern for their family members and other passions all stimulate trust responses. As much as it may sound like a homily, science has shown us that caring and honest behaviors increase trustworthiness (note the *and honest* in that sentence; the unconscious brain senses false caring as quickly as it does true caring).

On a companywide level, unconscious trust responses can be activated by what business knows as morale-building programs. Lifestyle programs like on-site child care, flextime, team-building outings, exercise facilities, and family leave are more than just good public relations; they actually raise oxytocin levels in the bloodstream, increasing employees' trust and productiveness. Even something as unconventional as on-site massage therapy (which, by the way, has been used by such touchy-feely employers as the U.S. government)[11] is amazingly effective. Not only does massage send a message that the company cares, but it translates that caring into human touch, a powerful stimulator of oxytocin response.

Strengthening social attachments is just another way of building strong interpersonal synapses with others in your stadium. These sorts of behaviors work especially well with those with whom you make direct contact. But I believe these principles scale also to teams, business units, and companies as a whole. These larger gestures can help to carry your Wave throughout the stadium, even reaching those in the outfield whom you have never met and do not know.

(A point of clarification here: Despite the fact that we talk about "interorganizational trust," organizations can't actually manifest trust for each other. Trust flows from individuals. As part of their research, Dyer and Chu point out that a person can place trust in another person or in a group of individuals, such as a partner organization. But a group of people can also collectively hold a trusting orientation toward people in another organization; thus "interorganizational trust describes the extent to which there is a collectively held trust orientation" from one company to another. Although companies cannot extend trust per se, they can act consistently in such a way so as to earn an institutional trust, trust that exists independent of the personnel who might be there at the time.)[12]

As Mike Fricklas's wife reminds him, it's a long, hard fall off the ladder of trust. Trust is destroyed by the suspicion that any person, group of people, or organization is acting in its own narrow interests without regard for mutuality and mutual advantage. The choices you make, as an individual or an organization, send strong messages to the marketplace, and the marketplace responds in countless ways, both easily quantifiable and more ephemeral. Mike also shared with me that he has made it a fundamental part of his professional approach to get to know and build trust with the general counsels of the other big media companies. "Through those relationships," he said, "we've both resolved amicably differences of view that had come up between our companies and been successful promoting issues where there is a commonality of interest across our industry, like antipiracy efforts or new compensation rules."

TRUST IS THE DRUG

In mid-2006, Jeffrey B. Kindler was named chief executive officer and then later chairman of the board of pharmaceutical giant Pfizer Inc. after several years in which the company experienced subpar performance in rapidly changing market conditions. It's fair to say he inherited a company operating in a low-trust environment, with the popular public perception of "Big Pharma" linked almost entirely to "big profits." "I was at a play recently, and there was a line that got great laughs about people going to a charity function to provide philanthropy for a disease invented by the pharmaceutical industry," Jeff told me. "I mean, when you get to the point where popular humor and popular culture accept the premise that we actually sit around trying to invent diseases so that we can then invent treatments for those diseases and make money, you know, it is appalling."[13]

Kindler has long been recognized not only for his business acumen, but also for his leadership in the areas of pro bono legal services, diversity, and corporate social responsibility during his tenure at General Electric and McDonald's. The board's selection expressed a conviction that he could take the company in a new direction, make it more nimble, less bureaucratic, and more responsive to the needs of the market. In a sense they were looking for someone to restore the trust necessary to launch Pfizer on a TRIP. To his credit, Jeff has tackled this challenge head-on. In his first public communication upon taking over the company, he promised Pfizer would do nothing less than "transform virtually every aspect of how we do business."[14]

When we spoke, I asked Jeff how he was approaching the monumental task of restoring trust with Pfizer's stakeholders and the public at large. "The first step is to listen to people," he said. "I have spent an enormous proportion of my time since I got this job listening to employees, listening to customers, listening to investors, listening to analysts, even listening to the media. My first objective is to find out what is on their minds, what bothers them about the industry, what bothers them about the company, what is frustrating them, and whether we are serving appropriate objectives. I'm trying to fully understand the source of the mistrust. Then I am trying with my team to build into our plans, our activities, and our decision making ways in which we can be responsive to those concerns, large and small. How are we going to be more customer focused? How are we going to not just *tell* patients that we care about them, but *demonstrate* that we care about them in actions that they will find credible?"

Though Jeff's challenge is to turn around a very large ship sailing in stormy seas, his journey is similar to the challenge any team of any size faces when trying to get a TRIP going, and it begins by knowing who you are and where you want to go. Listening—the first crucial step toward gaining trust—helped him establish stronger connections with those he hoped to lead. By showing that he understood and embraced the challenges everyone knew were ahead, he was able to begin the process of building strong synapses throughout the organization. Listening truly earned him the benefit of the doubt, the first step in fertilizing the soil in which true change can grow. He was then able to begin to express his vision for a new Pfizer, one dedicated to a highly focused and highly energized commitment to serving others. "I am constantly looking for ways to represent, stand for, and behave at all times consistent with the fundamental values that define who we are, culturally and otherwise," he said.

I asked Jeff for a specific example of how he planned to restore the market's trust in Pfizer. "Although the patients are the ultimate consumers of our drugs, a lot, if not most, of our products around the world are being paid for, to a large extent, by governments, insurance companies, or other commercial entities," he offered. "In the past, in situations where we had a really great drug, we could almost impose upon those payers a demand that they reimburse the product and make it available to the patients. We do not live in that world anymore, and so we must change. We have to be thinking about the payers not as adversaries that we have to argue with and push to solve our problems and address our business issues, but as partners. We need to understand what is driving their concerns and their issues to emerge with a win-win solution. Over time—not overnight, but over time—if we can demonstrate that we are open to that, that we are listening, that we care about their concerns, and that we are taking steps to respond to them, then I think we will engender trust."

What Jeff is attempting is pretty easy for leaders to say, but something altogether different to achieve. The pharmaceutical industry has many bridges to repair. Changing the way people perceive you and rebuilding trust doesn't happen overnight. It requires self-reflection and hard work, struggles in the Valley of C necessary to build a team that can really thrive in a hyperconnected world. Jeff's honesty in the face of this challenge is a powerful first step. "It is a long process," Jeff admitted. "It takes wrestling and struggling to change these behaviors, but if you really start to go to this gym and build muscle in this area, you will have much more mass around you, and you will outperform your competitors. A cornerstone of trust is credibility. If people think that either you do not acknowledge reality or you acknowledge it but don't admit to it, why would they trust you? You are saying things that are inconsistent with the reality that they see. So, obviously, an essential element of credibility—if not the entire essence of credibility—is being honest and open and realistic about things."

Keeping promises, acting in a consistent manner, building upon and extending the work of your predecessors (frequent shifts in policy and procedure create uncertainty in others and undermine the trust response), acting from principle, thinking in values terms and putting those values into operation, and pursuing activities of significance are all larger ideas that inspire trust in others. Filling the interpersonal synapses between you and others with trust-producing conduct will increase the profitability of those relationships, in both human and financial terms.

TRUST, BUT VERIFY

James Paul Lewis Jr. was a trusted man. A devout Mormon and churchgoer, for nearly 20 years he ran Financial Advisory Consultants (FAC) from its offices in Orange County, California, where he administered two investment funds aimed at those looking for a high rate of return on their retirement funds. His promotional material promised up to a 40 percent annual return in FAC's Growth Fund and an 18 percent annual return in its Income Fund. According to reports, Lewis "did not accept investments from anyone unless an existing investor referred them," and most of those investors were church members and clergy.[15] He ran a trust-based business, and people trusted him despite the fact that he was never very specific about what his funds were investing in to make such spectacular returns. If asked, Lewis would make vague references to distressed businesses, leased medical equipment, insurance premium financing, and other business activities. Investors received newsletters and monthly statements, many of which showed the returns that he promised. Over nearly 20 years, FAC raised about $311 million, of which exactly none was ever invested in any fund. The funds, quite simply, didn't exist.

Before he was apprehended in 2004 and sentenced to 30 years in prison, James Paul Lewis Jr., a trusted man, ran perhaps the biggest Ponzi scheme in U.S. financial history. He used the money he raised from new investors to pay returns to old ones, meanwhile skimming millions of dollars for personal use, including supporting the usual assortment of wives and girlfriends. Over the years, Lewis defrauded as many as 5,000 investors of the money they had earmarked for their retirement. (Ironically, he was eventually discovered by Barry Minkow, who had spent seven years in prison for defrauding investors as owner of ZZZZ Best carpet-cleaning company. Minkow is now a private fraud investigator.)[16]

Extending trust is a rational act. To whom you extend it, under what circumstances, and to what end are questions resolved in the complicated interstices where certainty, predictability, behavior, and opportunity meet. Sometimes the choice is made consciously, as an analytical calculation: "This guy has treated me fairly and conducted himself honestly, so I'll trust him." "This woman's reputation is impeccable. Surely, she can be trusted." Sometimes the decision comes from deep, unconscious triggers, a feeling that a certain person can be trusted. The oxytocin fires in your brain, and a doorway to trust opens. But even these unconscious beginnings must be backed up by a procession of trustworthy actions, or they, too, fall off the ladder.

Ponzi schemes, like all con jobs, thrive on trust. Trust is such a powerful thing that it fuels the worst in us as well as it does the best. The world is a dangerous place, and business, even in the best of times, can be rough as well. I don't want you to think me a Pollyanna, suggesting that if we all hold hands, trust one another, and sing Kumbaya that all will be well. Of course it will not. There will always be people out to game the system, abuse your trust, and operate out of limited self-interest and opportunism, and they often think that those who do not are either naive, fools, or both. We must be vigilant and wise, and perform our due diligence at all times and in all situations.

Although Ralph the doughnut guy ran a trust-based business, his daily presence acted as a built-in deterrent against wide-scale cheating and abuse. Within large organizations, everyone must be vigilant for incidences of fraud and abuse of trust, because no matter how much trust you extend, there will always be some small percentage of those who will cheat or game the system. "Somebody is doing something today at Berkshire that you and I would be unhappy about if we knew of it," Warren Buffett wrote in a 2006 memo to the Berkshire Hathaway's top managers. "That's inevitable. . . . But we can have a huge effect in minimizing such activities by jumping on anything immediately when there is the slightest odor of impropriety. Your attitude on such matters, expressed by behavior as well as words, will be the most important factor in how the culture of your business develops. And culture, more than rule books, determines how an organization behaves."[17] It would be impractical to run a large business without some sort of monitoring and compliance system, for instance; you would have anarchy. But how you maintain an environment of trust while catching and punishing malfeasance makes a difference. That's what the old Russian proverb, *doveryai, no proveryai*, "trust, but verify," is all about. (Although President Ronald Reagan made this something of a catchphrase that he applied regularly to diplomatic relations with the former Soviet Union, writer Damon Runyon is widely credited with first using it in English.)

At first blush, "trust, but verify" seems oxymoronic. If you are verifying, doesn't that mean you've stopped trusting? Let's work through an example using employee expense accounts and to see if this is true. (Not all of us make this kind of decision, but it provides a good example for anyone working within a team.) You are the head of the stadium, you have invited people in, and you've said, "In this stadium, I trust you." Then you institute an expense reporting system that relies on rules (forms, manager approvals, accounting sign-off, lots of hoops to jump through). As we have discussed, these rules create all the predictable antirule responses; people feel externally monitored, and respond accordingly. You words say one thing—"We trust you"—but your program says another.

If you take those rules away, however, don't you get anarchy? Actually, no. If you say to your employees, "Fill out your forms honestly and you will be reimbursed," your value-based statement sends a powerful message. "We are on this journey together," it says, "and we get there faster and more profitably when we work together and trust one another." By inserting trust into the relationship, you can trigger all the responses in others that we know lead to cost-saving efficiencies: less transactional costs to process reimbursements, higher voluntary compliance, and the social bonding that results in greater alignment. In doughnut terms, you let them make their own change. You even get increased internal vigilance, as those who see the benefits of the approach watch out for those who might jeopardize a good thing.

But what of the shirker, the cheater, the one looking to get over on you for a few extra bucks? You can't rationally assume that no one will cheat, so how do you protect against fraud? You verify randomly. Everyone knows that you have a vested interest in how money is being spent, so everyone knows you will be paying attention. Everyone also knows that the only way to find the people who betray your trust is to pay attention; attention is care as well. The key is to do so in a way that honors the needs of the company without undermining the commitment to trust. Random checks allow ongoing vigilance without imposing a compliance tax on the trustworthy. That's what it means to trust and verify.

When you do find a transgressor, how you respond makes all the difference. In a rules-based system, cheating is often immediately followed by an e-mail that says, " From now on, all expense vouchers must be . . ." followed by a new set of rules and regulations. This is a prime example of rules governing our past; someone has been caught cheating, and now everyone must pay though added bureaucratic busywork. It harkens back to elementary school discipline, when the teacher would say, "Because Johnny couldn't stay in his seat, the entire class will remain behind for five minutes." This primitive attempt at group-responsibility building in fact has exactly the opposite effect; it makes everyone hate Johnny, fracturing class cohesion. Similar responses occur in business when managers respond to the transgressions of an individual with added burden for the group. Rather than keep people in line, it encourages them to act as free agents, protecting their own space.

Steve Kerr, former CLO of GE and Goldman Sachs, showed me a better response: "An empowering leader, when she finds out that one of the ten has cheated, then micromanages that person. The transgressor will now feel externally treated, but he will deserve to be. If you ask him to evaluate his superior, he will probably say, 'Oh, she's an autocrat and is always on my back,' but the other nine people won't know what he's talking about. Their sense of trust will remain intact."[18] The penalty for breach of trust (provided that it is not severe enough to warrant the ultimate penalty of dismissal) is the withdrawal of trust. If adult Johnny is caught fudging his expense reports, then he must be externally monitored until trust can be reestablished. This also sends a powerful message to the rest of the stadium: Trust is not a gift to be taken lightly. We're all climbing the same ladder together.

TRUST

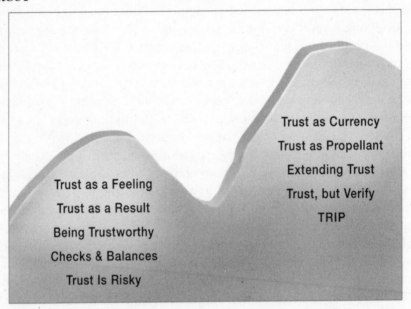

Trust as a Feeling

Trust as a Result

Being Trustworthy

Checks & Balances

Trust Is Risky

Trust as Currency

Trust as Propellant

Extending Trust

Trust, but Verify

TRIP

Understanding that the conditions of the world have changed in such a dramatic, *and specific*, way that trust has become the currency of the age, more powerful than ever, is perhaps the most crucial HOW of our connected world. Every day, the newly horizontal structure of business puts us into relationships less rigidly defined by hierarchical structures. These relationships, to be productive and Wave-producing, require us to focus more intently than ever before on what fills the spaces between us.

Trust powers a new TRIP, down a new path, a path that is more reliable, more generative, and more able to help you achieve long-term, sustained success than the dodgy dance of the past. Increasingly, those who engender and extend trust, who become actively transparent, who maintain their integrity in the face of countervailing forces, and who fill the Gaps and synapses around them with trust will see that trust returned to them, propelling their new TRIP toward progress.

CHAPTER **9**

Reputation, Reputation, Reputation

Reputation, reputation, reputation!
O, I have lost my reputation!
I have lost the immortal part of myself,
and what remains is bestial.
My reputation, Iago, my reputation!
—William Shakespeare, *Othello*, II, iii

On a traffic-free walking street in the Belgian city of Antwerp, a man pulls his long black coat more tightly around him to keep out the cold chill of the winter wind that blasts off the cobblestone street like a wave cracking against the rocks. As the wind gusts again, he quickly grabs his black hat to steady it on his head, and ducks into the doorway of a large building. Entering a long high-ceilinged room, he loosens his coat to free his long graying beard as he walks swiftly past the two dozen or so plain wooden tables that line the high-windowed wall. "I must hurry," he thinks to himself, "or I will not be home by sundown."

It is Friday, and for observant Jews, the Sabbath begins at dusk.

At a table near the back, he greets another man, dressed in a white shirt and black vest, and quickly takes a seat across the others. The hubbub of others, sitting at other tables, engaging in quiet conversation, fills the room.

The wife? *Der kinder*? They keep the small talk to a minimum as they begin an animated discussion conducted in a mix of Yiddish and English. They both know it is getting late. The vested man opens a thin black leather pouch and produces a small paper envelope no bigger than a postcard. Slipping off his coat, the visitor opens the envelope and extracts the folded piece of white tissue paper. He carefully unfolds it on the table, and then reaches into his pocket to get his ever-present loupe. Squinting through the small magnifying glass, he examines the envelope's precious contents: diamonds, one of the world's most valuable commodities.

The conversation continues unbroken as the visitor picks through the dozen stones, each worth more than $20,000, wholesale. With an expert eye that comes from a lifetime of training, he chooses eight. The vested man names a price. The visitor considers it for a moment, determines it fair, and then hands the vested man a small, handwritten piece of paper with an address on it. The vested man places six of the precious stones into an envelope with the address and puts both envelopes back in his pouch. The two remaining stones he twists into a tissue and hands to the buyer, who puts them in his pocket. To seal the deal, the men look each other in the eye, shake hands, and exchange the traditional final words of a deal between diamond traders, *mazel und brucha*, luck and blessing. With the stones in his pocket and the instruction given, the buyer bundles up and heads home for Sabbath supper.

On the next Monday, the seller will ship the six stones in the envelope to the address provided. The two diamonds in the buyer's pocket will go to a dealer in another city, and the seller will be paid. A $240,000 deal is transacted on a handshake and *mazel*, the pledge that money and goods will be delivered as promised. The only piece of paper exchanged between them: a handwritten address.

For centuries, stretching back into ancient times before the advent of regulated markets, whole economies organized and governed themselves based on trust and reputation. Personal affiliation, whether familial or with a foundation in the same religious or social group, formed the backbone of enterprise. Within these closed and semi-closed circles, word of misbehavior spread quickly. Those who cheated or betrayed a trust ran the very real risk of being permanently ostracized from their families, faith, and communities, their reputations—and thus their ability to transact business—destroyed. Though we tend to think of these sorts of business communities as feudal in nature, or existing today only where conditions of poverty or deprivation necessitate them, in fact this form of self-regulation exists to this day in the diamond trade, one of the richest economic markets known to man.

Over the centuries, Sephardic Jews, who after the Spanish Inquisition spread throughout Europe, where they were barred from most forms of economic activity save for moneylending, came to dominate the diamond trade. Diamonds had three things going for them that made them attractive to a transient community: They were highly valuable, universally desired, and easily hidden and transported on your person. Anywhere Jews were forced to move, they could take fortunes in diamonds with them and easily set up shop. Eventually, the "diamantaires" found their way to Antwerp, where they were welcome. Except for the relatively recent expansion to centers in London, Tel Aviv, and New York City, Antwerp has remained the diamond center of the world for 500 years.

Since diamond trade has always existed outside the bounds of traditional business, trust and reputation governed what contracts and law would not. From its inception, all deals were verbal and binding, sealed with a handshake and a proclamation of *"Mazel!"* Countless fortunes' worth of diamonds routinely exchanged hands on nothing more.

Diamonds today trade largely as they did in the fourteenth century. Your word is still as good as a legal contract and signals that the agreed-upon price for the agreed-upon stones is final and cannot be altered. While diamond cutters may rely on computers and lasers to help them shape the stones, the trade itself depends on each dealer's reputation and honesty, not on information technology and modern business practices. Dealers store diamonds in each other's safes, entrusting packages of glittering rocks without a contract, inventory, or appraisal, and ship stones to dealers who may simply order a number of carats at a certain grade, buying them sight unseen.

Traditionally, the only entry to this close-knit world came through relationships and reputation, but even the diamond trade has not been immune to the forces of globalization. In recent years, the Antwerp marketplace—where about 90 percent of the world's uncut diamonds and half of its polished diamonds are sold each year—adapted to a large influx of South Asian diamantaires from the Gujarat region of India.[1] Although marriage and faith (mostly Jain, an ancient ascetic practice) bind the majority of these newcomers, the Indians have been quick to assimilate. Many have learned Yiddish and Hebrew, they close deals with the traditional "*mazel*," and they routinely serve kosher food at social gatherings.

Two tightly knit groups—as different in custom, culture, and practice as one could imagine—deal in billions of dollars' worth of small, easily transported items each year, stones that to the naked eye almost all look the same. Their real currency, however, is trust and trust's sustaining by-product: reputation.

Think how great your advantage would be if you could close every deal with a handshake. While your competitors and their lawyers spend six weeks papering every deal to protect against every possible infraction, you could be moving ahead with the initiative. In Japan, a highly developed and regulated modern economy, business still recognizes the inability to foresee every eventuality, so the system still embraces the agreement between partners to treat each other honorably, and the business moves forward. Like the diamantaires, the Japanese have a business culture that reflects the traditions of their social culture, one of close community connections, long-term familial value, and the importance of personal responsibility to the group, within a modern reality.

REPUTATION IN A WIRED WORLD

Reputation is another of those soft things, like trust, that everyone wants but few think about how to get. For much of our history, the importance of reputation was largely self-evident. When most people lived in smaller, semiclosed communities, the proximity and familiarity of other people placed social pressure upon us to conduct ourselves within prevailing norms. As we moved from towns to cities and our day-to-day communities expanded in size, we maintained many of the closed community structures that kept behavior in check. The great

European and American cities of the eighteenth, nineteenth, and early twentieth centuries stayed organized in neighborhood structures that mimicked the small town and village traditions of feudal times. Multigenerational households were common, and families often stayed rooted in the same general locality for generations. People transacted most of their business on a local level, with known and trusted suppliers. Large businesses benefited from the slow pace of the world and were able to form trusting relationships over time upon which large enterprises could grow.

The last part of the twentieth century saw remarkable changes to the underlying structures of how we live. Increasing affluence, ease of transportation, expanding multinational business practices, and the transformation of economies from manufacturing/agricultural to information/service exerted tremendous pressure on the nuclear cohesion of communities. Families spread out. Neighborhoods whose character had been consistent for 100 years saw influxes of new people, new customs, and new wealth. Ironically, the increased connectivity made possible by advances in communications technologies allowed people to be further apart. Though your new job took you 2,000 miles from the town your family had lived in for three generations, you could still "reach out and touch someone" relatively cheaply.

These transformations broke the bonds of familiarity and tradition that placed high value on reputation. In a new city, or a new job, you could reinvent yourself. Identity became more fluid, opening up new opportunities for change and growth, but also removing some of the external pressures of conformity. More was possible, and so more was possible. Until about 20 years ago, for instance, it remained relatively difficult to thoroughly check someone's background and reputation. Until then, information was more controllable and, to some degree, avoidable. You could often elude that dark spot in your past with a change of locality and make a fresh start.

All that has changed. The world of business is faster, more spread out, more transient, and more fluid than ever before. Information flows. Yet, paradoxically, the overwhelming capacity of technology to connect us and transmit information to us instantly and cheaply binds us together as never before. It creates conditions of interdependence as high as if not higher than when locality bound us in commonality. In some sense, the whole world is now local (or *glocal*, as the current meme goes, both global and local at the same time). What does this mean for individuals and companies? From a reputation standpoint, what is old is new again. Reputation—how others think of you—is now more critical to your ability to build long-term sustained success than ever before.

Reputation is the sum total of your HOWS: What you stand for, what you can be trusted to do, your track record of accomplishment, the esteem you have earned, and how you have been experienced by others. In a transparent world, reputation leads. It enters the room before you do, and remains after you go, either enhanced or tarnished. It records your past, but also creates expectations for the future.

In a fractured world, reputation is also continuity. When people went to work for a company at an early age and had a reasonable expectation that they would continue to work for that company until they retired, public reputation, while valuable for promotion and advancement, was not as critical to career. The embrace of the company and the tradition of employment continuity sheltered individuals from the need to constantly represent themselves to the outside forces of the business world. Being able to say "I'm an IBM man" provided a lifetime of reputational capital. That is no longer the case. External structures, like a company, no longer provide personal continuity; only your reputation can. The average worker entering the job force now will work for an average of 10.5 companies over the course of a career.[2] As more and more members of the workforce become dedicated to knowledge-based work, it takes less to redefine your career. The specific industry or area of specialty is less important. Therefore, when employers evaluate new hires, they rely less on industry-specific job skills and more on personal characteristics and reputation to judge a person's potential. Your reputation and your Rolodex—the network of contacts and supporters—become a far more integral part of your personal package than they ever were before. Both are built over time by your HOWS.

Conversely, the company can no longer assume that its corporate reputation supercedes that of its personnel. In a transparent world, people can see between the lines of what you do and discern HOW you do it. Nuance becomes revealed, and reputation accrues to those companies whose individuals represent those nuances to the world. As we become more interconnected, more responsibility is shifted to frontline personnel, and more personnel are pushed to the front lines. They become the face of the company; through their actions, they have a profound effect on how the organization is experienced by the market. Thus a company becomes the reputational sum of its parts, and its reputation becomes more vulnerable to the actions, both positive and negative, of those individuals. The transgressions of a single actor can bring a company down.

To have a reputation that is worthy of merit, others have to impute something to you, that you are a good leader or a good executive, that you are consistently creative or a reliably hard worker, that you treat people well and fairly, or that you are honest. They only do that if they trust you, because *reputation is a series of mutual connections*. Consider reputation, therefore, as the sum of the trust circles you have developed over time, radiating out from you across companies, industries, and areas of endeavor. You build a good reputation when those who encounter you—employees, co-workers, and customers—trust you.

And whom do we trust? Those who are consistent, to whom we ascribe and impute integrity, those who say what they mean, mean what they say, and always follow through. "The ability to be consistent in life is one of the most precious and powerful things," famed Las Vegas developer and hotelier Steve Wynn told me. "Franchise comes from consistency, whether it's hamburgers or people." Over the course of the last 30-plus years, Wynn has built a series of high-risk projects—including the Mirage, Treasure Island, and Bellagio hotels—each more successful than the last, on the strength of his personal reputation. His personal brand has become so synonymous with a memorable experience that he autographed his latest project, the Wynn Las Vegas resort. "I've been successful because I've consistently given people an experience that is not only exciting, but occasionally unique. Consistency is a measure of predictability and integrity, and you can't make it without integrity." If you have integrity, Wynn is saying, you can generate trust, and if you have the trust, you can build a reputation.

To then extend that reputation—for others to contribute to it with high praise or support—they must in turn put *their* reputations on the line. If I call a manager in our New York office and ask her opinion of someone I am considering entrusting with an important project, her evaluation also reflects on my estimation of her. If she accords that individual high praise but the person does not measure up, that New York manager's reputation is going to take a hit in my book. I will have less confidence in her ability to evaluate talent. Her reputation is dependent on the strength of the trust circles she perpetuates. It may not be a critical hit, but it will be a hit nonetheless.

Acting in consonance with your reputation creates trust. The people you deal with begin their relationship with you aware of your reputation. If the interaction they have with you reinforces, extends, or at least is consistent with your reputation, they can more easily extend trust. Thus, reputation, combined with experiences that support it, propels trust. If, however, you fail to meet the expectations set by your reputation, you introduce dissonance into a relationship. The inconsistency between what is expected and what you deliver creates distraction. Dissonance and distraction, as we know, bring friction into play. Potential partners, confronted with conflicting messages, will raise their defenses and slow down the process of dealing with you in order to gain more time to evaluate the situation and make a wise choice.

Dave Chiu and Didier Hilhorst, young master's students at the Interaction Design Institute Ivrea, an Italian nonprofit organization dedicated to interactive design, recently developed a dream project they called RentAThing. A small, handheld device resembling an iPod, RentAThing "is a tool for negotiation that provides additional information about the reputation of the parties involved and enables smoother transactions." RentAThing represents one visionary step down the road to literally "trading on your reputation."[3] When two people want to transact a piece of business—Chiu and Hilhorst use the example of renting a rake—the person who owns the rake would consult his RentAThing to evaluate the other person's reputation for renting garden tools. Armed with this information, the owner could price the transaction according to relative risk; a lower reputational score would mean a higher rental price, and vice versa. The renter's rake score could be combined with other reputational scores—say, for returning library books on time or responding to phone messages in a timely fashion—in order to achieve a higher overall trust level, resulting in a lower rental price.

Chiu and Hilhorst look forward to a day, in the not-too-distant future, when wireless connectivity will allow machines and individuals to instantly share reputation scores, no different than a credit score, allowing the information in the RentAThing to apply to a variety of transactions. "Instead of silos of reputation, with various services, companies, and individuals developing isolated reputations," they write, "RentAThing provides a centralized means of managing and developing a single reputation."

In his 2003 novel, *Down and Out in the Magic Kingdom*, Canadian author and digital-rights activist Cory Doctorow posits a "post-scarcity" world in which everything is free, available based on a person's reputational score, which Doctorow calls "whuffie." Whuffie is accrued or depleted according to a person's favorable or unfavorable actions, and serves as actual currency in a world without money. Everyone knows everyone else's whuffie instantly (through a chip implanted in the head—isn't that always the case?), and everyone has the ability to increase or deplete someone's whuffie instantly. Conduct a great symphony? The audience loves you and you accrue whuffie from them all. Shove someone as you walk down the street? That dirty look he threw you now carries a cost. Doctorow imagines that because you achieve whuffie only by the evaluation of others, everyone will be more positively motivated to do useful and creative things to benefit others.[4]

Both of these fabulist visions find their roots at the real-life intersection of information technology and personal conduct. Reputation in the virtual world, the world of networked communication, can be calculated with exactitude. Computer science engineers rely on reputation systems to mathematically quantify trust in online communities. Everything from web site security to trading communities like eBay employs reputation-based computational models that evaluate behavior, calculate trust scores, and apply them to everything from security access to insurability. As more and more information about who we are and what we've done moves from the relatively safe confines of personal connections in semiclosed societies to the far more vast network of the Internet, our personal reputations begin to more closely resemble these abstract commercial ones. As the online world has a persistence of memory with no rival, HOW we do what we do—every day becomes far more important and integral to our ability to thrive.

Online, mathematical reputation systems, in fact, provide us with an interesting way of evaluating the value of reputation in life. Researchers at the University of Michigan and Harvard University conducted a study that aimed to do just that. First, they noted that in living, word-of-mouth reputational systems—the kind that work for or against us in business each day—much information is lost or omitted. Humans, as expressive as we are, are imperfect communication systems (ask anyone who ever played the game of "telephone" as a child). Online systems, like the one used on perhaps the most widely known application, eBay, forget nothing. Buyers and sellers on eBay rate each other with a feedback score and a short written comment. Not only does that score and comment remain forever, millions can access it for next to no expense (reputation on the Internet broadcasts your actions simultaneously to merchants in Beijing and housewives in Sweden).[5] To evaluate the precise value of this eBay reputation, the researchers set out to discover just how much a good reputation was worth to sellers in an online marketplace, where the traditional signifiers of a seller's reputation—the cost and appearance of a facility, longevity in a community, connection to known others—are absent. In cooperation with a known and respected dealer of collectible postcards, they sold identical lots of cards through the dealer's high-reputation main identity and through other, newly created, identities that had low reputational scores. They found that buyers, on average, were willing to pay 8.1 percent more to a seller with a good reputation than to a seller without one, for identical merchandise.

The presence of positive reputation was directly quantifiable. Like trust, it is a soft thing we take for granted, which the new conditions of the world have suddenly rendered hard. Who among us couldn't do with an 8 percent raise or an 8 percent premium for whatever we are selling?

REPUTATIONAL CAPITAL

Reputation comes in many forms. It can be, most obviously, the word-of-mouth messages that others receive and pass along about you. It can also be the proxies of your past achievements, like your resume or your past salary. Almost everyone can remember a time when, confronted with the knowledge of what someone they have just met earns or their previous job titles, responded with the thought "Wow, he sure doesn't seem like a $X per year kind of guy."

A friend of mine used to produce television commercials, an industry staffed mostly by freelancers paid day rates. As part of any particular job, he would routinely find himself hiring any number of staffers, from entry-level production assistants (PAs) to directors of photography (DPs), who came with a wide range of salary quotes. Staffs would form for short-term, high-budget projects—anywhere from a week to a month and up to a million dollars or more—and then disband again, making the process a sort of high-turnover microcosm of what human resources (HR) professionals go through when staffing longer-term enterprises. In a high-turnover situation like this, reputational capital increases dramatically. No work commitment lasts long, and success depends on sustaining repeat clients, people who hire you again and again.

The past achievements of top-level creative talent like DPs often speak to their artistic reputations (their WHATS); their HOWS—temperaments and personal qualities like grace under pressure, team skills, and communication skills—while important, seldom rise to a level of equal importance. In the creative leadership positions, talent often rules the day. Reputation made the most difference in the lower-skill positions like PAs, the entry-level worker bees critical to the smooth functioning of every film set.

"Breaking into the film industry and developing a freelance career is almost exclusively a reputational, word-of-mouth process. One producer recommends you to another, and they to yet another, in an informal network. Almost no one is hired unless someone vouches for them," my friend told me. When PAs receive a work call, however, they have another reputational component to manage: their quote, or salary rate. Day rates on film shoots can vary widely depending on budget, type of project, personal experience, and other factors, but PAs can quote any amount (within a range) they desire. "If I had a normal-sized budget, I would always trust the PA to quote me their rate," he said. "But the rate they quoted set an expectation of performance. If a PA quoted me [the then top day rate of] $200 per day, I expected him or her to show up on set and be really crack: motivated, self-generating, knowledgeable about equipment and procedure, and able to solve a lot of the many problems that plague a shoot on any given day. If they quoted me a lower rate, say, $125, then I would know that this was someone who needed more training. My expectations would be lower."

When the shoot day began, expectation became everything. "If you came in with a low quote and really performed, I was much more likely to invest time and effort in training and grooming you. I cut you more slack when things went wrong and created more opportunity for challenge when things were slow," he said "If you had a top quote, however, and you weren't on your game, the next day you were just gone. Not in a hostile way—you never have to fire anyone working freelance; you just got a warm thank-you, a handshake, and a 'Sorry, we don't need as many PAs tomorrow.'" (In the fast-paced environment of film production, no team has any allowance for friction or distraction, or anything that slows the process. If you don't measure up to the expectations set for you by the proximal reputation set by your quote, you are just out of work.)

Although hiring and firing in a corporate environment are usually longer processes than the handshake-and-smile of the film world, increasingly business finds itself unable to carry within it anything that slows down the machine. The bonds between people in common enterprise today are often thinner than before. Consultants, part-timers, freelancers, strategic partners, and all manner of other shorter-term commitments make up the variety of synapses between people in business. The world is mobile and information skills more adaptable and malleable to a wider range of opportunities. In such a world, we are often teamed in work situations where we must be productive with little of the time more traditional, longer-term work relationships have to build trust and continuity. Gaps between what you represent and what you deliver can cause almost instant mistrust, and, in a thin-bond world, end in a friendly handshake. Delivering reputational consonance—giving others the feeling that what you see is what you get—creates quicker acceptance, stronger synapses, and greater opportunity. This, in turn, contributes to your reputational capital by increasing the trust circles around you, and, increasingly, your reputational capital is the coin of the realm that affects your buy-in to the biggest games going.

MISMANAGING REPUTATION MANAGEMENT

In late 1983, in a conference room at brokerage house Drexel Burnham, five members of their high-yield bond department, including its head, Michael Milken, brainstormed an idea that would land on the global business community like a cluster bomb. Drexel decided to finance hostile takeovers of corporations using so-called junk bonds, low-rated, high-yield promissory notes, secured by the assets of the target company.[6] At that time in business history, hostile buyouts were rare and treated delicately. To take over a company against the wishes of the people who ran it was a highly aggressive play that, in fortress capitalism days, made you many enemies. The barriers to do so were commensurately high. Financing such deals was the province of conservative, white-shoe investment banks. Aggressors were usually large companies that used bank loans to take over smaller ones. Drexel's idea turned this model on its ear. Under their plan, many more companies and creditworthy investors, no matter how large or small, could take over another company, even one much larger than themselves, using the target company's assets as collateral for the high-yield bonds Drexel would sell to raise the money.

When they announced this new deal, in early 1984, it dramatically altered the structure of corporate endeavor forever. Suddenly, old-line, established corporations built on sound value over time saw their own assets used against them. Value was no longer the play; instead, short-term shareholder value became the dipstick by which every company was measured. Many of the prevailing attitudes in business (and many corporate downfalls) derive from this single, fateful action.

When the enormous fees that playing this new junk bond game could earn became clear, many rushed into the game, including most of the major brokerages and many corporations, large and small. But there were two noticeable exceptions to this orgy of short-term profit taking: investment bank Goldman Sachs announced it would not fund hostile takeovers, and Johnson & Johnson (J&J) decided it would never do one.[7] The reason for both decisions?

Reputation.

"Our CEO and president, Jim Burke, decided J&J would never do a hostile takeover," Roger Fine of Johnson & Johnson told me when we caught up one day in New York. Fine is a truly admired leader and someone with whom I have had the privilege to work closely since the early days of LRN. "He wanted us to have the reputation of never giving anyone else a bear hug, and never doing anything that the management of another company that we coveted didn't want to do. Now don't think we were pussycats; J&J is an aggressive acquisitive company that wants to benefit from the opportunities of the market-place as much as the next company. But Burke's theory was that if we established our reputation for never pursuing this kind of transaction, people would come negotiate with us as a matter of preference versus people they couldn't trust."[8]

Though reputation, like trust, is not a new concept in business, there has been an explosion of interest around the subject since the mid-1990s. Companies now see what J&J and Goldman Sachs recognized back then: Reputation is a competitive advantage. Their reputations for straight dealing and respect for the companies they sought to acquire closed the Certainty Gap between them and their negotiating partners and allowed the deals to close more quickly, with less friction and more cooperation. Now these advantages are becoming plain to all. In 1998, Harris Interactive, a major corporate and public interest research firm, in association with Charles Fombrun, executive director of the Reputation Institute at the Stern School of Business at New York University, designed something they called the Reputation Quotient (RQ), a research tool that captures perceptions of corporate reputations. Since then, they have published the results of their evaluations as an annual list of the 60 "most visible companies in America," ranked by their reputation. Achieving and maintaining a great corporate reputation is an increasing preoccupation with visionary corporate leaders. Jeffrey Immelt, chairman of the board and CEO of General Electric (GE), in his letter accompanying GE's 2002 Annual Report, made no bones about it. "We spend billions each year on improving our training, enforcing our compliance with ethical norms, and reinforcing our values," he said, "all to preserve our culture and protect one of our most valuable assets—our reputation."[9] When financier Warren Buffett took over troubled brokerage firm Salomon Brothers after securities violations threatened to wreck the company, he went before the U.S. Congress, apologized for the employees' transgressions, and issued a stern warning to any that might think of following in their footsteps. "Lose money for the firm," he told them, "and I will be understanding; lose a shred of reputation for the firm, and I will be ruthless."[10]

Unfortunately, a fair amount of the recent interest in reputation revolves around creating and managing corporate reputation as an extension of brand awareness in the marketplace, an effort colonized by public relations and corporate communications departments and consultants. When I recently Googled "reputation management," I got 68 million hits and 16 or so paid ads. Communication strategists, research companies, law firms, and consultants of all stripes and hues have sprung up to deal with managing and repairing reputation. Fine minds and strategic thinkers have broken it all down into "6 Dimensions," "18 Immutable Laws," and "Communication Gaps" that must be learned, mastered, adhered to, or filled.

Certainly, business in a hypermediated world has a place for reputation and crisis management. Kryptonite learned that lesson the hard way. Let us not forget that companies are the by-product of a lot of blood, sweat, and tears. When things go bad, a lot of human effort and resources are dissipated: real loss, real dissipation, degradation of value that was built on the backs of real people. Reputation, to the degree that stakeholders see it as an external surface representing all this effort, is an extension of brand, and the building of reputation in the marketplace is an essential component of any business strategy. But reputation is not the same as brand, and does not equate automatically with brand awareness. Think of the brand awareness built up in the marketplace by companies such as ExxonMobil, J&J, GE, and Microsoft. Each of these companies is known by everyone. All of these companies have achieved almost total brand saturation in their markets, but not all of them share the same reputations.

The problem with external approaches to corporate reputation, and by extension trust, is that they look at reputation as a silo to be managed, a story to be spun. The mentality of much of this thought seems to go like this: *The corporation is under siege from the marauding forces of information and transparency, and every company should be armed with a plan and a phalanx of experts ready to go to war on the great battlefield of public opinion, both proactively to extend the brand and reactively in times of PR crisis. Whoever can gain control of the message can prevail.* This thinking, with its roots in fortress capitalism, stands little chance of success today. To truly thrive in the internetworked world, business and the people who labor in business need to find a way to operate *within* the new conditions of transparency and interconnectedness that define the playing field of economic endeavor, to thrive *because of* and not *in spite of* these new conditions. Even a company like fast-food restaurateur McDonald's, which grew up in the pretransparent world to become a formidable and globally recognized brand, has embraced this new relationship with its stakeholders. "We welcome transparency," CEO Jim Skinner told me. "Transparency means that people have a very clear look at your behavior. They now make their own determination of whether or not your behavior adds value or whether it is significant relative to your success, and whether or not the behaviors are part of the integrity and ongoing culture of a company. That doesn't mean it comes without conflict or issues regarding how you behave as an organization. Someone might determine now, for any number of reasons, that they don't want to have anything to do with us or our brand. But I don't want them to think that what manifests our success was done in a way that would not have survived transparency earlier. The difference is that we now actively welcome people to see that."[11]

Great companies and leaders today know that their reputational capital is as valuable to their success as their physical capital. A recent LRN study of purchasing behavior revealed that half of Americans who own stocks independent of a 401(k) say they decided not to purchase stock in a company because they questioned its reputation.[12] Positive reputation binds you more closely to your stakeholders, be they customers, employees, or, most critically, recruits.

Joie Gregor is vice chairman of one of America's top executive recruiting firms, Heidrick & Struggles. Gregor recruits executives, CEOs, COOs, and board members for major corporations, and many consider her an expert in building global leadership teams. I worked closely with Joie on a recruiting assignment for LRN. She knows, before she takes on clients, that their reputations precede them into the marketplace for talent. "The great candidates or top talent look at companies and ask, 'Are they a great company?'" she says. "And it's almost never about just making the numbers. It is about the culture. I don't know that I've ever met any great executives who would go to a company that doesn't value their people, that lives on the edge of 'is it right or is it wrong.' They will ask those questions. They will investigate the reputation. And if they can't align, they don't join."[13]

In the working world today, most of us see ourselves as freelancers. We stay with a job or an organization as long as its goals—and the benefits we can accrue in the pursuit of them—remain tightly aligned with our own. It's harder to keep the best people solely by means of salaries and perquisites; there's often a better package just over the horizon. In this way "carrots" like compensation packages become very expensive to maintain. You can pay someone $20 to participate in your Wave, but they'll do so only as long as it seems worth it. The best people, as Gregor made clear, are looking for something more, a relationship built on stronger values than money and success.

"Reputation is who you are," Jeff Kindler, CEO of Pfizer, told me. "It's your character, it's your brand, it's your identity. Why work for one company versus another company? Really talented people who have lots of opportunities are not, in my experience, ultimately moved by an incremental difference in their paycheck. They are inspired by a couple of fairly simple things: (1) working in a place that gives them ample opportunity and resources with which to grow and develop as a person and make meaningful contributions; (2) working for and with people who share their belief system, their professional aspirations, and their objectives for what the enterprise can accomplish; and (3) working in an enterprise that is somehow making the world a better place in some dimension that is important to them. That is what inspires them to go the extra mile. To create such a place, you have to have a distinct culture, a distinct character, and a distinct set of values and objectives that resonate against that spectrum of motivations."[14]

Paul Robert came up through the ranks to become associate general counsel and director of contracts and compliance at United Technologies Corporation (UTC). In an age where talented executives like him are in high demand, Paul has spent nearly 20 years working at UTC. Mindful of what Jeff Kindler had said, I asked Paul what inspires him to go to work every day. "Every morning, like everyone else, I drag myself out of bed to go to work," he said. "Sometimes it's cold, and sometimes it's dark. What makes me do it is that I work for a company that makes skyscrapers possible. I work for a company that still powers 50 percent of the passenger aircraft on earth, that delivers people to Grandma during Thanksgiving at the rate of one take-off and four landings every 12 seconds. I work for a company that adopted a business ethics code in 1932, and if you look at that code, written by Willis Carrier, who was chairman of the board of Carrier Corporation, there is nothing new there. It has the same values we have today."[15]

Reputation is as important to recruiting at the entry level as it is at the top. David B. Montgomery of Stanford Graduate School of Business and Catherine A. Ramus of University of California, Santa Barbara, surveyed more than 800 MBAs from 11 leading North American and European schools. Amazingly, more than 97 percent said they were willing to forgo financial benefits to work for an organization with a better reputation for getting its HOWS right. How much would they forgo? On average, 14 percent of their expected income. A reputation for doing it right and for caring about employees both rose to the top third of the list of 14 attributes these MBAs most valued in a prospective employer, proving to be about 77 percent as important as the top criterion of intellectual challenge and only slightly below financial package in relative importance. "We were quite surprised by these results," said Montgomery, the Sebastian S. Kresge Professor of Marketing Strategy, Emeritus, and dean of the School of Business at Singapore Management University. "There were no previous empirical studies that indicated how important these additional job choice–related factors might be."[16]

Goran Lindahl, former CEO of Swiss industrial giant ABB, put it simply: "In the end," he said, "managers are not loyal to a particular boss or even to a company, but to a set of values they believe in and find satisfying."[17] Those values, manifested as behavior and performance throughout every facet of an enterprise's activity, provide the building blocks and mortar of reputation. They are the invisible added *something* that binds people together more powerfully than short-term gain. Instead of thinking of reputation and trust as just shiny surfaces on the walls of the fortress, we need to understand them as assets that provide the engine of our achievement.

"Reputation is not about spin. It is merging what is real with what people think about you," says Charles Fombrun of the Reputation Institute.[18] We know that the brain is exceptionally good at recognizing conflicting messages. Thus, integrity is a necessary component of any representation a company or an individual makes. If those to whom

you are communicating sense dissonance or apparent conflict between your carefully crafted message and the realities of your behavior, they will quickly turn away. When I think about reputation,
therefore, I think about something holistic and authentic, something
that fills the interpersonal synapses between one person and another,
between one company and another, and between every organization
and its various stakeholders. It begins with the individual and extends
out to the organization of which he or she is a part.

Values. Continuity. Reputation. To thrive in our transparent, connected world, we need to shift our thinking from *managing* reputation to *earning* it. Reputation cannot be spun like the gossamer
threads of a spider's web intended to catch flies, but must be built,
brick by brick—one communication and one interaction at a time—to
form a structure capable of sheltering the aspirations of those who
wish to live there. You cannot get to a good reputation by cutting corners; reputation is on the square, or not at all.

A SECOND CHANCE

Whereas it may take less now to redefine your career, you cannot
do much to redefine your reputation. You build reputation action by
action over the course of a business day. Over time, it tends to settle into place. Your reputation is not for your epitaph; it's like a
baseball player's batting average—very difficult to move up more
than a few points towards the end of a season. It takes a long-term
commitment to becoming a more consistent hitter and to improving
your ability to make contact with the ball, to raise your batting average year over year, over the course of a major league career. Reputation also kicks in much earlier in life than it once did. People used
to think of reputation as a legacy issue, something to be considered
in the second half of your career; after you became successful, you
worried about how your reputation would be viewed by others.
Now, employers check the MySpace pages of recruits just out of
college. It is as if your batting average is no longer limited to your
performance in the majors, but also includes how you swung the
bat in Little League; the things you do as a kid stay with you

throughout your career. Reputation is built one interaction, one gesture, and one event at a time throughout your life. Even someone like Steve Wynn, a man whose reputation was built on big successes, agrees that building reputation is about the little things, the simple, authentic impressions you make in each interaction. "It's not about home runs," he said. "It's about hitting singles and doubles, one meaningful experience at a time." In an age when your reputation is built on authentic impressions, the pressure is on to act authentically right from the start.

When Drexel Burnham fell and the high-flying stock market of the 1980s crashed on Black Monday, 1987, Michael Milken became the poster boy for 1980s greed and corporate avarice. Although there was little to suggest that this quiet financial genius was nearly the Machiavellian schemer the press, the Securities and Exchange Commission (SEC), and federal attorneys made him out to be (former New York City Mayor Rudolph Giuliani, then lead attorney for the prosecution, has since expressed full support for Milken's presidential pardon),[19] Milken paid the price. Years in jail, the largest fine ever levied in the history of U.S. securities laws at that time, and a lifelong ban from the thing he did best left Milken picking up the pieces of a shattered life and damaged reputation.[20] Now, years later, Milken's valuable philanthropic efforts on behalf of cancer research and public education through the activities of the Milken Family Foundation are helping him restore the reputation he lost, as he helps others.[21] It seems Milken evolved from a man motivated by the pursuit of success into a man inspired by the pursuit of significance, and in that transformation, that shift from a focus on the self to a focus on others, he was able to find a solid measure of redemption.

REPUTATION, REPUTATION, REPUTATION

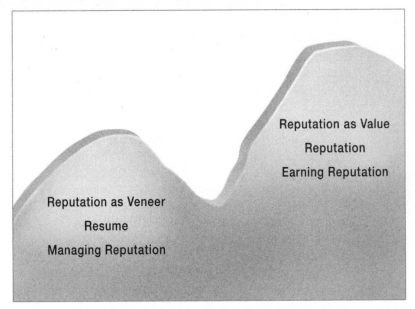

Second chances are harder to come by in a transparent world. It is easier for people to trip you up and, since times are full of uncertainty, harder for people to extend trust after it is broken. The fall down the ladder of trust is often long, and the landing particularly hard. Reputation is the only known antidote. It can inoculate you, to some degree, against the unease that others feel when suspicion enters a relationship. It buys you the benefit of the doubt.

In a world of connection and transparency, getting your hows right means making the shift from managing reputation to building it in everything you do. A good reputation is like a good rope and piton for a mountain climber. Every good climber is going to slip occasionally and sometimes even take a fall. However, when conditions get rough, only a good rope, well secured, will keep you from being blown off the mountain.

The Marlboro Man and Me

In 2001, David Greenberg became senior vice president and chief compliance officer of Altria Group, Inc., the parent company of Kraft Foods and
Philip Morris, among others.[22] "When I took my current job," David told me
recently with a laugh, "what I knew about compliance and ethics would have
fit in a thimble. Altria's conception of compliance training at that time involved lawyers standing up and lecturing people about rules and procedures."[23] Charged with creating an effective compliance and ethics program
for a sprawling organization of more than 190,000 employees, David got
turned on to the technology solutions emerging in the industry and began
reaching out.

David and I sat down recently at LRN's New York offices to recall the history of our relationship, a journey that for both of us has proven a profound
and meaningful experience. Though to this point in the book I have not
shared many stories directly about LRN, and certainly none as long as this, I
want to detour from the narrative to relate, with David's help, a story that
truly tested many of the values and principles I hold deeply, and that I think
also illuminates many of the ideas we have been discussing in this part.

During his search for solutions, David contacted LRN, and we began a series of informal discussions and information sharing. Altria, as the parent
company of cigarette maker Philip Morris, is a company facing reputational
challenges because, in the eyes of many, it misled its customers about products and betrayed their trust. But LRN is not in the WHAT business; it's in the
business of HOW, and when companies reach out to us, it is because they want
to embark on or further their journey toward getting their HOWS right. When
David contacted us, I saw a genuine opportunity for constructive engagement
with an organization and its 190,000 or so people around HOW they conduct
their business and pursue their goals. Through David's leadership, Altria
seemed to be committed to rebuilding trust by getting more of its HOWS right.

So after a time of general evaluation, David began a very formal process,
contacting potential vendors like us to make capabilities presentations. At
that point, LRN was seven years old, a leader in our field but still growing.
David was one of the leaders in the field crafting a very rigorous, compara-
tive, and thorough process of deciding what Altria would purchase and with
whom the firm would form a relationship. He set up a selection committee
and issued formal requirements, which he sent to all potential bidders or
partners. Though we were working with many large companies at the time,
many of our relationships were not won in formal, competitive beauty con-
tests; they just kind of happened. Early in the millennium, though, things

were changing rapidly for us, and as markets mature, systems formalize. Still, to us Altria was a Goliath, and establishing a relationship would have meant a lot to the growth of our business.

Unbeknownst to us at the time, six months earlier David had hired a small consulting firm to generally advise Altria in the area of compliance and, specifically, to help spearhead this selection process. Soon thereafter, a member of the LRN sales and services team brought to my attention that the principals of this advisory firm had a major stake in one of the vendors competing against us to supply the online training. "They were transparent about that," David told me, "and I believe it was as much an advantage to us as a conflict. Altria is a hundred-billion-dollar corporation and always does what's in its best interests. These partners had a lot of knowledge about the industry that could help us get up to speed, and I knew to ask about and assess their bias. The level of formality and structure in our process gave me even more comfort. We had a committee, we had a very elaborate process, we had standards and criteria, and we had lots of people who were going to be a part of the decision making who had absolutely no business relationship with or stake in this advisory firm."

LRN had invested a great deal of time and resources in getting to know David and his team. We were proud of our solution, felt that we could be a good partner for Altria, and had developed a lot of excitement around trying to become its partner. But the presence of these advisors seemed to us a clear conflict of interest, and when we found out about it, we really struggled with what to do. In a competitive situation, you obviously don't want your trade secrets revealed, and you don't want anything that you consider proprietary or confidential to wind up in the hands of a competitor. If this competitor obtained passwords and IDs to go online and review our courses, they would have insight into our material and our approach to adult learning and instructional design. They would be armed with things that companies do a lot to protect. Also, we were very unsettled that Altria hadn't disclosed the advisors' involvement at the beginning of the process, that we had to discover this on our own.

So I reached out to David, for whom I had developed some respect, and communicated our unease. I expressed our feeling that this looked like a conflict of interest on its face, and while the appearance of conflict doesn't always mean conflict, we certainly felt vulnerable in this instance. We argued back and forth. David saw it much like hiring a national law firm to help select a regional counsel. I saw it more like hiring one tobacco farmer to help you choose who to buy tobacco from, even though he grew tobacco

(Continued)

The Marlboro Man and Me *(Continued)*

himself. Finally, David suggested a compromise, offering to exclude the advisors when we talked about pricing and when we disclosed our passwords. It was reasonable common ground, so I agreed to proceed.

A short time later, however, we received an e-mail requesting our passwords, and Altria's advisors were on the distribution. The dissonance between the ground rules David tried to set up and what Altria did was a blow to the process. We lost confidence that our vulnerability could be protected, even as an administrative matter. "I thought that the information was controllable, that I had a choke point on the process, but I didn't," David said. "Someone probably hit "Reply All" on some e-mail, which let information into someone else, and maybe it ended up in the hands of someone who didn't know the agreement and innocently sent it along." More important, we grew deeply concerned about our competitor. Why would these advisors want to be in this potentially conflicted situation? They shouldn't *want* to see our passwords. These concerns multiplied, distracting us from our ability to move forward with passion and turning into real trepidations about Altria itself. Could we really trust these people?

I lost a lot of sleep over this. On the one hand, it is really hard to tell a Fortune 10 company to go jump in a lake; you want its business and you certainly don't want a competitor to get it. We were a leading company and I felt we had the solutions that a leading company like Altria needed. I felt we could win. Could I really sacrifice a big win, and all it would mean to the company, on the altar of a principle? On the other hand, there was something gnawing deeply at my belief system. Whether or not the people at Altria saw it as a conflict, David and his team didn't seem able to honor the fact that we did.

Ultimately, I felt that this was flat-out wrong and the advisors should not participate in the process. There was a conflict, and for us to go forward, they needed to go away. So I called David and made my case. I told him that although Altria didn't see the situation as a disabling conflict, LRN felt very disabled by it. We felt we would be unable to come to a meeting and be open and transparent, to discuss our strengths, weaknesses, and future plans in a candid way, or tell Altria everything it needed to know to understand who we were.

David took me seriously, but he told me that he had spoken to others about the issue and that he and his group felt they were going about this in an appropriate way and that was the way it was going to be. "I wasn't the sole decision maker, but I was the senior person on the team," David said. "I was so convinced that I would make the call on the merits and lead the team on the merits that, while everything Dov was saying was theoretically correct, I felt that if LRN was the best or if X was, the best was going to win. I think that one of the lessons here is that we were just dealing with such different realities. In my reality—probably arrogantly—I didn't think someone would walk away from competing for our business based on that set of facts; this was too attractive a proposition and our reputation for quality and performance would transparently give confidence to the world that no matter who knew whom, or who owned what, we were going to pick the best thing for Altria."

I consulted with the LRN team. There was a lot at stake on what we would do, not just for the company abstractly, but for individuals and their livelihood. I made the decision to formally notify David and Altria that we were withdrawing from the process. It was a painful and difficult decision. I sent a letter to David. I tried to be very careful in the letter to not impugn his integrity or be critical of David or Altria or its leadership. I said simply that I felt that there was a conflict that was disabling, that we'd thought deeply about it, and that based on our values, beliefs, and the constitution of our company, we felt withdrawing was the right thing to do.

"At the time, I was shocked," David said. "I didn't understand it. I felt very strongly about my fairness and ability to run a fair process and do the right thing for the company. I just could not accept that the words meant what they said. It felt irrational because not only did LRN have a full shot, I thought it might win. I didn't know what was really behind it; I just felt like it was a story that I'd probably never get to the bottom of. Then it occurred to me that it might be a tactic, that by calling our attention to these problems, LRN was trying to control some part of the process, to put us a little bit on the defensive and gain an advantage. Maybe LRN was attempting to differentiate itself by being *smart*. It never occurred to me to think it was simply a principled stance."

In response to the letter, David reached out to me. "I thought it was my obligation to Altria to not let one of the quality companies withdraw from the process," David said. The call impressed me; the letter didn't ask for it and he didn't need to make it. I said, "We withdraw," not "Call me if you want to discuss it." During the call, however, David got upset and at one point asked me if I was impugning his integrity. Perhaps because he thought we were just being clever, he began to find my position insulting. I took great pains to point out that I was not personalizing the situation, and that it was about

(Continued)

The Marlboro Man and Me *(Continued)*

LRN's belief system and not his integrity. LRN simply felt compelled to withdraw. "It was hard not to take personally," David said. "I was starting to get the message that here I am, the chief ethics officer, and in essence it's being pointed out to me that at least some people perceive something I'm doing has the appearance of a serious conflict of interest. It made me uncomfortable, defensive, or at least self-justifying and, you know, any number of other adjectives." We ended the conversation agreeing to disagree, and left it at that.

In retrospect, I think we failed to humanize each other at that time. That's too common in business; people see each other as human doings, not human beings. At that point, I saw David as a businessman, the type of guy who, when he got off the phone, went on to the next task. I didn't realize that he was the kind of guy I could hurt or easily insult. Conversely, he probably didn't see me as the kind of guy who anguished and lost sleep over a principle. "I think I saw you as a walking balance sheet," David said, "or a profit-and-loss statement. I found it hard to believe or accept that we had really offended any values or important LRN standards."

A couple of years went by. Altria picked a vendor. There was a lot of loss in the situation, for both LRN and Altria. I felt their pick should have withdrawn as well, and in my dourest moments I thought that maybe they kind of deserved each other. "I took the position that life is long, and let's move on," said David. "Neither of us had crossed any lines or said anything that we would regret, so we kept it distant and professional." During those years, David became an industry leader and something of a guru in this industry. He was often called upon to speak about his progress at Altria (which of course increased my disappointment at not being able to land the deal). I saw him speak at conferences and meetings. It was awkward. He would speak, and I would speak, but we didn't speak to each other. Our reputations grew, and we grew more familiar with each other's reputations. I was impressed by his passion and commitment; he seemed like a good guy.

Then one day, I got a voice mail from David suggesting a meeting. "At the time I called," David explained, "LRN was developing something that was new, advanced, different, and no one else had. I am not dogmatic in my beliefs, nor do I think I'm infallible. As I grew into my position and became part of the community, I started to understand more of what I didn't know. I took as my mandate that Altria needs to have the best possible program, so I reached out, despite our past. I saw it as the principled thing to do."

Although I was still smarting after all those years, I thought, "no harm, no foul." It was a new chapter. So we created a strong presentation customized to Altria's needs, and began a series of meetings between our teams. David kicked the tires, and then dug deeper into our approach and specific solution. We developed a rapport, and David extended me the honor to speak at one of Altria's global leadership conferences. "At that point," David said, "we had put aside the past, and we were proceeding on a professional, on-the-merits basis. Within my own team, it was a big deal to invite Dov to speak at one of our leadership meetings, and I was conscious of that on two levels. One, I thought there'd be learning, and that was the main thing. And two, I thought it was useful to say to the troops, 'I, David, am capable of learning, and we should not be standing on personal principle or history or anything else when it comes to doing the right thing for the company. We may have had an unfortunate experience with LRN, which left whatever scar tissue it left; but that was a few years ago, and we're still about doing the right and smart thing.'"

After the conference, our teams sat down and had a long dinner. During it, David got very open about his thoughts about leadership and what it was like to be a young executive officer with Altria and go work overseas and come back. It was a very sharing dinner about perspective and views on big business, big companies, and leadership. We got to know each other a little bit more just in the exchange of perspectives that night. David showed a lot of power in his ability to be vulnerable and reflective in front of his colleagues, and a lot of humility.

A couple of weeks later, he and I had dinner together, just the two of us, and during the meal, I had my briefcase open (I think I did it on purpose). At some point, I pulled out a copy of LRN's Leadership Framework, the constitution around which our company was built, and got very passionate. I shared our ideas about values-based leadership, our commitment to our beliefs, and how the framework governs all that we do. It was a great meal, where we both really opened up with each other. "As we were leaving the restaurant, I had my epiphany," David said. "I stopped Dov on the street and said, 'You know, it just occurred to me that you really believe in what you say, and that you were truly acting on principle back then, and I don't think I really believed it until right now.'" It was at that moment I felt complete closure. David and I stopped seeing each other as human doings, and started believing in each other as human beings. At that moment, Altria and LRN stopped being companies in business together, and started doing a Wave.

(Continued)

The Marlboro Man and Me *(Continued)*

In the ensuing months, David and I began to nurture a wide-ranging relationship of collaboration and innovation. During that same time, Altria's original contract with its vendor expired and Altria began a new formal selection process. "It became clear to me," said David, "that because of the way LRN perceived itself and runs its business, they were more likely to have real insights into values-based business and doing the right thing." It became clear to me that through our process of rediscovery and connection, David and I created, even if inadvertently, an atmosphere that allowed our respective teams to collaborate powerfully—with trust and understanding—and to forge a partnership to bring values-based solutions to Altria's operations worldwide.

David and I built our relationship one interaction at a time, over time, as we both learned more about each other and found a way to reach across the divide of business that had separated us. Along the way we both struggled in the Valley of C, and the things we held dearest to us—our principles, integrity, reputation, honesty—were put severely to the test. Yet despite all the challenges during the journey, neither of us strayed from what he most believed; we kept getting our HOWS right. Years later, we were able to reconnect because, though troubled and strained, the synapses between us were never fully broken. Both of us sensed something strong and authentic in the other and so, with the intercession of time and reflection, we were able to rebuild those connections and make them strong and lasting. Although the Wave we tried to start in the third inning petered out, by the seventh we were all waving our arms and cheering together.

Part IV

HOW WE GOVERN

INTRODUCTION: INNOVATING IN HOW

Business, simply put, is a vessel that contains and expresses the results of human endeavor. Within it pools much that we aspire to: meaning, success, significance, excellence, and contribution to the greater good. There, too, live greed, self-serving attitudes, covetousness, consumption, exploitation, and a host of our less savory qualities. A company or an organization forms to achieve a goal unattainable by an individual alone—a greater service to others, a larger product, or an advancement of human knowledge. For business to find its greatest expression and achieve its loftier aims, it must organize and govern itself in a manner that unleashes these higher forces in those who join within it. Every group faces the challenge of how best to accomplish this goal, an organizational premise that attracts the best and brightest, inspires them to achieve at the highest level, and generates sufficient reward—both monetary and nonmonetary—to compensate their efforts.

In Part One, we discussed the many forces and factors that have fundamentally changed the world in which business operates, placing a new and intense focus on HOW we do what we do. In Parts Two and Three, we examined in depth these new HOWs and explored ways we can, as individuals and groups, learn to master a way of acting and thinking about the world that aligns us more closely with these new realities. Taken together, these three parts provide a new lens through which to see and react to the challenges we face day to day. This leaves us with a profound question: If HOW is the new fuel of human connectedness and achievement, can we conceive of a new organizing principle, a new way of binding ourselves together, in order to create groups, teams, and organizations more capable of making Waves? In other words, can we embed HOW horizontally across every aspect of our organization and make it something that informs everything we do?

To illustrate what I mean by that, let's briefly discuss a concept that had a similar transformative effect on twentieth-century business: quality and process management, which I think of as the HOWS of WHAT. Since the mid-1980's or so, global business heartily embraced the concept of designed-in quality and process reengineering. The impetus for the shift came from the success of Japanese manufacturing techniques. Before Japan's rise as a manufacturing powerhouse, the rest of the world was stuck in the quagmire of the production triangle (see Figure IV.1).

FIGURE IV.1   The Production Triangle

Each point of the triangle represented either fast, cheap, or good. The idea was that you could pick two: You could have it good and fast, but it wouldn't be cheap; good and cheap, but it wouldn't be fast; or fast and cheap, but it wouldn't be good. The trap lay in the fact that quality was generally considered an end-of-the-line inspection point. Widgets would roll off the line, and someone standing at the end would inspect them for quality and throw the bad ones away. If there were 20 steps in the manufacturing process, quality was step 21; steps 1 to 20 didn't concern themselves with quality. Businesses could deliver high-quality products, but it was more costly to do so because it meant throwing away more products at the end of the line. More profoundly, businesses generally viewed quality as an aesthetic, a soft, amorphous characteristic that couldn't be easily quantified or measured. People thought, "I know good quality when I see it; but it's subjective." We did not have a common vernacular for it; *good* was in the eye of the beholder.

The Japanese came along and stood those concepts on their ear. They realized that quality defects were in fact inefficiencies, and by shifting the idea of quality from the back of the line to the front, they could create a process that manufactured high-quality products far more efficiently and economically. They did this initially by decentralizing the responsibility for quality from the top of the production pyramid, like auto assemblers Toyota and Mitsubishi, to their subassemblers, and then took the savings they accrued and invested in close collaborations with these subassemblers to improve quality in the production lines. Suddenly, they were able to deliver a high-quality product quickly at far less cost, giving the rest of the world a very loud wake-up call. They started winning, with quality as a key differentiator.[1]

Global business raced to catch up. Ford Motor Company proclaimed quality "Job #1."[2] Titans like General Electric embraced the process reengineering concepts of Total Quality Management (TQM) and six sigma to drastically reshape the focus of their corporate cultures.[3] Quality was no longer a vertical silo, the responsibility of some deputized quality assurance/quality control (QA/QC) person at the end of the line; it became the responsibility of every employee at every level of every task. Power shifted from the top of the hierarchy down to its base; anyone, at any stage of the process, could stop the line if they found quality compromised. By *designing in* quality at every stage of a business process, enterprises of all types were able to wring inefficiencies from their systems and greatly improve productivity.

The quality movement freed Western businesses from the tyranny of the production triangle and overcame the inverse relationship of cost/quality/time. Suddenly, a company could deliver all three: fast, cheap, *and* good. The best companies today do this every day because that is what it now takes to compete and to win. A Dell computer is not just cheaper; it is just as good as the expensive ones that IBM used to make. Southwest Airlines flies the same routes, under the same regulatory constraints and the same cost pressures as the majors, but found a better way to navigate through a difficult market. Southwest turns around planes faster, makes them perform more reliably, and delivers a high-quality service at a low price.

How did business do it? How did it take this aesthetic, quality, and turn it into a measurable process? First, it sat back and tried to gain some systematic understanding. What are the factors that influence quality? It developed deep knowledge around the forces and dynamics that correlate and cause quality to happen or not happen, and it developed a language in which to frame these thoughts. Armed with that understanding, it began to design, measure, and manage quality as a business process. It broke down the walls surrounding the QA/QC department at the end of the line and pumped the flow of quality throughout the system. In so doing, business took this immeasurable, amorphous thing, quality, and began quantifying it to infinitesimal, six sigma, levels. It gave awards for quality, built international awareness for the accomplishment, and monetized it. Consumers paid more attention to reliability statistics and a company's reputation for quality. More information about the long-term performance of products became readily available in the marketplace and the marketplace reacted accordingly. Companies started winning or losing on quality. The amazing economic growth since that time can be largely laid on the back of this revolution in the HOWS of WHAT of industry.

The closed-loop business approach to quality—based on quantifiable metrics, real-time information, and continual vigilance, which provide organizations a complete grasp on the people, processes, and information that impact manufacturing, sales, and other elements of their business—can be applied equally systematically to the HOWS of human conduct. To thrive in the world to come, we must approach the way interpersonal HOWS work in our organizations in the same way as we did quality. We need to find more ways of building strong synapses between people, getting everyone aligned on a common TRIP, create the environments in which more Waves can start, and develop approaches that transmit these values throughout our group endeavors. To do that, we need to understand systematically the way groups work. We need to understand *culture*.

There are almost as many different types of organizational cultures as there are groups of people working together; although many seem similar, each has its unique flavor. Anytime people come together to accomplish something larger than themselves, a culture grows. A corporate board has a culture, a business unit has a culture, and every team has its culture. Talking about culture, though—what it is made of, how it forms, how it influences group performance, and how it can be changed—has historically been another amorphous thing, and the province of the few who sit at the top of the organizational chart and worry about such things.

In a world of HOW, however, these issues are no longer hidden and no longer the province of the elite few. Everyone must learn to innovate in HOW; not the how of process, but HOW we do what we do. More and more of us work in teams, more and more of us get opportunities to lead and to start Waves, and more and more of us can influence the culture of the group every day. The powerful forces at loose in the networked world have made the understanding of these issues of critical importance to anyone who wants to thrive today. So in this part, we try to shed some light on what makes groups go. To truly succeed, everyone must open up the way we think about the people we work with to include questions of governance and culture.

CHAPTER

10

Doing Culture

I came to see, in my time at IBM,
that culture isn't just one aspect
of the game; it is the game.
—Lou Gerstner, former
Chairman of the Board
and CEO, IBM

The General Electric Aircraft Engine Assembly plant in Durham, North Carolina, produces some of the most powerful and technically complex aircraft engines in the world. Seen from the outside, there is little remarkable about this plant. Two hangar-sized buildings dominate 500 unlandscaped acres of the rolling North Carolina countryside, each with more than three acres of floor space and multistory ceilings. Before GE moved here, it was a steam-generator plant, and the corrugated metal walls and concrete floors betray little about this twenty-first-century enterprise. There are no offices, no recreation centers, and no fancy lunchrooms. Every year, more than 400 of the largest engines in the world roll out the door. These engines power large commercial aircraft, like the Boeing 777 and the Airbus A320, including the engines that keep Air Force One aloft. Each engine GE/Durham makes weighs 8.5 tons or more and has more than 10,000 parts.[1] Each part must be assembled to the most exacting specifications. Nuts as light as an ounce must be tightened to a specific tightness using a torque wrench. Gaskets three feet in diameter can be no more than half the width of a human hair out of round or they will malfunction, causing potential disaster. Each time one of these engines flies, hundreds of people rely on its perfection to arrive at their destination safely.

The special nature of GE/Durham does not reveal itself in its WHATS but rather in its HOWS, as a remarkable article in *Fast Company* magazine reported.[2] Over 200 people work at GE/Durham, a tiny part of a massive conglomerate, and nearly everyone, with the exception of a couple of dozen support personnel, is a Federal Aviation Administration (FAA)-rated technician. All work in teams of less than 20 techs whose only command from management is the date their engine is scheduled to ship. The team decides everything else, from the uncrating of the first part to the moment a team member hops on a forklift to deliver the completed engine to shipping. Each team selects one member to sit on each of nine councils to address issues such as human resources, materials, and training. Membership rotates regularly, and each council addresses a critical component of the principles that drive plant safety, quality, people, and processes.

There are a number of things conspicuously absent from the Durham plant. A time clock, for one. With the exception of a daily team meeting to allow the two shifts to synchronize activity, workers come and go as they like. There is no cleaning crew; everyone cleans up after themselves and the place is spotless. There is no tool lockup; if you can trust people to build an aircraft engine, you can trust them not to walk off with a torque wrench. There is only one boss at GE/Durham, the plant manager, and everyone reports to him. Or more accurately, they *don't* report to him.

GE/Durham builds some of the most sophisticated machines on the planet in a high-trust, high-communication environment with no bosses but one. What does he or she do? Paula Sims, who led the plant four of its first six years of operation, says she focused on the big picture, growth and improvement. She also focused on something GE/Durham has in abundance: trust. She learned that lesson the hard way. "Not long after I started here," she reported, "an employee came to me and said, 'Paula, you realize you don't need to follow up with us to make sure we're doing what we agreed to do. If we say we'll do something, we'll do it.' I sat back and thought, 'Wow. That's so simple. I'm sending the message that I don't trust people because I always follow up.'"

This seemingly ungoverned culture has achieved some remarkable things in its relatively short life. Over the course of five years in the late 1990s, GE/Durham reduced the cost of airplane engine assembly by over 50 percent. The plant reduced quality defects over 75 percent. One in four engines ships with just a single flaw—usually cosmetic—like a scratch or a misaligned wire. The rest are *perfect*. In 1999, they added a new engine to their line, the CFM56, a workhorse at that time used in 40 percent of jets flying more than 100 passengers and in production at other GE assembly plants for years. Within nine weeks, they delivered their first engine, 12 to 13 percent cheaper than plants that had built it for years. This amazed Bob McEwan, then general manager of GE's Evendale assembly operations, where they build the same engines. "Now, down in Durham, you don't hear about process improvement," he told *Fast Company* in the 1999 report. "They are constantly swinging away at it. . . . They have their washers all sorted into holders, like poker chips sorted into trays. You can easily get the washer you want. It's things like that. They don't ask anybody—they just go and do it. Down there, you can get more going in a week's time than you can here in a year." They have another leg up on their brethren as well. In 2002, Evendale released over 2,000 pounds of toxic chemicals into the air.[3] In Durham, they released 10 pounds. As of October 2005, they had gone eight years without a workers' compensation claim. They work smart, they work clean, and they work safe.

With its incredible performance metrics, you might easily assume that what GE/Durham does have is a highly incentivizing employee ownership structure, or at least a profit-sharing arrangement that motivates them to cut costs and improve quality, but that's another thing missing from the picture. There are just three pay grades at GE/Durham—tech-1, tech-2, and tech-3—and each is based on skill level and training. The only monetary incentive is to get better educated, which they call "multiskilling." Multiskilling allows teams to build technical continuity, so that when one tech-3 is on vacation, another can still build a turbine without him. Moreover, no one is trying to graduate into middle management, because there is no middle management. The technicians themselves are responsible for all scheduling, ordering, process management, and deliverables. And they are inspired. "It matters," said technician Bill Lane. "I've got a three-year-old daughter, and I figure that every plane we build engines for has someone with a three-year-old daughter riding on it."

Within the massive bureaucracy that is GE, GE/Durham stands as an outpost of team-oriented, consensus-based self-governance, a culture unto itself, inspired by common values and common purpose. "Upstairs, you've got wrench turners," said Bob McEwan of his Evendale plant. "In Durham, you've got people who think. I think what they've discovered in Durham is the value of the human being."

THE SUM OF ALL HOWS

The success of GE/Durham lies in the unique way people there have chosen to relate to each other, to organize their endeavors, and to govern themselves—in short, their culture. Culture is a company's DNA, the sum total of its history, values, aspirations, beliefs, and endeavors, the operating system, if you will, that defines and influences what occurs at the synapses between everyone working together in a group, large or small. Unlike an operating system, however, just inserting a piece of code—such as a compliance program or an innovation team—cannot change a culture; cultures are alive; they evolve and change over time. Organizational culture, then, is really more like an ecosystem, a highly sophisticated, interdependent cosmos of evolving organisms with a profusion of interrelationships. More simply defined, culture is the way things *really* work, the way decisions are *really* made, e-mails *really* composed, promotions *really* earned and meted out, and people *really* treated every day.

And it matters. Culture is a company's unique character, its lifeblood. It lives in each company's achievements, how its members have dealt with adversity, managed growth and contraction, made the hard choices, and celebrated their greatest victories. Much as some people say that character is one's destiny, culture can be thought of as the destiny of an organization. The culture that grows around any given group of people is unique to them and can't be copied. Others can perhaps duplicate your HOWS in general, but the specific texture and quality of what they total lives uniquely in the people who live by them.

Though cultures within large organizations often share many traits, group cultures are generally singular; they differ from organization to organization, from team to team, and from unit to unit. A large, multinational company that has grown though acquisitions, operates in highly regulated markets, and faces domestic and international risks, laws, and standards manifests a different sort of culture than a family-owned construction company that has grown organically. A family-owned business is by its nature transparent; a small group of people sit down at the table and eat together each night, sharing the life of the enterprise and furthering its culture over chicken and rice. For a larger organization, influencing culture is a more complex challenge.

If individuals' best response to the new global conditions of hypertransparency and hyperconnectedness lies in the mastery of their personal HOWs, the organization's best opportunity to thrive lies in the mastery of culture. "Business leaders and the financial and industry analysts that follow them have also come to recognize that establishing and fostering the right corporate culture is not simply a way of staying out of trouble," said Lou Gerstner of IBM on another occasion, "but represents a fundamental driver of sustainable differentiation and winning in the marketplace."

Mastering culture is no longer a job for just those at the top of the organizational chart. An organization's culture represents the collective action of all the individuals that comprise it, so on the journey to make the most of the new conditions of today, it is incumbent upon everyone who wants to do well to understand the intricacies of how culture works. Making HOW work for you every day requires the ability not only to change the interpersonal synapses between you and your direct associates, but to affect the synapses between everyone on your team. When the press is on to make the quarterly numbers, achieve a great product launch, or put together that great sales presentation, you want to be working in a stadium—whether filled with a half dozen people or a thousand—that can easily make a Wave. Moreover, the new conditions of the hyperconnected world put that ability in almost every worker, not just the top brass. You can approach it in a deliberate way and learn to see it as a system of HOWs that you can shape and influence, each element reinforcing the others in a powerful Wave of achievement. You, too, can master culture.

What? Master culture? Doesn't culture just sort of *happen*?

Well, culture is organic, but it does not grow willy-nilly. To see how all its parts work together in mutually reinforcing ways, let's first examine its components—the moving parts, if you will, that make the thing go. Let's begin by discussing the types of culture most common in business today. This discussion might seem a bit like homework to you, but if you can see the framework it describes, then the chapters that follow will give you a deep sense of how it applies to thriving on the journey ahead.

THE SPECTRUM OF CULTURE

Myriad details shape, influence, and direct the formation of group cultures. Some are intrinsic to the enterprise and cannot be altered. A warehouse operation in which everyone communicates face-to-face or via walkie-talkie and shouting will foment a different culture than a cubicle-filled office where most people communicate at meetings and via e-mail. Both of these will differ from a culture that grows out of the interaction of remote workers or teams working out of their homes or small satellite offices. The substance of the business—what it makes, sells, or serves—also bears a direct relation to culture. A company making transmission gears will grow a culture different from a business statistics and research group. A young, hungry company in a new industry will develop differently from a long-established market leader. Factors like people's age, what they wear, their attitude toward nepotism, or inclusion or exclusion of family in company functions all exert profound influence on the type of culture that grows there. These circumstantial factors are *tokens* of culture, and all influence the basic questions that culture seeks to answer: How are decisions made? How is power wielded? How does information flow? How do Waves happen?

Cultures in general tend to fall into four basic *types*. These types lie along a spectrum that, not coincidentally, also mirrors the historical development of organizational complexity and societal maturity, from the most simple and direct to the most complex and rational. I first spoke about this Spectrum of Culture in my testimony before the U.S. Federal Sentencing Commission in 2004.[4] These states are abstract, but as we discuss them, you will begin to see elements of them in almost every group culture in which you participate.

To get a sense of the broad strokes, let us pretend, for a moment, that we decide to go on a fact-finding mission to a series of factories where heavy and potentially dangerous machinery busily hums away, creating a brighter future for mankind (or just a bunch of well-made widgets that are highly profitable to sell). We want to tour these factories to get a sense of how they operate, so one day we set off to visit four of them.

At the first shop we visit, we meet the shop supervisor, who agrees to lead us around the factory. Grinding gears and large swinging booms whirl around us, and as we look around, the first thing we notice is that some people are wearing hard hats and other protective gear, but many are not. Ducking a low-hanging beam as we walk, we ask if we should perhaps wear something. "Do what you like," he says. "It's your life." As a shower of sparks flies over our heads, we decide that we treasure our vitality more than the information we can gather here at Factory One, and we beat a hasty retreat.

At Factory Two, we immediately notice that almost everyone wears a hard hat, but as the tour begins, no one offers one to us, and there don't seem to be any extras lying around. When we ask about this, the supervisor says, "Yeah, the boss makes us wear them. I hate them myself, but if he catches anyone without one, they get fired, and I need this job. He also makes us wear name tags and blue pants, because he can't remember anyone's name and his favorite color is blue. Go figure."

Factory Three is clean, bright, and well organized. On the wall as we walk in are a number of hard hats clearly labeled "Visitors," above which, on the wall, hang numerous posters spelling out safety procedures and regulations. "Everyone Must Wear a Hard Hat!" says one. "If You Do Not Run It, Do Not Touch It!" says another, and so on. We all immediately pick up bright yellow hats and put them on—all except our head salesperson, who turns to the supervisor and says, "Hey, I've got a meeting with a big client this afternoon and I don't want to mess up my hair with a hat. Is that okay?" The supervisor looks around to see who is watching and thinks to herself for a moment. "Does this person really need to wear a hat?" she asks herself. "He looks pretty important, and I bet my boss would want me to make him happy. I wonder which is going to be better for me, enforcing this rule or making my boss happy?" Clearly, we are important guests, she realizes, and she doesn't want to offend us, but the safety officer has been snooping around of late, and she decides against it this time. "I'd like to say okay," she says, "but there's a rule and I don't want to get busted. If it were up to me, I'd let you slide. Let me ask someone higher up." She disappears for about 15 minutes and then returns looking uneasy. "I couldn't find anyone who can okay it," she says, looking clearly like she doesn't want to offend us, "so I guess you don't have to wear it."

As we walk onto the shop floor at Factory Four, a worker walking by immediately stops what she's doing and hands us all hard hats and protective goggles. Just then, the supervisor walks up and greets us all warmly. The salesman, still concerned about his coif, makes the same appeal, but without hesitation the supervisor says, "At this company, we really believe in safety and if you are not wearing the proper equipment, I'm afraid I can't let you go past this point." The salesman, to our surprise, becomes incensed (he's a bit of a maverick with an overdeveloped sense of importance) and complains loudly that he is a friend of the plant's owner and he should be allowed to do as he pleases. "I'm sorry, sir," the foreman replies, "but I take personal responsibility that nothing happens to you. I don't want to offend you, and you can call my boss or the owner if you like, but I believe your safety and the safety of everyone are paramount."

THE FOUR TYPES OF CULTURE

The culture in Factory One views safety from a state of *anarchy and lawlessness*, a state where everyone acts in their own self-interest with little regard for the group dynamic or organizational ethos. Village markets, desert traders, and local artisans operated in these conditions long ago, independent operators unbound by formal organizational principles. Needless to say, the turnover rate at this factory is quite high (as is the incidence of missing limbs and major concussions), but no one seems to care because they have no health plan anyway and there are lots more workers waiting to take the place of the injured when they can no longer perform their jobs. These cultures, by their very nature, build little of the predictability and certainty that capital-based enterprise requires to thrive (you can't get people on a TRIP if they are all going their own way). Few of these cultures survive today in any significant way, though, as we will see, remnants of their habits and behaviors do.

Factory Two's culture treats safety as a matter of *blind obedience*. Blind obedience characterizes many of the traits we associate with early, industrial age capitalistic enterprises, the culture of the manufacturing facilities of nineteenth-century Europe and the old assembly-line factories of early twentieth-century America, as well as the culture of the feudal societies that preceded them. Labor was plentiful back then, largely unskilled or manual in nature, and jobs were few. Robber barons, industrialists, and monopolists fought to gain dominance over their spheres of influence, and ruled with an iron hand. In Factory Two, no one questions the boss and everyone does what they are told or faces the consequences. They do not necessarily understand why they wear those hard hats and blue pants, nor do they necessarily care. It is enough for each to achieve their individual goals, so they wear the blue pants and ask few questions.

Factory Three, as clean and efficient as it is, is infused with a culture of *informed acquiescence*. Informed acquiescence cultures are rules-based; those wishing to participate in the culture learn the rules and agree to abide by them. The rules are clearly spelled out for everyone, and workers either embrace the rules without qualm or spend time dancing with the rules as they try to make things work. Informed acquiescence cultures dominated twentieth-century capitalism, and for good reason. Rules-based cultures are efficient and scalable. In a top-down organizational model, management can issue directives and have them sift down through the organizational chart in predictable and controllable ways. As operations scale up, larger numbers of people can be trained and governed easily. The variables of individual behaviors are minimized. With organizational boxes clearly defined, they can be filled with qualified individuals who understand the box they have to fill, the rules of the game in which they fill it, and the road up the ladder to success. As such, informed acquiescence cultures tend to be management-oriented, with an established managing class and a well-entrenched bureaucracy.

Informed acquiescence represented a brilliant and innovative step forward from blind obedience. The majority of companies, until recently, ran fairly successful operations governed by these principles.

People could share more information (albeit in controlled ways), had a much higher degree of certainty and predictability, could collaborate better, and for the most part knew just where they stood. Informed acquiescence expresses the highest goals of rationalism. It treats people as rational agents: people who like carrots and hate sticks, people who like to be motivated because motivation leads to concrete results. Rationalism takes an impersonal approach to the vast complexity that is human behavior, in all its complicated glory. It strives for a world that is more black-and-white and contains fewer shades of gray; thus it is easier to manage and simpler to control. Workers are rationally informed about what is expected of them, their reward is clearly articulated, and they, in turn, acquiesce to those rules and expectations. Informed acquiescence lets us set our sights and strive. Trillions of dollars of wealth and value were created upon its back, great companies were built, humankind advanced, and many people progressed and improved their lives.

It is Factory Four, though, that most interests us. In Factory Four, everyone takes personal responsibility for maintaining a safe working environment, because they have come to believe that safety is in everyone's best interests. It is, in a word, *valuable*. This represents the fourth general type of culture, *values-based self-governance*. There is a difference between employees who believe in a value and ones who comply with a bunch of rules. The former are governed by *should*, as in "Keeping people safe is something I value, so everyone should wear a hard hat." They believe it; they act on their belief, and they self-govern in the name of it; when faced with a choice, the value they hold close guides them surely. The informed acquiescence employees, who are only concerned with rules, live in the world of *can*. Because the rules live outside of them, they work in a *gapped* relationship to regulations. Faced with a VIP who does not want to comply (or any situation that does not fit neatly within the rules), they are left to make decisions absent guidance other than enlightened self-interest. If they cannot decide, they call someone else to do so, a manager or boss, and so it goes up the line until someone makes a decision. Into the gap between the individual and the rules falls time, efficiency, and perhaps safety itself.

Informed acquiescence culture, with its hierarchical separation of functions, actually reinforces this gap. One department—say, compliance—might issue proscriptive regulations controlling what you can and can't say to the marketplace about your products and competition, and another—say, the sales department—might give guidance about what moves the product. In the middle, a salesperson is left to bridge the gap on her own. "I can't *say* that," she might think, "but the notion moves product. Perhaps I can *intimate* it instead." When something is expressed as a self-governing value, by contrast, no one tries to split the middle, because there is no middle. The value—in the salesperson's case, truthfulness—provides a clear *should* that is unambiguous. And she doesn't have to say, "I'll go check with my boss to see what I can say or do." She can act on her belief, immediately, efficiently, and rapidly. There is no gap, either personally or institutionally, between the individual and the best behavior (see Figure 10.1).

Values speak to the higher self. They have the power to inspire and not just motivate. They breed belief. Values-based self-governance, in turn, performs a remarkable double duty: It controls unwanted behavior

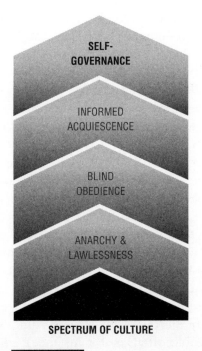

SPECTRUM OF CULTURE

FIGURE 10.1

while simultaneously inspiring higher conduct. In this way, values are actually a more efficient determiner of HOW we do what we do than are rules. When we embrace a value and weld it to our behavior, we believe in what we do. Business defined in values terms is business done for a higher purpose, inspired for the greater good. A person aligned with a company value will be less likely to betray that value, because to do so does not just break a company policy; it betrays the self. At the root of these cultures lies shared values, the HOWS that guide every interaction.

Business has become really good about safety since the early 1990s, in great measure because, perhaps without realizing it, it shifted safety from a set of rules and programs to a part of its core values system, and then found a way to transmit those values throughout the workforce. In other words, it changed safety from a vertical silo of WHAT into a horizontal force of HOW that powered every part of the operation, shifting it from a set of rules to a part of culture. And it succeeded. From 1992 to 2002, U.S. workplace fatalities declined 11 percent, and injuries and illness in private industry declined a remarkable 34 percent, not from more safety cops, but from more safety belief.[5]

Anarchy and lawlessness, blind obedience, informed acquiescence, and values-based self-governance represent the four basic types of group culture, but almost no company, team, or group is wholly one or another; they often contain bits of each in different measures. When that top salesperson decides that expense limits do not apply to him and orders the most expensive bottle of wine on the menu at his dinner meeting, he in a sense indulges anarchic impulses. "Rules are not for me," he seems to say. "I'll get it done my way." (Although such mavericks have a special place in the history of business, when most people organize to achieve something bigger than themselves they tend to embrace some sort of regulating system, so we will not focus much on anarchy and lawlessness for the purposes of this discussion.) When the boss writes that "Get it to me by 4:00 P.M." e-mail, she is relying on the autocratic authority and the threat of punitive reprisal characteristic of blind obedience cultures to coerce results.

There are no hard walls between these four basic cultures; most groups organize themselves in a progressive and evolutionary state embracing elements of all four. They require some of the coercion of blind obedience (fireable offenses, for instance); some rules and acquiescence to them (but not the stupid ones); maybe a skosh of anarchy now and again to stir the pot; and some measure of self-governance. Larger groups may have a number of different, related, cultures operating separately within a single organization. A corporate board might have a culture distinct from the management team, which in turn oversees smaller teams with unique characteristics. GE/Durham represents a distinct unit within the large panoply that is GE, as different from its parent as MTV Networks is from other units of Viacom.

Culture can seem an ephemeral thing, one of those soft things that are so difficult to get a grasp on sometimes. Now that we have an overview of the essential *types* of culture that dominate business, let's try to break it down further to understand the various *dimensions* of culture, the HOWS at work whenever a group forms for a common purpose. Let us explore ways to make something "soft" into something "hard" that we can do something about.

FIVE HOWS OF CULTURE

Culture occurs at the synapses where people interact. Synapses, as we know, are capable of receiving signals from many different sources at once, as a diamond can receive light from many angles and refract it in many directions. So let us imagine the processes of culture entering these synapses as light enters the facets of a diamond. The nature and character of the stone—thus, the culture—determine which light will get through, and in what direction it will travel. Though many things come to bear upon how culture grows and operates, some forces and structures are more influential than others. Figure 10.2 identifies 22 of what I think of as the most influential dimensions of culture, the facets through which human energy flows. Each dimension is defined by the way it manifests itself within the three types of cultures we are most concerned about. In order to better survey these dimensions, I have grouped them on a table into five HOWS: How We Know, How We Behave, How We Relate, How We Recognize, and How We Pursue (see Figure 10.2). The table provides the defining characteristics of each dimension for each of the three cultures we have discussed (the fourth, anarchy, I have inserted as a placeholder to remind you where it lives in the spectrum of culture, but left blank because it rarely relates to our lives today).

THE FIVE **HOW**S OF CULTURE

DIMENSIONS OF CULTURE		ANARCHY	BLIND OBEDIENCE
HOW WE KNOW	Use of Information		Hoarding
HOW WE BEHAVE	Organizational Structure		Silos & Fiefdoms
	Source of Behavior		Autocratic Leadership
	Reason for Behavior		Coercive
	Responsibility for Own & Others' Behavior		Central Policing Authority
	Source of Authority (Who Gets to Decide)		Power Figure—Arbitrary
	Magnitude of Authority		Authority without Recourse
	Source of Regulation		Externally Imposed
HOW WE RELATE	Roles & Types of Skills		Follower & Worker
	Personnel Development		Rote Learning
	Level of Trust		Heavy Inspection & Limited Delegation
	Rules vs. Values		Minimal Adherence —Loopholes
	Nature of Relationships (Employees)		Suspicion & Penalty Based
	Nature of Relationships (Customers)		Suspicion & Close Monitoring
	Nature of Relationships (Supplier/Third Party)		Arm's Length—Transactional
HOW WE RECOGNIZE	Rewards & Recognition		Conformity &/or Obedience
	Penalties & Discipline		Supervisor Determined—Fear
HOW WE PURSUE	Time Orientation		Short-Term
	Mission & Purpose for Existence		Survival—Coerced to Participate
	Determination & Definition of Significance		Significance Not a Concern, Human Doing
	Attention to Regulatory & Legal Requirements		Emphasis on Enforcement
	Attention to Market & Public Dynamics		Superficial Attention— Game the System

FIGURE 10.2   The Dimensions of Culture

INFORMED ACQUIESCENCE	SELF-GOVERNANCE
Need-to-Know Basis	Transparent
Division of Expertise & Functions	Integration with High Trust
Rules Based	Values & Principles Based
Motivated by Individual Self-Interest	Inspired for Greater Good
Individual Organizational Units	Universal Vigilance
Power Figure—Consistent with Rules	Individual—Values Based
Top-Down Decision Making	Empowerment & Individual Accountability
Voluntarily Adhered to Internal & External	Act on Shared Beliefs
Manager	Leader
Training	Education
Checks & Balances, Contracts	High Trust & Verify
Compliance with Requirements	Guided by What Is Right to Do
Honorable Work— Pay & Reward	Social Contract— Committed to Growth
Price It Fairly & Get Paid in Return	Add Value Beyond Expectation
Contractual, Fair, Impartial with Continuity	Mutual Collaboration— Make Each Other Better
Rewards for Personal & Organizational Success	Satisfaction in Achieving Mission & Significance
Established Structures & Procedures	Guilt from Self & Peer Pressure & Sanctions
Short-Term & Long-Term Goals	Driven by Legacy & Endurance for the Enterprise
Success Oriented— Reward for Achievement	Mission, Promise, & Significance
Journey of Success	Journey of Significance
Controlled by Rewards & Penalties	Proactive & Preventive
Highly Responsive & Reactionary	Lead & Transcend the Markets

How We Know

The first thing that distinguishes the nature of a culture is how it creates, communicates, and uses information. This single factor is so central and influential to our HOWs that it warrants a group by itself.

- Cultures of blind obedience hoard information in the hands of the elite few. Workers are primarily task-oriented. Bosses issue decrees from above with no explanation, and nothing strategic can be gained from letting others in on your secrets.

- As organizations and groups gain in complexity, informed acquiescence cultures require ways to transmit information in an efficient and orderly fashion. These companies go to extraordinary lengths to share necessary information—group members are well trained and can readily access the rules of conduct, for instance—but management still tightly controls other information and releases it on a need-to-know basis. The old maxim, "A little knowledge is a dangerous thing," lurks just below the surface of all operational decisions.

- Self-governing cultures, by contrast, require conditions of transparency to thrive. If individuals, inspired by the core values of the group, are to be truly trusted to self-govern then they must have free and unfettered access to the information they need to make sound and reasonable judgments. At Nordstrom, for example, new employees receive a very simple statement that tells them almost everything they need to know about the company's culture. First, it states Nordstrom's fundamental commitment, "To provide outstanding customer service." Then it lists the Nordstrom rules: "Use good judgment. We trust one another's integrity and ability. Our only rule: Use good judgment in all situations."[6] Perhaps no finer statement of self-governance exists today. But the key to the Nordstrom culture lies in the next statement, the last new employees receive: "Please feel free to ask your department manager, store manager, or division general manager any question at any time." Deeply imbedded within the self-governing culture of Nordstrom is the idea that all information is accessible to everyone, regardless of seniority or status.

How We Behave

There are three basic ways that people can compel action in others: (1) They can *coerce* them, bullying, threatening, or cajoling them to do something against their will; (2) they can *motivate* them, using promises of reward or fear and threats of repercussion to get them to willingly agree that the desired action is in their best interest; or (3) they can *inspire* them, connect with them in a way that the desired action become a common goal. The second HOW of culture broadly encompasses the source and reason for personal or group behavior. Why do people do what they do? What keeps them from doing A rather than B?

- In blind obedience cultures, people obey. Autocratic leaders keep people in line by coercing them to comply. "Wear blue pants or you'll be fired" is a clear indicator of a coercive relationship between leaders and followers. If you imagine a spectrum between internal and external control of behavior, blind obedience falls furthest toward the latter. The source of authority (i.e., who gets to decide things) falls to a power figure who can make unilateral decisions and wield that authority without recourse over those below them. To accommodate this sort of power structure, blind obedience cultures tend to have extremely vertical management structures, with authority concentrated in the hands of the few. Each boss rules his or her domain like an independent silo and fiefdom. The boss keeps everyone in line, decides what's right and wrong, and provides clear marching orders.

If this sounds like the Army, you would not be far from wrong. Modern military cultures, which grew out of the experience of World War I, made blind obedience culture into a high art, and with great success. Unquestioning submission to central authority, they believed, built the floors of certainty, predictability, and unit cohesion necessary for soldiers to lay down their lives for one another. Though it may not sound like the most appealing culture in which to work, you might be surprised to learn that the movie business grew up in the same model. The fledgling motion picture industry took off just after the First World War. Returning veterans, looking for new opportunity, flocked to the

West Coast to take up crew positions in this fast-growing new field. Film crews, like armies, are large mobile units that must move people and machinery from location to location in response to every changing demand. It made perfect sense for these new crew people to organize in the way they knew the best. Thus each department—sound, camera, lighting, sets, production, and so on—created its own autonomous fiefdom, with a rigid command-and-control structure. Though much more highly evolved, film crews today operate in much the same way around the world.

- Unlike blind obedience cultures, in which everyone defers to the boss, in informed acquiescence cultures everyone defers to the rules. Rules try to present an objective and fair guide for all behavior. These cultures tend to create organizational hierarchies based on expertise and function, promoting the most qualified to management roles where they manage by top-down decision making. Managers try to act consistently (and rationally) within the rules. The responsibility for monitoring fealty to the rules falls to a discrete organizational unit, often legal counsel or compliance officers, charged with training and monitoring compliance. Informed acquiescence relies on a reward and punishment structure to motivate people, and people follow because they see compliance to be in their own best interest. This central self-interest factor places informed acquiescence cultures in the center of the behavioral spectrum between internal and external control. People acquiesce to what is asked of them because they are primarily motivated by personal success, and they see doing what has been asked as a high-value step toward that goal. Leaders and managers in these cultures use carrots-and-sticks methods to motivate desired behavior.

- Self-governing cultures find their engine of behavior in values and principles. Values and principles are the source of inspiration, and when we are guided by them or acting on their behalf we believe in what we are doing and find significance within the effort. On the spectrum from internal to external behavioral control, self-governance relies on the internal resources of the individual for much of its power. Authority accrues to individuals in accordance with their alignment with group core values,

and the emphasis throughout the group is on personal enfranchisement and individual accountability. People joined together
by common inspiration and shared core values form tight, uncon-
ditional bonds, unlike the lighter, conditional bonds of carrot-and-
stick cultures. Organizational structure in self-governing cultures
is tightly integrated—flatter, if you will—and the synapses between individuals and teams operate in a state of high trust. Self-
governance requires universal vigilance; in self-governed groups,
the responsibility for one's own and others' behavior becomes
the job of everyone on the team. (As Thomas Jefferson, one of
the crafters of the U.S. Constitution and no stranger to the
concept of individual liberty, said, "The price of Freedom is
eternal vigilance."[7]) Acting on shared beliefs makes everyone
self-regulating with regard to both company priorities and external control. At GE/Durham, for example, no one has a "boss";
everyone is one. "I have 15 bosses," reported Keith McKee, a
team technician. "All of my teammates are my bosses." With
everyone accountable for the team's success, no one tolerates
slacking; the culture becomes self-enforcing and feedback becomes the name of the game.

How We Relate

The third HOW of culture describes the dimensions that govern and influence the interpersonal synapses between members of a group: the
roles and types of skills that each person manifests, the group's approach to developing those skills, the level of trust that fills the decision-
making process, the group's relationship to doing the right thing, and the
nature of the relationships between employees, customers, and suppliers—basically, how we all get along.

- Blind obedience cultures delegate little power down the chain of
  command. They fill their ranks with followers and workers who
  often feel subjected to heavy inspection of their efforts by bosses.
  Stiff penalties keep the rank and file marching in the lockstep
  necessary for the endeavor to move. Suspicion often fills the relationships between co-workers; the mercurial nature of autocratic

leadership leaves few feeling secure in their positions. The same suspicion is directed outside the organization's fortress walls at customers and suppliers, the former also viewed with suspicion and closely monitored, and the latter kept at arm's length. Partnership with outsiders is anathema in these cultures, so people tend to be transactional in nature and short-term in orientation.

- Cultures of informed acquiescence make individuals into managers of job function, consistent with its strict, hierarchical approach to organizational structure. Personnel development is achieved through a training approach to carefully tailor information to specific function and expertise. Emphasis is on performance and performance management. To develop yourself in informed acquiescence cultures, you would read a book called *The 14 Steps to This* or *The 50 Rules of Great That*. Trust flows between people as it is earned, but is often restricted by a system of checks and balances that keeps managers accountable for their underlings. These carrot-and-stick cultures reward honorable work consistent with company directives. This is capitalism as we know it, with customers and suppliers more often seen as vendors and suppliers than partners. Contracts rule external relationships, with lots of requests for proposals (RFPs) and multiple bids for services even when proven supplier relationships exist. These approaches strive for fairness and impartiality, and often achieve it within a controlled framework.

- In self-governing cultures, the role of every individual is to lead and be a leader. Each individual is called upon to make more values-based decisions, so people need the education and, more important, the experience of wrestling with issues and coming to their own conclusions. Rote learning and training approaches fall short of giving them the tools they need to be self-generating. This book, in many ways, takes an educational approach to HOW. It gives you few rules of thumb or exercises to impart its knowledge, but rather tries to lay out the broad picture of the issues it addresses and stories that illuminate the many ways the concepts can be applied. It might make it a little harder for you, the reader, to get quick and easy answers, but it does give you a perspective and knowledge from which you can evaluate things for yourself, a lens through which you can view the myriad and quick-changing events that make up a business day. In self-governing cultures, there is no one way to take the TRIP; to become self-governing is a continuous evolution unique to each individual and group. Someone can point the way, but you must traverse the hills (and spend some time in the Valley of C) on your own.

Self-governing cultures are high-trust cultures. As Paula Sims's experience at GE/Durham demonstrates, behaviors that sent signals of distrust undermine the enfranchisement of the individual. Trust begets trust, and the opposite is also true. In return for trust and autonomy, relationships between members of the group recognize the implicit social contract and include the greater good. Likewise, suppliers and customers are embraced as partners; mutual collaboration and improvement become the rule with suppliers, and added value the goal with customers. The language of values that drives these cultures can inspire behavior above the floor of contracts and agreements, adding the capacity to delight customers and exceed expectation in every relationship.

How We Recognize

The fourth HOW of culture is simply the way culture tends to reward achievement and discipline transgression.

- Blind obedience cultures, obviously, reward conformity and/or obedience. Supervisors, at their whim, mete out punishment, and the arbitrary nature of the discipline creates fear, which keeps people in line.
- Informed acquiescence cultures take a far more rational approach and attempt to create clear rules and standards by which reward and control are exercised. The rewards accrue to those who achieve individual or organizational success.
- Self-governing cultures reward those who further the mission and significance of the enterprise, even if it might cause short-term financial loss. That is because the interpersonal alignment

that makes these cultures successful is more valuable in the long run than a short-term opportunity. Preserving this alignment allows the culture to be largely self-policing, with deviation from common values met by the stigma from peers and that sense of betraying oneself we spoke about earlier.

The HOWS of celebration—who gets the awards, who gets featured in the company newsletter, who is feted by the team at the annual retreat—are often overlooked in group cultures, but they are vitally important to the nature of culture. Companies that want A, however, often reward B. My friend Steve Kerr, former chief learning officer at GE and Goldman Sachs, first wrote about this phenomenon more than 30 years ago in an article for the *Academy of Management Journal* called "On the Folly of Rewarding A, While Hoping for B."[8] "I built a nice little model that illustrates the effect of a reward system on culture," he told me one day. "If you take a chance based on the best information available and you get it right, you get a *small* reward. If you take a chance based on the best information you have and you get it wrong, you get a *medium-sized* punishment. If you take *no* chance, and just go along with the boss or go along with the majority, you get a small reward. So what would you do?"[9]

I had to think about it a moment; then I did the math and it became clear: Taking a chance and getting it right gets you about the same size reward as taking no chance. Taking no chance avoids the possibility of getting it wrong. "In such a system," Steve concluded, "you end up with tremendously risk-averse behaviors. The leaders, lacking self-awareness, don't realize they've caused this, and they complain about their 'gutless colleagues' who take no chances. But the culture flows from the rewards and punishments in place."

A recent WorkTrends study by Gantz Wiley Research revealed the deep schisms that lie at the heart of many business cultures. While six in 10 respondents believed "My company's senior management supports and practices high standards of ethical conduct," only a third felt that "Where I work, people do not get ahead unless their behavior clearly demonstrates my company's values."[10] A Workplace 2000 Employee Insight Survey revealed that, though workers want their work to make a difference, 75 percent of them do not think their company's mission statement has become the way it does business.[11]

Charles Hampden-Turner, who works with companies the world over on issues of culture, told me a great story about Hewlett-Packard (HP), a culture that, until its board scandal, was famous for getting its HOWs right. "My friend Carl Hodges at Hewlett-Packard got a gold medal for defiance from Dave Packard, the head of the company," he told me. "HP was doing R&D for the Apollo lunar landing module, and Packard wanted it out. 'I don't want to see it again,' he told Carl. So Carl got it out of research—he put it into production. And Packard was really upset with him. Later, he relented and supported the project, which allowed the descent on the moon and made a mint of money for HP. So Dave Packard gave Carl Hodges a gold medal for defiance, and he delivered it in front of everyone, so everyone knew that he was wrong and Carl was right."[12]

How We Pursue

We have agreed that groups come together to achieve a higher goal, one greater than individuals can achieve alone. The final, and perhaps most important, HOW of culture deals with the dimensions that express *why* we do what we do, the nature and purpose of our efforts. Foremost among these dimensions is our relationship to time.

- Individuals working within a blind obedience culture find success in a short-term relationship to their efforts. They are generally task-oriented, and spend little time considering the future or the long-term implications of their endeavors. If your short-term focus is on conquering and controlling as much as you can, you feel little compulsion to consider the long-term effects of your pursuits on resources, physical or psychic. Blind obedience cultures pay little attention to the market as a whole or the public dynamics of their interactions; they follow their leaders and go where they are told. Leaders tend to view power and success as achievable though control, and anything that gets in the way of that effort—government regulation or public opinion—is just an obstacle to be conquered or avoided whenever possible. This leads to all sorts of back-room dealing and hostile approaches to competitors.

The mission and purpose of cultures like this is survival, and the members of the group are generally coerced into the journey. Little in blind obedience cultures concerns itself with transcendence, and the pursuit of significance is largely absent from everyday endeavor. This is human doing, not human being—execution, not pursuit. A short-term temporal orientation is not unique to industrial age efforts. An Internet start-up, or similar such new enterprise, struggling to gain a foothold in a fast-changing landscape can find itself in a similar relationship to time. The race to obtain funding or appease the financial market might bring this same cultural dimension into play, causing people to ignore the long-term ramifications of their choices in favor of getting it done *now*. Unless these efforts can be seen within a longer-range goal, some of the forces of blind obedience can seep into even the most well-intentioned cultures.

- Informed acquiescence cultures attempt to balance short-term orientation with long-term goals. Long-term goals key them into the market and create a great sensitivity to public dynamics, so these cultures are highly responsive to the needs of the marketplace and react quickly to changes and new demands. Carrots-and-sticks approaches motivate people internally, and the culture responds to regulatory and legal requirements in the same way, looking for ways to dance with the rules in order to gain the maximum amount of carrots. Informed acquiescence cultures are compliance cultures, with specialized compliance officers attempting to regulate behavior through rewards and penalties. Thus, the pursuit of goals is always subject to external scrutiny and the limiting nature of rules-based approaches. Informed acquiescence cultures are on a journey of success. They reward achievement and measure that success by the financial return of their endeavors.

- Self-governing cultures, in order to achieve the close values alignment required for real cohesion, necessarily think about the long-term. The culture must be driven and defined by the legacy and endurance of the enterprise and its quest for significant goals. It must keep one foot always in the future to inspire common pursuit in its highly trusted individuals. This future orientation puts self-governing cultures ahead of the time curve in many areas. It creates the conditions by which they can lead and transcend the markets, and, because of the *should* nature of values-driven endeavors, it creates a proactive and preventative relationship toward regulatory and legal requirements. Self-governing cultures coalesce around mission, promise, and the pursuit of significance, a journey that is, in many ways, its own reward.

DOING CULTURE

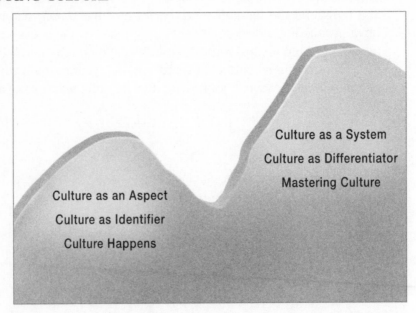

Culture as a System
Culture as Differentiator
Mastering Culture

Culture as an Aspect
Culture as Identifier
Culture Happens

In this chapter, we've broken culture down into its constituent parts and developed a vocabulary with which to understand the way groups in an enterprise function. These various dimensions of culture combine in myriad and infinite ways to create unique and diverse group cultures, as impossible to replicate as a snowflake. This tremendous variety means culture can become a key source of long-term differentiation.

We've also taken the first steps toward an understanding of both the importance of culture to our ability to thrive and the fact that culture is something we do, and can do, in an active way. Culture is made of the little things that pass between people every day. Taken as a whole, these HOWS form an organic ecosystem that can be planted, watered, fertilized, weeded, and given plenty of encouragement to grow. Grasping how culture works gives you the building blocks to grow a culture that can really outbehave the competition.

In the next chapter, we chart a path forward toward a new model for group culture that can best equip us for the road ahead: values-based self-governance.

11

The Case for Self-Governing Cultures

*If from lawlessness or fickleness, from folly
or self-indulgence, [we] refuse to govern
[our]selves, then assuredly in the end [we]
will have to be governed from the outside.*
—Theodore Roosevelt, 1907

C ulture lies in the synapses between individual units of a system, whether that be neurons in the brain, individuals in a group, or units in a conglomerate. Now that we understand something about the general types of culture at work in most business endeavors today, and the various dimensions that define and influence how these cultures function, what do we do with that knowledge? How does it help us make Waves, go on TRIPs, and continue to thrive in the new conditions of twenty-first-century business?

Blind obedience, informed acquiescence, and values-based self-governance are not just types of culture; they also describe an approach to governing—how organizations create the rules, structures, policies, and procedures that shape the way people behave and perform. As we discussed, blind obedience and informed acquiescence cultures place most governance outside the individual, in the hands of a boss or a set of rules. They seek to control things the same way the guardrails in a bowling alley are used to keep kids' balls from rolling into the gutter; roll the ball and the guardrails keep it on the lane and moving in the right direction. Transparency and connectedness, however, make cultures based on one form of external control or another less ideal for our new world. It is no longer enough to just get the ball to the pins; because everyone is watching, we must now bowl strikes. Few would deny that in a horizontal, hyperconnected, and hypertransparent world, to bowl strikes we need a working environment that connects people and groups more intensely, is powered by communication and information flow, and enfranchises individuals at all levels of the company to act quickly and autonomously when presented with new opportunities by the fast-moving marketplace.

But as the rapid changes in technology since the mid-1990s created a new type of hyperconnected worker, little has changed in the underlying structures of how we organize and govern ourselves to truly take advantage of our new reality. The guardrails are still in place. To thrive in the new conditions of twenty-first-century capitalism, groups must learn to place the structures of governance in each individual's hands. At the heart of this process lies a fundamentally different relationship between governance—the way we seek to control things—and culture—the way things really happen. Instead of achieving culture through governance, companies must learn to govern *through* culture, to put the guardrails of governance within the culture itself.

To govern through culture is to govern through HOWS, through the internal structures that influence every action and relationship in an organization. This represents a profound shift in focus from blind obedience and informed acquiescence, the two governing systems with which we are most familiar. It moves governance higher up the food chain, if you will, while also distributing it throughout the diverse parts of the variegated whole. Rather than governing with a matrix of rules and authorities laid over the organization, governing through culture is about governing from within the corpus. When governing through culture, rules don't work well, values do; motivation does not bind people together, beliefs will; external controls are less effective, and self-governance is more efficient. A culture of HOW, one that uniquely transforms new conditions into new opportunities, as we have already learned, has a name: values-based self-governance.

SELF-GOVERNANCE ON THE SHOP FLOOR

We have three compelling reasons to embrace the idea of governing through culture: We can, we must, and we should do so.

We Can

The evolution in transparency and communication, the breakdown of the fortress, and everything else we have discussed about the new conditions in the twenty-first century enable us to see and affect culture on every level. We can identify, quantify, and systematize the dimensions of culture as never before, allowing us a unique opportunity to unleash its power and efficiency.

We Must

When I was asked to testify before the U.S. Federal Sentencing Commission when the committee was considering revisions to the Federal Sentencing Guidelines, I made a passionate argument about the centrality of culture to business governance.[1] The committee heard from many other experts as well, and they incorporated these ideas into their new recommendations to judges dealing with corporate malfeasance.[2] The newest guidelines direct judges determining a company's culpability for wrongdoing to evaluate an organization's commitment to "promote an organizational culture that encourages ethical conduct and a commitment to compliance with the law."[3] The U.S. Department of Justice, interpreting the committee's findings, made it even more clear, saying, "A corporation is directed by its management and *management is responsible for a corporate culture* in which criminal conduct is either discouraged or tacitly encouraged."[4] [italics added]

"Our work on the commission was nothing less than a battle for the hearts and minds of the people who work at companies," Judge Ruben Castillo told me when we visited with each other in his chambers in Chicago.[5] Castillo is vice chair of the commission and has served as a U.S. district judge for the Northern District of Illinois since 1994. "The guidelines became more than just a way to reduce [incidents calling for] fines and punishment; they aspire to induce higher values and bring the business community to higher levels of conduct." As we move forward into an ever more transparent world, culture—the character of an organization—is now everyone's responsibility.

We Should

Culture can't be copied. The collective experience of any group of people forms a unique narrative, a story that lives and breathes in the halls, offices, and factories of that enterprise. The way people connect, spark against one another to create new ideas or refine old ones, solve problems, and overcome adversity builds the synapses that make an organization thrive or die, and no two groups conglomerate these experiences alike. Each is as unique as any family; the number of children can be the same but the ties that bind them will always be unique. Because of this singularity, culture, as an expression of the collective HOWs of a group or enterprise, gives us our greatest opportunity for differentiation. Many of the people I spoke to agreed. "Culture is a competitive advantage that's very, very hard to imitate," Charles Hampden-Turner told me. "If you have a particular culture, another company can come along and seize your patent and try to imitate your product, but your culture has the huge advantage of both being real to the people who understand it and of being almost impossible to emulate. It doesn't 'scale up,' as people like to say, because it is a process rather than a product."[6]

Just like we all know that one family can't copy another, one company can't copy another's culture. I put this precise question to Massimo Ferragamo, chairman of Ferragamo USA, Inc., a subsidiary of Salvatore Ferragamo Italia, which controls sales and distribution of Ferragamo high-fashion products in North America. "Families cannot copy one another and companies cannot copy each other," he told me.[7] Massimo is the youngest of six children of Salvatore and Wanda Ferragamo.[8] It was Salvatore Ferragamo who started the family shoemaking business at age 15 in Italy. Massimo followed in his father's footsteps and began working in the family company at age 12, putting shoes into boxes. Today, he, his mother, his siblings, their children, and a slew of other relatives preside over a luxury fashion empire with more than

200 retail locations around the world. As they embark on the journey to take the company public, Massimo has had ample opportunity to think about what will make the family business endure in the new millennium. And for him, it boils down to culture. "It is the culture that is not copiable. It is values and deep things that are very hard to duplicate. Those values are established by someone naturally in the life of the company, often without them even knowing it, and then gets carried through the threads of people who embrace those values and culture. I would venture to say this: Our U.S. company and our Japanese company and our Italian company, in three different parts of the world, stand a much greater chance of having a similar culture that two unrelated companies that occupy the same building in Florence."

Organizations can win through culture, by getting their HOWS right and setting off Waves of creativity and purpose throughout their workforce. Winning today requires surpassing expectation because great companies don't just fulfill contracts; they exceed them. They outbehave the competition. "It means giving an experience that no one else can do," Ferragamo told me, "and it is very, very challenging. It means excellence to the *n*th degree."

I asked Massimo for an example of how he thinks he can outbehave his competition. "I was talking to a lovely lady who works in our company," he said. "She was on holiday and passed by one of our stores that was extremely busy. She doesn't work in our retail stores, but she went in and said, 'Let me give you a hand.' It was 10:30 in the morning and she didn't leave until 5:30 that evening, and this was her *vacation*. During the day, a customer came in and said to her, 'I have my Christmas shopping to do and I do not know what to do, and I am in a hurry.' She said, 'Look, do you have a list?' He gave it to her. To make a long story short, he sat down with a drink and she just brought over things. He left with a six- or seven-thousand-dollar purchase, and I am sure she made his day. The challenge for me is how do I duplicate that commitment, not as a happenstance, but as a standard? How do I create a culture where we can play a great game and keep on scoring so that everyone can still be that excited by the game? That is how you outbehave competition."

In an informed acquiescence culture, you could do everything that the carrots and sticks require, play by the rules, and still never *delight* or *surprise* anyone. Self-governance is about giving people the freedom to act individually and creatively, to uncork their ability to surprise people and create delight. In a world where your HOWs matter most, governing through culture puts the opportunity to exceed expectations in the hands of those who can make the difference.

FREEDOM IS JUST ANOTHER WORD

When most people first think of self-governance in the abstract, it seems all well and good. But when they think about it concretely, fear creeps in. How can an organization function, they ask, when workers are free to do what they want?

But what is freedom? Some people think that freedom is an absence of constraint. "If I could just do exactly what I want," they think, "I could really get something done." Danish philosopher Soren Kierkegaard had a different thought: "Anxiety is the dizziness of freedom," he said.[9]

Researchers at the University of Erfurt in Germany set up an investment game to discover exactly what freedom means to people—in dollars and cents. They recruited 84 players and gave them 20 tokens each. To make it interesting, and to ensure a real profit motive, they told the players they could redeem their tokens for real money at the end of the game. In each of a number of rounds, players could choose whether to invest some or none of their tokens in a fund. The fund had a guaranteed return, and after every round, the profit would be distributed to the entire group equally, including those free riders who chose not to invest.[10] The game was totally transparent; everyone could see what everyone else did. Those were the ground rules.

Next (and here is where it gets interesting), they established two different types of groups: those that permitted members to penalize other members and those that did not—in other words, groups that had a self-governing system and those in which participants were totally free to do as they liked. Players had to choose a group with which to invest, and after each round they could change groups if they wanted to.

Perhaps not surprisingly (given most people's misperception of freedom as an absence of restraint), about 65 percent of the players initially chose a group that had no regulatory procedures. By the fifth round, however, things began to change; about half of them switched to self-governed groups. A smaller number migrated in the opposite direction. By round 20, nearly everyone had moved to self-governed communities. The "free" groups were empty. The greatest profits were to be had in groups with self-regulating cultures. Given a choice, it seems, groups without regulatory mechanisms attract exploitative people who tend to undermine cooperation. Early on, those who wanted a free ride to collect profit without risk gravitated toward the unregulated groups. Then people caught on; the threat of penalty by the group tended to draw people not afraid to cooperate. In these groups, more people invested and everyone earned more profit.

It turns out that people in pursuit of something, when given the choice between cultures where they are free to do as they please and cultures that have self-regulating mechanisms, choose those with self-governing principles. "[We found] that when you have people with shared standards, and some that have the moral courage to sanction others, informally," said Bettina Rockenbach, the study's senior author, to the *New York Times*, "then this kind of society manages very successfully."[11]

Freedom does not mean anarchy. The freedom to self-govern actually binds people together around stated values and the desire to accomplish common goals. "A financial analyst once asked me if I was afraid of losing control of our organization," wrote Herb Kelleher, executive chairman and former CEO of Southwest Airlines, a company whose workers thrive on autonomy. "I told him I've never had control and I never wanted it. If you create an environment where the people truly participate, you don't need control. They know what needs to be done, and they do it. And the more that people will devote themselves to your cause on a voluntary basis, a willing basis, the fewer hierarchies and control mechanisms you need. We're not looking for blind obedience. We're looking for people who on their own initiative want to be doing what they're doing because they consider it to be a worthy objective. I have always believed that the best leader is the best server. And if you're a servant, by definition you're not controlling."[12]

The rationale for centralized, top-down decision making—control, direction, and compliance—melts away when individuals are tightly aligned with the company's values and goals, accountable for their actions, and self-regulated. Because values-based governance is positive governance—given to what is desirable rather than what is prohibited—

it presents a proactive solution to achieving corporate aims. As opposed to the heavy enforcement apparatus of blind obedience cultures or the reactive, make-another-rule solution of informed acquiescence, values-based self-governance provides constitutional principles that can be applied again and again to situations as they arise. It addresses the wide range of possible human conduct more comprehensively and puts the values of the company out in front of behavior.

TAKING CULTURE FOR A TEST-DRIVE

Joe Stallard is the vice president of human resources at Sewell Automotive Companies, which has become one of the largest family-owned car dealerships in the United States in large part because Sewell does culture. The 1,500 people who work at Sewell sell and service new and used vehicles, and their success depends on not only delivering a good product, but also building relationships with their customers. Since 1911, Sewell has thrived by delivering a customer experience that goes far beyond what most people expect from car dealerships. "We certainly have elements of self-governance in our culture," Joe told me when I asked him about the company culture, "and we have elements of informed acquiescence. I've always said it is very effective, if you need something done fast, to just coerce people to do it, but it's not going to be very long-standing. When you take the time for people to understand the *whys* and *hows* to get things done—and more importantly, to get them to *believe* in them—you are much more effective."[13]

There are very few rules at Sewell. "I think that a lot of rules implies no trust in many ways," Joe said. "You have to put rules or a stick in place—'If you do this, I'll do this to you'—if you don't trust people. We have three guiding spirits at Sewell, and I always say that if we get these three things right, we don't have to have a lot of rules." Those "guiding spirits" represent the core values that bind everyone at Sewell in common enterprise: Act Professionally in Everything You Do, Be Genuinely Caring, and Maintain the Highest Ethical Standard. "If everyone has some strong, guiding principles," Joe said, "it allows them to be creative, to be innovative, to be flexible, and to get out there and really do some things differently."

There are just three values, but for Sewell they cover a lot of ground. When you bring your car into a Sewell repair shop, a team of technicians trained to work bumper to bumper does all the work required on that vehicle. Each team elects a group leader who guides the work flow, but other than that the team is almost entirely self-governing. Frontline technicians make every decision necessary to fulfill those three values, up to and including spending company money to do so. "Let's say you brought in your Lexus. It is out of warranty, the window regulator went out, and you feel we should have caught it," Joe offered by way of example. "Most technicians would have to talk to a service manager, who would review the records and maybe talk to his supervisor before making a decision, or something like that. At our dealership, the person that you first dealt with can make the decision to fix it. Now, you might ask why we would do that; won't they just spend all your money? Actually they won't. In fact, they'll spend less than you hope."

Spend less? Frontline personnel, with no profit-and-loss (P&L) responsibility and no commission structure, when allowed to freely spend company money, spend less?

"Yes. Think about it. If you give most people the power to spend freely, what are their concerns now that it's their responsibility? 'I hope I don't do too much. I hope they don't look at my goodwill account and say it's huge.' So they will worry about it almost more than we would like them to. Sometimes new hires will come back and tell the assistant service manager that they noticed the taillights are out on a car and they are worried this customer could be upset. We ask them, 'If it was your mother, what would you want us to do? What do you think we *should* do?' They want the reassurance at first. Over time, as they gain trust, they make these decisions themselves. If you give them the checkbook, they're a lot more thrifty than if you took it away.

"Are we more vulnerable because we have fewer rules?" Joe continued. "Sure. But let me give an example. We give all of our sales associates a car, gas, and insurance. First day you start, if you work at a Lexus store, you're going to get a new Lexus to drive. Now are we vulnerable? Could we have somebody go out, get drunk, and total our car or kill somebody and leave our dealership open to tremendous amounts of liability? That could happen, but it never has. Most other dealers tell us, 'You're crazy. Why would you do that? How do you keep somebody from not doing that?' And we say, 'Well, we start with great people.' They honor that trust."

Everything about Sewell culture reinforces its three basic "spirits," and they celebrate them every chance they get. "We tell lots of stories here," Joe says, stating what has already become obvious to me in the course of our conversation. One of their favorites involves a technician who had recently been hired from one of their competitors. "The technician charged a customer for work that he hadn't done. One of the other technicians went over to him and said, 'Hey, what are you doing? You can't do that here.' And he said, 'Oh, at the last place I worked, that's the way we made a little extra money.' So the technician told him that we don't do that here, and he apologized and said, 'I just didn't know.' So the group watched him a little bit, and the next day they caught him doing it again. This time a few guys went over to him and said, 'Hey, we told you we don't do this here.' He replied, 'Okay, I'm sorry. I got it. It's a bad habit.' So now the group watched him a lot. The third day they caught him doing it again. This time, they spread-eagled him on the back of a car, told him to get his tools, get his truck, and get out. No supervisor, no manager; they just said, 'We're not going to let a guy like that mess up our business,' and they fired him."

Now that may seem a little rough to you if you work in a cubicle, but if you work in a service garage, the culture can tolerate a different set of behaviors. Joe admits that the fired technician could have raised a fuss, but he just went away. He realized that he just didn't belong.

To "Be Genuinely Caring" can be rough, but it also brings inspiration. When a team member suffering from an illness had to go on disability and discovered that his insurance didn't kick in until he was off the job a month, his fellow group members all donated a paid hour of their own time to support him. When Hurricane Katrina wiped out Sewell's one New Orleans dealership (located between the Superdome and the Civic Center), over 40 of the 114 associates working there lost their homes and possessions. Associates in Dallas/Fort Worth, despite not knowing any of the affected families personally, canceled that year's parties and awards, quickly raised $168,000, donated use of their summer homes and cabins, found apartments and housing, and helped those associates rebuild their lives. Although they didn't know them, they considered them a part of the Sewell family.

Self-governing cultures both inspire alignment and eject elements that don't fit in. That's one of the many reasons that Sewell, in an industry that typically sees 184 percent turnover each year, enjoys just

22 percent turnover. "We reinforce behaviors by celebrating them in stories," Joe said, "but we also reward for them. One of the big measurements in the automotive industry is the customer satisfaction index (CSI). We pay every person in the dealership—whether you mop the floors, answer the phones, or sell cars—on how well the store does in CSI, because we believe everyone has an impact on customer satisfaction. We break it down and post it in all the different work areas. Everyone knows, for instance, if the customer satisfaction index in the pre-owned car department is low, and we have people from accounting saying, 'How can we help you get that up?'"

Values-based self-governance is not an end in itself; it is a way to influence the creation of winning cultures for the twenty-first century. Through culture, companies have the opportunity to grow more varied and diverse while simultaneously remaining tightly aligned in a common purpose. There are no hard walls in cultures; they are progressive and evolutionary, growing and changing at all times. Sewell's culture, for example, is not purely self-governing; by Stallard's own admission it has elements of coercion and instances where rules provide the best way to get things done. But by building on the core of self-governing principles, Sewell is able to keep these external controls peripheral to the central effort of the group, keeping everyone inspired and propelled by the values that lie at the center of all they do. In those instances when senior leadership does have to throw up some guardrails, everyone at the company trusts that those external protections extend from the same set of core values as everything else they do.

CLOSING GAPS

Streamlining authority and putting information and decision making in the hands of those closest to the challenge make a team nimble and responsive, two qualities critical to thriving in a fast-moving market. More than front-loading decision making, however, self-governance holds the key to the next great leap in corporate efficiency: *It closes the gap between the individual and the company*.

Businesses do *gap analysis* of initiatives all the time to discover the difference between expected outcomes, standard outcomes, and the competition. So let's look at the costs of compliance with the rules and regulations of the U.S. government's latest attempt to regulate corporate behavior, the Sarbanes-Oxley rules. "Even before the most expensive Sarbanes-Oxley rules take effect," reports the *Wall Street Journal*, "companies say their audit costs are increasing by as much as 30 percent or more this year due to tougher audit and accounting standards. . . . Companies also are paying steep fees to fund a new accounting-oversight board—as much as $2 million apiece annually for some large businesses."[14] A study by Financial Executives International estimated the labor invested in new compliance procedures by small companies with revenues less than $25 million at almost 2,000 man-hours; at $5 billion in revenue the number was 41,000 man-hours.[15] What has all this new investment achieved? PricewaterhouseCoopers found that of the 85 percent of multinational corporations that have new compliance controls and procedures, only 4 percent report significant changes in behavior.[16] Business has spent madly to close the gap between rules and conduct, instituting new programs and training to raise the level of regulatory compliance. Yet despite these Herculean efforts, there has been little real reduction in regulatory enforcement action and prosecution.[17]

"We have great training, great systems, and great policies and controls," Douglas Lankler, chief compliance officer, senior vice president, and associate general counsel of the pharmaceutical company Pfizer told me when we met at Pfizer's New York headquarters, "and yet we still end up with compliance problems."[18] Lankler is the son of an assistant district attorney. He grew up listening to and idolizing the stories his father told him about putting bad guys in jail. They so impressed him that he went on to become an assistant U.S. attorney so he could do the same. Pfizer, one of the largest health companies in the world, has a best-practice, state-of-the-art commitment to compliance and achieving higher standards of conduct and corporate responsibility, and yet even Lankler recognizes the challenges posed by rules-based compliance. "People are giving a lot more attention in the year 2007 to compliance issues and understanding of their importance and the real exposures that exist than they did in 2001, and yet the hotline is still ringing at about the same pace that it was ringing in 2001. And it is not just that people feel more comfortable talking about it, we're still hearing about things you would think we would be able to move on from. And I think unequivocally that every company does the same; Pfizer is not unique in this."

It has been said that insanity is doing the same thing over and over again and expecting different results. This is the trap in which business finds itself with regard to compliance. How much falls through the gap between the ways people conduct themselves and the rules? How much time and confusion does the need for external regulation by a management-oriented bureaucracy create around every decision or initiative? Organizations spend 98 percent of their time and enforcement resources on the 2 percent of their employees responsible for compliance failures, and still have not substantially reduced those failures. Herein lies the essential flaw in informed acquiescence cultures: the gap between people and what's expected of them, people and the rules, and people and what their boss wants. Gaps are the inevitable end result of external governance. "It's like an arms race," said Lankler. "You can keep tightening the controls, but businesses will get more aggressive and try to figure out a way around them; then you tighten the controls more and hire more people to enforce them, and they get even more aggressive, and it never ends."

Self-governance closes the gap. It puts 100 percent of your resources into 98 percent of your organization, giving them the inspiration, trust, and opportunity to achieve at their highest level. Why will employees do the right thing? They will do the right thing because in self-governing cultures, not to do the right thing no longer betrays just the company; it betrays the individual's own values. Rules control and limit how we do what we do; only values-based self-governance can simultaneously control behavior and inspire us to do more. When companies and workers align on values, workers then act on their own beliefs. Nothing is more powerful than that. Betraying oneself brings distraction, those pesky little voices in your head that cause friction and diminish your productivity and effectiveness. (We'll discuss the non-compliance percent in a few pages.) Values-based self-governance creates a culture of consonance.

Imagine how much can be gained by eliminating dissonance at the very core of corporate governance and creating a culture of consonance. The time, energy, and expense formerly dedicated to closing the gap between the individual and the corporation disappears. "To me," said Lankler, "what I want to be saying to our sales force is, 'I'm not interested in rules and policies and procedures and restrictions anymore. I'm not interested in bounds, what you can do, what you can't do. You people get it, you are big boys and girls, you have integrity, you understand that we expect you to do the right thing. We don't have to have these artificial restrictions; we can trust you.' If we can get the culture right so this is what we reward every day at Pfizer and this is what we look most highly upon, we can operate with even more freedom and be even more aggressive. That, to me, is the holy grail."

When you introduce more self-governance into a culture, you diminish the need for rules and procedures and policies. You also diminish the need for carrots and sticks to motivate compliance (another efficiency; carrots and sticks are expensive). In their place, you get alignment to values, more inspiration, and less time and effort lost down the rabbit hole gap between people and rules. Self-governance is the most efficient way to get everyone on the same page, aligned to organizational values and goals, and doing the right thing to achieve them. Compliance is about surviving; self-governance is about thriving.

Michael Monts is vice president, business practices, at United Technologies Corporation (UTC) and a thoughtful and respected leader within the defense industry. UTC was an early leader in trying to create a values-based governance culture, and Michael helped the company see the limits of compliance-based solutions to corporate behavior. He brought this point home to me forcefully. "Creating a compliance program—the external structure, rules, and what have you—will definitely improve your overall compliance results, but ultimately you reach a plateau. Values-based programs take things to the next level. First, they help people get away from loophole hunting. More importantly, if you look at it from the vantage point of leadership, values-based approaches inspire people to accomplish great things. It's not fear that moves people; it's the aspiration toward accomplishing something wonderful. When you combine your vision, values, mission, and leadership, you can capture the imaginations of your employees and harness their power in a collaborative effort. It's what you want, and it's exactly what they want. At bottom, it's not just a cost-benefit equation. They want to feel like they are a part of something that is big."[19]

VALUES IN ACTION

Values-based self-governance begins, of course, with values, a clearly articulated set of principles that define the nature and purpose of an organization in human terms. At GE/Durham, they use the phrase

"Guiding Principles," and it titles a document they consider their constitution.[20] In it, they articulate values of diversity and respect, a commitment to a learning and teaching culture, a dedication to keeping promises, responsibility for the environment, and an attitude toward resolving conflict in a way that corrects and not punishes unacceptable behavior. At Sewell Automotive, they have their "guiding spirits": Act Professionally in Everything You Do, Be Genuinely Caring, and Maintain the Highest Ethical Standard. These values form the basis for its entire culture. Every structure, process, and decision in both these groups flows from their commitment to a set of HOWs.

Sewell and GE/Durham are relatively small enterprises, so a natural question to ask is: "How can this work for a big corporation?" Luckily, we have examples around us both old and new. Johnson & Johnson has long been a leader in integrating values into its corporate culture. Robert Wood Johnson, the son of the founder, who later became known as General Johnson after his service as a brigadier general in World War II, took over direction of the company in 1932 and 10 years later wrote a one-page document that came to be known as the Credo. It codified the company's socially responsible approach to conducting business.[21] The Credo states that the company's first responsibility is to the people who use its products and services; the second responsibility is to its employees; the third is to the community and environment; and the fourth is to the stockholders. This revolutionary document upended the traditionally held view that a company's first responsibility is to its shareholders. General Johnson and his successors in managing the business have believed that if the Credo's first three responsibilities are met, the stockholders should be well served.

Since the day it was written, the Credo has become a living, breathing part of everything J&J does, not because it sits framed on the wall of every office, but because it sits enshrined in the day-to-day discussions of everyone at the company. "We don't talk about the Credo for five minutes in every meeting," Roger Fine of J&J told me. "We have no such rule. The way I first heard about the Credo when I joined the company in 1974 is more typical. I was in a meeting with about 8 or 10 executives and all of the sudden somebody said, 'That's a Credo issue.' That's a classic line at J&J, and it acts like a trump card. When somebody says, 'That's a Credo issue,' the conversation stops, whatever the business subject is, and the entire conversation turns to 'Okay, let's talk about the

Credo issue. What is the issue? What are the pros and cons? What's the dilemma, if there is an initial dilemma? Then we try to resolve it."[22]

When Roger first told me this, it sounded like the Credo was a burden, an extra tax on the system that needed to be periodically paid. I pointed out to him that business moves quickly, and no one wants to be encumbered by the albatross of having to stop a meeting to discuss this extra thing. "I travel around the world each year speaking to dozens of groups about the Credo," he explained to me. "When I do, I usually talk about four or five misconceptions people have about it, and I save this one for last. This is the craziest fallacy of them all. We want to be real hard competitors, and we want to compete, and that's what everybody at J&J should do. But they need to do it informed and inspired by the Credo. The last sentence of the Credo, you see, is the most important sentence of the Credo. It says, 'When we operate according to these principles, the stockholders *should* realize a fair return.' What that means is that the Credo is not a brake on our success; it's the engine of our success. Everything in J&J's history proves the General right."

More recently, Xerox Corporation made "Living our values" one of its five central performance objectives, and chairman and CEO Anne Mulcahy credits it as part of the company's remarkable turnaround. "Corporate values helped save Xerox during the worst crisis in our history," Mulcahy said at the Annual Conference of Business for Corporate Social Responsibility in 2004. Xerox went far beyond a vague statement of purpose and infused its central values into every facet of the organization, with a high level of accountability and vigilance. "Far from words on a piece of paper," she said, "[our values] are accompanied by specific objectives and hard measures."[23]

Clearly articulated values keep everyone on the same course. *Values place governance within each person rather than in persons or rule sets external to them, establishing the conditions for a very different type of culture to grow.*

A JOURNEY TO CULTURE

How does a culture become more self-governing? Methodist Hospital System in Houston tackled that challenge in a very systematic way. In

1998, the board came to the conclusion that the nonprofit hospital chain had become too much like a for-profit enterprise, managing to the bottom line, and had lost touch with its values-based roots. To rectify this drift, they embarked on a major effort to change the nature of HOW they do WHAT they do. Rather than institute new rules, policies, and procedures or simply plaster the walls with inspirational posters, they chose to approach the challenge from the inside out, to govern through culture. *Workforce Management* magazine reported their compelling story in early 2005.[24]

They began their process where it counted the most, with the 8,600 employees who would live and breathe it every day. Through ongoing workshops, they developed three documents: a vision statement, a belief statement, and a new mission statement, all based on the idea of integrating spiritual values—broadly and inclusively defined—throughout the workplace. The core values they came up with made an appropriate acronym for a hospital, ICARE: integrity, compassion, accountability, respect, and excellence.

Values-based self-governing cultures, as we have discussed, require dedication to education and vigilance, so Methodist's next step was to develop a system that built an understanding of these new values in meaningful ways. They polled their employees extensively and developed a clear baseline matrix against which to measure their progress toward their goal of values integration. This matrix later became a powerful HR educational tool used throughout the organization.

Most important to increasing self-governance around these values was helping each group of employees translate ICARE into daily behaviors and decision making, in a sense marrying a HOW to every WHAT. Putting values into action, after all, is the core effort of self-governing cultures. They asked each employee work group to interpret and apply each value to their specific discipline. What does compassion look like? How do we express respect every day? Every discipline came up with its own answers. Nurses internalized accountability with, "Don't ask why; ask why not. Follow though and correct mistakes," while the information technology (IT) department forwarded, "If I do not understand, I will ask questions." Pharmacy workers tackled integrity by vowing, "We will always do our best whether the boss is here or not," while no less than the CEOs of the five-hospital system dared themselves to "challenge each other with respect." This process helped to turn values into self-governable behaviors that could be embraced and applied by each worker on a daily basis.

Given how difficult it sometimes seems to quantify the results of attempting to govern through cultural change, some might be tempted to say that Methodist's initiative was a leap of faith. Even Tom Daugherty, who directed the initiative, admitted skepticism. "You can't always identify a clear line of sight between cultural change and operational performance," he said. But at Methodist, the results speak for themselves. Employee turnover dropped 38 percent, from 24 percent to 15 percent, in less than two years. Vacancy rates fell by half. Satisfaction levels for patients, doctors, and staff hit all-time highs. *U.S. News & World Report* named Methodist one of the top 100 hospitals in the country and, in 2007, *Fortune* magazine ranked them number nine on their list of the 100 Best Companies to Work For.[25]

Methodist is a fairly small company, as corporations go, and concentrated on serving a single locality. So I asked Douglas Lankler of Pfizer how he would go about pursuing his vision of "the holy grail" in a large, multinational organization. "I think it's easy," he immediately replied. "You ease it in. Let's say we have a cap on the amount of money that we will let a particular regional sales force give to a group of doctors for educational speaking events, say $100,000. The law doesn't require it, but we put that cap in place because we feared that without it there would be anarchy and people might just pour money at the doctors. That would put us in a situation where we're essentially paying for prescriptions, and we can't have that; we can only fund education-based speaking programs that are designed to get medical information out to doctors and patients who need that information. So you say to that region, 'We're going to move that cap to $200 grand, but at the same time we're going to help you see the *right* way to use these funds, and trust you to do so in accordance with our values.' You make them more self-governing. If they can do that, their sales are going to go up because more information is getting out to the communities, to the physicians and patients, and compliance is going to go up also because the sales reps know they are being trusted to do the right thing. Then we reward them when they do."

Leadership is key to this process. "We have a lot of leaders who have turned around difficult markets," Lankler said. "For example, the area president of Asia, a region that is wracked with corruption, took over a situation where, from 2000 to 2003, we were having 90-some-odd compliance issues per year, and got it down to one or two. He really drove the notion of values and integrity and his expectation that first and foremost you do it right. 'We can sell like there's no tomorrow and surpass our numbers,' he told his team, 'but if we're doing it in an improper way that's unethical or illegal, then we haven't achieved what we need to achieve.' He was able to back it with his own well-grounded and well-demonstrated integrity."

Increasing self-governance means moving values to the center of your efforts and making it clear—in how you reward, celebrate, communicate, and pursue—that those values form the guiding spirit of the enterprise. This is not just an effort for appointed leaders and managers. Everyone has the opportunity to do something about culture, to evolve it, make it better, and make it more responsive to the needs of today. Corporate culture, after all, is not monolithic. A board can have a culture, a team can have a culture, and a unit can have a culture. The culture of GE/Durham differs dramatically from cultures of other GE units, but the fact that it embraces and sustains the core values of its parent keeps it congruent with its sister parts.

How leaders beget HOW leaders, like our fictional caveman Ook begat lots of collaborative little baby Ooks. Self-governing cultures grow as people begin to see, model, and then adopt the HOWS that build strong synapses. To be more self-governing is to realize that *culture is something that you do, not something that does to you.* Everyone needs to engage in the cultural dimension of what they do. Like oarsmen on a boat, we can all pull together to make culture happen. You need a critical mass of leaders to start Waves, and in a self-governing culture, leadership begins with you.

WHY SELF-GOVERNANCE IS THE FUTURE OF BUSINESS

There are many more reasons why getting more values-based self-governance into every culture makes sense.

A Horizontal World Calls for a Horizontal Governance Architecture

Values-based self-governance minimizes the layers of hierarchy within an organization. At GE/Durham, decision making eschews middle management because there is none. There are no silos and there is little separation of functions; all governance functions reside within each individual. Almost nothing happens without a chance for everyone's input; thus almost every initiative is an expression of the group. At Sewell, each self-governed team takes responsibility for every aspect of a vehicle, which allows them to deliver a superior experience to their customers in a more efficient and responsive way.

Self-Governing Cultures Thrive on the Free Flow of Information

Unlike the hoarding or need-to-know information flow of blind obedience and informed acquiescence cultures, values-based self-governance requires that information be readily available to all when they need it. Information unleashes ability. To unleash the power and creativity of a workforce of inspired leaders, you must create an environment that unleashes the information they need to succeed. Transparency between people at all levels in all transactions actually makes these cultures stronger and more effective, and the free flow of information makes cultures more self-governing by increasing trust.

A Leading Company Needs to Be a Company of Leaders

To push the bounds of creativity and innovation, you need people to live out there every day. Rules-based cultures contain an inherent tension between outside-the-box thinking and inside-the-box compliance. Self-governing requires each individual to step up and lead, to take responsibility both for their own work and for the performance of others. They live outside the box because there is no box to contain them, only values to guide them. At GE/Durham, for example, each person works in, and is responsible for, their own team, but each also belongs to shopwide councils that address larger issues of the unit.

Council membership rotates so everyone is exposed to and responsible for the complete range of functions in the factory. By making each employee both individually responsible and accountable to the group, self-governing cultures encourage a leadership orientation.

Values-Based Self-Governing Cultures Encourage Employee Development

Blind obedience and informed acquiescence cultures tend to build their workforce skills through rote learning and through training programs, respectively. While these approaches to worker knowledge can be an efficient way to disseminate black-and-white, easily quantifiable information—like maximum pollution levels or safety performance metrics—they don't do enough to prepare people to wrestle with the infinite shades of gray they now face in the course of a working day. You cannot train someone to struggle in the Valley of C, but you can develop their ability to do so. You *train* a dog, but you *develop* leaders.

Thomas R. McCormick, director, global ethics and compliance for the Dow Chemical Company and one of the true thought leaders on the relationship between values and business performance, told me a story about how Dow is investing in the education of its team. "We are asking every supervisor in the company—there are about 2,000 of them—to have a face-to-face education session with their employees to take them through three or four scenarios (such as conflicts of interest), really tough, gray-area issues that would be relevant to that work group, whether it is a business or a function or a geographic location or whatever," he said. "The goal is to really have people talk through some of these areas where there aren't any good black-and-white answers, and collectively explore how they would handle the situation. It's educational, but it also sets a tone. They see their leader talking through it with them, and that reinforces what leadership expectations are. All of that is designed to help people manage the gray, which you can only do by making values-based decisions."[26]

The conditions of the networked world make pushing vast amounts of information to workers' fingertips cheap and easy, but it must come with a concomitant dedication to education. At GE/Durham, it means multiskilling. At Sewell, it means the rich stories, told again and again, and modeled in everyday behavior.

Self-Governance Builds Universal Vigilance

There are times when individuals can join an organization but not embrace its goals. In groups governed by informed acquiescence, these people can skate by or game the system to some degree, fly under the radar so to speak, and create drag on the system. They might even be part of the 2 percent that compliance efforts are currently focused on containing. In values-based self-governed groups, however, they can't fool the culture; the vigilance of the group identifies them and makes them feel uncomfortable. In a self-governing group, the person who does not truly align with the values of the group will not feel at home, and be ejected. The overcharging technician at Sewell learned that lesson the hard way. Thus, the 98 percent take care of the 2 percent, ejecting the non-aligned before they can create the kinds of compliance failures that can bring a company down.

Greater than simply preventing compliance failures, though, the universal vigilance of a self-governing group maintains alignment over time. If someone is not performing, it becomes incumbent on everyone else to raise the issue and then solve it as a group, with a focus on fixing the problem, not assigning blame. With everyone accountable to the team's success, slacking is not tolerated.

Global fast-food giant McDonald's organizes itself more like an ecosystem than an organization with strong central control. CEO Jim Skinner likens the culture to a three-legged stool supported by the franchises, the suppliers, and the vast employee pool. But it is a strong commitment to values that keeps all these various and dispersed stakeholders aligned with a common purpose, and the culture it breeds exerts a similar self-regulating influence on all levels of the organization. "People talk about 'tissue rejection,'" Skinner told me. "It occurs when people join us at too high a level from outside the organization without paying their dues, if you will, in order to understand our culture. It's not really a rejection by the business itself, but by our culture. People in a sense say, 'I don't care how bright you are or what capabilities you have; you have to be able to understand all of what we stand for.'"[27]

Cultures like these are self-enforcing, and this reduces the need for external management controls. Honest feedback becomes the name of the game, and this form of self-governance takes advantage of the collective intelligence of the group to regulate the culture as a whole.

Self-Governance Shifts Decision Making from the Pragmatic to the Principled

Reputation, consistency, promise keeping—all the factors we've discussed necessary to achieve personal and corporate continuity in a transparent world—stem from the ability to make decisions based on principle, rather than what is immediately pragmatic. Values-based self-governing cultures are inspired by mission and steered by values. They enshrine long-term principles in place of short-term thinking, and challenge each decision maker to fulfill those principles in every act they perform. Decisions made on the basis of sound principles provide a steady rudder in stormy seas.

Self-Governance Is a Higher Concept

Like the trust, belief, and values it relies on, values-based self-governance speaks to the higher self. It governs in the name of principles and values, not rules, and only principles and values have the ability to inspire. Isn't it more inspiring to think that you are your own legislature? More inspiring to self-govern rather than acquiesce to someone in authority?

There is a touch of inspiration in all these concepts. Values-based self-governance relies on structures and rhetoric that *speaks* to people. It speaks the language of *should* rather than *can*. Inspiration comes from holding a set of beliefs, and we all want to believe in what we do. This is why values-based self-governance provides such an outstanding model for the future. It calls us forth to marry our highest goals and aspirations to how we do what we do each day.

THE CASE FOR SELF-GOVERNING CULTURES

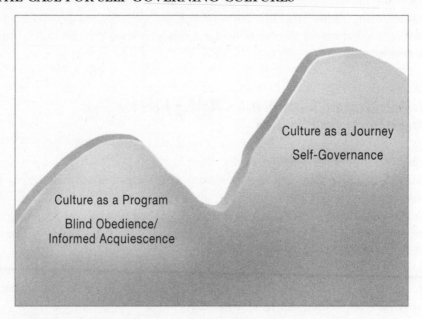

If values become the engine of culture, self-governance provides the scaffolding that allows everyone throughout the hierarchy to embrace and put into operation those values daily in everything that they do. Different subunits, like the various specialties at Methodist Hospital System, can internalize those values in ways that are specific to their form and function; global businesses can extend horizontally across borders, open back-room operations to embrace and collaborate with new partners, and diversify in new ways while maintaining the integrity of their missions; and the myriad combinations of freelancers, consultants, full-timers, telecommuters, and other thinly bound people who make up the workforce of today can align more tightly around common values. Since values provide a stronger, more adaptable navigation system than do rules and procedures, values-based self-governance provides a system that allows an organization to grow, adapt, mutate, and evolve in the marketplace without losing sight of its core mission or straying too far from its chosen path.

Cultures stay healthy only if they pursue and stay true to their missions, a purpose beyond themselves, a noble mission. Culture means journey. Because cultures are alive—growing and changing as they adapt to challenge and celebrate success—they are in a constant state of *becoming*. To embrace the notion of doing culture, then, means to accept that you are on a journey, every day, to build stronger connections with those around you. Embracing the importance of self-governance—that how your group interrelates begins with you and HOW you do WHAT you do—is the first step on that journey.

You don't need a memo from headquarters that says "We are now a self-governing company" to begin to change the culture around you. You can begin by getting your HOWS right, by extending and engendering more trust, by being more actively transparent, by aligning more closely with group values and acting from those values in everything you do, and by defining your journey—whether it be laying bricks or managing a team—as one with a mission greater than success. Pursuing a noble mission can take you—and your organization—on the journey from WHAT to HOW, from rules to values, from defense to offense, from informed acquiescence to self-governance, from brand awareness to brand promise, and from a road to success to a journey of significance that should (in the J&J Credo sense), in turn, beget success.

12

The Leadership Framework

We are what we repeatedly do.
Excellence, therefore, is not an act, but a habit.
—Aristotle

We have probed in great detail the fundamental influences that fill the spaces between us. We've considered HOW we think, HOW we behave, HOW we govern ourselves as groups, and HOW the world has changed to put new emphasis on these ideas. If you agree with the view I have presented, you no doubt have already begun to notice the HOWS around you through a different lens (unless you've read this through in a single sitting). Perhaps you have noticed how something the boss said set off voices in you that you recognized as distracting, or perhaps you noted some dissonant messages coming from your work group. Perhaps you reexamined an e-mail you received or sent and took an extra moment to think about how it affected you or would affect another person. Maybe you were treated at a store in a way that made you feel richer or poorer for the experience, and you began to think about why, or that there might be a better way. These perceptions are the first step in your journey up the Hill of A toward a deep and meaningful understanding of the HOWS with which we fill the interpersonal synapses in the world, and others do as well.

But I am also cognizant of the fact that you might still be wondering what this all means, or more precisely, how do you *do* HOW? I wouldn't blame you for that. After all, you have worked through a couple of hundred pages of a book, and I almost never told you how to *do* anything. I have not provided you with instructions on how to write a better e-mail or greet another person, or elucidated the manner in which you should speak. In short, I have not provided specific steps or actions that you can take to employ in your daily working life the concepts I've presented.

The reason I haven't done this is, quite simply, because I am not able to, or, more precisely, because the very nature of what we have been talking about renders writing such an instruction manual impossible. If you remember, I told you early on that I didn't have a "Manual of How" filled with *Six Rules for This, or 24 Steps to That*. Much to your credit, you have kept reading anyway. I have tried to provide you instead with a way of looking at the world, a lens through which to see everything we do with new weight and meaning. These ideas simply cannot be summed up in a list of things to do.

And yet, for a system of thought to be truly useful, we must find a way of bringing it to bear on every moment of our lives, to put thoughts into action, in our case, to *do* HOW. I can't give you rules, but I can give you a framework, a way of focusing your efforts, time, thought, and passion on behaviors and approaches that will help you make the choices that will set off Waves all around you. At LRN, we call it the Leadership Framework, and we use it to guide our HOWS every day. I developed it in the early days of the company and refined it since then.[1] It now encapsulates all the concepts that we have covered in this book and provides a way to put them into action in everything you do.

Why leadership? Because to be a self-governing individual you must lead yourself and approach everything you do from a leadership perspective. You can write an e-mail as a leader, attend a meeting as a leader, or build a report as a leader. You lead your own journey of significance every day, in how you choose to act, treat others, and see the world. A leadership mentality brings you into an active relationship with the forces and circumstances in your personal sphere of influence. It helps you to reach out to others, to create the kinds of strong interpersonal synapses so crucial to thriving in a hyperconnected world, and to inspire those around you to do the same.

LEADERSHIP

Let's talk for a moment about leadership. On May 25, 1961, U.S. President John F. Kennedy stood before a special joint session of Congress and asked for a number of special appropriations to address "urgent national needs." He spoke for about 45 minutes, but few remember most of what he said. What the whole world remembers, in one way or another, is that for about eight of those 45 minutes, JFK shared his vision for landing on the moon. In about a thousand words, he launched an effort that would involve hundreds of thousands of people for the next decade and more. On that night, and in the days that followed, people coalesced around this common idea. He did not say it would be easy. "It is a heavy burden," he said, "and there is no sense in agreeing or desiring that the United States take an affirmative position in outer space, unless we are prepared to do the work and bear the burdens to make it successful. . . . This decision demands a major national commitment of scientific and technical manpower, material, and facilities, and the possibility of their diversion from other important activities where they are already thinly spread. It means a degree of dedication, organization, and discipline which have not always characterized our research and development efforts." But JFK spoke not just for the scientists, contractors, and astronauts who would make the journey. He spoke for the nation. "In a very real sense," he said, "it will not be one man going to the moon—if we make this judgment affirmatively, it will be an entire nation. For all of us must work to put him there."[2] In just eight minutes, JFK changed the world.

That is leadership: not simply having the vision of landing on the moon, but doing everything it takes for the roughly one million people who came together around this effort to speak the same language, to have a common consciousness, and to pursue a mission that is greater than any individual. Would America have landed on the moon if most people had said, "I'm interested in going to the moon, but it *depends*. I would go to the moon if I could sit in the spacecraft, in the front row, on the right side. Where I sit matters more than landing on the moon." If everyone wanted to jam into the spacecraft but no one wanted to work at Cape Canaveral and do a different job, we would not have reached New Jersey, let alone the moon. So a million people had to come together in a mutually reinforcing system to convert that vision into reality.

An organization, as we have said, is simply that: a group of people who come together in a mutually reinforcing system to accomplish something greater than any individual. So leadership is not just for people who have "president" in their title. Leadership is an attitude, a disposition, and a way of approaching the challenges you face every day. It is not a title on your business card. Though many people are formally empowered to lead others, many more of us—and in our increasingly horizontal world that number grows every day—work in teams without formal hierarchical structures. And this trend is bound to continue, with more and more of our achievements the result of our ability to be effective in groups of relative equals. Self-governance is also a leadership orientation; it begins by leading yourself. To become more self-governing and to participate in and foment more self-governing cultures around yourself, you must accept the challenge to become your own legislature, to look inside for answers and be guided by your alignment to the values you find there. This framework can help you develop the orientation to do this well.

As we go through the elements of the framework in the pages that follow and hear from many people who lead, remember that great leaders became leaders precisely because they either consciously or by their very nature embodied those behaviors that make Waves, that move those around them to do great things, and that work powerfully with others for change. That is the essence of leadership, and it begins with leading yourself.

We began this book with a story about a person I think is one of the greatest leaders ever, Krazy George Henderson, the man who invented the Wave. To thrive in the internetworked world of twenty-first-century business, you don't need one big Wave; you need to make Waves every day, and like that stadium cheer, anyone can make one at any time. It could be a question in a town hall meeting that would make it a better meeting, or an e-mail that inspires others to take up the cause at hand. Leadership is getting your HOWS right, and you can look at anything through the prism of leadership. You can brush your teeth because it is something your parents made you do as a child, or you can brush your teeth because you have a vision of dental health and a winning smile. Leadership is about starting and making Waves contagious in everything you do.

The Leadership Framework is not a set of rules or edicts you must memorize or comply with, *cans* and *can'ts* that live outside of you; the Leadership Framework lives in the world of *shoulds*. It begins with core values and then gives you ways of approaching each decision or action to bring those values to bear on others. It provides a foundation from which to make decisions every day and brings values to life in behaviors. These behaviors, consistently done, reinforce each other to create an upward spiral of energy that propels endeavor. If you divide life into WHAT you do and HOW you do it, the Leadership Framework describes an approach to HOW: how you communicate, how you work, how you treat others, how you make decisions, how you interact in the marketplace, and how you can act consistently. It governs, guides, and inspires HOW we do things. A framework is another way to describe a system; each part mutually enforces every other part. Like the studs, rafters, and beams of a house, or pieces on a chessboard, the strength of each is magnified tenfold when they work together.

Though I call it the Leadership Framework, you can also think of it as a lens, the Lens of How. When you see the world through it and act accordingly, you will engender more trust, build a stronger and more enduring reputation, become more actively transparent, think more clearly, act more spontaneously, and make more Waves with those around you. You won't have to worry about all those things individually, because they will make perfect sense when seen as a whole. You will begin to affect culture, to lead and model a standard of conduct that will speak to the higher selves of those around you, and lift their efforts as well. The lens of HOW will inspire you by rendering clear the terrain you must navigate on your journey to climb the Hill of A, and many hills beyond.

This framework is not the only possible framework you could construct for this journey; it was designed for the types of high-information, person-to-person efforts that go on at LRN every day. It represents the amalgamation of many of the thoughts and concepts I have picked up or developed over the years, and that apply well to our core activities.[3] If you work on a shop floor or in some other specific environment, some of the ideas here might be superfluous to your efforts. No matter what you do, however, understanding the behaviors and dispositions described here will begin to give you a visceral experience of what getting your HOWS right is all about.

WALKING THE TALK

Perhaps not surprisingly, the Leadership Framework draws some of its power from a disposition toward language. We know from the research we discussed in Chapter 5 that language exerts a powerful influence on the way we think about things. There is, for example, a vast difference in the influence of the word *enlist* versus the word *sell*. When you sell, the object in play is the product, a thing that lives outside both you and the buyer; when you enlist, you invite a relationship in which the product is but one stage today on a journey of innovation tomorrow. The behaviors, thoughts, and consciousness that follow from being in touch with *enlist* are entirely different from embracing *sell*. Similarly, do you have *customers* or do you have *partners*? What does the word *partner* say about that person across the table from you differently than the words *customer*, *vendor*, or *supplier*? Will that affect how you negotiate? How you define success in that negotiation?

Like *can* versus *should*, language has the power to contain or inspire, and the language you adopt and employ either locks you in rigid relationships or frees you to new possibilities of connection. In other words, if we broaden our vocabulary, we have access to a bigger world with more options. I also believe that the people who will become the leaders of tomorrow—those who will thrive and excel in our hypertransparent, hyperconnected world—will be the ones who embrace this language and unlock its transformative power.

THE FIRST FIVE HOWS OF LEADERSHIP

To help you see how the concepts in the framework interrelate and build upon one another, I have assembled them in graphic form in Figure 12.1.

You see that it is organized into three concentric spaces. At the center of the lens, at its point of sharpest focus, lies a set of Core Values. In the illustration, I have used the values that we embrace at LRN as central to our mission. You can easily substitute your own, but they must be the deep sorts of values like justice, honesty, integrity, community, and honor that truly inspire the highest in human conduct and interrelations. You'll find the list of possible choices is not long. The most important things about whatever values lie at the center of the circle are that they express the highest aspirations and fundamental beliefs of the group to which you belong; that they are truly the core; and that everyone can agree, embrace, and align themselves with them. They are the guiding principles that unite you in common endeavor.

Surrounding the central core are Leadership Attributes, the behaviors, attitudes, and orientation of a self-governing individual. It is these attributes we will primarily focus on and explore in the pages that follow. Surrounding these is a set of Nonleadership Attributes, behaviors that often result when you abdicate your pursuit of HOW.

Let us begin at the beginning of the framework and see where it leads. (I know, a circle has no beginning—that is part of its unique character—so I have numbered a starting place at about nine o'clock on the circle to get us on track.) Feel free to refer back to the illustration frequently to better follow the narrative.

Vision

The Leadership Framework begins with five essential attributes, five keystones of behavior upon which the entire structure rests. The first is *vision*. A self-governing person spends some time in another realm, the future. Having a leadership disposition means mentally envisioning a better future for yourself, the tasks at hand, and those with whom you labor. Leadership starts with vision, and leaders envision every moment. You could have big visions or little ones, envision a

LEADERSHIP FRAMEWORK

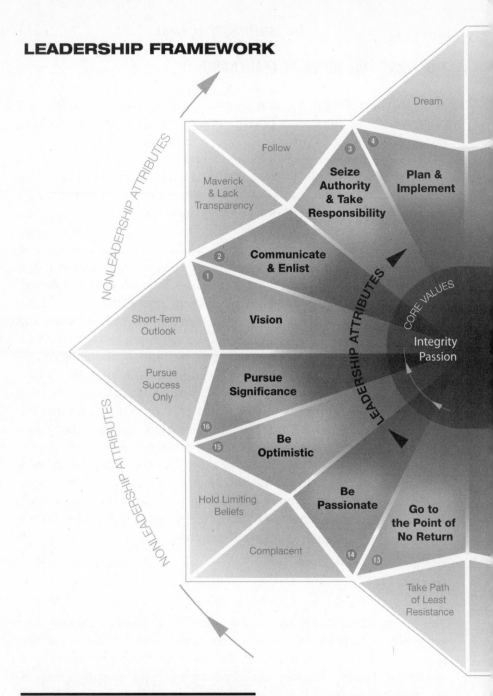

FIGURE 12.1   The Leadership Framework

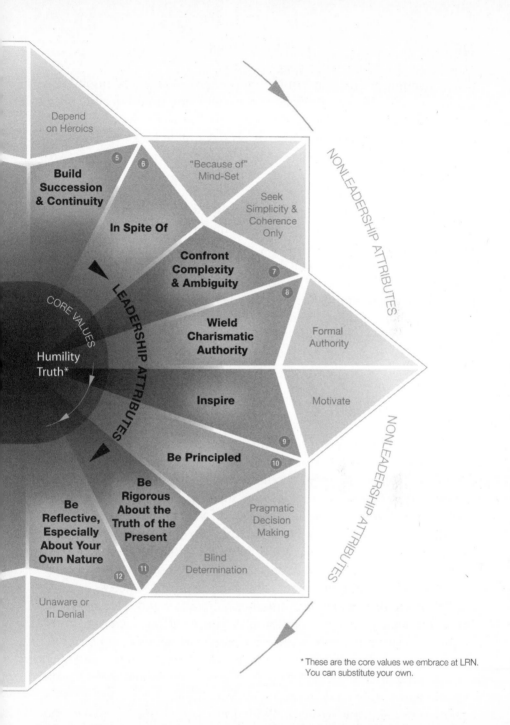

Depend
on Heroics

⑤ ⑥

**Build
Succession
& Continuity**

"Because of"
Mind-Set

Seek
Simplicity &
Coherence
Only

In Spite Of

**Confront
Complexity
& Ambiguity**

⑦

⑧

CORE VALUES

LEADERSHIP ATTRIBUTES

**Wield
Charismatic
Authority**

Formal
Authority

Humility
Truth*

Inspire

Motivate

Be Principled

⑨

⑩

**Be
Rigorous
About the
Truth of the
Present**

**Be
Reflective,
Especially
About Your
Own Nature**

Pragmatic
Decision
Making

⑪

⑫

Blind
Determination

Unaware or
In Denial

NONLEADERSHIP ATTRIBUTES

NONLEADERSHIP ATTRIBUTES

* These are the core values we embrace at LRN.
You can substitute your own.

275

better meeting or envision inspiring thousands of workers around the world to make better decisions. You could envision a feature in a technological platform, or envision a whole new product, or simply envision a way to make someone else's day a little bit better. You can create a new vision or embrace someone else's and make it your own.

Envisioning represents a proactive stance toward achievement; it is an activity, a behavior, and a disposition toward pursuing your goals. If you don't have a vision, then you fall outside the lens of HOW and are a short-term manager: task-oriented, obedient, and obsessed with and limited to what you can see right under your nose. Short-term managers tend to be reactive by nature and find themselves putting out fires more often than they light the beacons that show the way. It is a defensive posture and worries more about appeasing others than about engaging them. To get your HOWS right you must be focused on others, and vision is the crucial first disposition toward achieving that goal.

Communicate and Enlist

Most visions that are worth pursuing are greater than any one of us, so if you have a vision and you feel it truly has content that could make for a better future, then you should *share* it with somebody else. The question then becomes: HOW do you share it? What is the quality of your effort? If you browbeat somebody, if you talk *at* them, you are not sharing. Sharing, at its heart, attempts to make your vision into everyone's vision, to make a Wave. Uniting a group of people behind a single goal or set of goals presents the greatest challenge to any leader; achieving that alignment results in the greatest success.

To reach this goal you must *enlist* those around you and help them see what you see. To truly enlist you must be open and forthcoming about your motives, be transparent in your communication, and reach out to others in a way that they feel you've truly shared.

Consider the last 50 e-mails you received. Which ones enlist? Which, when you read them, make you think, "Yes, I get it. This makes sense. I want to help." Which ones, by contrast, make you think, "What is this all about? This is not what we agreed to. Why did you cc: my boss? What are you up to?" The ones that enlist create connections. They build strong synapses between the sender and you. They make you want to participate, belong, or assist in the effort.

In every e-mail, instant message, phone call, teleconference, or face-to-face encounter you can communicate to enlist and share, or you can do something else. Ask yourself, when you write an e-mail, do you have a vision to make it effective? A vision for the response? Leaders reach out to others with a quality of communication that allows people to share, to be enlisted, and to make your vision theirs. Taking this additional moment before you hit the send button is not an extra something, a burden or tax for you to contend with. Instead, it makes everything you do more effective. If others embrace your communication and make its goals their own, more gets done. Think of it this way: You go on a diet to lose five pounds. Dieting is not an added burden; it takes no more time to eat one way than another way. Dieting is a series of choices to eat one thing and not another, and a good diet regimen provides you with guidance—based on a set of beliefs about health, exercise, and nutrition—to help you make those choices and achieve your goal. When you reach out to others, you can choose to enlist them, or you can choose to respond in way that has little effect but to clear your in-box for the time being. One starts a Wave; the other kills one.

If you don't share your vision with others, you are acting as a *maverick*. Your vision will remain yours alone. There is nothing wrong with being a maverick (in fact, we admire many of them), just as there is nothing wrong with many of the behaviors that occupy the outer circle of the Leadership Framework. From time to time, they may even be the most useful or appropriate behaviors to practice. However, they are not self-governing, *leadership* behaviors, behaviors that can start TRIPs or make things happen in a hyperconnected world. Since the conditions of the world have changed in such specific and remarkable ways so as to place new, higher value on connection and interrelation, it is those behaviors that best capitalize on the conditions that we are concerned with here. These are the behaviors codified in the Leadership Framework.

Seize Authority and Take Responsibility

Self-governing leaders step forward. They raise their hands at meetings. They say, "I have an idea," "I'd like to run this task force," "I'd like to complete that assignment," or "I think we should land on Mars and not Venus." Leaders stand up for what they envision, and are not afraid to occasionally take center stage. They offer themselves up. They seize the authority and take the responsibility that comes with leadership. *Carpe diem* is the watchword of their faith. If you never step up, you consign yourself to a career of always following.

Having a leadership orientation does not necessarily mean you must lead in every instance; you can maintain a leadership disposition and still follow the leadership of others. Within any team or work group, certain people will take the overall lead, but within that effort opportunities arise for everyone to lead. You could envision yourself disseminating project metrics in a way that enlists others in the team goals or step forward to provide them with essential data to make better decisions. Though you work within a group or have natural or appointed superiors, a leadership disposition opens you up to a greater level of contribution and achievement. A self-governing leadership culture allows everyone to take these opportunities to lead, and when you step up and seize the moment, the moment seizes you.

Plan and Implement

Walt Disney was a visionary. He imagined an anthropomorphic mouse and he put that mouse into action, changing the face of animation, film-making, merchandising, amusement parks, and family entertainment. But he didn't create one of the largest entertainment companies in the world solely by his dreams. "The way to get started," he famously said, "is to quit talking and begin doing."[4] Leadership is ideas put into action.

If you have a vision and you share and enlist others in it, the next step requires that you plan and implement its achievement. The gutters of business are littered with the great ideas of those who envision but cannot implement. They are the dreamers of the world. They talk a good game, but when push comes to shove, they don't have what it takes to get things done. Many people have imagined a business they wanted to start, a project that would make lives easier, or simply a better way to reach a goal; many have imagined landing on the moon in one way or another. You meet many people with dreams, but you also meet those who work with others as a team to make their vision real.

In a world of HOW, these are the winners. A small vision achieved is worth ten grand notions unimplemented.

Self-governing people step up, seize the moment, and find ways to get things done. Though this may seem at first a recipe for doubling your workload, in fact the opposite is often true. This basic eagerness to plan and implement their visions or the visions of others serves as a powerful example to those around them. When others see these sorts of HOWs in action, they feel similarly inspired and join in. More gets done with less effort because the whole team pulls together. In football, when a running back is crashing the line with extra effort, his tackles block extra hard, his quarterback makes better handoffs, and everyone on the team steps up with the extra effort needed to help him score a touchdown.

Build Succession and Continuity

I collect mechanical wristwatches. It's a hobby. I find them very beautiful, a profound expression of our desire to order the world around us, and objects that embody the deep tradition of man striving for perfection, to make many small and intricate parts operate as a constant whole. If you ask me the time, however, I usually reach into my pocket and pull out my cell phone. It is in continual contact with an atomic timeserver and is the most accurate information I can put my hands on. I'm the CEO of my company, the ultimate leader there, if you will. If I show up late to a meeting, can the people waiting for me there find out the time? Of course they can.

Metaphorically, leaders don't show up and tell you perfect time; as James C. Collins and Jerry I. Porras told us so brilliantly in *Built to Last*, leaders build clocks that keep telling the time whether they are there or not.[5] If landing on the moon depended on JFK, what would have happened when he was tragically assassinated? Leaders are not superheroes; they build succession and continuity into everything that they do. They don't build anything that depends on a single person to show up and tell perfect time.

This idea is one of the most central and powerful ideas in the Leadership Framework, and the one most often underestimated. I think it is because saying the world doesn't need heroes contradicts most of our experience. Business often calls on us to be heroic, to go the extra mile, burn the midnight oil, or pull the extra shift in order to meet our goals. And I agree. The world certainly needs heroes. You can't get the train out of the station without some hard pushing, without heroism sometimes. The paradox is that though we need heroism from time to time, to truly thrive we must build self-sustaining approaches at the same time. Understanding the need for systems that generate energy as they achieve, rather than depleting resources to do so, leads you to a disposition that does not depend on heroics. You cannot build a great, enduring, significant company on the backs of superheroes. No matter how strong they are, eventually they will collapse under the weight. To build a skyscraper of an idea, hundreds of floors stacked on one another, you need a foundation of continuity that can grow as you do.

In 1964, Disney began to buy unproductive orange groves near Orlando, Florida, for what was called the "Florida Project." It was one of Walt's grandest notions. But, as the project developed, he developed lung cancer and soon died. His brother Roy and a team of Disney's hand-selected and trained designers picked up the ball and saw it through to completion; Walt Disney World opened in 1971, the largest theme park ever imagined. He had enlisted them in his vision and they had made it their own. Roy Disney died three months later, but succession plans were in place, and Donn Tatum became the first non-Disney family member to be chairman and CEO of The Walt Disney Company.[6] The dream lived on.

Ask yourself a practical question: Do you want to be promoted from your current position? Now put yourself in your superior's shoes for a moment. Can he or she promote you if you are the only person who can do what you do? If the job won't get done unless you stay there and continue to be the hero, it makes no sense for the business to ever promote you. If heroism is what's getting the job done, you will stay right where you are to keep getting the job done. If, however, you build a self-sustaining approach to your job, a clock that can tell time without you, it is far more likely that you can get promoted—in fact, more likely that you *will*. Not only will you have excelled at the discharge of your responsibilities, but also you will have built something larger than yourself and made a contribution to the whole organization.

For example, many large and medium-sized businesses require sales and services teams to use a web-based customer relationship management (CRM) application like Salesforce.com. Essentially a centralized database platform, these tools provide each company rep a way of recording and storing detailed information about sales contacts, leads, and ongoing negotiations in which they are involved. Too often, I think, a tool like this is perceived as busywork, an administrative tax on the hardworking reps who, after a long week on planes, trains, automobiles, cell phones, and BlackBerrys, must then spend additional hours plugging all their notes into the system. Seen through the lens of HOW, however, this is a leadership opportunity, a chance to build continuity, to inform and enlist the team. Should you catch the flu a day before a closing pitch, the continuity you've built into the CRM application enables someone else on the team to easily step up, grab the ball, and bring home the business.

If you build a system that can be run by others, train others so that they may step up and take more responsibility, or enlist those around you in a team-based approach that is more efficient and profitable, a superior can then say, "The business doesn't seem to need you as much to accomplish that goal; we could use you better in this new position." The key ingredient to progress, to getting ahead, is to leave a foundation behind.

CIRCLES IN CIRCLES (A THOUGHT)

These five behaviors—envision, communicate and enlist, seize authority and take responsibility, plan and implement, and build succession and continuity—form the foundation of a self-governing disposition. The rest of the Leadership Framework amplifies, refines, and reinforces these basic concepts, creating a circle of leadership attributes.

A thought here about circles: Waves, we know, go *around*. Studies show us they start much more easily in closed-loop stadiums where everyone can see one another, and much less easily in, for instance, motor speedways, where the audience lines one side of the stadium. Leadership, in some way, mirrors this geometry. The Leadership Framework creates a self-perpetuating circle of energy, like a Wave in a stadium. When two kids hold hands, lean back (trusting one another not to let go), and spin around, they can achieve great speed with little effort, and the energy between them continues to grow as long as they hold on. When they let go, all that energy disburses. The Leadership

Framework mirrors that idea. As we talk through the Leadership Framework, you will notice that for everything a leader *is*, there is something he or she *is not*. When your actions take you out of the framework, you sacrifice its self-propelling energy and, like those dizzy kids, crumple in a heap on the grass.

The other remarkable thing about the framework is that it allows us to be really aggressive and fiercely competitive in pursuit of our goals. Its interlocking nature leaves us freer to innovate, to take chances, and to act spontaneously without losing sight of our core values, the center around which we spin. Because it helps us see things through our core, we can see the shortest, most expedient path to achievement. Though the wild uncertainties of daily business can sometimes leave us lost in unfamiliar terrain, the Leadership Framework always tells us where home is, and helps us see the sure path to get there. By holding on tightly to the circularity of the framework, we can generate that much more speed and energy on our journey.

THE LEADERSHIP FRAMEWORK, CONTINUED

In Spite Of

Everything worth doing encounters resistance along the way. To move a big rock requires you to fight gravity and inertia. To climb a mountain requires you to overcome the effects of thin air. Say, for instance, you return from giving a presentation to a potential partner. The discussions went well and you feel the prospect should be doing business with you and not your competitor. But one person in the meeting announced to the room that the company doesn't have room in its budget this year. What is your attitude when you hear this? What is your disposition to obstacles?

In 1905, Madam C. J. Walker started selling a scalp conditioning and healing formula, Madam Walker's Wonderful Hair Grower, door-to-door to African-American women throughout the South and Southeastern United States. Walker, the daughter of former slaves, had been orphaned at age 7, married at 14, and widowed with a child at 19. She worked doing laundry to put her daughter through school before she envisioned a new life for herself. "I got my start by giving myself a start," Walker said. In spite of obstacles far greater than any that most can imagine, Walker grew her enterprise into a company that employed 3,000 people. She became the first known African-American woman to become a millionaire. "I am a woman who came from the cotton fields of the South," she was fond of saying. "From there I was promoted to the washtub. From there I was promoted to the cook kitchen. And from there I promoted myself into the business of manufacturing hair goods and preparations. I have built my own factory on my own ground."[7]

It would be hard to imagine anyone who envisioned and accomplished so much in the face of seemingly overwhelming obstacles than C. J. Walker. She pursued her vision *in spite of* obstacles, and this deeply ingrained attitude was central to her ability to thrive. If you want to make a Wave happen and the person to your right doesn't want to stand up, are you done? Do you sit back down Waveless? Yet we've all seen Waves happen in which people at first don't want to stand up, but then get caught up in it. It becomes a great Wave. This can occur only when its leaders persevere in spite of initial resistance. A self-governing leadership disposition helps you ask the question, "How do we help our partner find the budget they need to support the program?"

I've never met a good sailor who hasn't sailed in rough waters, and I have never seen a vision, never heard an interview, and never read a biography about someone who achieved something worthwhile that did not include stories about gutting out rough times, overcoming obstacles, and getting there *in spite of* all that got in the way. It's a fact that you will face obstacles; it is a constant of life. What matters is not the obstacle, but HOW you think about obstacles, HOW you approach them, and HOW you behave in the face of them. Leaders believe they will find a way *in spite of* the forces aligned against them. They never walk away because of a problem. Sometimes you won't succeed despite your best efforts, but if you don't start with the *in spite of* disposition, you will seldom win.

Confront Complexity and Ambiguity

We live in a world full of conflict. Had we infinite resources, perhaps we could say yes to everything and wouldn't need to make tough choices. Perhaps we wouldn't even need a Leadership Framework.

But the world is full of conflict, full of competing desires, interests, objectives, agendas, and possibilities. So, much as we need to cultivate an *in spite of* disposition, we must also embrace the complexity and ambiguity. Even the best-made plans can go awry, and to expect smooth sailing and steady winds sets you up to struggle when inevitable adversity hits. Over dinner in Los Angeles, venture capitalist Alan Spoon told me, "There is always going to be good news and bad news. The good news takes care of itself; it's the bad news that takes work. That's where you'll spend your time."[8] Leaders know this going in; they understand that conflict is natural, and anticipate the need to lead in the midst of conflict.

Again, it boils down to disposition. Leaders stare in the face of conflicting desires and individual interests, and of limited, not unlimited, budgets. They open some doors and they close others. They make principled decisions in the face of conflict and so set a steady course through rough seas. Leaders are thirsty for truth and they go after it. By definition, the future that they have envisioned and the present are in conflict; change must occur to achieve something new. Within this tension lies the opportunity to thrive, but only in the hands of those willing to confront it.

Similarly, leaders eschew essentialism and reductionism in the approach to their goals. The goal is never about one thing, like profits or productivity or quality. Leaders acknowledge the inherent complexity of every journey. They balance many voices and many goals and seek to fulfill the needs of the many stakeholders in every effort. In the face of a multitude of choices, the self-governing person looks wisely and deeply to the core values at the center of their framework and makes considered decisions about the best way to uphold them.

Wield Charismatic Authority

We have taken as one of our foundational attributes that leaders seize authority. But what kind of authority? Stand up or I'll punch you? Do this because I'm your mother or father, or because I'm your boss? In Japan during World War II, the Japanese military began sending their airmen, known as kamikazes, on *tokko*: suicide missions. Many young Japanese men died during these missions, but a few lived to tell the tale of what it was like. One of them was a Japanese Navy pilot named Shigeyoshi Hamazono. In his wartime memoir, *Suiheisen* (*The Horizon*), Hamazono describes being prepared to die for his country, but recalls an encounter he had before leaving on a mission on April 6, 1945. He tells of Vice Admiral Ugaki, who gave a farewell speech to the Kokubu No. 1 Air Base kamikaze pilots, of whom Hamazono was one. Ugaki shook their hands and said, "Please die for your country." After finishing his remarks, he asked if anyone had any questions. A veteran pilot, whom Hamazono respected, stepped forward and said, "I am confident that I can sink two enemy transport ships with just the bombs carried by my plane. If I sink them, may I return?" Ugaki reportedly answered, "Please die."[9]

Authority typically comes in two forms: charismatic authority and formal authority.[10] Formal authority derives from reference to power, usually hierarchical power. "I'm your parent. In my house, I'm right, even when I'm wrong." That is formal authority (and also the reason why most of us grow up and leave home).

Many young men died on both sides of that brutal war, and Ugaki is an extreme example, but we see examples of formal authority like "Please die because I ordered you to" wielded every day in matters from the mundane to the sublime. You get an e-mail that consists of one sentence, "Do this by four o'clock." The implication is clear: "because I'm the boss." Are you enlisted? Or has the wielding of formal authority introduced friction into the relationship? You might acquiesce for any number of rational reasons—you are new at the company, your boss is quite senior, she could help your career—but are you enlisted? Are you inspired? Formal authority lacks the ability to inspire and enlist. It can, at best, demand acquiescence, a grudging or even willing going along with the order. Each time leaders wield formal authority they deplete their store of it. It's like a bank account; the more you withdraw the less you have. Eventually, willing acquiescence turns to grudging acquiescence, which turns to subtle undermining, and even outright rebellion. The delays and distractions of those you lead in that way steadily mount, and their productivity and responsiveness steadily decline.

Charismatic authority, in contrast, compounds itself. What if, instead, that four o'clock e-mail says, "If you can get this done by four o'clock, it will help our team win in these three ways." The e-mail enlists you by sharing how the task fits the larger vision; what originally seemed an arbitrary deadline now becomes an integral part of a vision to succeed. Vision and enlistment breed charismatic authority. Charismatic authority derives not from power but from principled action toward others, from referencing beliefs and principles and reaching out to others with them, and from a desire to get your HOWS right and make Waves. It is earned every day, in every HOW. You build charismatic authority with every action toward others, so rather than deplete their bank account of authority, you build it. Sometimes it takes a little extra time, but the time is an investment that is paid back with interest, a short-term cost for long-term gain. Thus authority itself becomes a Wave, self-sustaining, going around and around until no one can remember where it started but everyone is glad they were a part of it.[11]

Say what you will about Krazy George Henderson, but there is no denying that he is a paragon of charismatic leadership. No one participates in his Waves because he is hired by the stadium to start them, nor do they follow because he bangs his drum loudly. They follow because he reaches out to them, shares his vision, enlists them in the big picture, and perseveres in spite of those who think he's a crackpot or who would rather eat their hot dogs in peace. And he gets things done; people stand and cheer.

Inspire

We know that rational people, for the most part, avoid pain and seek pleasure. Rational people, the common thinking says, will be motivated by more pleasure and less pain, more money and less censure. When you are in a position of authority, then, and you want to get things done, you give people more carrots and fewer sticks, right? Informed acquiescence cultures are built on this simple thought. Motivational thinking, in the form of carrots and sticks, dominates these organizations. While we can't deny the reality that no one works solely because they enjoy it or it fulfills them (or we would call it "play" rather than "work"), *motivation* as a leadership principle is not self-sustaining. The person who hands out $20 bills in order to make a Wave eventually either runs out of money or the cooperation of recipients who decide that $20 isn't really enough. Motivation requires an *object* of motivation, a carrot or a stick, some external means by which to propel or compel action. Motivation has its place, but we know that in a world of HOW motivation is not enough. A leader seeks a self-sustaining method of generating action. To make Waves, you must seek to *inspire*.

Inspiration comes from a dedication to beliefs and values, the pursuit of big ideas and significant contributions to others, and a commitment to communicating this dedication and pursuit to others. Isn't it different to be inspired than to be motivated? Everyone knows what it is like to be inspired. You can be inspired by a movie, by a book, or by an experience that happened to you, inspired by what you want to accomplish, or inspired by the actions and efforts of others. Values are inspirational, as is the pursuit of goals greater than yourself. Inspiration calls forth your best efforts and your most creative thinking. If you are inspired to land on the moon, or inspired to start or participate in a Wave, you don't care about carrots and sticks; you have a higher calling. Just as trust elicits trust, inspiration elicits belief. Informed belief—the marriage of the questioning and unquestioning parts of the mind—is a powerful, self-sustaining force. Like everything else in the Leadership Framework, inspiration circles back on you. Seeing others inspired inspires you in return. Leadership is about inspiration. Leaders inspire, and seek to keep the atmosphere of inspiration—the call to significance—alive in others. You don't have to be the boss to do this; anyone can, and in a world of HOW, where the quality of your effort is as important as its end result, everyone should.

Be Principled

In the wake of Hurricane Katrina and the destruction of the city of New Orleans, the U.S. Federal Emergency Management Agency (FEMA) handed out money to people in a helter-skelter fashion with almost no basic fraud-prevention systems. Emergency aid was subsequently used to purchase season tickets to the New Orleans Saints football games, a large dinner at a Hooters restaurant in San Antonio, a $200 bottle of Dom Pérignon, an all-inclusive weeklong Caribbean vacation, and several "Girls Gone Wild" videos. Thousands of incarcerated criminals received emergency housing allowances.[12] "We just made the calculated decision that we were going to help as many people as we could," said Donna Dannels, acting deputy director of recovery for FEMA, speaking to a Congressional oversight committee a year later, "and go back [later to] identify those people who we either paid in error or [who] defrauded us."[13] Dannels made this statement after a nonpartisan Government Accounting Office study revealed that as much as $1.4 billion—one-quarter of the total monies FEMA distributed in the wake of the disaster—was lost to fraud and abuse.

Decision making, in general, flows from one of two sources: pragmatism or principle. Pragmatic decisions seek to solve the immediate problem in the most expedient manner, like FEMA in the face of Katrina. Pragmatic thinking tends to embrace short-term benefits and alleviate immediate pain, but it produces unintended consequences with often long-term ramifications. If FEMA were a for-profit company, for instance, its losses from fraud would be dwarfed by the loss of its credibility and reputation. Who would choose to invest in an insurance company that reimbursed the purchase of "Girls Gone Wild" videos? What possible explanation can remediate the impression that choice leaves on the market?

In the course of a business day, we are all called upon to make countless decisions. If we are self-governing and adopt a leadership disposition, we make even more. What kind of spacecraft do we build? What should the design look like? What kind of people should we hire? What should I say when I return this phone call? Leaders are constantly making decisions, and a given team or organization might make hundreds, if not thousands, of decisions each day. If each one of us makes decisions based on short-term, pragmatic considerations—what will sound good, what will make the problem go away, what will close this deal—the errors of unintended consequences— like *Girls Gone Wild*—just spiral out of control. We can't control or imagine the ramifications of all those short-term decisions.

What would happen, for instance, if, after a successful quarter of doing or saying whatever it took to make your numbers, you put all of your customers in a room and walked out. What would they think of you if they started to compare notes?

"Hmmm, they let you do a six-month pilot? They told me they don't do pilots."

"You got a three-year contract? They told me they would only do a five-year contract, no matter what."

In a transparent, connected world, this happens every day, both physically and virtually. And not just about company practices, but about your individual behavior, as well. Comparing notes is cheap and easy, and we do it countless times a day via the vast store of information and communication technology easily at our fingertips. That puts a premium on consistency. The world of HOW calls for conduct that creates long-term, self-sustaining continuity, which builds trust and further alignment between you and the world around you. I propose a corollary to Mark Twain's famous quote about telling the truth (though not as eloquently phrased): "Always act on principle. That way, you won't have to keep track of all the intended and unintended consequences of your actions."

Seeing through the lens of HOW leads you to make decisions based on principle—a sound, central core of beliefs that expresses long-term values. In a transparent world, where everything that can be known will be known, only principled decision making can guide the kind of consistency of purpose you need to build trust and reputation. Acting from principle rather than pragmatism also makes you more efficient and nimble. Because you will not spend as much time dancing with rules or comparing short-term gains, you can act more intuitively and with more clarity rather than in a slow and calculated fashion. The best possible decision will be more immediately apparent to you because it will spring from your deepest values. You will act with more certainty, confidence, and trust in your choices.

If you want to become enduring and self-sustaining, you must focus your thinking through the lens of principled thought, and let those values-based considerations inform everything you do or say.

Be Rigorous about the Truth of the Present

Shortly after Steve Wynn opened the eponymous Wynn Las Vegas resort in 2005 to great fanfare and acclaim, he realized he had a problem.[14] Dealers and floor people in Wynn's casinos are usually the best-paid in the industry and derive most of their income from tips that are pooled and divided among the frontline service personnel who run the gaming tables. "I made a mistake," he told me from Macau, where he was working on his newest project. "It turned out, unfortunately, that the dealers were making all of the tips and the floor people and supervisors who serve the customers side by side with the dealers were not receiving any, meaning the dealers were making more than their supervisors. This disparity caused dissatisfaction and resentment among the floor people, who thought it unfair. Plus, because of the inverted compensation structure, I had difficulty recruiting dealers to step up and become supervisors. The casino was suffering."[15]

You can only take risks, as we know, when you have a strong foundation of trust. Trust enables risk, which allows innovation and leads to progress: TRIP. But when mistakes are made and realized, a leader has only two choices: to let them be and absorb the cost or to expend the resources necessary to correct them. In Wynn's case, he had to choose between an inverted and unfair compensation structure that was detrimental to the growth of his operation, and disrupting the morale of his dealers by altering their pay package and jeopardizing their trust. "It was a terrible scenario," Wynn said. "I thought about it for months, but I couldn't let it stand. This was the first time in my whole career that I had to double back and do something that would hurt my employees' compensation package. It felt like cutting off one of my fingers."

No matter how painful or personally embarrassing the truth may be, leaders step up and face it head-on. Over the course of many face-to-face meetings, Wynn told his dealers he was revamping the way the tip pool was divided to create greater rewards for those who stepped up and accepted more responsibility. "I told them I had made a mistake, that it was my job to treat everyone fairly, that a group of them were getting screwed, and that I was going to make a change. I said, 'Look, I'm here, and I'm going to meet with every employee in this company, every dealer, because I owe you now and forever an explanation of the thinking behind our decisions, especially one that impacts your life.'"

Despite his transparency, the dealers were predictably (and perhaps understandably) upset. Even after many discussions, some of them filed suit in the district courts and with the Labor Commission. Ultimately, those lawsuits were dismissed. Even after the rigors and combativeness of a lawsuit, however, Wynn did something remarkable. "I took the guys who sued me for coffee," he said. "I told them how much I respected them for standing up for what they thought was right. I told them that not only did I not have any hard feelings, but I actually felt they were correct to promote what they thought was right, and to have the guts to stand up for it and not just grouse in the back room. I am also meeting with all the employees to tell them how proud I am that, even though they disagreed with me and even though they thought that I had made the wrong decision, they never, ever took it out on the floor of the casino with the customers."

Wynn, and anyone in his position when a problem is found, had many ways he could have avoided taking action directly. Many of us have been on the receiving end of memos, e-mails, or delegated proclamations from the top of the organization giving us bad news about our jobs. But Wynn chose to deal with the problem head-on and directly. I asked him why he chose that road. "When you make a decision that you feel is the right decision for the long-term benefit of the enterprise, it still may be wrong," he said. "It could explode in your face; it could be embarrassing, humiliating, or even catastrophic; but that is absolutely not an excuse for not making that decision, nor standing up for it in front of others. That's probably at the heart of leadership."

You can't build a skyscraper like Wynn Las Vegas on a foundation that is not solid, or worse, that you "sort of believe" is solid. You can't land a rocket in the Sea of Tranquility if you don't know whether the surface is rock or powder. A leader needs to know, so a leader is rigorous about the truth of the present. The more rigorous you can be about the truth of your present condition—what is solid and what is not, what works and what malfunctions—the better you can pursue the future. A leader peels the onion to get to the truth, no matter how difficult or evanescent that truth may be. Leaders believe it is healthy to ask the tough questions, toss ideas back and forth, confront problems when they arise, and wrestle truth to the ground. Getting bad news, understanding what is broken, understanding what's shaking, understanding where the house of cards is and where real killers of the future lurk. To make your visions reality, you must not be afraid to see everything there is to see.

The opposite of rigorous truth means indulging some blind spots or living in a state of plausible deniability and superficiality, a habit that leaders should banish from their thinking and approach. Leaders must know how solid is the foundation before they take leaps, build skyscrapers, and innovate, and be rigorous about the journey along the way.

Be Reflective, Especially about Your Own Nature

As much as most of us relish conditions of harmony, simplicity, synthesis, and coherence, nowhere do they exist at all times. Even monks who live on mountains have to struggle to get a decent meal now and again (though they produce much spiritual calm, their P&Ls leave something to be desired). More often, our world is full of conflict, complexity, and ambiguity. To become a person capable of getting your HOWs right, of focusing not just on the WHAT of the outcome, but simultaneously on the HOW you do WHAT you do, you must learn to feel comfortable within these conditions. To be self-governing means to be reflective, especially about your own nature.

Our virtues are typically our vices. Lawyers are trained to argue and tend to win a lot of arguments. People disposed to winning arguments, however, often face a challenge in the realm of personal relationships, because relationships are rarely about winning or losing. So seeing through the lens of HOW, a lawyer devoted to strengthening her synapses with others reflects: When do I talk too much? When do I listen? When am I argumentative? When am I zealously advocating? Am I enlisting? Am I not? Is the Wave really happening? Are people really getting up because they're inspired or are they getting up because I motivated them? We must reflect about our virtues and our vices and be rigorous about our own truths.

"Shortly after I became CEO of Pfizer," Jeff Kindler told me, "I was being interviewed on internal video for our more than 100,000 employees. They were asking me about changes to the company, and I said something like, 'There may be a need to make important changes in the company; we may need to take up a lot of actions to change,' and blah blah blah blah. I was using a lot of buzzwords and corporate-speak. And then I realized what I was doing. I was on the border of spinning, and I interrupted myself and said, 'Wait a minute, let me correct myself. Let me be clear about what I am talking about here. There will be cost cutting, and there will be layoffs, and people will lose their jobs.'" It was Kindler's first major communication with his company, and it was his first opportunity to show what kind of a leader he was going to be. Though it meant being vulnerable in front of 100,000 people, Kindler's ability to reflect in the moment allowed him to set a true course of change for his company. "It was harsh language," he admitted, "but it was truthful, and I think people respected the fact that I was not giving them a load of baloney in corporate-speak. Since then, I have received comments that people at Pfizer appreciate that somebody is talking straight to them, that I am acknowledging that we have serious challenges and serious issues we need to face."[16]

Self-reflection lights the way on a journey of self-improvement, guiding you through both the good times on the Hill of A and the struggles in the Valley of C. Governing yourself means working on yourself and trying to do things better year over year and week over week. Like the monks, we will never achieve perfection, but if we reflect not only will we improve, but we will develop the sort of simultaneous consciousness that Jeff Kindler has, the ability to see the HOWS in everything we do, as we do them.

A lack of reflection leaves you superficial and determined. You may win a lot of arguments, motivate a lot of action, show the superficial characteristics of corporate-speak leadership, and even achieve some success, but you will work harder to do so, and eventually people will begin to see your limitations as a leader.

Go to the Point of No Return

Do you remember the first time you went to the edge of a very high diving board at a swimming pool? Goaded there by your friends who, despite all sense, yelled for you to jump, you inched your way to the edge, looked down, and immediately wished you were somewhere else. In that moment, you realized, perhaps for the first time in your life, that you had consciously taken yourself to the point of no return. If you crawled back and didn't jump, you realized, your friends would call you a bunch of names you didn't want to be called. If you jumped, however, you felt you might die. Butterflies in your stomach, trying hard not to giggle, there was nothing comfortable about that moment. Nothing was more terrifying.

Some of us jumped. Some of us crawled back, only to return another day and succeed. Some of us, to this day, have never taken the plunge. But to envision, by definition, means to explore the unknown, to go to new, risky, and potentially frightening places. You can't land on the moon if you don't go farther than the hill behind your house. If you are trying to bring about a better future, you must every day go someplace you have not been before, to the point of no return. What happens every time you go to the point of no return? You push past your limits and open up new terrains of possibility. Each challenge accepted leads to greater ability when you confront the next. Taking the first step off the Hill of B, leaving the easy and comfortable knowledge there to pursue mastery on the Hill of A is a point of no return. Forcing yourself to ask the question this week that you were too shy to ask last week is a point of no return. When you take that step, you know that tough times lie ahead in the Valley of C. Those who cannot bring themselves to take that step confine themselves to the path of least resistance. A leadership disposition guides you to take the path of most resistance and turn it into the path of least resistance.

Be Passionate and Optimistic

LRN is headquartered a few miles from the Pacific Ocean in Los Angeles, and since I started the company in 1994, I have worked hard to personally recruit the most talented people I could find. Inevitably, when I identify and pursue a potential recruit who lives in another city, we end up in a pros-and-cons-type debate about the relative merits of wherever they live and Los Angeles. Each time I have this discussion, it sounds eerily the same. *Their* city has great culture, *my* city has great culture; *their* city has great restaurants, *my* city has great restaurants; and back and forth we go in this ledger of pluses and minuses. But in the end, when all has been tallied, I play my trump card. "Both cities are great," I say, "but all else being equal, my city gets an extra boost, because in Los Angeles we have the sun, and the sun is that one thing that shines through all the other qualities, making them that much better." In business, that is what passion does. Passion is like the sun shining through everything; it makes it that much better.

Passion is the difference between a morning wake-me-up and a global corporation. Starbucks chairman Howard Schultz makes a good cup of coffee, but he is passionate about creating a workplace full of dignity and respect for his employees, customers, and suppliers. Schultz's passion wafts through the company and its many shops like the scent of roasting coffee beans, inspiring everyone who catches a whiff. And that makes all the difference in the world.

"You either have a tremendous love for what you do, and passion for it, or you don't," Schultz told *BusinessWeek*. "So whether I'm talking to a barista, a customer, or an investor, I really communicate how I feel about our company, our mission, and our values. It's our collective passion that provides a competitive advantage in the marketplace because we love what we do and we're inspired to do it better. When you're around people who share a collective passion around a common purpose, there's no telling what you can do."[17]

You need passion to start a Wave. You've got to turn to the person to your right and have real conviction that if we make this Wave we can help our team win. If you're not passionate about that, then it will never happen. Without passion, you grow complacent, and complacency leads nowhere. "Passion is everything," Steve Wynn told me. "It springs from strange places in the human psyche, from a kind of introspective, deep, and penetrating consideration of what you do, and it unleashes a phenomenal amount of energy that leads to higher insights and a deeper understanding of your customers or your employees. And it strikes a happy, deep, self-satisfying chord. It resonates. And when it does, you're off on a hunt. You don't think that you're tired or even working. You're just consumed with the notion that if you can get this done, it's significant; it's wonderful, and off you go. That's the thing we call passion."

You can express your passion in any way you want. You can write an e-mail with passion, you can speak with passion, or you can create a spreadsheet with passion. Passion is the spice that enhances all other ingredients with greatness. Some people express their passion by just showing up, every day, on time, steady as a rock. Passion fuels enlistment and alignment and communication. Have you ever been truly persuaded by an argument that wasn't put forward passionately? Passion is the sun, and leaders are passionate. "You take two runners," Massimo Ferragamo told me, "one with an incredible physique and the other who runs with passion, and the second one you know will win even if it kills him. Working with passion is an engine that is unbelievable. A person with drive and passion does three times the job of another person. But it is not so much the quantity of the job; that is not the point. The point is that they draw crowds; they have followers; they push, and lead, and so achieve much more."[18]

Optimism lives hand in hand with passion. Would the United States have spent 10 years trying to land on the moon if we believed there was a chance we would take off and miss? "I am an optimist,"

Sir Winston Churchill once said. "It does not seem too much use being anything else."[19] Self-governing people don't allow themselves to entertain the notion of not landing on the moon. They don't keep the vote in their mind to say, "I choose success versus failure." They only envision how they are going to land on the moon. They've got that positive, passionate energy.

That last thought may seem—well—optimistic. But there is an important power lurking in optimism, the power of unlimited belief. Pessimists hold limited beliefs. The doubt and fear of failure that are natural to everyone trying to achieve something great creeps into their brains and ossifies there, creating friction and dissonance and bottling up the amazing power that brains can unleash when filled with belief. The only way to get to the next level, to reach the point of no return and to push past it, is to spend zero time contemplating the alternative. "Perpetual optimism is a force multiplier," said former U.S. Chairman of the Joint Chiefs of Staff General Colin Powell.[20] Helen Keller, who had vision greater than eyesight and was no stranger to the point of no return, said, "No pessimist ever discovered the secrets of the stars, or sailed to an uncharted land, or opened a new heaven to the human spirit."[21]

Pursue Significance

When Bill Gates was in high school, he and his friends would sit around marveling at what they thought was the undeniable future. "We couldn't believe that everyone else didn't see what we saw," he said in a recent television interview, "that personal computers were going to change the world." This was long before the fateful meeting with IBM when Gates and Paul Allen realized that if they just had an operating system, they could change the world (so they went out and bought one, which they resold to IBM, and Microsoft was born).

It's virtually impossible to be inspired and generate passion unless you have an important mission. The journey to self-governance is inspired by the pursuit of significance. Leaders believe that landing on the moon will benefit mankind, not just profit the company. Leaders believe in ideas. I founded LRN on the idea that the world would be a better place if more people did the right thing. Leaders think of themselves as cathedral builders, not bricklayers. Mission, whether personal or organizational, needs to be important, something worthy of your inspiration or your passion. It could be number two on your list or it could be number three, but it's got to be on your list of important things. You will never find enduring, self-perpetuating power by pursuing the mundane. Passion and optimism compel those who assume a leadership disposition to engage in enterprises of transcendental importance.

Significance means different things at different stages of your life. The young, for instance, often have less time and resources to devote to giving back to their community than those who are older and more established in life. The most successful among us might feel that our achievements alone add up to a life of significance. But the pursuit of significance I am talking about is a disposition toward serving others, toward devoting some measure of every stage of your life to improving lives. Even the most successful need to always measure their efforts against the higher standard of service to others. To make that shift, to envision your efforts in service of a better world, creates a disposition that leads you beyond the immediate and mundane toward the extraordinary and exceptional. If you can pursue significance in this way, then, and only then, can you achieve true success.

Circles in Circles, Part Two

And so we have circumnavigated the lens of HOW and returned to where we began, envisioning a better future through the pursuit of significance. And so we go around again.

Like a ship's sextant aimed at the stars, this lens—the Leadership Framework—can help you navigate your way through a world of HOW. By developing a leadership disposition and focusing your efforts and perspectives on the areas we have discussed, you will begin to fill the synapses around you with trust, alignment, transparency, inspiration, and passion. You will begin to make Waves, perhaps little ones at first, but their effects will be immediate and long lasting. More than just a way of seeing, the Leadership Framework has all the qualities I have tried to put in this book: It is a system whose many parts are mutually reinforcing; it is a framework of ideas on which you can build structures of understanding; it is a constitution, informed and driven by a values-based approach to the world; and it is steeped deeply in the notion of self-governance, the thought that ultimate success will never come from without, but rather from within.

As the Leadership Framework circles back on itself, so too now does this book. We began our journey together with the story of Krazy George Henderson and the first Wave, and if you flip back now to that first story and reread George's description of that fateful day, you will see that without consciously knowing it, George was as alive to the ideas of the world of HOW and the Leadership Framework as you now are. He knew that there was a way of pursuing his goals—a set of HOWs—that was more powerful, more effective, more self-sustaining, and more significant than other ways. I would reprint that story for you here, but it is probably easier for you to just flip back to the Prologue and read it again.

Besides, everything has to end somewhere.

THE LEADERSHIP FRAMEWORK

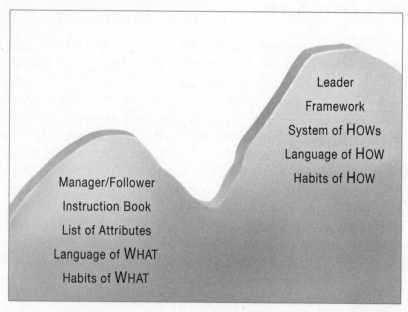

Leader
Framework
System of HOWs
Language of HOW
Habits of HOW

Manager/Follower
Instruction Book
List of Attributes
Language of WHAT
Habits of WHAT

Afterword

We can be knowledgeable with other men's knowledge
but we cannot be wise with other men's wisdom.
—Michel de Montaigne, essayist (1533–1592)

You would expect a restaurateur to understand service, but Danny Meyer, founder of New York City's Union Square Cafe, one of America's most successful culinary restaurant organizations, goes further. "We are in a very new business era," says Meyer in his book, *Setting the Table*. "I'm convinced that this is now a hospitality economy, no longer the service era. If you simply have a superior product or deliver on your promises, that's not enough to distinguish your business. There will always be someone else who can do it or make it as well as you. It's how you make your customers feel while using your products that distinguishes you. . . . Service is a monologue: we decide on standards for service. Hospitality is a dialogue: to listen to a customer's needs and meet them. It takes both great service and hospitality to be at the top."[1]

Hospitality. How your customers *feel*. These concepts transcend the restaurant business and apply to all business in a world of HOW. Meyer is talking about an *experience*. In a dialogic society, answering the phone on the second ring or always having a smile on your face is no longer enough; a connected, transparent world now looks past the proxies of service and looks to how the companies and people with whom they do business engage and interact with them. Experience

299

matters in a world where interrelationships matter. And not just customer experience, but supplier, employee, colleague, vendor, competitor, regulator, and media experience matters, all the interactions with everyone you encounter throughout the business day. Experience is becoming the great differentiator.

Can you *do* experience? Can you write a guidebook of best practices that deliver a consistent interpersonal experience throughout your organization or team? Is *experience* something you do, or is it something more ephemeral, more dependent on each individual's ability to act independently and consistently in the group's best interest?

Let me ask a different question. In their seminal study of the habits and practices of visionary companies, *Built to Last*, Jim Collins and Jerry Porras survey what they call the "core ideologies of visionary companies."[2] As they define them, core ideologies give "guidance and inspiration to people *inside that company*" (italics theirs). Here are some of the things they list:

- 3M: innovation, tolerance.
- American Express: heroic customer service.
- Citicorp: expansionism, being out in front, aggressiveness, self-confidence.
- Philip Morris: winning.
- Procter & Gamble (P&G): continuous self-improvement.
- Merck: excellence.

These are all amazing companies, each with a long history of success and achievement. But I ask: Can you *do* innovation? Expansionism? Winning? Can you *do* excellence? Can winning or heroic customer service inspire you? Can you be guided in your everyday efforts by aggressiveness and self-confidence? As groundbreaking as was Collins and Porras's book in its time (and I built LRN on many of its precepts), the world has evolved substantially since then. While *Built to Last* remains a visionary work and its approach fundamentally sound, we can now see more deeply into what lives at the true core of successful enterprises. The new lens of HOW shows us that what Collins and Porras saw as "core ideologies" are not *core* enough for the road ahead. I don't think you can *do*, be *guided by*, or most importantly, be *inspired by* any of these things. They are results, things you *get* when you innovate in HOW.

You can't *do* self-improvement, but if in every e-mail, conversation, meeting, and task you are thinking like a leader, you will improve. You can't *do* tolerance, but if in every interaction you strive to fill the spaces between you and others with trust, you will *get* tolerance, and a whole lot more. You can't *do* excellence or winning, but, if you believe in a set of core values and you pursue the expression of those values in everything you do, you will deliver more excellence to others and, in a world of HOW, win. We've seen this in other areas of business. Human resources long ago learned that you can't *do* employee retention; employees stay or leave in relation to their inspiration, reward, and fulfillment with their work. The quality movement showed that you couldn't *do* quality; you *get* quality from a commitment to eliminating inefficiencies in the process of creation. The lens of HOW lets us see more deeply into the true core of what brings perpetual and perennial success, past the *doing* to the values and beliefs that truly form the common bonds and inspiration of group endeavor.

So let us return to the first question: Can you *do* experience? Obviously, no. Great experiences result from great interactions, and great interactions come from getting your HOWS right, from building strong synapses with all those around you, and from inspiring those around you to do the same. Look at some of the big shifts in business today:

- From brand awareness to brand promise.
- From customer service to customer experience.
- From managing reputation to earning reputational value.

All these big shifts result when you get your HOWS right, when you connect to something deeper than ideas, something that unleashes the power to make Waves in everything you do: values. And all these shifts are happening and newly critical to success because the sea change in connectivity and transparency since the beginning of the twenty-first century has brought them to the fore.

Philosopher Henry Sidgwick spoke about the Paradox of Hedonism, the idea that if you pursue happiness directly it tends to elude you, but if you pursue some higher, more meaningful purpose, you can achieve it.[3] The problem with Collins and Porras' core ideologies is that they are about going at the benefit directly, aiming at just the "IP" (innovation and progress) in TRIP and neglecting what it takes to get there. Like happiness, if one seeks such ends as innovation, progress, and winning, one can best achieve them by pursuing the values that can get you there: trust, honesty, integrity, consistency, and transparency. Values inspire, and are deeper and more powerful than ideologies.

How do you measure success? By how much money you have? How many awards you win? How much respect you earn from peers? What you contribute to the world? The love of your family and friends? How many things you own? How many lives you save? If you are like most people, it is probably some mix of these things and others, in varying degrees and proportions. But when does it all add up to success? Early on in the book, we spoke about the paradox of journey, how sometimes you must struggle with new ideas and new perspectives until you internalize them and make them an "artless art," and how this period of struggle often signifies effort beyond easy knowledge and competence. When you put this book down, you may have that experience with these ideas as well, for though this book nears its end, your journey into the world of HOW just begins.

Before we part company, I want to leave you with one more paradox, the paradox of success, and it's a corollary to the paradox of happiness. You cannot *do* success; you cannot achieve it by pursuing it directly. Success is something you get when you pursue something greater than yourself, and the word I use to describe that something is *significance*. All measures of success share one commonality: They signify the value of your passage through life. You can go on a journey of significance—a journey to do, make, extend, create, and support value in the world; and I believe, in the spirit of the Johnson & Johnson Credo, it is this journey that *should* bring you success, however you measure it

Pursuing significance, in the end, is the ultimate HOW.

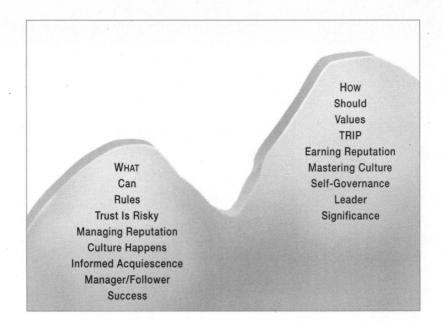

WHAT
Can
Rules
Trust Is Risky
Managing Reputation
Culture Happens
Informed Acquiescence
Manager/Follower
Success

How
Should
Values
TRIP
Earning Reputation
Mastering Culture
Self-Governance
Leader
Significance

Hows Matter

When *HOW* was first published, I was conscious that the world moves faster than books. I wrote on this very page that the pages in *HOW* had only managed to catch my best thinking and the most current information at my disposal as of the moment we originally went to press. But at almost every stage of the writing process—draft, revision, polish, proofreading, and publication—and in the days and months that followed, our hyperconnected, hypertransparent world continued to add new dynamics and issues to consider. That is as it should be and certainly how it turned out to be. And undoubtedly how it will continue to be.

How is a lens, a way of seeing and understanding these changes as they happen. That's why I launched www.HowsMatter.com to continue the dialogue online on all things HOW. Many of the thought leaders featured in this book and countless others making Waves in this world through HOW have since contributed to the discussion.

With this edition of *HOW*, I am committed to keeping the conversation going and bringing renewed energy to it. Please join us online.

Our online effort will attempt to capture in real time the lively multidisciplinary conversation embodied in these pages. We'll also continue to provide useful tools—downloadable color versions of the frameworks in this book, an online interactive HOW course, further studies that support and data that confirms the hypotheses in *HOW*, interviews, videos, articles, and more—all to help augment and deepen your understanding of HOW.

We hope to see you at **www.HowsMatter.com**.

DOV SEIDMAN

Acknowledgments

Writing a book is a journey unlike any other I have ever taken, and, as with most journeys, it would not have been possible without the love, support, encouragement, feedback, and tireless efforts of the many people who made the journey with me. I know I will have the chance to sit down with each of them and express my profound gratitude for what their contribution has meant to me. In the meantime, I'd like to thank them here.

Joni Evans, originally my agent at William Morris and now a dear friend. You gave me the belief and confidence that I had a book in me, and that it would prove useful to others. Your ongoing mentorship and guidance, substantive help, enthusiasm, and inspiration have provided a rare form of encouragement. You have been there every step of the way. I'm deeply grateful. The world needs more like you.

Jennifer Rudolph Walsh and Jay Mandel. Along with the team at William Morris, you stepped into the project and embraced it with the same passion and commitment, and saw me through to the finish line. I feel fortunate to have you both in my corner.

Pamela van Giessen, my editor at John Wiley & Sons. You believed in me, and more important, had a vision for this book far more significant than the one I brought you. You saw that HOW is for people, not just the institutions for which they work. You felt the resonance of this material, shaped and formed it as we went along, and then kept me from running off the track. Perhaps most important, you promised to blue-pencil the word ethics if I ever put it on the page, forcing me to think about these issues in deeper and more universal ways. You were, in a word, visionary. Thanks also to the whole team at John Wiley & Sons, especially Jennifer MacDonald, Nancy Rothschild, Alison Bamberger, and the extraordinary Mary Daniello, for their care and efforts in seeing this book onto the shelves.

Nelson Handel made unique editorial contributions throughout. You helped me better tell the story and lay out the ideas. Our collaboration—intellectual and literary—was intense, and the book is much better for it. No one argues with me like you do. Thank you.

No book that attempts to cover this much ground would be possible without a resourceful and enthusiastic team of researchers. Your passion for the message and relentless digging brought to light many gems that helped the story shine. Liza Foreman, Lisa Derrick, Maureen Brackey, Brian Hong, and especially Diane Wright for her meticulous efforts, I am grateful to each of you for your contributions. I'd also like to thank Catherine Fredman and Mark Ebner for your additional editorial contributions; Adam Turteltaub for your thoughtful research and support; Caroline Heald, thank you for your caring assistance; and Dave Lambertsen for your illustrations.

I am fortunate to have benefited from the uncommon intellect and erudition of Eric Pinckert. At the beginning, when the book was taking shape, and at the end, when it needed to stay in shape, you were invaluable. Mark Detelich, thank you for your unique enhancements. Rob Shavell, thank you for our various collaborations, especially the last one, which resulted in the subtitle of this book.

Ideas never come in a vacuum, and I have been honored over the years for the inspiration and challenges of many brilliant thinkers. Steve Kerr, you are foremost among them. We have been on an intellectual journey together for years, and you have had a profound influence on me. If anything times zero is zero, than anything times you is nearly infinite. You are one of those rare people with whom nascent ideas begin and bloom. When this book came about, you became an active participant, helping me refine and extend the work, make each idea more precise, and make each principle more grounded. I'm proud to call you friend.

My thanks also go to Marcus Buckingham for your wise perspective as I began this effort and helpful feedback near the finish line. Having been there many times before, you helped me stay focused on the book's promise and you stepped in at key moments to help me deliver it.

My friend Tom Friedman, you sat me down in Aspen one day and said the things that a new writer needs to hear in a way no one else could have, and our ongoing conversations since then have been invaluable. What a special privilege for me. Through our "Aristotelian days" on the gondolas and the slopes, Aspen will never seem the same.

Murray Hidary, thank you for our close friendship especially during the journey of discovering this book in myself. Our many conversations on life's issues through the lens of HOW have been illuminating.

Ben Sherwood, my dear friend of 20 years, your inspirational example showed me that you can write a book and still keep your day job. Then you introduced me to Joni. For what more can a friend ask? Thanks for your rare sensibilities, wise advice, and for pushing me past the points of no return.

Among the many things I learned from a great teacher of mine, Rabbi David Ellenson, is the expression from the Mishnah, "make for yourself a rabbi, and acquire for yourself a friend." David, I am honored to be able to call you my rabbi and blessed to be able to call you a dear friend. I cherish our many meaningful conversations on matters of HOW.

I am grateful to all the people with whom I spoke about the ideas in this book, from business executives and thought leaders to line and middle managers to professional cheerleaders, some of whom read and commented on various drafts, some of whom were interviewed, and all of whose insight and experiences have helped shape my thinking, including Keven Bellows, William Broyles Jr., Judge Ruben Castillo, Jack Daly, Keith Darcy, Paula Desio, David Ellen, Patti Ellis, Massimo Ferragamo, Roger Fine, Mike Fricklas, Pat Gnazzo, David Greenberg, Joie Gregor, Charles Hampden-Turner, Patricia Harned, George Henderson, Dr. Michael Hoffman, Dr. Richard Joyce, Jeff Kindler, Rich Korn, Mats Lederhausen, Doug Lankler, Tom McCormick, Michael Monts, Paul Robert, Adam Rosman, Timothy Schultz, Jim Skinner, Joe Stallard, Robert Steele, Patricia Swann, Dr. Kerry Sulkowicz, David Toms, Chris Weiss, Marianne Williamson, Linda Wolf, Steve Wynn, and Paul Zak. It is impossible to remember and properly thank all the other people who, through casual conversation, spirited debate, or a glass of good wine also contributed to my thinking. If I have neglected to mention you now, I thank you for all you have given.

I'd like to thank Philosophy, without which I would never have read a book from cover to cover or learned that ideas can change the world. Thanks to all my professors and mentors, patient and loving people, who helped me see through the words to the profound ideas that lay beneath them. And thanks especially to my dear friend, professor Herb Morris from UCLA, who went the extra mile to mentor and help me through life, and still does.

The ideas in this book grew most directly from my experience with my colleagues at LRN (where all of our conference rooms are named after philosophers). At some level, every member of the LRN team over the past 13 years has contributed to how I think about and approach human achievement in both business and life. This book would not have been possible without the day-to-day, head-to-head interactions that have characterized our journey together. I want to thank you all for giving me the opportunity to work with you and to grow and learn by so doing, for your transparency, your trust, and for allowing me to join with you to transform these ideas from notions into real-world HOWS. So much of what I am today results from our mutual journey. I'd also like to thank the distinguished current and former members of the LRN board of directors, Senator Bill Bradley, Rex Golding, Alan Silverman, Alan Spoon, Sheli Rosenberg, Joe Mandel, and Lee Feldman for believing in the book and its relevance to our mission.

My deepest appreciation also extends to all of LRN's customers. Through my interactions with you over the years and the collaborations with your finest minds, you have given me the opportunity to solve real problems of ethics, compliance, leadership, and culture—real HOWS for a real world. You will see the fruits of our collaboration hanging amply throughout this book.

Family shapes you as nothing else. My mother, Sydelle Seidman, underpinned my life with values. You gave me a home base, and through our many adventures, the courage to venture widely yet never leave home behind. You helped me see the power of instinct and intuition, and believed in me when others did not. I love you.

My brother Ari and sister Goldee, thanks for your solidarity and love as we adapted together to all that life threw at us. I love you both. Being sandwiched between you, I got my first and most lasting lessons of HOW. Alex and Gabi, my niece and nephew, your resiliency and spirit show that our family's next generation will also know HOW. I love being your uncle.

My father, Alex Seidman, who lives in memory, gave me the love of knowledge and connected me to the lessons of history, both others' and our own. What he sacrificed for us inspires me still.

Yury and Vicky Parad, my wife's parents, who, had I a choice of in-laws, would be my favorites among all possible in-laws. I am blessed by your sense of what it means to be family. Thanks for all your caring support, Russian remedies, and Yury, for your careful reading and mind-map of the book. And thanks to my lovely sister-in-law, Michele, for being a shining example of nice people finishing first.

Finally for these acknowledgments but first in my book of life, Maria Seidman, my wife, my constant content. Throughout the journey, from cover to cover, you have been the other voice in my head, reading, reflecting, pushing, and helping me to get it right. You have also been a loving and constant source of energy and support. Above all, you are my constant inspiration that the ideas in this book extend beyond business to life itself. I know no truer partner. I love you.

As I sit here today looking back, one final nod to all those seeming curses that turned out to be blessings in disguise.

And to all those people who questioned how I was going make a living with philosophy: This is HOW.

DOV SEIDMAN
April 2007

When *HOW* was published, I embarked on a journey of connecting with people around the world through the ideas in it. It was clear to me then, as it remains now, that *HOW* is not a book with a beginning and an end, but rather a living philosophy of human endeavor that would be further shaped as we applied its principles to our changing world. That has certainly turned out and continues to be the case. I feel fortunate that the people I named in the original Acknowledgments were there not just to help me create and launch *HOW*; they have been some of its greatest champions. I'd like to thank each of you anew. So many others, especially readers, collaborators, and friends—many more than I can properly thank individually—have been helpful and supportive of my conscious efforts to refine the HOW philosophy and amplify its message. It has been a rich and rewarding adventure. I am humbled by all of this and grateful to each of you.

I'd like nonetheless to thank Eric Krell and Richard Murphy for your editorial contributions to this edition, and others who have generously commented on it. My colleague Katy Brennan deserves special recognition. Thank you, Katy, for passionately and supportively standing up with me in our efforts to inspire a HOW Wave. It is no coincidence that your name starts with *K*, as, like Krazy George, you too are "Krazy" with a *K*.

Being on a TRIP with my colleagues at LRN as we pursue significance together continues to be a source of learning, growth, and meaning for me. I am deeply grateful to each of you for your commitment to "Living HOW" and for your collaboration as we endeavor to inspire principled performance in the world. On behalf of all of us, I am thankful to LRN's community of partners for your continued confidence that in our work together we can build enterprises that are too sustainable to fail.

I'm profoundly honored and privileged that President Bill Clinton chose to contribute a Foreword to this edition of *HOW*. Mr. President, your leadership and many examples, especially the work of the Clinton Global Initiative (CGI), are a source of inspiration to me and evidence that collective action is possible in order to meet the challenges of creating sustainable prosperity in our interdependent world. CGI's focus on "answering the HOW question" has allowed for a special bond with many dedicated members of the wonderful team at CGI. Thank you for *how* you have meaningfully involved me in various CGI initiatives. I'd like to acknowledge Bob Harrison and Christina Sass, true ambassadors of CGI, for your inspirational leadership and collaboration around this edition of *HOW*.

My wife, Maria, to whom this book is dedicated, thank you for your loving support of my journey with HOW. I'm most grateful for our shared journey of life, especially as we together embrace what at times makes life bittersweet. Just a few months after *HOW* was published, my brother, sister, and I lost our beloved mother, to whom this book is also dedicated—though now in her loving memory. A few months later Maria and I welcomed our son Lev Tov into our lives.

We named our son after my mother, and we believe we gave him a good name. But it is not enough to have a good name. In this Era of Behavior he has to *earn* his good name. When it comes to his behavior, so far it turns out that coercion and motivation, even a little bribery, work best with him. It is my greatest hope that as he grows up we will inspire in him the sustainable values that will guide his pursuit of significance. Lev, it is a privilege as your father to help you earn your good name. You inspire me to get my HOWS right first at home and then in everything I do. Thank you for deepening my conviction that HOW matters and thereby my commitment to making the world a better place.

DOV SEIDMAN
July 2011

Notes

PREFACE

1. Norimitsu Onishi, "Making Honesty a Policy in Indonesia Cafes," *New York Times*, June 15, 2009.
2. Stephen Linaweaver, Michael Keating, and Brad Bate, "Conspicuous, but Not Consuming," *Good*, June 20, 2009.
3. AFP profile of Vicente del Bosque, 2010.
4. Michael Eisen, "A New Look: Head Coach Tom Coughlin Has Changed His Ways in 2008," Giants.com, January 30, 2008.
5. John Tierney, "How Happy Are You? In a Boston Suburb, It's a Census Question," *New York Times*, May 2, 2011.

PROLOGUE: Making Waves

1. George M. Henderson, interview, 2005.
2. I. Farkas et al., "Mexican Waves in an Excitable Medium," *Nature* 419 (September 12, 2002).
3. Ibid.

PART ONE   How We Have Been, How We Have Changed

1. J. Madeleine Nash, "Fertile Minds," *Time*, February 3, 1997.
2. Netscape, "Netscape Communications Offers New Network Navigator Free on the Internet," news release, October 13, 1994.

Chapter 1   From Land to Information

1. "Revision Summaries: The Hundred Years' War—1337–1453," Arnold House School, www.arnoldhouse.co.uk/site/pub/Pupils/history/history _rs_100yearswar.html.

2. "The Queen at 80," CBC News, April 20, 2006.

3. Adam Smith, *The Wealth of Nations* (New York: Bantam Classics, 2003).

4. Daniel Gross, "In Praise of Bubbles," *Wired*, February 2006.

5. "Google Company Overview," www.google.com/corporate/.

6. Thomas L. Friedman, *The World Is Flat: A Brief History of the Twenty-First Century* (New York: Farrar Straus and Giroux, 2006).

7. In the interest of transparency and full disclosure, it should be known that I have long-standing collaborations and commercial relationships with some of the companies that appear in one form or another in the book. I have tried to be fair and impartial in my analysis of them and their activities and to be truthful when selecting quotes and anecdotes to illustrate my points. It is, in many ways, precisely because of these relationships that I have been able to see more deeply into a wide assortment of business practices in order to share that insight and access with you, the reader. These companies are: 3M; Altria Group, Inc./Kraft Foods; Citigroup Inc./Citicorp; Computer Associates (CA); The Dow Chemical Company; eBay Inc.; Ford Motor Company; Fox Entertainment Group/ Fox Searchlight Pictures/MySpace; Harris Interactive Inc./Wirthlin Worldwide; Johnson & Johnson; JPMorgan Chase & Co.; MCI/WorldCom; Mitsubishi Motors Corp.; The New York Times Company; The Paramount Motion Picture Group/Paramount Studios; Pfizer Inc.; Philip Morris USA; Procter & Gamble; Toshiba America Inc.; Toyota Motor Sales, U.S.A., Inc.; Tribune Company/Los Angeles Times; Tyco International Ltd.; United Technologies Corporation; Viacom International Inc.; The Walt Disney Company; Wynn Las Vegas.

8. Matthew Hamblen, "CA's Swainson Outlines Customer Advocate Cuts," *Computerworld*, November 16, 2005.

Chapter 2   Technology's Trespass

1. David Hume, *A Treatise of Human Nature*, new ed. (New York: Oxford University Press, 2000; orig. pub. 1739–1740).

2. Terence H. Hull, *People, Population, and Policy in Indonesia* (Jakarta: Equinox Publishing, 2005).

3. Charles Hampden-Turner and Fons Trompenaars, *Building Cross-Culture Competence* (New York: John Wiley & Sons, 2001).

4. Charles Hampden-Turner, interview, 2006.

5. Peg McDonald, "Globalization—Business Opportunity and KM Challenge," *KM World*, February 1, 2001.

6. Jack M. Germain, "Online Consumers Window Shop More Than Impulse Buy," www.ecommercetimes.com/story/42761.html.

7. Lev Grossman and Hannah Beech, "Google under the Gun," *Time*, February 5, 2006.
8. Heather Landy, "RadioShack CEO Admits 'Misstatements,'" *Forth Worth Star-Telegram*, February 16, 2006.
9. "Veritas CFO Resigns over Falsified Resume," TheStreet.com, www .thestreet.com/markets/marketfeatures/10045724.html.
10. "Academic, Athletic Irregularities Force Resignation," ESPN, December 14, 2001.
11. Rob Wright, "A Monster.com of a Problem," *VARBusiness*, February 13, 2003.
12. *The New Oxford American Dictionary*, 2nd ed., s.v. "Google."
13. Madlen Read, "Should I Worry about Prospective Employers 'Googling' Me?," *Pittsburgh Post-Gazette*, March 5, 2005.
14. Lizette Alvarez, "(Name Here) Is a Liar and a Cheat," *New York Times*, February 16, 2006.
15. Peter Wallsten and Tom Hamburger, "Two Parties Far Apart in Turnout Tactics Too," *Los Angeles Times*, November 6, 2006.
16. "Anger Over Big Brother 'Racism,'" *BBC News*, January 16, 2007.
17. Landy, "RadioShack CEO."
18. Andrew Ross Sorkin, "An E-Mail Boast to Friends Puts Executive out of Work," *New York Times*, sec. C, May 22, 2001, late edition.
19. "The Wayback Machine," The Internet Archive, www.archive.org/ web/web.php.
20. According to "Mark Twain Quotations, Newspaper Collections, & Related Resources" (www.twainquotes.com/Lies.html), "This quote has been attributed to Mark Twain, but it has never been verified as originating with Twain. This quote may have originated with Charles Haddon Spurgeon (1834–92) who attributed it to an old proverb in a sermon delivered on Sunday morning, April 1, 1855. Spurgeon was a celebrated English fundamentalist Baptist preacher. His words were: 'A lie will go round the world while truth is pulling its boots on.'"
21. Eulynn Shiu and Amanda Lenhart, "How Americans Use Instant Messaging" (Pew Internet & American Life Project, Washington, D.C., 2004).

Chapter 3   The Journey to How

1. *Jerry Maguire*, DVD, directed by Cameron Crowe (Sony Pictures, 1996).
2. "All-Time Worldwide Boxoffice," Internet Movie Database, www .imdb.com/boxoffice/alltimegross?region=world-wide.

3. Harvey Araton, "Athletes Toe the Nike Line, but Students Apply Pressure," *New York Times*, November 22, 1997; Steven Greenhouse, "Nike Shoe Plant in Vietnam Is Called Unsafe for Workers," *New York Times*, November 8, 1997.

4. Claudia H. Deutsch, "Take Your Best Shot: New Surveys Show That Big Business Has a P.R. Problem," *New York Times*, December 9, 2005, late edition (East Coast).

5. LRN/Wirthlin Worldwide, "Attitudes toward Ethical Behavior in Corporate America Still Suffer from a Gaping Divide among Executives and Rank-and-File Employees," November 18, 2003.

6. "The Joy of Postal Service Dress Regulations," *Morning Edition*, National Public Radio, November 13, 2006.

7. Jyoti Thottam, "Thank God It's Monday!," *Time*, January 17, 2005.

8. "Occupational Outlook Handbook—Engineers," United States Department of Labor, Bureau of Labor Statistics, August 4, 2006.

9. "The Story of Xerography," Xerox Corporation, www.xerox.com/downloads/usa/en/s/Storyofxerography.pdf.

10. "Playmakers Part II: Play-Doh," Parents' Choice Foundation, www.parents-choice.org/full_abstract.cfm?art_id=236&the_page=editorials.

11. Henry Petroski, "Painful Design," *American Scientist* 93, no. 2 (2005): 113.

12. Brad Stone and Robert Stein, "Is TiVo's Time Up?," *Newsweek*, March 20, 2006.

13. Steve Kerr, interview, 2005.

14. Ibid.

15. Mary J. Benner and Michael Tushman, "Process Management and Technological Innovation: A Longitudinal Study of the Photography and Paint Industries," Johnson Graduate School, Cornell University, Ithaca, New York, 2002.

16. Barbara Ross et al., "The Great Tyco Robbery," *New York Daily News*, September 12, 2002.

17. Steve Kerr, interview, 2005.

18. "Merriam-Webster's Words of the Year 2005," Merriam-Webster, www.m-w.com/info/05words.htm.

PART TWO   How We Think

1. Daisetz T. Suzuki, in *Zen in the Art of Archery* (New York: Vintage Books, 1981).

2. David Crystal and Nuala O'Sullivan, "First Steps on a Journey with Words," *Guardian Weekly*, May 26, 2006.

Chapter 4 Playing to Your Strengths

1. William Broyles Jr., *Cast Away* (New York: Newmarket Press, 2000).

2. William Broyles Jr., e-mail message to author, 2006.

3. For further reading on the subject, consult such texts as: Michael S. Gazzaniga, *The Ethical Brain* (Washington, DC: Dana Press, 2005); Brain Research Bulletin 67 (2005); "Scientists Create 'Trust Potion,'" BBC News, June 2, 2005.

4. Felix Warneken and Michael Tomasello, "Altruistic Helping in Human Infants and Young Chimpanzees," *Science* 311 (2006): 1301–1303.

5. Erika Tyner Allen, "The Kennedy-Nixon Presidential Debates, 1960," Museum of Broadcast Communications, www.museum.tv/archives/etv/K/htmlK/kennedy-nixon/kennedy-nixon.htm.

6. Earl Mazzo, "The Great Debates," *The Great Debate and Beyond: The History of Televised Presidential Debates*, www.museum.tv/debateweb/html/greatdebate/e_mazzo.htm.

7. Peter Kirsch et al., "Oxytocin Modulates Neural Circuitry for Social Cognition and Fear in Humans," *Journal of Neuroscience* 25, no. 49 (2005): 11489–11493.

8. Joyce Berg et al., "Trust, Reciprocity, and Social History," *Games and Economic Behavior* 10, no. 1 (1995): 122–142.

9. *A Beautiful Mind*, DVD, directed by Ron Howard (Dreamworks SKG, 2001), based on Sylvia Nasar, *A Beautiful Mind* (New York: Simon & Schuster, 1998).

10. "Nash Equilibrium," Wolfram MathWorld, http://mathworld.wolfram.com/NashEquilibrium.html.

11. Paul J. Zak, "Trust," *Journal of Financial Transformation* 7 (April, 2003): 20.

12. Paul J. Zak, interview, 2006.

13. Ibid.

14. Joseph Shepher, "Mate Selection among Second Generation Kibbutz Adolescents and Adults: Incest Avoidance and Negative Imprinting," *Archives of Sexual Behavior* 1, no. 4 (1971): 293–307.

15. Richard Joyce, *The Evolution of Morality* (Cambridge, MA: MIT Press, 2006).

16. Richard Joyce, interview, 2006.

17. Matthew D. Lieberman et al., "The Neural Correlates of Placebo Effects: A Disruption Account," *NeuroImage* 22 (2004): 447–455.

18. Melanie Thernstrom, "My Pain, My Brain," *New York Times Magazine*, May 14, 2006.

Chapter 5   *From* Can *to* Should

1. Jim Saxton, "Individuals and the Compliance Costs of Taxation: A Joint Economic Committee Study," Joint Economic Committee, United States Congress (November 2005).
2. Daniel Gross, "Hummer vs. Prius," *Slate*, February 26, 2004.
3. "Young Canadians and the Voting Age: Should It Be Lowered?," Canadian Policy Research Networks, www.cprn.com/en/diversity-voting.cfm.
4. Jeffrey Hart, *The Making of the American Conservative Mind: National Review and Its Times* (Wilmington, DE: ISI Books, 2005).
5. "Organizational Guidelines," United States Sentencing Commission, www.ussc.gov/orgguide.htm.
6. Laurie Sullivan, "Compliance Spending to Reach $28 Billion by 2007," *Information Week*, March 2, 2006.
7. Michael Parsons and Jo Best, "EU Slaps Record Fine on Microsoft," *ZDNet*, March 24, 2004.
8. Leo Durocher and Ed Linn, *Nice Guys Finish Last* (New York: Simon & Schuster, 1975).
9. Jim Puzzanghera, "HP's Dunn Details Role in Scandal," *Los Angeles Times*, September 28, 2006.
10. *Harper's Magazine*, sec. Readings, January 2007.
11. "Bhartrihari," *The Internet Encyclopedia of Philosophy*, www.iep.utm.edu/b/bhartrihari.htm.
12. Edward Sapir, "The Status of Linguistics as a Science," in *Culture, Language and Personality*, ed. David G. Mandelbaum (Berkeley: University of California Press, 1986).
13. Michael Janosfsky, "Olympics Coaches Concede That Steroids Fueled East Germany's Success in Swimming," *New York Times*, December 3, 1991.
14. Craig Lord, "Drug Claim Could Be a Bitter Pill," *Times* Online, March 3, 2005.
15. Daniel Eisenberg, "When Doctors Say, 'We're Sorry,'" *Time*, August 15, 2005.
16. "Drug Company to Pay for E. German Doping," *Science Daily*, December 21, 2006; "East German Doping Victims to Get Money," *MSN Money*, December 13, 2006; "Drug Firm Jenapharm Compensates Doped Athletes," *Deutsche Welle*, December 12, 2006.
17. "Strategic Principles," University of Michigan Hospitals and Health System, www.med.umich.edu/strategic/princ.htm.
18. University of Michigan Hospitals and Health System, "University of Michigan Hospitals and Health Centers Recognized as Top Performer in

the 2006 UHC Quality and Accountability Ranking," news release, October 24, 2006.

19. "Levi Strauss & Co," www.levistrauss.com/Company/ValuesAndVision .aspx.

20. Boeing Company, "Boeing CEO Harry Stonecipher Resigns," news release, March 7, 2005.

21. Jim Skinner, interview, 2006.

Chapter 6   Keeping Your Head in the Game

1. Mark Nessmith, "David Toms Bails on British Open," TravelGolf .com,www.travelgolf.com/blogs/mark.nessmith/2005/07/15/david_toms_ bails_on_british_open_reeling.

2. David Toms, interview, 2006.

3. "Google Taps into Search Patterns," BBC News, December 22, 2005.

4. "Deja Two: Vinatieri, Patriots Do It Again," NFL.com, February 1, 2004.

5. "CBS Dealt Record Fine over Janet," CBS News, September 22, 2004.

6. Julie Rawe, "Why Your Boss May Start Sweating the Small Stuff," *Time*, March 20, 2006.

7. P. C. Burns et al., "How Dangerous Is Driving with a Mobile Phone? Benchmarking the Impairment to Alcohol" (Transport Research Laboratory, Crowthorne, Berkshire, UK, September 2002).

8. Chris Weiss, interview, 2006.

9. Em Griffin, "Cognitive Dissonance Theory of Leon Festinger," in *A First Look at Communication Theory* (New York: McGraw-Hill, 1997).

10. "Emory Study Lights Up the Political Brain," *Science Daily*, January 31, 2006.

11. "Jean Piaget," GSI Teaching & Resource Center, University of California, Berkeley, http://gsi.berkeley.edu/textonly/resources/learning/piaget .html#top.

12. "Emory Study Lights Up the Political Brain," *Science Daily*, January 31, 2006.

13. James Atherton, "Resistance to Learning," www.learningandteaching .info/learning/resistan.htm.

14. David Sirota et al., "Why Your Employees Are Losing Motivation," Harvard Management Update, http://hbswk.hbs.edu/archive/5289.html.

15. John K. Borchardt, "Who Puts Bad Apples in the Barrel?," *Today's Chemist at Work* 10, no. 4 (2001): 33–34, 36.

16. Ibid.

17. Aaron J. Louis, "The Role of Cognitive Dissonance in Decision Making," www.yetiarts.com/aaron/science/cogdiss.shtml.

18. Ibid.

PART THREE How We Behave

1. Adam Rosman, interview, 2006.
2. David Ellen, interview, 2006.

Chapter 7 Doing Transparency

1. "*Bicycling* Magazine's Editor's Choice—New York 3000," Bicycling.com as quoted on Kryptonite.com.
2. Kryptonite, www.kryptonitelock.com.
3. Patricia Swann, "Internet Postings and Blogger Videos: Bic This!" (Association for Education in Journalism and Mass Communication, San Antonio, Texas, August 10, 2005).
4. Ibid.
5. Patricia Swann, interview, 2006.
6. Kevin Kelly, "Scan This Book!," *New York Times Magazine*, sec. 6, May 14, 2006, late edition.
7. "CNN Live Today," CNN, December 14, 2004.
8. Ibid.
9. Constance L. Hays, "Jurors Discuss the Verdict against Stewart," *New York Times*, March 7, 2004; Constance L. Hays and David Carr, "Before Facing Judge, Stewart Is Out and About," *New York Times*, July 15, 2004; "Stewart Convicted on All Charges," *CNN Money*, March 5, 2004.
10. "Hotel Queen Gets 4 Years: Judge Tells Leona Helmsley No One Is Above Law," *Orlando Sentinel*, December 13, 1989.
11. Marcy Gordon, "Fannie Mae Fined $400M for Bad Accounting," *Washington Post*, May 24, 2006.
12. Reuters, "US Blames Fannie Management," news release, May 23, 2006.
13. "The Mortgage Giant Fannie Mae Accused of Deception and Mismanagement," PBS, www.pbs.org/newshour/bb/business/jan-june06/fanniemae _05-23.html.
14. "LRN Ethics Study: The Effect of Ethics on Ability to Attract, Retain and Engage Employees," LRN. June 26, 2006.
15. James A. Brickley et al., "Business Ethics and Organizational Architecture" (Working Paper, University of Rochester, William E. Simon Graduate School of Business Administration, 2000).
16. Robin Johnson, "American Food Century, 1900–2000; Non-Food Product Jingles," www.geocities.com/foodedge/jingles6.html.
17. John Horn, "Spreading the Word," Entertainment News, *Los Angeles Times*, August 25, 2006.
18. Ibid.

19. Chris Gaither, "Where Everyone Is a Critic," *Los Angeles Times*, August 25, 2006.

20. Dave Scott, "Digital Revolution Changes News Business," *Akron Beacon Journal*, April 26, 2006.

21. "Word of Mouth 101: An Introduction to Word of Mouth Marketing," WOMMA, www.womma.org/wom101.htm.

22. "Types of Word of Mouth Marketing," WOMMA, www.womma.org/wom 101/02/.

23. "(Lack of) Trust in Mass Media News," WOMMA, http://ads.womma .org/2005/09/lack_of_trust_i.html.

24. Pete Blackshaw et al., "Measuring Word of Mouth" (lecture, Ad-Tech NY, New York, November 8, 2004).

25. "Wachovia Apologizes for Slavery Ties," *CNN Money*, June 2, 2005.

26. Wachovia Corporation, "Wachovia Completes Research," news release, 2005.

27. David Teather, "Bank Admits It Owned Slaves," *Guardian*, January 22, 2005.

28. "Apple's Special Committee Reports Findings of Stock Option Investigation," news release, October 4, 2006.

29. Chris Penttila, "My Bad!," *Entrepreneur* (March, 2005).

30. "Citigroup CEO Charles Prince Discusses the Future of Global Banking," Japan Society, www2.japansociety.org/global_affairs/event_corp_note.cfm ?id_note=449304821.

31. Larry Johnson, interviewed by Alex Witt, MSNBC, August 27, 2004.

32. Keith Darcé, "Media Ethicist Cites Power of Cyberspace," *San Diego Union-Tribune*, May 14, 2006.

33. Dave McIntyre, interviewed by Sean Cole, *Marketplace*, American Public Media, May 11, 2006.

34. Ibid.

35. Edward C. Tomlinson et al., "The Road to Reconciliation: Antecedents of Victim Willingness to Reconcile Following a Broken Promise," *Journal of Management* 30, no. 2 (2004): 165–187.

36. John K. Borchardt, "Who Puts Bad Apples in the Barrel?," *Today's Chemist at Work* 10, no. 4 (2001): 33–34, 36.

37. "Resume 'Padding,'" HRM Guide USA, www.hrmguide.net/usa/recruitment/ resume_padding.htm.

38. Lisa Takeuchi Cullen, "Getting Wise to Lies," *Time*, April 24, 2006.

39. "Connecting Organizational Communication to Financial Performance— 2003/2004 Communication ROI Study™," Watson Wyatt Worldwide (2004).

40. Yvon Chouinard, interviewed by Cheryl Glaser, *Marketplace*, American Public Media, October 31, 2005.
41. Mark Twain, "Mark Twain Quotations, Newspaper Collections, & Related Resources," www.twainquotes.com/Truth.html.

Chapter 8 Trust

1. Jason Kottke, "Business Lessons from the Donut and Coffee Guy," www.kottke.org/03/07/business-lessons-donut-guy.
2. Warren E. Buffett, e-mail message to Berkshire Hathaway managers ("The All-Stars"), September 27, 2006.
3. Jeffrey H. Dyer and Wujin Chu, "The Role of Trustworthiness in Reducing Transaction Costs and Improving Performance: Empirical Evidence from the United States, Japan, and Korea," *Organization Science* 14, no. 1 (2002): 57.
4. Mike Fricklas, interview, 2006.
5. Francis Fukuyama, *Trust: The Social Virtues and the Creation of Prosperity* (New York: Free Press Paperbacks, 1995): 7.
6. Paul J. Zak, "Trust," *Journal of Financial Transformation* 7 (April, 2003): 20.
7. Dr. Peter Kollock, "The Emergence of Exchange Structures: An Experimental Study of Uncertainty, Commitment, and Trust," *American Journal of Sociology* 100 (1994): 313–345.
8. Ana Cristina Costa, "Work Team Trust and Effectiveness," *Personnel Review* 32, no. 5 (October 2003).
9. Roger Fine, interview, 2005.
10. Mike Fricklas, interview, 2006.
11. Zak, "Trust."
12. Jeffrey H. Dyer and Wujin Chu, "The Determinants of Trust in Supplier-Automaker Relationships in the U.S., Japan, and Korea," *Journal of International Business Studies* 31, no. 2 (2000): 259.
13. Jeffrey B. Kindler, interview, 2006.
14. "Tufts Graduate Named CEO of Pfizer," Tufts e-news, www.tufts.edu/communications/stories/081406TuftsGraduateNamedCEOofPfizer.htm.
15. Federal Bureau of Investigation, Los Angeles Division, "James Paul Lewis, Doing Business as Financial Advisory Consultants in Orange County, California, Arrested by Agents in Houston, Texas, for Operating 20 Year 'Ponzi' Scheme with Losses in Excess of 800 Million Dollars," news release, January 22, 2004.
16. Don Thompson, "Investors Fear They'll Lose Millions in Alleged Ponzi Scam," Fraud Discovery Institute, www.frauddiscovery.net/fac.html.
17. Warren E. Buffett, e-mail message, 2006.
18. Steve Kerr, interview, 2005.

Chapter 9 Reputation, Reputation, Reputation

1. Dan Bilefsky, "Indians Unseat Antwerp's Jews as the Biggest Diamond Traders," *Wall Street Journal*, May 27, 2003.
2. "Number of Jobs Held, Labor Market Activity, and Earnings Growth among the Youngest Baby Boomers: Results from a Longitudinal Survey" (United States Department of Labor, Bureau of Labor Statistics, Washington, D.C., August 25, 2006).
3. "RentAThing," www.rentathing.org.
4. Cory Doctorow, *Down and Out in the Magic Kingdom* (New York: Tor Books, 2003).
5. Chrysanthos Dellarocas and Paul Resnick, "Online Reputation Mechanisms: A Roadmap for Future Research" (lecture, First Interdisciplinary Symposium on Online Reputation Mechanisms, Cambridge, Massachusetts, April 26–27, 2003).
6. James B. Stewart, *Den of Thieves* (New York: Touchstone, 1992).
7. Roger Fine, interview, 2005.
8. Ibid.
9. General Electric Company, "GE 2002 Annual Report," news release, 2002.
10. Paul B. Farrell, "Warren Buffett, America's Greatest Story-Teller," *MarketWatch*, March 21, 2006.
11. Jim Skinner, interview, 2006.
12. "LRN Ethics Study: Purchasing Behavior" (Opinion Research Corporation, Princeton, New Jersey, January 30, 2006).
13. Joie Gregor, interview, 2006.
14. Jeff Kindler, interview, 2006.
15. Paul Robert, interview, 2005.
16. Alice LaPlante, "MBAs Seek Caring, Ethical Employers," *Stanford Business* (May 2004).
17. Goran Lindahl as quoted in *Purpose: The Starting Point of Great Companies* by Nikos Mourkogiannis (New York: Palgrave Macmillan, 2006).
18. Scott Westcott, "The Importance of Reputation," ProfitGuide.com (February 24, 2005).
19. Dorothy Rabinowitz, "Mr. Giuliani and Mr. Milken," *Wall Street Journal*, April 17, 2001.
20. Stewart, *Den of Thieves*.
21. "Michael Milken Biography," www.mikemilken.com.
22. "Our Management," Altria, www.altria.com/about_altria/biography/01_03_07_Greenberg.asp.
23. David Greenberg, interview, 2006.

PART FOUR   How We Govern

1. James M. Hagen and Soonkyoo Choe, "Trust in Japanese Interfirm Relations: Institutional Sanctions Matter," *Academy of Management Review* 23, no. 3 (1998): 589.
2. "Ford Sustainability Report 2004/5: Policy Letters and Directives," Ford Motor Company (December 2005).
3. "Quality," General Electric Company (2006), www.ge.com/en/company/companyinfo/quality/whatis.htm.

Chapter 10   Doing Culture

1. Chuck Williams, "GE Aircraft Engines, Durham Engine Facility" (lecture, WorldBlu Forum, Washington, D.C., October 2005).
2. Charles Fishman, "Engines of Democracy," *Fast Company* 28 (September, 1999): 174.
3. "The Toxic 100: Top Corporate Air Polluters in the United States," Political Economy Research Institute, University of Massachusetts, Amherst (2002).
4. "Testimony of Dov L. Seidman to the U.S. Sentencing Commission" (public hearing, Washington, D.C., March 17, 2004).
5. "1992–2002 Census of Fatal Occupational Injuries" (U.S. Department of Labor, Bureau of Labor Statistics, January 7, 2005).
6. "Our Culture," Nordstrom, http://careers.nordstrom.com/company/culture/index.asp.
7. United States. 2004. "America after 9/11 freedom preserved or freedom lost?" (hearing before the Committee on the Judiciary, United States Senate, One Hundred Eighth Congress, first session, November 18, 2003). Washington: U.S. G.P.O.
8. Steve Kerr, "On the Folly of Rewarding A, While Hoping for B," *Academy of Management Journal* 18, no. 4 (1975); updated for *Academy of Management Executive* 9, no. 1 (1995): 7–14.
9. Steve Kerr, interview, 2005.
10. Jonathan Pont, "Doing the Right Thing to Instill Business Ethics," *Workforce Management* (April 1, 2005).
11. Tom Terez, "Workplace 2000 Employee Insight Survey," Meaningful Workplace.com, August 29, 2000.
12. Charles Hampden-Turner, interview, 2006.

Chapter 11   The Case for Self-Governing Cultures

1. "Testimony of Dov L. Seidman to the U.S. Sentencing Commission" (public hearing, Washington, D.C., March 17, 2004).

2. Richard Bednar et al., "Report of the Ad Hoc Advisory Group on the Organizational Sentencing Guidelines," United States Sentencing Commission (October 7, 2003).

3. "Chapter Eight—Sentencing of Organizations—Federal Sentencing Guidelines Manual and Appendices (2005)," United States Sentencing Commission (November 1, 2004).

4. Larry D. Thompson, "Principles of Federal Prosecution of Business Organizations," United States Department of Justice (January 20, 2003).

5. Judge Ruben Castillo, interview, 2006.

6. Charles Hampden-Turner, interview, 2006.

7. Massimo Ferragamo, interview, 2006.

8. Joy Sewing, "Style and Feeling Guide Massimo Ferragamo," *Houston Chronicle*, April 29, 2004.

9. Hannay, Alastair, *Kierkegaard: A Biography*, ed. and trans. Reidar Thomte with Albert B. Anderson (Cambridge: Cambridge University Press, 2001).

10. Benedict Carey, "Study Links Punishment to an Ability to Profit," *New York Times*, April 7, 2006.

11. Ibid.

12. Herb Kelleher, "A Culture of Commitment," *Leader to Leader* 4 (Spring 1997): 20–24.

13. Joe Stallard, interview, 2006.

14. Deborah Solomon and Cassell Bryan-Low, "Companies Complain about Cost of Corporate-Governance Rules," *Wall Street Journal*, February 10, 2004, Eastern edition.

15. "Size Matters: Larger Companies Will Spend More for Sarbanes-Oxley Compliance Requirements" (Financial Executives International, February 10, 2004).

16. "Management Barometer," PricewaterhouseCoopers (March 2003).

17. "Annual Reports and Statistical Sourcebooks," United States Sentencing Commission (2000–2005).

18. Douglas Lankler, interview, 2006.

19. Michael Monts, interview, 2006.

20. Chuck Williams, "GE Aircraft Engines, Durham Engine Facility" (lecture, WorldBlu Forum, Washington, D.C., October 2005).

21. "Our Company: Growth & Expansion," Johnson & Johnson, www.jnj.com/our_company/history/history_section_2.htm.

22. Roger Fine, interview, 2005.

23. Reggie Van Lee et al., "The Value of Corporate Values," *Strategy + Business* (Summer 2005).

24. Matthew Gilbert, "True Believers at Methodist Hospital," *Workforce Management* (February 2005): 67–69.

25. "Top 10 Best Companies to Work for," *CNN Money*, 2007.

26. Thomas R. McCormick, interview, 2005.

27. Jim Skinner, interview, 2006.

Chapter 12   The Leadership Framework

1. The version of the Leadership Framework that appears here has been adapted from the original LRN Leadership Framework in order to better serve this book.

2. John F. Kennedy, "Special Message to the Congress on Urgent National Needs," John F. Kennedy Presidential Library & Museum, www.jfklibrary .org/Historical+Resources/Archives/Reference+Desk/Speeches/JFK/003P OF03NationalNeeds05251961.htm.

3. Not all of these ideas about leadership dispositions and attributes are original; some I have absorbed from others or from things I have read over the course of my career. During my studies as a Wexner Fellow, I learned from Rabbi Nathan Laufer, for instance, the effectiveness of describing leadership attributes both positively and negatively, as what they are and are not. Among the many books I read about leadership, *The Corporate Mystic* by Hendricks and Ludeman influenced me to think more rigorously about it. Though I didn't invent all these ideas, I believe I first assembled them and then refined them over the years with my colleagues at LRN in an original fashion uniquely suited to thriving in a world of HOW.

4. Roxy Sass, "Roxy Boldly Takes On 'The Happiest Place on Earth,'" *Stanford Daily* (August 5, 2004).

5. James C. Collins and Jerry I. Porras, *Built to Last: Successful Habits of Visionary Companies* (New York: HarperCollins, 1994): 88.

6. "Company History," Walt Disney Company, http://corporate.disney .go.com/corporate/complete_history_1.html.

7. A'Lelia Bundles, "Madam C. J. Walker—A Short Biography," Madam C. J. Walker: The Official Website, www.madamecjwalker.com.

8. Alan Spoon, interview, 2006.

9. Bill Gordon, "Kamikaze Images," http://wgordon.web.wesleyan.edu/ kamikaze/books/japanese/hamazono/index.htm.

10. "Max Weber," Department of Sociology, University of Chicago, http://ssr1 .uchicago.edu/PRELIMS/Theory/weber.html.

11. Ibid.

12. "FEMA Assistance Paid for Saints Tickets, Vacation, Divorce Lawyer," KTBS, www.ktbs.com/news/local/3053051.html.

13. *Paula Zahn Now*, CNN (June 14, 2006).

14. Wynn Resorts, "Steve Wynn's Newest Resort, Wynn Las Vegas, Now Taking Room Reservations," news release, January 14, 2005.

15. Steve Wynn, interview, 2006.

16. Jeff Kindler, interview, 2006.

17. Carmine Gallo, "Starbucks' Secret Ingredient," BusinessWeek, May 5, 2006.

18. Massimo Ferragamo, interview, 2006.

19. Winston S. Churchill, Never Give In: The Best of Winston Churchill's Speeches (New York: Hyperion Books, 2003).

20. Brian Duffy, "The Kid of No Promise," *U.S. News & World Report*, October 31, 2005.

21. Helen Keller, Helen Keller Foundation for Research & Education, www.helenkellerfoundation.org/research.asp.

Afterword

1. Lisa McLaughlin, "The Business of Hospitality (Your Time; Money)," *Time*, October 2, 2006.

2. James C. Collins and Jerry I. Porras, *Built to Last: Successful Habits of Visionary Companies* (New York: HarperCollins, 1994): 88.

3. Barton Schultz, "Henry Sidgwick," *Stanford Encyclopedia of Philosophy*, http://plato.stanford.edu/entries/sidgwick/.

Selected Bibliography

Alsop, Ronald. "Recruiters Are Holding MBAs to Higher Standards of Integrity." *MSN Encarta*. http://encarta.msn.com/encnet/departments/elearning/Default .aspx?article=MBAIntegrity.

Araton, Harvey. "Athletes Toe the Nike Line, but Students Apply Pressure." *New York Times*, November 22, 1997.

Aristotle. *Nicomachean Ethics*. 350 B.C.E.

Atherton, James. "Resistance to Learning." www.learningandteaching.info/ learning/resistan.htm.

"Athletes to Go to Court over Doping Programme." *Yahoo! UK & Ireland Sports*. http://uk.sports.yahoo.com/060406/2/immn.html.

Bagli, Charles V. "Developer's High-Rise Plan Stirs Concern in the Diamond District." *Wired New York*. www.wirednewyork.com/forum/showthread .php?t=8727.

Berlin, Isaiah. *The Crooked Timber of Humanity*. Princeton, NJ: Princeton University Press, 1990.

Blass, Thomas. StanleyMilgram.com. www.stanleymilgram.com.

Brandeis, Justice Louis. "Sunlight Is the Best Disinfectant." *Brandeis Institute for Investigative Journalism*. www.brandeis.edu/investigate/sunlight/.

Brin, David. Interview, 2006.

———. "A Dangerous World: Transparency, Security and Privacy." www.davidbrin.com/privacyarticles.html.

———. "Three Cheers for the Surveillance Society!" *Salon*, August 4, 2004.

———. *The Transparent Society: Will Technology Force US to Choose between Privacy and Freedom?* New York: Perseus Books, 1998.

Buckingham, Marcus. *First, Break All the Rules: What the World's Greatest Managers Do Differently*. New York: Simon & Schuster, 1999.

———. *Now, Discover Your Strengths*. New York: Free Press, 2001.

————. *The One Thing You Need to Know: About Great Managing, Great Leading, and Sustained Individual Success.* New York: Free Press, 2005.

"Business across Cultures: Equality in the Workplace." *Living in Indonesia, A Site for Expatriates.* www.expat.or.id/business/equality.html.

Business Ethics. www.business-ethics.com.

Capurro, Rafael. "Between Trust and Anxiety: On the Moods of Information Society." www.capurro.de/lincoln.html.

————. "Ethical Challenges of the Information Society in the 21st Century." Academic Press, December 2000.

"Causes of Hundred Years' War." *Killeen Harker Heights Connections.* http://killeenroos.com/2/100YEARS.htm.

Center for Ethical Business Cultures. www.cebcglobal.org.

"Center for Neuroeconomics Studies." www.pauljzak.com/index.php.

Cherniss, Cary, Daniel Goleman, Robert Emmerling, Kimberly Cowan, and Mitchel Adler. "Bringing Emotional Intelligence to the Workplace," Piscataway, NJ: Consortium for Research on Emotional Intelligence in Organizations, October 7, 1998.

Day, Peter. "Get Rid of the Hierarchies." BBC News, November 28, 2005.

"Death on the Job: The Toll of Neglect." AFL-CIO, April 2006.

The Defense Industry Initiative on Business Ethics and Conduct. www.dii.org.

"Do It Right: A Noted Author Explains Why an Ethical Business Is a Profitable Business." *Bentley Surveys.*

"Does Superior Governance Still Lead to Better Financial Performance?" *Bentley Surveys.*

Driscoll, Dawn-Marie, and W. Michael Hoffman. *Ethics Matters: How to Implement Values-Driven Management.* Waltham, MA: Bentley College Center for Business Ethics, 1999.

Einstein, Albert. ThinkExist.com. http://en.thinkexist.com/quotes/albert_einstein/.

Eliot, T. S. 1934. "Choruses from the Rock." In *Complete Poems and Plays: 1909–1950.* New York: Harcourt Brace & Company, 1952.

"Engadget: Kryptonite Evolution 2000 U-Lock Hacked by a Bic Pen." www.businessblogconsulting.com/2004/09/engadget_a_href.html.

Epstein, Edward Jay. "The Jewish Connection." http://edwardjayepstein.com/diamond/chap8.htm.

Esty, Amos. "The Bookshelf Talks with Michael Gazzaniga." *American Scientist Online.* www.americanscientist.org/template/InterviewTypeDetail/assetid/44271.

"*Ethical Consumer* Magazine's Online Shoppers' Guide." Ethical Consumer Research Association. www.ethiscore.org/.

Ethics & Compliance Officer Association. www.theecoa.org.

Ethics Resource Center. www.ethics.org.

Fairtlough, Gerard. *The Three Ways of Getting Things Done: Hierarchy, Heterarchy and Responsible Autonomy in Organizations.* Axminster, Devon, UK: Triarchy Press, 2005.

"Fortune 100 Best Companies to Work for 2006." *CNN Money,* 2006.

"Fortune 100 Best Companies to Work for 2006: Nordstrom." *CNN Money,* 2006.

Gazzaniga, Michael S. Interview, 2006.

———. *The Ethical Brain.* Washington, DC: Dana Press, 2005.

Geffner, David. "A Sparkling Life: Three Generations of Family Shine in L.A.'s Jewelry Trade." *Jewish Journal,* August 15, 2003.

Gerstner, Lou. "Lou Gerstner's Turnaround Tales at IBM." The Wharton School of the University of Pennsylvania, December 18, 2002.

Greenhouse, Steven. "Nike Shoe Plant in Vietnam Is Called Unsafe for Workers." *New York Times,* November 8, 1997.

"Greenspan's Not-So-Modest Book Proposal." *New York Times,* March 2, 2006, sec. DealBook.

Haines, James. "Corporate Governance, Business Ethics, and Individual Responsibility." Fall 2004 Anderson Chandler Lecture, Lawrence, Kansas, November 8, 2004.

Hausman, Daniel M. "Trust in Game Theory." Paper for Discussion, University of Wisconsin–Madison, Philosophy Department, 1997.

Hays, Constance L. "Jurors Discuss the Verdict against Stewart." *New York Times,* March 7, 2004.

Hays, Constance L., and David Carr. "Before Facing Judge, Stewart Is Out and About." *New York Times,* July 15, 2004.

Heidrick & Struggles. www.heidrick.com/default.aspx.

Helliwell, John F., and Haifang Huang. "How`s the Job? Well-Being and Social Capital in the Workplace." Social Science Research Network, November 2005.

Henderson, George M. "Wave Statement." www.krazygeorge.com/wave.html.

Hendricks, Gay, and Kate Ludeman. *The Corporate Mystic: A Guidebook for Visionaries with Their Feet on the Ground.* New York: Bantam, 1997.

Hyatt, James C. "Birth of the Ethics Industry." *Business Ethics,* Summer 2005.

International Center for Information Ethics. www.i-r-i-e.net/index.htm.

"J&J Is People's Favorite." *CNN Money,* December 6, 2005.

Jones, Dan. "Exploring the Moral Maze." *New Scientist,* November 26, 2005.

"Kryptonite Cylinder Locks Opened with Bic Pens." *Bicycle Retailer and Industry News,* September 16, 2004.

"Linda S. Wolf." Forbes.com. www.forbes.com/finance/mktguideapps/person info/FromPersonIdPersonTearsheet.jhtml?passedPersonId=929909.

Lipton, Eric. "Study Finds Huge Fraud in the Wake of Hurricanes." *New York Times*, June 14, 2006, Late Edition—Final.

LRN. www.lrn.com.

Maher, Kris. "Wanted: Ethical Employer; Job Hunters, Seeking to Avoid an Enron or an Andersen, Find It Isn't Always Easy." *Wall Street Journal*, July 9, 2002, sec. Career Journal.

Masum, Hassan, and Yi-Cheng Zhang. "Manifesto for the Reputation Society." *First Monday*, July 2004.

Meakem, Glen. Speech. The Joseph M. Katz Graduate School of Business, University of Pittsburgh Commencement, Pittsburgh, June 14, 2002.

"Media Holds Its Own in Trust Poll." BBC News, May 3, 2006.

Mencken, H. L. "Quotes Related to the Fundamental Values of Academic Integrity." Center for Academic Integrity, Kenan Institute for Ethics, Duke University. www.academicintegrity.org/quotes.asp.

Meyer, Danny. *Setting the Table: The Transforming Power of Hospitality in Business.* New York: HarperCollins, 2006.

Milgram, Stanley. "The Perils of Obedience." http://home.swbell.net/revscat/perilsOfObedience.html.

Montaigne, Michel de. "Essays of Michel de Montaigne." *Project Gutenberg.* www.gutenberg.org/files/3600/3600-h/3600-h.htm (alternate translation from the French).

"The Moral Brain." www.themoralbrain.be.

"Morals on the Brain." BBC News, October 19, 1999, sec. Sci/Tech.

Moss, Stephen. "Idleness Is Good." *Guardian*, April 17, 2003.

"The Nature of a Wave: Waves and Wavelike Motion." *The Physics Classroom.* www.physicsclassroom.com/Class/waves/U10L1a.html.

"100 Best Corporate Citizens for 2005."*Business Ethics*, Spring 2005.

"Our Favourite Case Study Tells Their Side: Kryptonite Speaks." *Business Blog Consulting.* www.businessblogconsulting.com/2005/07/our_favourite_c.html.

"ParEcon." *ZNet.* www.zmag.org/parecon/indexnew.htm.

Patsuris, Penelope. "The Corporate Scandal Sheet." *Forbes*, August 26, 2002.

Pavlina, Steve. "List of Values." StevePavlina.com. www.stevepavlina.com/articles/list-of-values.htm.

Pew Internet & American Life Project. www.pewinternet.org.

Picasso, Pablo. In *Uncommon Wisdom,* Kansas City: Andrews McMeel Publishing, 1999.

"Predicting Hits: What's the Buzz?" *Los Angeles Times*, February 10, 2006, sec. Calendar.

Ramsey, Geoff. "Ten Reasons Why Word-of-Mouth Marketing Works." *Online Media Daily.* http://publications.mediapost.com/index.cfm?fuseaction=Articles.showArticleHomePage&art_aid=34339.

"The Real Link to Demand Creation." *Sirius Decisions.* www.siriusdecisions .com/newsletter/newsletter20/index.html.

Reckard, E. Scott. "Ex-Money Manager Gets 30 Years." *Los Angeles Times,* May 27, 2006, Home Edition.

Reputation Institute. www.reputationinstitute.com.

Resnick, Paul, Richard Zeckhauser, John Swanson, and Kate Lockwood. "The Value of Reputation on eBay: A Controlled Experiment." *Experimental Economics,* June 2006.

"Responsible Shopper." *Co-op America.* www.coopamerica.org/programs/rs/.

Rheingold, Howard. "Important New Book on Sharing Economies." www .smartmobs.com/archive/2005/05/18/important_new_b.html.

"Richard Joyce." Philosophy Program, Research School of Social Sciences, Australian National University. http://philrsss.anu.edu.au/people-defaults/ rjoyce/index.php3.

Roosevelt, Theodore. "The Opening of the Jamestown Exposition." Speech, Norfolk, Virginia, April 26, 1907.

Rubel, Steve. "Kryptonite Lock's Blog Crisis Leaps into the Press." *Micro Persuasion.* www.micropersuasion.com/2004/09/kryptonite_lock.html.

Scoble, Robert, and Shel Israel. "Kryptonite Argues Its Case." *Naked Cases.* http://redcouch.typepad.com/weblog/2005/07/kryptonite_argu.html.

Seglin, Jeffrey L. "Business with a Conscience: Do It Right." *MBA Jungle Magazine,* November 1, 2001.

Shakespeare, William. *Othello.* New York: Washington Square Press, 2004.

Shirky, Clay. "Reputation and Society." *Corante.* http://many.corante.com/ archives/2004/07/19/reputation_and_society.php.

Socrates. ThinkExist.com. http://en.thinkexist.com/quotes/socrates/.

"Stewart Convicted on All Charges." *CNN Money,* March 5, 2004.

"Surveillance Campaign." American Civil Liberties Union. www.aclu.org/ pizza/.

"Theories about Decision-Making." ChangingMinds.org. http://changingminds .org/explanations/theories/a_decision.htm.

"The Toxic 100: Top Corporate Air Polluters in the United States." Political Economy Research Institute, 2002.

"TQM, ISO 9000, Six Sigma: Do Process Management Programs Discourage Innovation?" *Knowledge@Wharton,* November 30, 2005.

"Triarchy Press—Articles." www.triarchypress.co.uk/pages/articles/articles.htm.

"Trust in Employees Significantly Higher Than in CEOs, Edelman Trust Barometer Finds." Edelman, January 23, 2006.

Ulrich, Dave, Steve Kerr, and Ron Ashkenas. *The GE Work-Out.* New York: McGraw-Hill, 2002.

Vedantam, Shankar. "Study Ties Political Leanings to Hidden Biases." *Washington Post,* January 30, 2006.

Webley, Simon, and Elise More. "Does Business Ethics Pay?" Institute of Business Ethics. www.ibe.org.uk/DBEPsumm.htm.

Whiteley, Richard. *The Corporate Shaman: A Business Fable.* New York: HarperCollins, 2006.

Whitfield, George B., III. "Conflict Resolution Strategies in Indonesia." *Living in Indonesia, A Site for Expatriates.* www.expat.or.id/business/conflict resolution.html.

Wiedemann, Erich. "Jews Surrender Gem Trade to Indians." *Spiegel Magazine*, May 15, 2006.

Wooden, John. ThinkExist.com. http://en.thinkexist.com/quotes/john_wooden/ 2.html.

"World Values Survey." www.worldvaluessurvey.org.

Zuboff, Shoshana. "From Subject to Citizen." *Fast Company*, May 2004.

Index

Honor, 273
Horizontal, generally:
  business models, 23–24, 100
  communication, 153
  governance architecture, 260
  specialty, 61
  world, 167, 180, 242
Hospitality, 299–300
How We Behave, as dimension of culture, 227–229, 231–233
How We Know, as dimension of culture, 227–230
How We Pursue, as dimension of culture, 227–229, 237–239
How We Recognize, as dimension of culture, 227–229, 235–237
How We Relate, as dimension of culture, 227–229, 233–235
Human behavior, influential factors, 14. *See also* Human instinct; Human nature
Human instinct, 169
Human nature, 52–53, 78, 80, 88, 108
Human networks, development of, 72
Human resources information system (HRIS), 52
Hume, David, 28
Humility, 98
Hunsaker, Kevin, 89
Hurricane Katrina, 250, 287
Hyperconnectedness, 41–42, 48, 61, 93, 127, 175, 219, 242, 272
Hyperconnection, 87, 167–168, 272, 277
Hypertransparency, 61, 87, 150, 167–168, 219, 242, 272

IBM, 25–26
Ideal capitalist enterprises, 75
Immelt, Jeffrey, 194
Implementation, 278–279
Incorporation, 24
Independent contractors, 26–27
Industrial age, 18, 43, 84, 135, 223, 238
Information, generally:
  accessibility of, 25, 131, 136–137, 143–144, 230
  age, 15, 20, 38, 44, 87
  democratization of, 38
  economy, 21–22, 102
  flow, 19–22, 38–39, 122, 152–153, 242, 260
  networks, 54
  reputation and, 195
  skills, 192
  technology, 38, 150, 189
  transparency (*see* Transparency)
Information sharing, 21–22, 160, 230, 276
Informed acquiescence culture, 223–226, 229–230, 232, 234–235, 238, 241–242, 245, 248, 253, 265

Info Screening Services, 150
Innovation, 22–23, 49–52, 54, 59, 96–97, 99, 110, 165, 167, 131, 209, 213, 290, 302
Insecurity, 108, 165
Inspiration, 98, 263, 286–287, 296–297, 302
Integration, importance of, 10
Integrity, 44, 54, 94, 98, 106, 108, 117, 123, 127, 136, 151, 187, 209, 253, 257, 264, 302
Intellectual journey, 58
Intellectual property, 51
Interaction Design Institute Ivrea, 188
Interactive advertising, 142
Interconnectedness, 186
Interdependence, 185–186
International customers, 29
Internet/internetworked world, impact of, 129–131, 135–136, 196, 270
Interorganizational trust, 173
Interpersonal, generally:
  alignment, 235–236
  interaction, 14–15
  synapses, 64, 72, 80, 89, 95, 120–121, 124, 127, 131, 172, 199, 209, 213, 268, 277
  transparency, 132, 148–152
Interpersonal relationships, 111, 122
Interrelationships, 26–27, 31. *See also* Interpersonal relationships
Invention/inventors, 49–50, 131

Japan:
  business culture, 184
  kamikazes analogy, 284–285
  manufacturing techniques, 210–211
JetBlue Airlines, 22, 299
Job hunting, 149–150
Jobs, Steve, 145
Job skills, information-based, 152
Johnson, Robert Wood, 255
Johnson & Johnson (J&J), 50, 169, 193–195, 255–256, 265, 302
Joint ventures, 26, 35–36
Journal, online, 36. *See also* Blogs/blogging
Journey, nature of, 60. *See also* Hills of Knowledge paradox; Intellectual journey
Joyce, Dr. Richard, 72–75
JPMorgan Chase & Co., 145
Judgment, 67–68, 78, 99, 133–136, 169
Junk bonds, 193
Jury system, 169
Just Do It era, 41–45, 48, 55, 61, 88
Justice, 98, 273. *See also* Judgment
Just-in-time (JIT) inventory, 52
JVE Jenapharm, 92, 94, 97, 112, 146

Kaizen, 52
Kamikazes analogy, 284–285
Kartchner, Chris, 126–127